D0856776

THE MISSISSIPPI STATE
SOVEREIGNTY COMMISSION

THE MISSISSIPPI STATE SOVEREIGNTY COMMISSION

Civil Rights and States' Rights

Yasuhiro Katagiri

University Press of Mississippi
Jackson

www.upress.state.ms.us

Copyright © 2001 by University Press of Mississippi
All rights reserved
Manufactured in the United States of America

09 08 07 06 05 04 03 02 01   4 3 2 1
∞
Library of Congress Cataloging-in-Publication Data

Katagiri, Yasuhiro, 1960–
The Mississippi State Sovereignty Commission : civil rights and states' rights/
Yasuhiro Katagiri.
p.   cm.
Includes bibliographical references and index.
ISBN 1-57806-388-4 (cloth : alk. paper)
1. African Americans—Civil rights—Mississippi—History—20th century.   2. African
Americans—Segregation—Mississippi—History—20th century.   3. Mississippi State Sovereignty
Commission—History.   4. State rights—History—20th century.   5. Mississippi—Politics and
government—1951–   6. Mississippi—Race relations.   7. Civil rights
movements—Mississippi—History—20th century.   I. Title.

E185.93.M6 K38 2001
323.1′1960730762′06—dc21
2001026090

British Library Cataloging-in-Publication Data available

Lovingly dedicated to
my mentor and friend, Makoto Saito;
my parents, Yasohachi and Mikiko;
my parents-in-law, Charles and Shirley Modesitt;
my wife, Brenda;
our son, Akira Reuben; and
our twin daughters, Aya Rebekah and Ann Rachel,
who are proud Mississippians

Once a government is committed to the principle of silencing the voice of opposition, it has only one way to go, and that is down the path of increasingly repressive measures, until it becomes a source of terror to all its citizens. . . .

—Harry S. Truman

CONTENTS

Contents

PREFACE

This book deals with the institutional history of the Mississippi State Sovereignty Commission from its inception in 1956 to its virtual demise in 1973 and describes its emphatic but eventually failed attempt to resist the civil rights crusades in the Magnolia State. My primary objectives in writing the book have been to pose and attempt to answer the following questions: Why was the Sovereignty Commission created, and what were some of the political and social backgrounds which affected its creation? What kind of activities did the Sovereignty Commission engage in during its seventeen-year existence? What kind of impact did the Sovereignty Commission have on the course of recent Mississippi history, particularly the state's civil rights movement? In light of the fact that other southern states also resisted the civil rights movement and operated governmental agencies similar to the Mississippi State Sovereignty Commission during the 1950s and the 1960s, readers of this book may wonder why the Sovereignty Commission in Mississippi should be warranted as its subject matter. In answering this valid question, I would like to suggest some reasons why my work's subject matter merits an extended examination and evaluation of this particular state agency. Offering these reasons, furthermore, relates to my intended purposes of writing this work.

First, in terms of its culture and politics, Mississippi has exemplified the very essence of the American South, which W. J. Cash once depicted in *The*

Mind of the South as being "not quite a nation within a nation, but the next thing to it."[1] The state, more precisely, serves as a classic representation—in terms of both positive and negative aspects—of Deep South states. No state fought harder, for instance, than Mississippi to thwart the racial integration process after the United States Supreme Court's school desegregation ruling in 1954. Thus, the story of Mississippi's "massive resistance" contains substantial elements of the entire region's anti–civil rights crusades.

Second, the birth of the Mississippi State Sovereignty Commission embodied the mind-set of most white Mississippians, who were determined to resist any meaningful change in the state's racial status quo. The Sovereignty Commission, in other words, was a product of Mississippi society of the 1950s and the 1960s—a society where the fears, angers, and sometimes unreasonable reactions of the white citizenry in pursuit of their dogmatic cause of white supremacy dominated the course of the state's politics. We ordinarily assert our faith in constitutional government. But when confronted with a constitutional crisis, we often become frightened, turn to dictatorial tactics, and lose our faith in freedoms—freedom of speech, freedom of assembly, and academic freedom. As a result, our intelligence, kind hearts, and even sanity vanish in the name of conformity. Unfortunately, this is exactly what plagued Mississippi in the wake of the Supreme Court's 1954 desegregation mandate, with its Sovereignty Commission being a product and playing a role as keeper of the state's rigid racial conformity. In this regard, Pete Daniel contends in *Standing at the Crossroads: Southern Life in the Twentieth Century* that "[m]ost discussions of the civil-rights movement fail to deal with the fears of whites."[2] In a similar vein, Charles W. Eagles observes in the *Journal of Southern History* that civil rights scholars have generally ignored "white southerners' hates, fears, and pride" and thus have failed "to develop more comprehensive and complex accounts" of the civil rights era in the South.[3] I readily agree, and in presenting the history of the Mississippi State Sovereignty Commission, I have attempted to record some of the fears and uncertainties that shackled white Mississippians.

Third, as mentioned, Mississippi was not the sole southern state where administrative commissions and/or legislative committees were created for the purpose of devising legal and extralegal means to circumvent the Supreme Court's desegregation rulings, propagandizing the vindication of states' rights theory and racial segregation, and suffocating any dissenters from their racial norms. However, it should be noted that Mississippi was the very first to reinstate the word "sovereignty" in naming its anti–civil rights state agency, and the Mississippi State Sovereignty Commission, moreover, eventually became the most active pro-segregation and pro–states' rights governmental agency throughout the South. In addition, not until the creation of the Mississippi State Sovereignty Commission was there any substantial public propaganda program carried out by the southern states on the issues of race relations and states' rights.

Fourth, the history of the Mississippi State Sovereignty Commission shows us the best example of how a state political structure and a private organization could forge a strong relationship in defense of their "segregated way of life." This intricate relationship became quite evident in the early 1960s when the Sovereignty Commission retained ties with the Citizens' Council—an ostensibly "nonpolitical" and "grassroots" private pro-segregation organization. However, although their relationship throughout the life of the Commission was fairly amiable, it was not always cooperative. For one thing, rivalry instead of cooperation had developed between the two organizations over which group could better carry Mississippi's segregationist message to the North and the West.

Fifth, through a closer look at the history of the Sovereignty Commission, I came to realize that white Mississippians had never constituted a monolithic entity in resisting racial integration, manifesting disagreements among themselves as to what tactics to employ to deal with the assault upon their racial norms. In fact, the birth of the Sovereignty Commission, contrary to some conventional understanding, was an uneasy process, and while laying itself open to criticisms voiced by both ends of the racial spectrum—namely, integrationists and die-hard segregationists—the Commission found itself repeatedly plunged into life-threatening situations by the state's white politicians. Dissenting voices, in addition, were raised even among members of the Sovereignty Commission itself from time to time, and this internal strife became apparent in the late 1960s when the agency's prominence was fading away.

Sixth, it is somewhat ironic that while the Sovereignty Commission kept its watchful eyes on Mississippi's civil rights activities, the agency's functions underwent some unmarked shifts in the middle of the 1960s. After Mississippi experienced a series of traumatic and rapid-fire incidents on the state's civil rights front, the Sovereignty Commission—the state's keeper of its "closed society"—grudgingly and painfully began to transform itself to a pragmatic accommodator to the state's "open"—or more accurately, "opened"—society. To be sure, this neither indicates that the Sovereignty Commission was converted to an advocate of the advancement of civil rights in the state nor implies that the indelible blot on Mississippi's history left by the Commission should be offset in any way. After all, the birth, life, and death of the Mississippi State Sovereignty Commission were the result of an abominable and unsavory segregationist enterprise staged by leading Mississippi white officials, and the very tragedy of its existence was that the agency used the constitutional mantle of "state sovereignty" to try to perpetuate white Mississippi's inhumane treatment of the state's black citizens. At the same time, however, I think that the Sovereignty Commission's heretofore unrecognized deeds to try to make the state's white citizenry realize the importance of a nonviolent accommodation to the reality of the 1960s also merits recording.

The last reason that I would like to offer is a more practical one. No southern state has preserved such a nearly complete set of official records of a similar type of pro-segregation state agency as Mississippi has done at its Department of Archives and History in Jackson. A sad truth for contemporary historians as well as the general public is that the official records of some of the South's state commissions and committees that carried out their "massive resistance" no longer exist. Most of the documents of the Louisiana State Sovereignty Commission and the Louisiana State Joint Legislative Committee on Un-American Activities, for example, were apparently burned sometime after they became defunct. As a result, the only remainder housed at the Louisiana State Archives in Baton Rouge today is one-cubic-foot of materials generated by the latter committee. Having said this, I readily admit that reconstructing the entire history of the Mississippi State Sovereignty Commission was like trying to complete a huge jigsaw puzzle with tiny pieces being scattered around in the official records, and I often encountered some "missing pieces" in other manuscript collections, such as the Paul B. Johnson Family Papers housed at the University of Southern Mississippi.

The celebrated southern historian C. Vann Woodward once observed that white southerners "have yet to achieve articulate expression of their uniquely un-American experience."[4] Regrettably, not only as a non-Mississippian, nonsoutherner, and non-American, but also as a nonnative English speaker, I may not be best qualified to articulate this "uniquely un-American experience" that blemished recent Mississippi history. But as a foreign scholar of the American South who, since my graduate school days, has grown to adore the Magnolia State and the region to which the state belongs, I genuinely wish that my work will make some contribution to a further understanding of Mississippi's counterrevolutionary experience in the face of the South's Second Reconstruction. "History is kept alive," Woodward also wrote, "by change, by challenge, and by reinterpretation."[5] I cannot agree with him more, and in the following pages I offer my own interpretation of the life and death of the Mississippi State Sovereignty Commission.

ACKNOWLEDGMENTS

Like any other scholarly enterprise, writing a book is basically a lonely task. Anyone who is trying to write a book must feel, at least once or twice, as if one were a marathon runner who sometimes wonders how and when he or she can reach the goal. It is also true, however, that the writer has many wonderful spectators along the road who encourage and cheer him or her on to victory. While the entire responsibility for this book rests upon me, I wish to express my sincere appreciation to a number of people and institutions both in Japan and in the United States for their aid and support.

The origin of this book can be traced back to my doctoral dissertation written under the direction of Makoto Saito at International Christian University in Tokyo. Though this book is a vastly revised version of the dissertation due to my further research trips to Mississippi and has little vestige of its original form, I am greatly indebted to his persevering guidance and valuable suggestions, which contributed to whatever merit this book possesses.

To the Japan–United States Educational Commission (the Fulbright Commission) both in Tokyo and in Washington, D.C., I would like to express my special gratitude for enabling me to conduct the initial phase of my research for this book in the United States.

In addition to the Fulbright Commission, I owe an immense debt to my host institution in the United States—the University of Southern Mississippi in Hattiesburg—where I had the privilege to study as a Fulbright graduate scholar. Throughout my one and a half years with the Department of History, Neil R. McMillen, Orazio A. Ciccarelli, and William K. Scarborough were especially generous in providing me with their academic support. Terry S. Latour (presently at Delta State University in Cleveland, Mississippi), Bobs M. Tusa, and Yvonne Arnold at the William D. McCain Library and Archives elicit my highest regards for their professionalism. Their diligence and courtesy always made my research process much easier and pleasant. The fact that almost all Mississippi newspapers do not have subject indexes required me to look at a considerable amount of microfilm at the Joseph A. Cook Memorial Library. In that dark "molehill" at the library's microfilms section, Eleanor Robin and her student assistants gave me their unlimited help. Charles C. Bolton, Shana L. Walton, and Marie Sykes at the Center for Oral History and Cultural Heritage on campus showed me the fascinating world of oral history. Their invaluable suggestions, travel funding, transcribing and editing services, and, most of all, friendships are all deeply appreciated.

The acknowledgments will never fully reveal the extent of the contribution made by the Mississippi Department of Archives and History in Jackson to the publication of this book. Anne S. Webster, Hank T. Holmes, and Sandra E. Boyd never failed in making me feel at home every time I visited them. Sarah Rowe-Sims and De'Niecechsi Comans Layton endured my repeated requests for shipping to me countless pages of copied documents from the official records of the Mississippi State Sovereignty Commission in the final stage of preparing this book.

I am also grateful for the splendid assistance that I received from the following Mississippi institutions and their staffs: the Mitchell Memorial Library at Mississippi State University in Mississippi State and, particularly, Mattie L. Sink; the John D. Williams Library at the University of Mississippi in University; and the L. Zenobia Coleman Library at Tougaloo College in Tougaloo.

To many institutions outside of Mississippi as well, I am indebted immensely in preparing this book. They include the Alabama Department of Archives and History in Montgomery; the Lyndon B. Johnson Presidential Library in Austin, Texas; the John F. Kennedy Presidential Library in Boston; the Louisiana State Archives and the Hill Memorial Library at Louisiana

State University in Baton Rouge; the Seeley G. Mudd Manuscript Library at Princeton University in Princeton, New Jersey; the State Historical Society of Wisconsin in Madison; the Harry S. Truman Presidential Library in Independence, Missouri; and the Davidson Library at the University of California at Santa Barbara.

The individuals who participated in my oral history interviews in Mississippi were generous with their time and willingness to discuss the issues and events described in this book: Mary Jane Barber of Jackson, Michael L. Carr Jr. of Brookhaven, Horace H. Harned Jr. of Starkville, the late Erle E. Johnston Jr. of Forest, Edwin King of Jackson, James H. Meredith of Jackson, the late Frank E. Smith of Jackson, the late Kenneth O. Williams of Clarksdale, William F. Winter of Jackson, and Joseph E. Wroten of Aberdeen.

I must take special note of the kindness of other numerous individuals who shared their thoughts with me and contributed to the completion of this book. In Mississippi, the late Frank D. Barber of Jackson, William G. Burgin Jr. of Columbus, William H. Johnson Jr. of Decatur, John C. McLaurin of Brandon, Dick Molpus of Philadelphia, and Joseph G. Moss of Raymond were all helpful. Jane Adams at Southern Illinois University in Carbondale; Jack Bass at the College of Charleston in Charleston, South Carolina; Douglas Brinkley at the University of New Orleans; the late Lindsey H. Cox of Memphis; the late Delmar D. Dennis of Sevierville, Tennessee; Reid S. Derr at East Georgia College in Swainsboro; John A. Dittmer at DePauw University in Greencastle, Indiana; L. Gerald Fielder of Waco, Texas; Mark H. Leff at the University of Illinois at Urbana-Champaign; Charles C. Payne at Northwestern University in Evanston, Illinois; and Christopher Waldrep at San Francisco State University provided valuable assistance.

My profound debts to the members of Woodland Presbyterian Church in Hattiesburg are also warmly acknowledged. During the several months when my wife was repeatedly hospitalized due to her pregnancy with our twins, these wonderful people helped us immensely in cooking, cleaning, and taking care of our baby son, so that I could go to school and dig into the many piles of the archival papers. Their physical, spiritual, and financial support was a true embodiment of not only the famed "southern hospitality" but also love in Christ.

My highest gratitude and respect goes to Seetha Srinivasan, editor-in-chief at the University Press of Mississippi, whose friendship I shall always treasure. Without her enthusiasm for this book, constant counsel, encouragement to attain the best, and trust in me, my manuscript could have never been converted into a book. As they promised me, Anne Stascavage, editor; Walter Biggins, editorial assistant; and Shane Gong, production coordinator, at the Press made my first experience of English book publishing a memorable one. I would also like to express my deepest appreciation to my copy-editor, Robert Burchfield of Iowa City, Iowa, for his thoughtful advice and to my indexer, Dorothy Young of Garland, Texas, for her splendid indexing skills. The time and effort rendered by the two anonymous readers for the Press are greatly appreciated as well.

Last but not least, I would like to thank my family members. I am very grateful to my parents, Yasohachi and Mikiko of Tokyo. My love and respect for them cannot possibly be expressed adequately here. Similarly, special mention must be made of the encouragement, friendship, and love of my parents-in-law, Charles and Shirley Modesitt of Fort Worth, Texas. For daily reminders that there is certainly more to life than writing a book, I thank our precious son, Akira Reuben, and our beautiful twin daughters, Aya Rebekah and Ann Rachel. The Mississippi birth of our twins has established a lasting bond between my family and the state that I am proud of. Most important of all was the constant encouragement, support, patience, and love of my wife, Brenda. Several years ago, in the acknowledgments of my dissertation, I wrote that I could not have pursued my doctoral study without the countless sacrifices my wife had made. That still holds true today, and to her and our little ones who have always deserved better, this book is lovingly dedicated.

Introduction

FOR THE PURITY OF WHITE BLOOD

The Dixiecrat Revolt and the Creation of the
Legal Educational Advisory Committee in Mississippi

During the years of World War II, more than 237,000 Mississippians served in the armed forces, and among them, some 85,000 black Mississippians were in service to defend what President Franklin D. Roosevelt in early 1941 termed the "Four Freedoms"—freedom of speech, freedom of religion, freedom from want, and freedom from fear of armed aggression.[1] As a nation, the United States had roughly three million black men and women serving in the armed forces during the war, and approximately half a million of them went overseas. "Among the numerous adjustments the American people had to make at the end of World War II," John Hope Franklin wrote, "was adaptation to a new position of African Americans in the United States."[2] As a state with the highest proportion of black people to white in the Union—54 percent in the 1940 census—Mississippi was also put in a position to adapt to this new reality. Many Mississippi veterans did not come home "with the same provincial and insulated attitudes after traveling over the United States and overseas." "In short," John R. Skates, a Mississippi historian, argued, "Mississippians during the war were introduced to the country, and the country discovered Mississippi, and, psychologically, things could never be the same."[3] Particularly, for those black Mississippians who fought overseas, the war was an emotional watershed. After all, these black veterans fought for the cause of freedom and democracy. But when they returned home in triumph, what they saw was the unchanged, stern realities of Mississippi's "segregated way of life."

In spite of some progressive ideas that the state had enjoyed during the war, white Mississippians in general assumed that their black peers should resume their subservient places. It was of no concern for most of them how many black Americans fought and died as soldiers of the world's "arsenal of democracy" during World War II or how many black African delegates met in New York to adopt the United Nations' Universal Declaration of Human Rights in late 1948. The issue of race relations, which had been "relatively dormant" during the New Deal and the following war years, naturally resurfaced in Mississippi, with most of its "peculiar racial customs intact."[4] The dominant mood of the state's politicians and white citizenry was hostility toward the probable increase of black civil rights activities in the state and, much more than that, toward the comprehensive civil rights programs being advanced by the national Democratic Party. The most immediate source of this hostility was the report issued by the President's Committee on Civil Rights and the subsequent actions taken by President Harry S. Truman. In the report, the committee listed thirty-five recommendations for both congressional and administrative actions—the enactment of an anti–poll tax law, the prohibition of segregation in interstate transportation facilities, and the renewal of the Fair Employment Practice Committee (FEPC), among others—to protect the civil rights of black Americans and to begin to eliminate racial segregation from American life.[5]

The white political leaders in Mississippi despised these civil rights proposals and their chief proponent, President Truman, who became the first modern president to recommend comprehensive civil rights legislation. About two weeks after the president delivered his State of the Union message, where he urged Congress to adopt his civil rights package, Mississippians celebrated the inauguration of their new governor, Fielding L. Wright, on January 20, 1948. However, the jubilant mood of the inauguration day soon disappeared once Governor Wright began his inaugural address:

> In Mississippi, and I think in the other states known as the South, we feel that our rights are being threatened by enemies of the South who are in fact also enemies of the nation. . . .

> As a life-long Democrat, as a descendant of Democrats, as the governor of this nation's most Democratic state, I would regret to see the day come when Mississippi or the South should break with the Democratic party in a national election. But vital principles and eternal truths transcend party lines, and the day is now at hand when determined action must be taken.[6]

Converting his inaugural address into a clarion call for a states' rights crusade, Governor Wright warned President Truman and other leaders of the national Democratic Party that Mississippi and other southern states "mean precisely what we say, and . . . if necessary, [will] implement our words with positive action." "We warn them now," he concluded, "to take heed."[7] The governor was ready for offensive action, and on Lincoln's birthday, February 12, Wright called for a meeting of Mississippi Democrats in Jackson. The state legislature, which was then in regular session, adopted a concurrent resolution to "dispense with all business" for the day.[8] The meeting resolved that the State Democratic Executive Committee would call a conference of "all true white Jeffersonian Democrats" from throughout the South to assemble later in Jackson.[9]

Those "true white Jeffersonian Democrats" from Mississippi and nine other southern states subsequently met in Jackson on February 22 and May 10 to hear Governor Wright's ideas of the South's continuing fight against the Truman-initiated civil rights programs. The keynote speaker at the latter gathering was Governor Strom Thurmond of South Carolina, who declared before the enthusiastic audience crowded into Jackson's city auditorium: "All the laws of Washington, and all the bayonets of the Army cannot force the negroes into their [white southerners'] homes, their schools, their churches and their places of recreation and amusement."[10] Before the conference's adjournment, the gathered delegates decided that they would meet again in Birmingham, Alabama, after the Democratic National Convention if and when their pro–states' rights demands were not met there.[11] Meanwhile, calling for southern unity to bury "the miserable mess" of the Truman administration's civil rights initiative, the Mississippi State Democratic Party's eight-page pamphlet declared on its cover page: "Give the Government Back to the People and to the States—FIGHT FOR STATES' RIGHTS!" "It is said that rebellion here will defeat the Party at the next election," it went on, "[and] [i]f so, we will defeat our enemies."[12]

Finally, on July 12, the Mississippi Democrats' worst nightmare came true in Philadelphia, Pennsylvania—the City of Brotherly Love—for the Democratic National Convention, in spite of southern protest, adopted the strongest civil rights plank ever. "We highly commend President Harry S. Truman for his courageous stand on the issue of civil rights," read the civil rights plank of the Democratic platform of 1948.[13] When the presidential balloting began, the entire twenty-three-member Mississippi delegation, led by Governor Wright and former Governor Hugh L. White, walked out of the convention. They were joined by thirteen members of the Alabama delegation. The Alabama walkouts were soon replaced by alternates, but the Mississippi delegation left no one behind.[14] Defeated, Governor Wright and the Mississippi Democrats were in no mood for compromise. No sooner had Wright come home from the national convention than he issued a statement calling on southern Democrats to meet in Birmingham for designating a States' Rights Democratic candidate for president. The meeting date was set for July 17. Only a few days after the close of the Democratic National Convention, a disgruntled group of some six thousand southern delegates from thirteen states gathered in Birmingham and began their rump convention. A number of Confederate battle flags and even a portrait of General Robert E. Lee were held aloft above the marching delegates. At the convention, the delegates of the newly organized States' Rights Democratic Party, or the Dixiecrat Party, chose Governor Thurmond as their presidential nominee and Governor Wright as the nominee for vice president. "[T]he most intense support for the 1948 southern revolt," V. O. Key Jr. wrote in his *Southern Politics in State and Nation* a year after the 1948 presidential election, "came from the areas with most Negroes." "The foundations of the revolt," he went on, "were symbolized in its presidential and vice-presidential candidates . . . [who were] chief executives of the two states with the highest proportions of Negro population."[15] Mississippi and South Carolina would soon be joined by Louisiana and Alabama—which ranked third and fourth, respectively, in percentages of black people to total population—in casting their electoral votes for the Dixiecrat Party.[16]

The platform adopted by the Dixiecrats in Birmingham was barely a thousand words long, but it forcefully presented the case for states' rights. While the platform itself stressed the importance of such concepts as laissez-faire economics, "home rule," and "local self-government," the core of these

Dixiecrats' propositions revolved around their racial fears. The disgruntled southern politicians, in essence, resolved to defend their "southern way of life" from the "totalitarian government" of President Truman and the national Democratic Party.[17] Governor Thurmond articulated this point in the acceptance speech of his presidential nomination: "I know that one of those proposals, that's been advocated, is a breakdown of segregation. I wanna tell you here now that the states of this nation should not be interfered [with by the federal government] in handling the matter of segregation. California knows what's best out there in handling the Japanese and some other problem. . . . But I can tell the people of the United States that we, people in the South, know what is best for the Southland. . . ."[18]

Thurmond, who would later convert from a Democrat to a Republican, also had words for the Democratic Party's national leadership: "[W]e are disappointed and disgusted to the core [with the party]. . . . We must prove to the nation that the South means business this year. . . . [And] we have just begun to fight."[19] In the presidential election on November 2, the States' Rights Democratic Party received 1,169,134 out of 48,692,442 popular votes and 39 out of 531 electoral votes. The party only carried four of the five Deep South states—Mississippi, Alabama, South Carolina, and Louisiana (it did not carry Georgia). About 87 percent of Mississippi voters cast their votes for the Dixiecrat ticket, which was the highest percentage among the four southern states, followed by Alabama's 80 percent.[20] In the end, the Dixiecrat revolt of 1948 turned out to be, as Numan V. Bartley called it, "a premature expression" of the subsequent southern "massive resistance" to the region's Second Reconstruction.[21] As Thurmond declared at the Dixiecrat convention, white southerners had "just begun to fight."

In the midst of the continuing enthusiasm for the states' rights movement launched four years earlier, Governor White, who walked out of the 1948 Democratic National Convention, took the helm of the state in 1952 for a second time. Reminding Mississippians that the state stood "where she stood in 1948," White, a successful lumber businessperson and the "Father of Balance Agriculture With Industry (BAWI) Program" in the state, declared in his inaugural address on January 22 that Mississippi "must stand firmly against usurpation of the Federal Government of the powers reserved to the states."[22] With the blessing of the governor, the state legislature at the 1952 regular session appointed a study committee that was "authorized to conduct a detailed study of the state's school situation and to draft the necessary legislation to reorganize the state's school districts."[23] In sum, the committee's responsibility was to equalize the educational standards for black pupils with those for whites in the state's elementary and secondary educational system in the hope that this "equalization movement" would influence the expected United States Supreme Court's school desegregation decision and, if possible, circumvent any federal court rulings unfavorable to the continuation of racial segregation in the public schools in Mississippi.

The school equalization plan, in truth, had been a smoldering issue in Mississippi since the state legislature took up the matter during its 1946 regular session mostly to pacify the state's black educators' growing demands for equal educational opportunities.[24] But this time, prompted by the Court's impending desegregation ruling and forced to make a forthright admission that black schools had indeed been "separate and unequal," the 1952 legislature decided to organize the special study committee. Officially called the Legislative Recess Education Committee, the group was created by House Concurrent Resolution No. 32, sponsored by State Representative Ney M. Gore Jr. of Marks, Quitman County, in the Mississippi Delta.[25]

In proposing the creation of the legislative study committee, the resolution took into consideration the fact that racial segregation in the state's public school system "has been, and is, the subject of criticism and attack by alien interests from outside the state and South," that "certain suits involving segregation in the public school system of various southern states are now pending" in the Supreme Court, and that white Mississippians were "convinced of the desirability of segregation of the races in the public school system of the state." While the House resolution vested the eighteen-member committee, which consisted of ten members from the House and eight members from the Senate, with authority to study the state's school laws, programs, and policies, the committee was also expected to make "necessary and proper" recommendations to the legislature in order to "maintain segregation of the races in the public schools" of Mississippi. More important, the resolution squarely acknowledged that "there is a great necessity" in the state to "provide equal school facilities for the races."[26] Mississippi, for instance, spent $117.43 for each white public school student while it only spent $35.27 for each black student in 1952.[27] Gore became secretary of the committee, whose report was submitted to the special session of the legislature called by Governor White in November 1953.[28] In his address to the opening session on November 3, White told the gathered lawmakers: "The most we can hope to salvage from a court decision would be a holding that we can separately educate the races provided we afford each race equality of educational opportunity. All past decisions [by the Supreme Court] have required that, and it may well be that our acknowledged failure in the past in this regard is the cause of our present emergency."[29]

During this special session, at the request of the Legislative Recess Education Committee, the state legislature created the new State Education Finance Commission, which would supervise expenditures for construction of new public schools and the consolidation of school districts. The equalization program adopted by the legislature on December 28, 1953, called for "equal salaries for white and Negro teachers, equal buildings, equal transportation, and the same educational opportunities of all children, regardless of race." The initial construction bonds totaled approximately $30 million, of which about 65 percent was earmarked for the construction of black schools.[30] Governor White hoped that black Mississippians "would be content with a promise to upgrade" the state's black public schools "while keeping them separate" from the white ones.[31] Even with the school equalization program being earnestly envisioned, which was not implemented until 1955, white leadership began to tighten the state's segregation policy.[32] In pursuing a carrot-and-stick policy, if the creation of the State Education Finance Commission could be construed as the "carrot," the "stick" was the organization of the Legal Educational Advisory Committee (LEAC) in the 1954 regular legislative session. Proposed by House Speaker Walter Sillers, the bill to create the committee was introduced into the House on April 5, 1954.[33]

LEAC was vested with authority to "formulate a plan or plans of legislation, prepare drafts of suggested laws" and constitutional amendments, and "recommend courses of action for consideration by the Legislature" whereby Mississippi could "maintain separate education and separate schools for the white and colored races" and "preserve and promote the best interests of both races and the public welfare." The twenty-five-member LEAC was composed of thirteen ex officio members, including Governor White; Carroll Gartin, lieutenant governor; House Speaker Sillers; James P. Coleman, attorney general; Judge Harvey McGehee, chief justice of the state supreme court; Jackson M. "Jack" Tubb, state superintendent of public education; and State

Senator Earl Evans Jr. of Canton, Madison County, chair of the Senate Finance Committee. The rest of the members of LEAC were composed of one state senator appointed by the lieutenant governor, two state representatives appointed by the House Speaker, the president of the Mississippi State Bar Association, and two "outstanding" constitutional lawyers and six "outstanding" citizens appointed by the governor. Governor White became chair of LEAC, and the committee designated Speaker Sillers as vice chair. Gore, who served as secretary of the Legislative Recess Education Committee during 1952 and 1953, was appointed as secretary.[34] LEAC's expenses were paid out of the contingent funds of the House and Senate.[35]

When LEAC was standing by in Mississippi awaiting the governor's eight appointees, the Supreme Court in Washington finally spoke out. On Monday, May 17, 1954, the Court outlawed legally imposed racial segregation in public schools in the epoch-making *Brown v. Board of Education of Topeka* ruling. Reversing the Court's own 1896 precedent that established the doctrine of "separate but equal," Chief Justice Earl Warren concluded in the unanimous opinion that the doctrine "has no place" in the field of public education. "Separate educational facilities," the chief justice added, "are inherently unequal."[36] Upon hearing the Court's decision, the *Jackson Daily News* predicted that "human blood may stain Southern soil in many places because of this decision but the dark red stains of that blood will be on the marble steps of the United States Supreme Court building." Governor White, nonetheless, urged that a "slow" and "cautious" approach be taken to maintain the racial segregation in the state's public schools. A few days later, the governor hurriedly appointed two lawyers and six citizens to the newly created LEAC.[37] Meanwhile, on the floor of the United States House of Representatives on May 19, Representative John Bell Williams from Mississippi, a future governor of the state, called the day of the *Brown* decision "Black Monday"—a phrase that "was to stick as a Southern epithet."[38] However, the Mississippian who rendered the greatest contribution to making the phrase "Black Monday" so popular in the entire South was State Circuit Judge Thomas P. "Tom" Brady. Soon after the Supreme Court issued its *Brown* decree, Judge Brady, who had walked out of the 1948 Democratic National Convention as one of the state's delegates six years earlier, delivered his address entitled "Black Monday" before the chapter of the Sons of the American Revolution in Greenwood, Mississippi. Later, Elliot Lawrence, owner of the Lawrence Printing Company in Greenwood, obtained a copy of Brady's address through a newspaper reporter. At Lawrence's request, the judge then extended his address into a pamphlet by. the same title, and Lawrence subsequently printed several hundred copies of it with Brady's consent.[39] In *Black Monday*, though the judge graciously indicated that he did not intend to "ridicule or abuse" the black race, Brady's viciousness was abundantly revealed:

> [Y]ou can dress a chimpanzee . . . and teach him to use a knife and fork,
> but it will take countless generations of evolutionary development, if ever,
> before you can convince him that a caterpillar or a cockroach is not a delicacy.
> Likewise, the social, political, economic, and religious preferences of the Negro
> remain close to the caterpillar and the cockroach. . . . There is nothing funda-
> mentally wrong with the caterpillar or the cockroach. It is merely a matter of
> taste. A cockroach or caterpillar remains proper food for a chimpanzee.[40]

While Brady's book was well received in the state, the harshest reaction to the *Brown* ruling came from salvoes fired by United States Senator James O. Eastland from Mississippi. On the day the *Brown* decision was handed down, Senator Eastland asserted that the South "will not abide by nor obey this legislative decision by a political court." "Any attempt to integrate our schools," the senator warned, "would cause great strife and turmoil."[41] Ten days later the Mississippi senator launched one of his strongest attacks against the nation's highest court. Standing on the floor of the Senate, Eastland accused the Supreme Court of its "reckless disregard of official oath and public duty" because "[w]hat the Court has done has been to legislate addi-tional civil rights, which [was] admittedly not heretofore authorized by the Constitution or by Congress." "Mr. President," Eastland proclaimed, "let me make this very clear: The South will retain segregation."[42]

A significant feature of the 1954 *Brown* decision was that the Supreme Court did not issue any enforcement order. In the Court's unanimous ruling, Chief Justice Warren admitted that "the formulation of decrees in these cases presents problems of considerable complexity" because of "the wide applicability of this decision, and because of the great variety of local condi-tions."[43] Having not been able to pronounce any immediate remedy, the Court decided to hear further arguments on the means of implementing its decision. "No matter what delayed plan the Supreme Court may propose for enforcement of its decision," Fred Sullens, editor of the *Jackson Daily News*, wrote on June 15, "that plan is not going to be accepted in Mississippi."[44] Echoing Sullens's resolve, fourteen white Mississippians met at the home of David H. Hawkins, manager of a cotton compress company, in Indianola, Sunflower County, on July 11. The purpose of the meeting, which was called by Robert B. Patterson, a cotton and cattle farmer from nearby Holly Ridge, was to "set out to organize a pressure group that would be a counterbalance" to the National Association for the Advancement of Colored People (NAACP).[45] Before they held their first official meeting, the founders of this "counterbalance" to the NAACP pondered naming their new group the Sons of the White Camellia as a composite name of the two Reconstruction-era white secret organizations in the occupied South—the Sons of Midnight and the Knights of White Camellia. But in the end they decided to call their new organization the Citizens' Council. The founders then asked the author of *Black Monday*, Judge Brady, to assist them in writing the charter and by-laws of the Council and later invited him to speak at the first official meeting.[46]

Immediately after the *Brown* decision was announced, disaffected white southerners began to organize a number of segregationist and anti-*Brown* private organizations throughout the South. Among these, the Citizens' Council was destined to become the most vocal and widespread organization in the region, particularly in the five Deep South states. Unlike the bulk of the members of some violence-prone Ku Klux Klan–type segregationist groups, the Council members enjoyed relatively high community status, and most of them were thought of as "respectable" citizens. The Council soon attracted lawyers, doctors, bankers, businesspeople, state and federal judges, state and national lawmakers, and even southern governors. In fact, when the Council founders met in Indianola to organize the group, they were determined "to retain control of resistance to desegregation in the hands of the 'better people.' "[47] As one Council movement observer wrote, their membership rosters "read like a Southern 'Who's Who,' " and "a halo of respectability hovers over them."[48] Avoiding the use of hooded violence, these "respectable" members preferred subtler and more sophisticated forms of resistance, which included propaganda activities using the mass media, economic reprisals, and nonviolent interference with the activities of the NAACP. Although the Council leadership steadfastly maintained that it was "not the intent or purpose" of their organization "to be (or to be used) as a political machine," each chapter of the Council had four major committees, including a Political and Elections Committee. According to a mimeographed form sent to prospective Council members in Mississippi, the stated aims of the committee were to "screen all candidates in local and state elections against those who might be seeking the Negro vote" and to "discourage Negro [voter] registration by every legal means."[49] As early as 1955, the Council's political influence began to steal over the government of "the Council's mother state," to borrow the words of Neil R. McMillen.[50]

Even after the Supreme Court rendered what Richard Kluger termed "simple justice" in the school desegregation ruling, Governor White was still hopeful that he could persuade black Mississippians to cooperate with the state's white leaders in keeping its public schools segregated.[51] On July 30, White called a statewide biracial meeting and, conferring with about ninety black leaders along with the members of LEAC, the governor urged the black leaders to endorse a "voluntary" segregation plan for the perpetuation of the state's segregated school system.[52] However, led by Dr. T. R. M. Howard of the all-black town of Mound Bayou in Bolivar County, who organized the Regional Council of Negro Leadership in 1951, the gathered black attendees opposed the governor's plan.[53] Expressing his "greatest shock" and "greatest disappointment," Governor White later recollected the meeting with disgust: "It [the "voluntary" segregation plan] won't work. I have been shaken, my faith [in the state's black leaders] is gone, and it's gone as a result of [what] I have heard [from the black leaders] with my own ears."[54] Following the failure of this biracial meeting, Governor White called a meeting of LEAC on the very same day. There, all twenty-five committee members voted to support the governor in calling a special session of the state legislature in September, whose main purpose would be to consider a constitutional amendment abolishing the state's public school system.[55] On August 12, another meeting was held in the House chamber between the LEAC members and Mississippi's public school officials from all eighty-two counties. Mindful that many of the gathered school officials did not appreciate, or at least were suspicious of, his scheme to abolish the state's public school system altogether, Governor White asked them for their "cooperation" and "sympathy" in his efforts to deal with "the biggest problem that has ever confronted Mississippi since Reconstruction days." "And, remember too, that we are a

Sovereign State," the governor went on, "[and] that we do have certain powers, and should it ever become necessary to exercise that power, that power is going to be used." One member of the Jasper County School Board, who was a retired Methodist minister, responded: "I am ready to follow our leaders. We have got to follow our leaders. The thing that we are fighting for, above everything else, is the purity of our white blood."[56]

The planned 1954 special legislative session started on September 7. In his message delivered to the joint assembly of the House and Senate, Governor White reiterated that he was "most positively and unexpectedly disappointed" with the results of his meeting with the state's black leaders. The governor then asked the legislature to adopt the constitutional amendment that would abolish the public schools as "a last resort" to prevent racial integration in the state.[57] By this time, LEAC had announced that, unless the amendment was approved, there would be no equalization program for the state's black public schools. Moreover, its chair, Governor White, also declared that he would not call the state legislature into another special session in early 1955 to consider school funds for the 1955–56 school year if the legislature was not given the "last resort" authority to close the schools.[58] Upon hearing the governor's message, on the first day of the special session, fifty-five state representatives introduced a concurrent resolution that provided that the legislature would submit a constitutional amendment to the state's voters. If approved, the amendment would authorize the legislature "to abolish the public schools" in Mississippi by a two-thirds vote of those present and voting in each House.[59] On September 10, the resolution was adopted in the House by a vote of 105 to 14, and the Senate concurred on September 16 by a vote of 37 to 0.[60] The legislature then submitted the amendment to the voters' approval, and on December 21 it was passed by more than a two to one majority. Geopolitically, the strongest support for the amendment came from the Mississippi Delta counties. Sunflower County, home of Senator Eastland, for example, voted 2,465 for and 78 against the amendment.[61] The twenty-six counties where it was known that chapters of the Citizens' Council had been organized solidly supported the amendment's ratification, providing the state legislature with one of the most formidable "stand-by" powers to combat racial integration in Mississippi.[62]

Five months later the Supreme Court issued the implementation decision of its 1954 *Brown* ruling, which would later be referred to as *Brown II*. Before the Court handed down the *Brown II* decision, in April 1955 it held oral arguments on the means of implementing the original *Brown* decree. Although the Court invited all states that would be affected by the *Brown* ruling to participate in the hearing, only six states—Arkansas, Florida, Maryland, North Carolina, Oklahoma, and Texas—accepted the Court's invitation.[63] Aside from South Carolina, which had already been involved in the initial *Brown* decision, the rest of the Deep South states rejected the invitation "on the grounds that such participation might imply an obligation to comply or that it was futile to debate implementing a decision which was not recognized as valid in the first place."[64] Admitting that implementation of the principles of the *Brown* ruling would "require solution of varied local school problems," Chief Justice Warren confirmed on May 31, 1955, that "the primary responsibility for elucidating, assessing, and solving" the school segregation problems would rest with local school authorities. At the same time, the Court made it clear that the lower federal courts would have responsibilities "to consider whether the action of school authorities constitutes good faith implementation of the governing constitutional principles." The Court's unanimous opinion concluded: "[T]he cases are remanded to the District Courts to take such proceedings and enter such orders and decrees consistent with this opinion as are necessary and proper to admit to public schools on a racially non-discriminatory basis with all deliberate speed the parties to these cases. . . ."[65]

In a legal sense, the Supreme Court showed its self-contradiction in handing down the first and second *Brown* decisions. While the Court declared in the first *Brown* decision that segregated black schoolchildren had a right to attend racially nonsegregated public schools under the Fourteenth Amendment to the Constitution, the same Court virtually "denied these same children a full and instant implementation of this constitutional right" in *Brown II*.[66] This self-contradiction and perhaps the Court's agony were accurately expressed in the brief phrase, "with all deliberate speed." As a result, the Supreme Court ended up suggesting a policy of gradualism, which in turn granted white southerners sufficient time to organize against what they termed "federal encroachment" on their "segregated way of life."[67]

Propelled by the Court's implementation decision, black Mississippians for the first time began to file school desegregation petitions in the summer of 1955 in such cities as Jackson, Vicksburg, Yazoo City, Natchez, and

Clarksdale under the auspices of the NAACP. The Vicksburg school desegregation petition was drafted by Thurgood Marshall, chief counsel for the NAACP in New York. However, no action other than "received and filed" was taken by the school board in Vicksburg, and in each community where the petition drives were launched the local chapters of the Citizens' Council dutifully crushed them. In Yazoo City, out of the total of fifty-two who signed the petition, fifty eventually lost their employment and two others left the state.[68]

As the summer of 1955 was drawing nearer, Mississippi was getting ready for its gubernatorial election, with racial segregation being an important issue. State Attorney General James Coleman won the state Democratic Party's second primary on August 23 and was elected to the governorship without Republican challenge.[69] After graduating from the University of Mississippi in 1935, Coleman went to Washington, D.C., as a legislative assistant to Mississippi Representative Aaron Ford, where he was exposed to the world of national politics. Upon returning to his hometown, Ackerman in Choctaw County, he opened a law office. Thereafter, he was elected state district attorney, state circuit judge, commissioner of the Mississippi State Supreme Court, and state attorney general.[70] Shortly after the gubernatorial election, Governor-Elect Coleman submitted a six-point program to LEAC for the purpose of strengthening Mississippi's fortress to preserve racial segregation. The Coleman-sponsored program included these proposals:

1. To prohibit common law marriages by statute.
2. To repeal the compulsory school attendance law.
3. To provide penalties for illegal bargain made by an outsider with a party to a suit and to punish "agitation court suits" to end segregation.
4. To provide penalties for abusive and obscene telephone calls and strengthen the law on criminal libel.
5. To provide penalties for persons interfering with state law under color of federal authority.
6. To create a permanent authority for maintenance of racial segregation with a full staff and funds for its operation to come out of tax money.[71]

Subsequently, one more proposal, which would require "all teachers paid from public funds to make affidavits as to all organizations they hold membership in," was added to the initial six. All seven proposals were readily approved at LEAC's December 14 meeting and were to be submitted to the

1956 state legislature.[72] The Jackson chapter of the Citizens' Council promptly passed a resolution endorsing the seven proposals and called upon the state legislature for their immediate passage. William J. Simmons, secretary of the Jackson Citizens' Council and future administrator of the Citizens' Councils of America, praised the state's white leadership in a letter to White: "A giant stride has been made on our side of the struggle, and we are heartened by this evidence of courageous and intelligent leadership. We offer the full and active support of our council in implementing your program."[73] As the cloud of racial conformity began to cover Mississippi, the state's political leaders were getting ready to "create a permanent authority for maintenance of racial segregation," which would replace LEAC as a full-time state agency.

THE MISSISSIPPI STATE
SOVEREIGNTY COMMISSION

Chapter 1

TO PROTECT THE SOVEREIGNTY
OF THE STATE OF MISSISSIPPI

The Origins of the State Sovereignty Commission

On January 17, 1956, James Coleman was sworn in as the fifty-second governor of Mississippi. After Chief Justice Harvey McGehee of the Mississippi State Supreme Court administered the oath of office to Coleman, the state's new chief executive began to deliver his inaugural address in the presence of the joint legislative assembly. Referring to his resolve to maintain "the continued separation of the white and negro races" in Mississippi, the governor proclaimed: "I say to this audience . . . that I have not the slightest fear that four years hence when my successor stands on this same spot to assume his official oath, the separation of the races in Mississippi will be left intact and will still be in full force and effect in exactly the same manner and form as we know it today."[1]

Though Coleman made a solemn vow that he would stand fast to defend "Mississippi's way of life," the new governor hastened to add that "this is no task for the amateur or the hothead" and reminded Mississippians that they "must keep cool heads and calm judgement" in dealing with "all the provocation which is being hurled" upon them "from almost every direction."[2] Notwithstanding the new governor's plea for calmness, an overwhelming

3

mood of defiance to the federal government dominated the state legislative session, which began on January 3, and the session would soon witness the introduction of a parade of bills and resolutions designed to protect Mississippi's racial customs and its sovereignty. All of the seven segregationist proposals devised and recommended by the Legal Educational Advisory Committee (LEAC) the previous year were introduced in the session in the form of specific bills. By the end of February, four of these bills had been passed by both Houses and signed into law by Governor Coleman.[3] One of the bills, which received the governor's blessing on February 24, repealed the state's compulsory education laws, whereby the state would be able to renounce its authority and responsibility to educate the Mississippi children if and when the state was forced to do so under the circumstances of racial integration.[4] However, the legislature's strongest determination to defend the state against the "illegal encroachment" of the federal government was expressed in its adoption of the interposition resolution.

The preparation for the interposition resolution began on January 26 when House Concurrent Resolution No. 12 was introduced, providing for the appointment of a thirteen-member joint legislative committee to draft the resolution. The House adopted the concurrent resolution that day, and four days later the Senate followed suit.[5] Senator Earl Evans, the president pro tempore of the upper House, became chair of the joint committee, or the Committee on Interposition, and Senator Bland Hayden Campbell of Jackson headed a subcommittee to which the actual task of drafting the interposition resolution was conferred.[6] On February 29, in submitting the committee's preliminary report to the legislature, Evans, standing on the Senate floor, elaborated that the "only [legal] approach" that Mississippi would be able to depend upon in defense of its state sovereignty and racial integrity was found "in what Jefferson, Madison, and Calhoun and many others termed 'the Right of Interposition,'" which "still remains [effective] though it has not been used in some eighty years."[7] Evans then asked the entire Senate to introduce and approve his committee's draft of the interposition resolution in the form of a Senate concurrent resolution. Rising to the occasion, Lieutenant Governor Carroll Gartin, the presiding officer of the Senate, stepped from his platform to speak for the Senate's adoption of Evans's elevated proposal: "We are not willing to sit idly by and see rights reserved unto us trampled under foot and taken away by the Supreme Court.

By all honorable and legal methods, we are going to wage a great fight to keep our traditions."[8]

Following the lieutenant governor's plea, as if to show its strong determination, the entire forty-nine-member Senate introduced and approved the state's interposition resolution, which provided: "That the State of Mississippi has at no time, through the Fourteenth Amendment to the Constitution of the United States, or in any manner whatsoever, delegated to the Federal Government its right to educate and nurture its youth and its power and right of control over its schools, colleges, educational and other public institutions and facilities, and to prescribe the rules, regulations and conditions under which they shall be conducted."[9] Noting further that "a question of contested power has arisen" between the state government of Mississippi and the federal government, it declared that Mississippi had the right "to interpose for arresting the progress of the evil." Finally, the resolution asserted the state's "firm intention to take all appropriate measures honorably and constitutionally available" to "void this illegal encroachment" upon the rights reserved to Mississippi and invited all states "to join in taking such steps as are necessary to settle the grave question of contested sovereignty."[10]

The interposition resolution was immediately sent to the House for its consideration, and the lower House also concurred by a vote of 137 to 0.[11] When the bill passed, five House members stood up and broke into a chorus of "Dixie."[12] Thus, the interposition resolution—the state's virtual official declaration to refuse to recognize the Supreme Court's anti-segregation decisions—easily passed both Houses, and copies of the resolution were transmitted, through the governor's office, to President Dwight D. Eisenhower, the governors of the other forty-seven states, all members of Congress, and all nine justices of the Supreme Court.[13]

With the defiance of the federal government at its height, Mississippi lawmakers turned to creating a tax-supported implementation agency of the resolves expressed in the interposition resolution, seeking to materialize the initiation of "a permanent authority for maintenance of racial segregation" advocated by LEAC in September 1955. On March 20, led by House Speaker Walter Sillers, fifty-eight state representatives introduced House Bill No. 880 providing for the creation of the Mississippi State Sovereignty Commission as part of the executive branch of the state government.[14] Defining the purpose of the Sovereignty Commission, Section 5 of the bill read:

⅄   It shall be the duty of the commission to do and perform any and all acts and things deemed necessary and proper to protect the sovereignty of the State of Mississippi, and her sister states, from encroachment thereon by the Federal Government . . . and to resist the usurpation of the rights and powers reserved to this state and our sister states by the Federal Government or any branch, department or agency thereof.[15]

Despite the fact that the Sovereignty Commission was soon to be identified as Mississippi's "segregation watchdog agency," neither the word "segregation" nor the word "integration" appeared in the carefully crafted bill. But to be sure, federal "encroachment" was a periphrasis implying "forced racial integration," and "to protect the sovereignty of the State of Mississippi" from that "encroachment" was a sophisticated roundabout expression of the state's resolve "to preserve and protect the racial segregation in the state." With the aura of sophistication and respectability emanating from the word "sovereignty," the Commission, for all practical purposes, was expected "to maintain segregation in the State of Mississippi" and to wreck "the NAACP and any other organization which is attempting to advocate integration and trampling" the rights reserved to the state.[16]

While the bill further provided in Section 6 that "the commission may co-operate with one or more of the states of the Union, or any agency or agencies, commission or commissions thereof, or with any person or persons, corporation or corporations, [and] organization or organizations" in achieving its objectives, it also empowered the state agency to carry out public relations activities on behalf of the state. Section 13 read that the agency "may expend . . . its funds deemed necessary for advertisement" and for employment of "speakers and other persons and agencies" to spread the virtue of Mississippi's "segregated way of life." The next to last section of the bill dealt with the protective measures for the bill itself. "If any section, paragraph, sentence, or clause of this act shall be held to be unconstitutional or invalid," it provided, "the same shall not effect [*sic*] any other part, portion or provision of this act, but such other part shall remain in full force and effect." Finally, the bill spelled out that the Commission would be composed of twelve members, including four ex officio members: the governor, the lieutenant governor, the House Speaker, and the attorney general. In addition, there would be two members of the Senate appointed by the lieutenant governor, three members of the House appointed by the Speaker, and three citizen members appointed by the governor. The governor and the lieutenant governor would serve as chair and vice chair of the state agency, respectively.[17] The segregationist *Jackson Daily News* and the liberal *Greenville Delta Democrat-Times* both agreed that the powers to be vested in the Sovereignty Commission "virtually amount to a blank check."[18]

When the Sovereignty Commission bill was introduced into the lower chamber by all-powerful House Speaker Sillers and a host of his like-minded colleagues, its passage in the legislature seemed an easy task. Though that turned out to be the case in the Senate, the bill had a rather uneasy beginning in the House. In the first vote taken there on March 21, only two representatives—George W. Rogers Jr. of Vicksburg, Warren County, and Woodrow Wilson "Woody" Hewitt of Meadville, Franklin County—opposed the bill. Neither of them took the floor to debate the bill's substance. However, during the afternoon session on the same day, Rogers and three other lawmakers, including Joseph E. Wroten of Greenville, Washington County, entered "a motion to reconsider" the first vote.[19] Wroten, who was destined to become an almost lone dissenter in the state's "massive resistance" policies, recollected later: "When the bill was first presented, it was presented as if it were just a group which would advocate constitutional government, orderly disposition of concerns about race relationships and the like." "And indeed," he added, "there was even an illustration of it as being the counterpart of a group . . . called the Virginia Commission [on] Constitutional Government." But the Greenville representative and some of his colleagues soon learned that the bill "was something that was being sponsored" by the Citizens' Council. On the following day, having realized the probability that, if the Sovereignty Commission was created, "it would be misused . . . [and] would serve as a handmaiden" for the Council, Representatives Wroten, Karl Wiesenburg of Pascagoula, Jackson County, and William F. Winter of Grenada, Grenada County, a future governor of the state, joined twenty other lawmakers in voting against the bill. In the end, ninety-one representatives favored the bill, and twenty-three House members were against it, with twenty-six others being recorded as either "absent" or simply "not voting."[20] The next day, Wroten, Winter, and seven other representatives entered the following explanation concerning their votes on the Sovereignty Commission bill in the

Journal of the House of Representatives: "The language of Section 6 may be susceptible of the construction that expenditures of state tax funds could be made in support of and under the partial control of private persons, corporations or organizations. Desiring to offer an amendment for the purpose of removing this possibility, we therefore voted to reconsider the bill for that purpose."[21]

Notwithstanding their expressed concern, Section 6 remained intact in the Senate, and the Sovereignty Commission bill was unanimously adopted in the upper House by a vote of forty-eight to zero.[22] The fears entertained by Representatives Wroten, Winter, and others would become a reality within four years under the administration of Coleman's successor. On March 29, 1956, with the blessing of Governor Coleman, Mississippi created the Mississippi State Sovereignty Commission.[23] The grand task conferred upon the new state agency was "to protect the sovereignty of the State of Mississippi." While the words "encroachment" and "usurpation" embodied the state's watchwords of the day, white Mississippians, in the eyes of the nation, became an embattled minority. A week later, the fledgling Sovereignty Commission was given a two-year appropriation of $250,000 by the state legislature, and with that the Commission officially replaced the two-year-old LEAC.[24] In the middle of April, fulfilling his duty, Governor Coleman announced the appointment of "three of the state's outstanding lawyers" to the newly organized state agency: Will S. Henley of Hazlehurst, Copiah County, a former member of the now defunct LEAC and a past president of the Mississippi State Bar Association; Hugh N. Clayton of New Albany, Union County, the newly elected president of the state's bar association; and George J. Thornton of Kosciusko, Attala County, a member of the state Democratic Party's executive committee.[25] Later, in February 1959, Thornton resigned from the Commission to take a post as a member of the State Oil and Gas Board. Governor Coleman eventually filled Thornton's place with "one of the outstanding school superintendents in the State of Mississippi"—H. V. Cooper of Vicksburg, Warren County—"to give the school people representation on the Sovereignty Commission."[26] Following a conference with Coleman, Lieutenant Governor Gratin and House Speaker Sillers appointed two senators and three representatives, respectively, to the Sovereignty Commission on April 28. Gartin's choices were Senators Evans and William G. Burgin Jr. of Columbus, Lowndes County. Senator Evans, who was a special agent of the Federal Bureau of Investigation (FBI) before he began his political career as a state lawmaker, had been a member of LEAC and served as chair of the joint legislative Committee on Interposition. Meanwhile, Sillers's appointees were Representatives George Payne Cossar of Charleston, Tallahatchie County; William H. Johnson Jr. of Decatur, Newton County; and Joseph W. Hopkins of Clarksdale, Coahoma County, who also had been a member of LEAC. The four ex officio members of the Commission included Coleman, Gartin, Sillers, and Attorney General Joe T. Patterson.[27]

After an organizational meeting held in Governor Coleman's office on May 2, the Sovereignty Commission announced its plan to set up a publicity office within the agency. At the same meeting, the Commission members also contemplated the employment of "a special attorney" with "wide federal court experience" who would "co-operate with the attorney general's office and take over any segregation litigation" filed against Mississippi. Subsequently, however, the Commission dropped its plan to hire an attorney, instead endorsing the idea of employing investigators for the state agency.[28] On May 15, at the third meeting in two weeks, the Commission decided to hire a full-time director "who shall keep a record of the proceedings of the commission" and a public relations director and two investigators who would be expected "to carry out the objectives and purposes" of the agency. As the first director of Mississippi's "segregation watchdog agency," Governor Coleman appointed Representative Ney Gore, who had served as secretary of LEAC, to the $7,200-a-year post. Hal C. DeCell, editor of the weekly *Deer Creek Pilot* in the small Delta town of Rolling Fork and publicity manager for the Coleman camp in the 1955 gubernatorial campaign, was appointed public relations director. Previously, DeCell had expressed his eagerness to the governor to have a share in initiating the state's public relations programs to give "Mississippi a voice in presenting its side." "I've been polishing some ideas for potential campaigns . . . in anticipation of the day when I can finally hitch up the horses," the former publicity manager wrote to Coleman in February 1956, promising the governor that "within six months after we hitch up the horses you'll be able to see direct and tangible results." With a maximum salary of $6,500 a year, DeCell was expected to combat "the animosities against the state" that had been "generated by vicious and slanderous misrepresentations and falsehoods appearing in national publications at the behest of . . . antagonistic pressure groups" represented by the NAACP.[29]

Along with the public relations department, the governor recommended the creation of the investigative department within the Commission that would "serve as the eyes and the ears" in the state's fight against racial integration.[30] To head this department, which the *Daily News* called the "intelligence corps" against the "enemy camp," Leonard C. Hicks was chosen as the Commission's chief investigator. Hicks, who resigned as head of the Mississippi State Highway Patrol to accept the new assignment, was a former sheriff of Sharkey County in the Mississippi Delta and a brother-in-law of former Governor Fielding Wright.[31] The Sovereignty Commission members initially hoped that they would be able to employ an additional investigator who would work under Hicks, but that did not materialize until October 1, 1958, when Zack J. Van Landingham was added to the department.[32] As for the Commission's initial clerical staff, the members employed Mildred Curry and Ruby B. Weeks as full-time secretaries and Bobbye Howell as a part-time secretary.[33] In addition, Governor Coleman appointed a three-member steering committee within the Commission to draft and submit policies to the full Commission. That committee was composed of Patterson, Evans, and Henley.[34]

With its membership being filled and two departments being organized, the new state agency seemed to be in perfect shape. But as soon as the governor appointed Representative Gore as director, the Commission was drawn into the center of a controversy that revolved around the state's traditional "double-dipping" practice—a practice where legislators could assume executive posts without renouncing their legislative positions. Under the Coleman administration, as many as fourteen state legislators worked in the executive agencies between regular legislative sessions, which were then held only once every two years.[35] After consulting with the state auditor, Gore offered his resignation as director of the new Sovereignty Commission to the governor in late May 1956, foreseeing that his continued employment at the Commission as a state lawmaker might "hinder its work by causing public dissension and conflict." Governor Coleman, however, wanted him to stay.[36] Two months later, Jack Armstrong Jr., a Scott County automobile dealer and farmer, and several others from the county brought suit to challenge Gore's right to serve as director of the Commission. The legal problem for the Armstrong party was Section 45 of the state constitution, which read that no state legislator, "during the term for which he was elected, shall be eligible to any office of profit which shall have been created." According to this provision, Gore, who was a member of the 1956 state legislature that created the Sovereignty Commission, should be banned from serving in the state agency. When *Jack Armstrong v. State Auditor Boyd Golding* was filed at the Hinds County Chancery Court in Jackson, Senator Burgin, a member of the Sovereignty Commission, offered his legal services to defend Gore. Meanwhile, in Armstrong's home county, Erle E. Johnston Jr., editor of the weekly *Scott County Times* in Forest and a future director of the Sovereignty Commission, vigorously supported the legal challenge.[37]

In September Attorney General Patterson filed a demurrer at the chancery court, questioning whether the state's taxpayers had the right to challenge Gore's job status and asserting that only his office, in the name of the state of Mississippi, had the right to take such legal action. Chancery Judge L. Arnold Pyle sustained the demurrer and declared that the plaintiffs had "no standing in court." However, the lawsuit dragged on with an appeal to the Mississippi State Supreme Court, and finally, in the middle of October 1957, more than fifteen months after Armstrong and others filed their initial lawsuit, the state's high court rejected the plaintiffs' challenge. Holding that Representative Gore was "a mere employe[e] working at the pleasure and under the direction" of the members of the Sovereignty Commission, the court ruled that Gore's position was not an "office" defined in the state constitution.[38] Ironically, shortly after the court upheld his right to hold the directorship, Gore resigned from the position on November 4. "In view of the length of time which I must devote to the legislature . . . and . . . of several incidents which have transpired during my employment by the commission," his resignation letter read, "I have concluded that the interests of the state and of the commission will be best served by my resignation."[39] After Gore left the Commission, Public Relations Director DeCell became the agency's acting director.[40]

Though many state legislators expected that the Sovereignty Commission would serve as Mississippi's high-powered investigatory "counter agency" to the NAACP when they created it, as the agency's first official report in the fall of 1957 revealed, since its inception the "greater part of the activities of the Commission" had concentrated on "the field of Public Relations."[41] During this period, the primary function of the Sovereignty Commission became that of "a study and propaganda center," and the agency channeled its energies into public relations activities to "give the South's side" in the segregation-integration controversies with a "Voice of Mississippi" program being directed above the Mason-Dixon line.[42] The Commission's initial posture was endorsed enthusiastically not only by Senator James Eastland but also by Sillers, the all-powerful House Speaker. Within a month after the creation of the Sovereignty Commission, speaking before a combined meeting of some local civic clubs in McComb, Pike County, Sillers declared: "[W]e can't win this battle in Mississippi or the South, [for] it must be won in 31 states north of the Mason and Dixon line." The Speaker elaborated his point:

> We will never win it on the race issue alone. It must be won by pointing out to the other states of the union that unless the reserved powers of the states are protected against unlawful usurpation by the federal government . . . the states will be stripped of their sovereign powers, and will exist only as vassals subservient to the will and sufferance of the federal government. . . .
>
> We must win . . . by convincing the people of other states that our cause is not merely racial, but fundamental in that we are fighting for the existence of our form of government. . . .[43]

In the Sovereignty Commission's first activity report submitted to the state legislature, considerable space was given to its public relations projects carried out by DeCell, who once explained that the grand purpose of his department was to "counteract . . . the misinformation that has been spread by poisoned pens" of nonsoutherners.[44] An early example of DeCell's counterattacks was his involvement in editing a documentary film that depicted the public school situation in Clarksdale, Coahoma County, and the nationally publicized 1955 Emmett Till murder case in Money, Leflore County. In the summer of 1956, at the request of the Citizens' Council, the public relations director became involved in the filmmaking process, which was then being pursued by a documentary producer, James Peck, and was underwritten by the Fund for the Republic, Inc.[45]

Officially organized in 1954 to foster the nation's cause of civil rights and civil liberties with some $15 million in grants given by the Ford Foundation, the Fund for the Republic helped rebuild the financially drained Atlanta-based Southern Regional Council (SRC). Chartered as a nonprofit and nonpolitical civil rights organization in Georgia, the SRC began its mission in January 1944 to "make 'separate but equal more equal' " for black southerners, preferring to "work within the system of racial separation" rather than openly opposing the practice in the region. However, in late 1951 the SRC adopted a policy to take "an explicit anti-segregation position," and as its "ultimate hope and aim," the SRC sought to create "the atmosphere in which artificial distinctions and discriminations based upon race will no longer persist" in the South. The Fund for the Republic also provided generous monetary support to the Vanderbilt University School of Law in its undertaking to publish the *Race Relations Law Reporter*.[46]

Using Peck's film made in Clarksdale as the groundwork, Director George M. Martin Jr. of the Newsfilm Project at the Fund for the Republic decided in October to make a comprehensive documentary that, the civil rights organization hoped, would address the contemporary "state of interracial communication" and "the general desegregation problem" in the South.[47] Martin, a former producer at NBC in Hollywood, took the helm of the filmmaking at the Fund's Los Angeles office while Peck, who was invited by the Newsfilm Project to serve under Martin as a consultant, worked at its New York office.[48]

At a glance, the relationship between Mississippi's segregationist agency and the civil rights organization was an unlikely one for, as DeCell once admitted, he and the Fund for the Republic were "separated by a seemingly wide gulf of opinion." But the Sovereignty Commission's public relations director had his own agenda.[49] In late November the Fund's Newsfilm Project asked Governor Coleman to make DeCell "available" to its work for the purpose of "insur[ing] the authenticity" of the documentary on the South. "Hal could be most helpful to us as a technical advisor," Peck wrote to the Mississippi governor on November 30, "in . . . accurately presenting the point of view he represents."[50] Within a month DeCell visited Los Angeles and "conferred at length" with Martin and Peck, where the Commission's public relations officer "contributed many suggestions which he felt would improve acceptance of the film in the South." During DeCell's visit, the Newsfilm Project also arranged a meeting for the publicity director with the Fund's president, Robert M. Hutchins. In the hope of "getting the Fund for the Republic completely off Mississippi's neck," the Sovereignty Commission's shrewd publicist nonchalantly spent the Mississippi taxpayers' money to "entertain" the Fund's officials and employees in Los Angeles.[51] Designated and acting as a "technical advisor" to the producers, DeCell fully exercised his "advisory rights" during the film's editing process in order to ascertain its "complete objectivity" while inducing Martin and Peck to change the film's original title of *Crisis in the South* to *Segregation and the South*.[52]

In May 1957 the Newsfilm Project previewed the nearly completed documentary in Atlanta to "various television and film experts," including De-Cell.[53] After the preview and in the last stage of preparing the film's final script, the Commission official raised an objection to the fact that the documentary reflected "the absence of Negro extremists," as well as to the Fund's "assumption implied in [its] use of the term 'when' rather than 'if' in connection with ultimate desegregation" in Mississippi. In response, Martin pointed out to DeCell that those "Negro extremists" were "almost impossible to find" and, as the official archives of the Fund for the Republic attest, the " 'when' or 'if' " controversy was settled in favor of the Newsfilm Project. Believing that he deserved to be recognized as a "technical advisor" to the Fund for the Republic, DeCell also urged Martin to alter the end titles of the film so that they would also give him "credit." Despite the Mississippi official's insistence, the documentary's final script indicates that the project director refused to include DeCell's name in the credits.[54] Nevertheless, reporting to Commission Director Gore that he had just completed his work on the documentary film, DeCell boasted in late May that his "efforts have been successful almost one hundred per cent" in convincing both the producers and the Fund for the Republic "to remove and delete the objectionable parts of the film dealing with Mississippi" and "to insert portions of [other] film[s] giving our side of the situation." "I have managed to make them remove the Till Case," the public relations director continued, "and have persuaded them to insert sections on Conwell Sykes, Chairman of the Greenville Citizens' Council . . . [and] excerpts from the governor's [Coleman's] Inaugural Address."[55] *Segregation and the South*, to which DeCell succeeded in adding what he termed "pro-segregation interview[s]," was eventually broadcast by ABC in New York and its affiliated stations throughout the nation on June 16, 1957.[56] By then, the Fund for the Republic had announced its board's decision to terminate the Newsfilm Project at the end of June, citing the civil rights organization's "emphasis change" from "direct info[rmation] operation" to "research-study projects."[57] "I was sort of disappointed to learn," DeCell wrote to President Hutchins of the Fund, "that you are giving up the News Film [*sic*] Project."[58] Along with this cajolery, however, the public relations director forwarded his memorandums to Gore in the middle of June jubilantly informing him of the decision made by the "fifteen[-]million[-]dollar organization" to withdraw from its "integration efforts in Mississippi."[59] "I personally am thoroughly satisfied with our success and progress in dealing with what could have been a block-buster against us," the self-praising publicist proclaimed.[60]

While DeCell was keeping busy trying to prevent the "blockbuster" against his native state from exploding, in the fall of 1956 he also organized the Commission's most publicized propaganda stunt under the Coleman administration in the agency's efforts to neutralize the "poisoned pens" of northern journalists. Earlier, DeCell attended a convention of the New England Press Association held in Cape Cod, Massachusetts, and invited some newspaper editors to visit Mississippi and "see the [state's racial] situation for themselves."[61] Through DeCell's efforts, a group of twenty small-town New England newspaper editors and publishers came to Mississippi at the state's expense. The group included seven editors from Massachusetts, five from Connecticut, three from New Hampshire, two each from Maine and Vermont, and one from New York. From October 6 to October 14 the editors toured the state as guests of the Sovereignty Commission. The grand purpose of the tour, as the Commission later reported, "was to breach the wall of sensational journalism which has stood for so long between the South and a national understanding of its problems."[62] "We just wanted to let you see for yourselves," DeCell told the touring editors, "that Mississippians are not like the pictures painted by some Northern publications," and he promised to show them whatever they would want to see because the state had "nothing to cover up."[63] Welcoming the editors, Governor Coleman told them on their first day in Mississippi that there would be no racial integration in the state for at least "50 years." "This is not based on hatred for the colored people," the governor hastened to add, "but the situation is such that we must have segregation if we are going to have any public education at all."[64]

After the brief conference with Coleman, the New Englanders boarded a bus chartered by the Sovereignty Commission and headed out on a week-long tour. Their itinerary included a two-day visit to the heavily black-populated Mississippi Delta region, a visit to the all-black town of Mound Bayou in Bolivar County, a steamer trip down the Mississippi River from Vicksburg to Natchez, and a weekend visit to Biloxi, a resort area on the Gulf Coast.[65] As the end of the tour approached, a few of the participants, such as J. Clark Samuel, president of the Massachusetts Press Association and editor of the *Foxboro Reporter*, began to realize that "there will never be integration" in the state and that "Mississippi's way of life will remain as it is."[66] But most of the editors believed that racial segregation was on the way out even in Mississippi. Paul C. Cummings Jr., editor and publisher of the *Peterborough Transcript* in New Hampshire, was one of the critics of "Mississippi's way of life." "Too many Mississippians are like the ostrich who buries his head in the sand," Cummings offered, "[and] [y]ou can't solve the problem that way, by intimating that it doesn't exist."[67] Having noted that Mississippi was seized by "a fear complex on the part of the white," William B. Rotch, another visitor from New Hampshire as editor of the *Milford Cabinet*, wrote in early 1957: "We promise[d] [ourselves] many times during the trip not to try to tell the South how to settle its difficulties." But he went on to admit that he could not resist making some comments on what impressed him "as the major social problem" of the South and, particularly, of Mississippi. Rotch contended that Mississippi's "major social problem" would not be solved "by pretending it does not exist" or "by blaming difficulties on 'outside agitators' and 'northern radicals.' "[68] In spite of these criticisms, the self-contented Sovereignty Commission prided itself on the tour's success in its own report:

> It is true that a certain national news magazine [*Time*] used only the worst comments it could find in its story, but after all, Mississippians have learned long ago to expect no more from such publishers. . . .
> It is our opinion that the tour was tremendously successful and will prove of great benefit to the state for years to come.[69]

The vast majority of the newspaper editors in Mississippi also praised the Commission's publicity scheme, and many of them eagerly quoted some of the favorable writings about the state offered by the Yankee editors. There were, however, a few dissenting voices heard in the state. Mary D. Cain, editor and publisher of the weekly *Summit Sun*, was one of the vocal dissenters. Daring to call the Commission-sponsored tour a "boo-boo," Cain criticized the agency's entire publicity stunt as a "great waste of time, money and effort." Another scornful reaction was exhibited by Curtis Mullen and Philip Mullen, copublishers of the weekly *Madison County Herald*, who described the tour in their editorial as one for which "our hard earned tax money [was] thrown away."[70] By the time the Sovereignty Commission published its report on the tour, entitled *Report to the People*, in a handsome thirty-page booklet form, it claimed that "over five hundred full pages of newspaper space over the nation" had been devoted to the articles written by those twenty editors from New England on the Mississippi tour.[71] While glorifying its *Report to the People* as "[o]ne of the [agency's] most impressive pamphlets," the Commission later clapped for itself: "It is this type of reawakening and educating those who have been brainwashed in other sections of the country which we are seeking."[72] For the purpose of "educating" the twenty northerners to understand that Mississippi would not need "outside agitators" in solving its own racial problems, the self-righteous state agency expended a total of $2,007.56, which included $1,500.01 for the participants' "transportation to [the] state," $302.40 for a "charter bus," and $36.40 for providing "meal[s] aboard [a] government steamer."[73]

In addition to DeCell's endeavors to "indoctrinate" Yankee reporters who covered the state's race relations, the dissemination of a large quantity of direct mail outside the South was another grand public relations project that the Sovereignty Commission carried out in its efforts "to educate the rest of the country . . . on Mississippi's problem with reference to segregation and the progress the negro is making in this State."[74] By the fall of 1957, more than 200,000 pamphlets and other forms of direct mail had been sent to the newspaper editors, television stations, and state lawmakers above the Mason-Dixon line.[75] One of the Commission's pamphlets, which was distributed in the early stages of its direct mailing project, was entitled *Don't Stone Her until You Hear Her Side*. Its front cover bore a caricature of a white woman—the personifying figure for Mississippi—who was being stoned by three white men representing "Pressure Groups" from the North. It also depicted the same woman being criticized by another white man with a club in his hand, who embodied "National Circulation Seekers." Seven thousand copies of the pamphlet were mailed to "non-southern hometown newspapers and radio and television stations" by the public relations department, with DeCell's personal invitation to visit Mississippi to "see the [state's racial] situation for themselves."[76]

The pamphlet, whose subtitle read *All Mississippi Asks Is Fairness and a Chance to Present Its Side of the Case*, further explained that "the continuation of utterly false accusations against our state and its people" had led to "the creation of a Public Relations Department" of the Sovereignty Commission in order "to aid in the dissemination of the truth about Mississippi to fair-minded citizens of the nation." The department's objective, it added, was "not to obscure the bad, but to give equal attention to the good that abound[s] in Mississippi." Urging people outside the state to write DeCell whenever they would make trips to or through Mississippi, the Commission promised that it would gladly "aid" them "in meeting the people in every section of the state."[77]

In mapping out its public relations strategies, the Sovereignty Commission did not pass over the influence of the state's black opinion leaders, such as clergy, newspaper publishers, and educators. As early as the summer of 1956 the Commission conceived a plan to utilize some black conservatives in the state to propagate the sanity of racial segregation, many of whom would soon be mustered as the agency's quasi-investigators and informants. While suggesting that "the direct mail method be used" by the Sovereignty Commission "for the dissemination of literature," Senator Burgin brought up the agency's possible use of black opinion leaders for the first time at the Commission's June 20 meeting. At the conclusion of the meeting, Burgin made a motion asking both Gore and DeCell "to determine what arrangements could be made" with Rev. Henry Harrison "H. H." Humes of Greenville, Percy Greene of Jackson, and Rev. J. W. Jones of New Albany for "securing the services of their newspapers as disseminators of favorable publicity for the Commission." The motion was unanimously approved.[78]

Rev. Humes was pastor of the New Hope Baptist Church, and he also edited a weekly newspaper called the *Delta Leader*.[79] The minister, whom DeCell often referred to as "a negro leader who is on our side," would soon become the Sovereignty Commission's principal paid informant. Through an arrangement made by the Commission's publicity director, Humes also appeared in *Segregation and the South* produced by the Fund for the Republic, along with "another negro segregationist from Greenville" by the name of Levi Chappell. "Segregation has proven," Humes declared in the film, "that

Negroes in the South . . . have done a fine job in making themselves secure by building his [*sic*] society and . . . an economic strength."[80]

Percy Greene was editor and publisher of the weekly *Jackson Advocate* founded in 1938. Recognized as somewhat of an "Uncle Tom" by many black citizens, Greene, in his numerous editorials, frequently called attention to the social and economic progress that black Mississippians had achieved under the segregated system in the state. He later became a vigorous critic of any "outside agitators," including Martin Luther King Jr., who, he claimed, came into Mississippi "to dictate the conduct of its affair[s] and force acceptance of such dictates by violence-provoking boycotts and demonstrations."[81] In the summer of 1958 the Commission's public relations department mailed out reprints of one of Greene's editorials—where he endorsed "the continued practice of segregation of the races in Mississippi"—to the agency's "national mailing lists." In exchange for his contribution to the state's segregationist cause, Greene made the Sovereignty Commission subscribe to his *Jackson Advocate* for the purpose of sending his paper to Mississippi's public school libraries. Under the Coleman administration, the Commission had paid an annual fee of $437 to the black newspaperman for a total of 175 subscriptions. Moreover, during 1958 alone, Greene received a total of $3,230 from the state agency; he was paid on seventeen different occasions for either "investigations" or "advertisement."[82]

To a lesser extent than Greene, whose relations with the Sovereignty Commission would last until the end of the 1960s, Rev. J. W. Jones, editor and publisher of the *Community Citizen* in New Albany, Union County, also worked for the state agency. Since founding the paper in December 1949, Jones had been the sole staff of the semimonthly paper, whose masthead proclaimed: "This Is a Negro Paper Dedicated to the Maintenance of Peace, Goodwill, Order, and Domestic Tranquility in Our State." The paper's typical issue usually contained "editorial support for segregation" and some reprints from conservative magazines and newspapers such as *U.S. News and World Report*, Georgia's *Augusta Courier*, the morning *Jackson Clarion-Ledger*, and the evening *Daily News*.[83] The Sovereignty Commission's relations with Jones began when DeCell made an investigative trip to New Albany in April 1957 and "went through" Jones's office files "in quest of editorials to be used in an upcoming mailing piece."[84] Among the Commission members, Sillers, who not only was a subscriber to the *Community Citizen* but also had "entertained admiration and respect" for Jones, was most enthusiastic about forming a liaison between the state agency and the editor. Strongly recommending that the Sovereignty Commission "give financial assistance to this worthy publication," Sillers wrote to Governor Coleman that "Jones needs our help and we need Jones' help."[85] Thereafter, beginning in November 1957, the state agency started to send a $75 monthly contribution to the New Albany editor which, as Jones explained, was spent for distributing the *Community Citizen* "among members of my race aside from a few copies which we send to white supporters to keep them informed of what we are doing." "Every article we write is for the instruction of my people, trying to inform them of the danger of listening to outside agitation and the propaganda of the NAACP," Jones once wrote to Governor Coleman, "[and] [w]e . . . assure you that we will continue . . . to support the social-traditional way of life in our State."[86] On another occasion, Jones wrote to the Commission office asking for "a recommendation" in order for him to solicit financial contributions from the white residents in his community. "I have for some time now watched with a great deal of interest the editorial policy and the attitude of the newspaper . . . edited by J. W. Jones," expressed the agency's investigator who prepared a statement in response. "The advice and counsel of Jones to members of his race as reflected in this newspaper is [*sic*] very instrumental," the Commission's recommendation read, "in combatting influence of the NAACP and in maintaining a healthy relationship between the races in the State of Mississippi." Having said this, the letter concluded that Jones was "doing an excellent job in this respect" and was "worthy of all the support" that he could "obtain from the people of Mississippi."[87] It cannot be determined how effective the Commission's official recommendation was in helping Jones's financial situation. But one can assume that it must have been profitable since Jones would later count upon the same scheme at least two more times.[88] The Sovereignty Commission kept retaining Jones's "services," which were "always along the line of advising negroes to maintain segregation" in Mississippi, and their relationship would last until November 1968 under the three consecutive administrations.[89]

Though not a Mississippian, another notable black who threw himself under the Sovereignty Commission's wing was Rev. M. L. Young, president of an organization called the Mutual Association of Colored People, South, in Memphis, Tennessee. Young's monetary ties with the Commission began in 1957 when he put out the *Mississippi Negro Progress Edition*, a thirty-nine-page booklet that "contained the photographs of numerous Negro schools . . . as well as of Negro personalities" in the state and "attempted to depict the progress of the Negro in education" under the system of racial segregation.[90] As in the case of Greene and Jones, the relations between Young and the Commission lasted until the latter half of the 1960s, when the Commission belatedly found out that Young was "a professional con man" who had been "supported by whites in return for [haphazard] information about civil rights workers" in both Mississippi and Tennessee.[91] For Young, who once inadvertently addressed a letter "Solving Commission" when writing to the Sovereignty Commission, the Mississippi agency was in fact a "solving commission" that took care of his financial needs.[92]

During its formative period, the Sovereignty Commission also contemplated creating a speakers bureau to sell the virtue of Mississippi's "segregated way of life" in the North. The matter was duly discussed at the Commission meetings in June and September 1956, but the plan to initiate the bureau did not receive the approval of Governor Coleman, who feared that such a program would only "stir up a hornet's nest." Clayton sided with Coleman. "The less publicity we have, the better off we are," the governor's appointee persuaded the other unsatisfied members at the September meeting. In the end, the eventual materialization of the Commission's hope to operate its own speakers bureau program needed to wait four years.[93]

Reflecting the governor's policy of avoiding stirring up "a hornet's nest," the state agency's cooperation with other southern states was also finite, notwithstanding its having been given a "blank check" to "protect the sovereignty of the State of Mississippi, and her sister states" from the "encroachment" and "usurpation" by the federal government. At its June 1956 meeting, Henley moved that the Sovereignty Commission "establish liaison" with "commissions and committees similar to this Commission in other states," which were "attempting to maintain state sovereignty." Sillers was another enthusiast who was eager to cultivate such a "liaison." At the Commission's September 1956 meeting, the House Speaker reiterated that the Mississippi agency should immediately begin "contacting other states on the question of cooperating with each other" and "on the proposition of working together to maintain segregation."[94] Prompted by these suggestions, the

Sovereignty Commission invited public relations officials from eight former Confederate states—Alabama, Arkansas, Georgia, Louisiana, North Carolina, South Carolina, Tennessee, and Virginia—and Kentucky to hold a meeting in New Orleans on September 27 and 28, 1956. The Mississippi agency sent both Gore and DeCell to the meeting, where the gathered representatives "expressed interest and enthusiasm" in organizing a cooperative "Voice of the South" program. Besides Mississippi, of those southern states represented at the New Orleans conference, Georgia was the most enthusiastic in embracing the Sovereignty Commission's "idea of an organization of Southern States Publicity Men." However, to the disappointment of Sillers and some other Commission members, this grand idea did not take form.[95]

While the Commission's DeCell-crafted public relations activities appeared to be in good shape, the state auditor was troubled by the public relations director's extravagance and "abuses" of the state funds. DeCell, who frequently attended various meetings and conventions all over the nation in an official capacity, habitually submitted wrongful accounting reports to the State Department of Audit. The items consisting of "charges for hotel rooms" that could not be accounted for by receipts and "erroneous charges for meals" abounded in these reports. For the fiscal year ending in June 1957, the public relations director, who had expended a total of $5,066.51 for "travel expense" during the period between May 15, 1956, and June 30, 1957, was ordered by the audit department to refund $132.02 to the Commission's treasury.[96] Concerned, both State Auditor E. Boyd Golding and Director J. Dexter Barr of the Department of Audit appeared at the Commission's October 1957 meeting and discussed with the members "certain expense vouchers filed by the Director of Public Relations of the Commission." Though in the end no action was taken, the commissioners voted to invite some members of the Mississippi State General Legislative Investigating Committee to attend the next Commission meeting "to discuss this situation."[97] DeCell indifferently continued to make his "business" trips to Dallas, Miami, New Orleans, and other places. His habitual "abuses" were hard to cure, even though Governor Coleman personally directed the publicity officer not to engage in "any more expensive travel in behalf of the Sovereignty Commission" unless his travel plans were submitted to and approved by the full Commission "in advance."[98] "We regret to report that we continue to find similar abuses in the travel expense accounts for the fiscal year ended June 30, 1958," the director of the Department of Audit wrote to the Commission on September 17, 1958. Asking for a clarification of DeCell's accounting items on "the expenditures for entertainment," Barr explained that "no determination can be made as to the number of persons entertained or the type of entertainment offered and therefore no basis can be arrived at as to the reasonableness of the charge."[99]

DeCell's extravagance, in fact, ran to excess. For example, in November 1957 he attended a convention of the Radio and Television News Directors' Association held in Miami, accompanied by Richard R. "Dick" Sanders, news director of a Jackson television station, WLBT. While his trip to the Florida resort cost the Commission a total of $302.95, well over half of the cost— $163.60—was expended on unaccountable "entertainment."[100] Moreover, the state auditor's "detailed check of telephone bills" revealed that "many calls were made at state expense" even though they appeared "to have no connection with the commission's activities."[101]

Finally, Barr was obliged to recommend that "rules and regulations regarding travel expense and telephone calls be adopted" immediately by the Commission "in order that these abuses can be corrected."[102] The audit department's exhortation eventually prompted Maurice L. Malone of Lucedale, George County, who had recently been appointed as the Commission's new director, to call a conference of the agency's employees. At the meeting held on October 13, 1958, Curry, one of the Commission's secretaries, was instructed "to set up a telephone log" for the purpose of "recording all long distance calls made on the part of any employees" of the Commission. It was also made clear that "all travelling by employees both within the State of Mississippi and . . . to a point outside the State" must be "first approved by the Director of the State Sovereignty Commission."[103] Two weeks later Malone sent a memorandum to DeCell, informing him that the director would thereafter "require a copy of the Program of each Convention" to "figure reasonable amounts necessary to be expended" for the publicity director's future trips. Stressing that the Sovereignty Commission should not "receive any {more} complaint from anyone" regarding its accounting, Malone told DeCell that his future "cooperation" would be "greatly appreciated."[104] The controversial public relations director would eventually resign from his position in the early summer of 1959. The outward reason for his departure was due to "the necessity of having to give full time to the operation of his newspaper in Rolling Fork."[105]

For the first one and a half years of the Sovereignty Commission's existence, Mississippi found itself in a relatively "calm frame of mind."[106] After all, the state's public schools were still segregated notwithstanding the Supreme Court's *Brown* rulings, and no immediate counteroffensive by the state NAACP could be detected. However, while the Commission was busy trying to correct the "false accusations" directed at Mississippi and its people, a segregation-integration issue suddenly flared up from an unlikely quarter that would eventually develop into one of the marked controversies during the Coleman administration. The matter revolved around the administration's decision as to whether the state should donate land to the federal government for the construction of a new Veterans Administration (VA) hospital in Jackson, which was expected to be racially integrated. The state legislature had already authorized the governor to sign the deed to convey the designated land to the federal government, but as word got around the state that the proposed VA hospital would be fully integrated, fierce opposition to the construction plan suddenly developed. The State Building Commission, chaired by Governor Coleman, had the actual authority over any state-owned land and was expected to handle this case. But because of the issues involved, the members of the Building Commission felt that the matter should be handled by the Sovereignty Commission and subsequently turned it over to the state's "segregation watchdog agency."[107]

"[D]eeply concerned" with "the situation at the Veteran's [*sic*] Hospital," Senator Evans wrote to Commission Director Gore on August 2, 1956, asking him to "obtain authority from a majority of the Commission" to take necessary steps to avoid the "intolerable situation," which the state might face with the coming of the prospective integration. Evans asserted that if the Sovereignty Commission failed "to take aggressive action" in dealing with the VA hospital controversy, the state agency would be "not only displaying a serious inconsistence" in its fight to maintain segregation but also violating the trust of the state legislature that had created it. "It is inconceivable, inconsistent and ridiculous for the people of Mississippi," the Commission member's strong words continued, "to resist by every 'lawful means' integration of the races in one phase of our social life and to accept, without a fight, non-segregation in another and equally vital part of our southern way of life."[108] As for himself, the senator was ready to "fight."

Forced by Evans to "effectuate a reasonable, aggressive and immediate plan of action," Governor Coleman presented the issue for discussion at the Sovereignty Commission meeting held on September 5.[109] The governor made it clear that he was in favor of the new hospital, stating that "he felt there was a big difference between grown people being integrated in hospitals and little children being in the integrated schools." Lieutenant Governor Gartin and Attorney General Patterson sided with him. "Integration is practiced in the armed forces," Gartin told the commissioners, "and there is nothing we can do about it." Then, the lieutenant governor posed a question: "How can the State of Mississippi say to a [white] veteran [that] 'You served with them [black soldiers] in the Army, but now we are going to deny you the hospital for treatment that you need?'" House Speaker Sillers, however, vigorously opposed the construction project because "every time a [federal] government agency comes into our state" Mississippians were forced to "surrender a portion of our sovereignty to the Federal Government." Reminding other members that the Sovereignty Commission was created "to preserve segregation" in Mississippi, Evans plumped for the Speaker. Sillers then suggested that the Commission "pass a resolution to confer with the heads of the veterans['] organizations" in the state, and Governor Coleman appointed a three-member subcommittee to probe into the matter. Patterson, Evans, and Representative Johnson were chosen for the task.[110]

Eight months later, on May 7, 1957, the Commission members heard a report submitted by the subcommittee. Patterson told the gathered members that the subcommittee met with a total of eleven representatives from the American Legion, the Veterans of Foreign Wars, and the Disabled American Veterans on October 29, 1956, at the Sovereignty Commission office, and he reported that those leaders were "unanimous" in recommending the donation of the state land for the new hospital regardless of its racial policies.[111] Still unconvinced, Evans, who served as a member of the subcommittee, continued to oppose the plan. He reiterated that the Sovereignty Commission was "created for the purpose of maintaining segregation" and was now "becoming a party to creating integration."[112] Flying into a fury, the senator went on: "Here a state agency created to keep segregation is in the position of being a part in the creation of an integrated facility. We're in the position

25

of either endorsing an integrated facility or denying medical facilities to the veterans of Mississippi." "That's exactly the position we're in," Governor Coleman chipped in: "It would put us in a bad light over the country to deny . . . the veterans these facilities just to prove we're segregationists."[113] Finally, the Sovereignty Commission, by a vote of six to one, approved the agency's recommendation that the State Building Commission give "favorable consideration" to "the effort to locate" the VA hospital in Jackson. Gartin, Patterson, Burgin, Hopkins, Clayton, and Henley voted to approve the recommendation. The sole dissenter, Evans, "requested that his negative vote be recorded" in the meeting's minutes. Though Governor Coleman, following custom, did not cast his vote, he also demanded that the minutes reflect that "had he been entitled to vote," he "would have voted in favor" of the recommendation.[114]

Obviously, not everyone was satisfied with the governor's argument. Sillers, who was absent from the meeting, later stated that he would "rather have no hospital at all" in the whole state of Mississippi than having one racially integrated hospital.[115] Representative C. B. "Buddie" Newman of Valley Park, Issaquena County, in the Mississippi Delta, called on the Sovereignty Commission members to reconsider their decision. If the Commission's action was not rescinded, Newman predicted, "it will forever be a black blot that will stain the history of Mississippi from now to eternity." Contrary to the attorney general's appraisal of the situation, some dissenting voices began to be heard even among the veterans of Mississippi. The Yazoo County post of the Veterans of Foreign Wars accused the Sovereignty Commission of yielding to "federal blackmail to get the veterans to accept integration," and a member of the Walnut, Tippah County, post of the same organization registered his vehement opposition to the "proposed race-mixing plant" in the capital city. "If we Mississippi veterans must be integrated to get hospitalization," he wrote to Clayton, "[we] had rather be disgraced in some other state." Blasting the commissioners for being "unscrupulous politicians" who trod upon "the finest white people on earth," the veteran dared to add: "The V.F.W. knows all about fighting."[116] The Commission's unpopular ruling also motivated Jimmy Ward, editor of the *Jackson Daily News*, to erupt with an emotional editorial, declaring that the day of May 7, 1957, be remembered as "Munich Day in Mississippi":

Except to entertain one group of northern weekly newspaper editors on a
jaunt into Mississippi the only other major accomplishment performed by the
Sovereignty Commission was to kneel down on May 7 and pay homage to
Washington bureaucracy and kiss the feet on liberalism. . . .

Having so thoroughly yielded to Federal political seduction, the commission should close its doors, disband, refrain from spending any more of its
funds which were assessed upon an already tax-weary people and fade away
without a single kiss of regret in her passing.[117]

Accusing the Commission of "swallowing the lure of Federal funds like a
hungry bass at dawn," the editor even suggested that the state agency
change its name to the "State Surrender Commission" only if it did not
want to disband itself.[118] Meanwhile, the Association of Citizens' Councils of
Mississippi adopted a resolution on May 16 insisting that the "humiliation"
of racial integration at the new VA hospital would cause "deep psychological
reactions on physically helpless war veterans." The Council went further to
urge Congress to "enact legislation as they deem fit to cause Veterans Hospitals to be operated in conformity with the customs, traditions and laws of
the States wherein they are located."[119]

By the time the VA hospital episode ended in an uproar, the existence of
an "undeclared war" between Governor Coleman and the Citizens' Council
had gradually begun to surface. Since his inauguration, Coleman had emphasized that though one of his primary tasks as governor was "to preserve
segregation in Mississippi," he wanted to be in a position to "keep a bunch
of self-appointed, volunteer 'doctors' from taking over" his native state and
driving Mississippians "headlong into disaster." The governor had also made
it clear that he would not join those who were "invoking the methods of
hatred, malice, or ridicule toward the negro race" in Mississippi, explicitly
criticizing the Council leadership.[120] As an illustration of Coleman's waging
the "undeclared war" against what he once termed Mississippi's " 'hidden'
government," when Robert Patterson, executive secretary of the Association
of Citizens' Councils of Mississippi, asked the governor in the summer of
1957 "if the Sovereignty Commission would agree to pick up the tab" for
Judge Tom Brady's speaking engagement at the Commonwealth Club of
California in San Francisco, Coleman flatly refused, stating that the travel
expenses to be incurred by the Council's favorite son "would not justify the
expenditure of taxpayers' funds."[121]

While the Citizens' Council's relationships with Governor Coleman continued to be "fairly cool," as succinctly described by William Simmons, the kingpin of Mississippi's Council movement, the white supremacist organization initiated a weekly television and radio series in April 1957 "to acquaint the public with the serious problems affecting states' rights and race relations, and with steps being taken to meet them." The series, entitled the *Citizens' Council Forum*, consisted of fifteen-minute telecasts and five-minute radio programs with conservative southern politicians and some "experts" explaining their lofty views on states' rights and constitutional government, as well as detailing their outlandish stories on "the worldwide Communist conspiracy" in the civil rights struggle, alleged black inferiority, and the "vice" of interracial dating and marriages. Richard D. "Dick" Morphew, who served as public relations director of the Citizens' Councils of America, became both executive producer and host of the television programs. At the series' inception, the *Forum* tapes were made in Jackson, and its first program was broadcast over television station WLBT in the capital city on April 29, 1957. But in June 1958, Simmons announced that the tapes would be produced thereafter in Washington, D.C. The reason for the move was both simple and expedient. Mississippi Representative John Bell Williams, an ardent supporter of the Council movement, secured the services of the House recording studios for the *Forum* tapes to be produced there. By the end of the same year, according to the Council, the *Forum* program had reached audiences in the former eleven Confederate states and the nation's capital.[122]

No sooner had Mississippi trembled over the Sovereignty Commission's decision to "surrender a portion" of its sovereignty to the federal government than the entire nation witnessed the first dramatic confrontation between a state and the federal government over school desegregation in Little Rock, Arkansas. The historical importance of the Little Rock crisis of September 1957, where nine courageous black students desegregated traditionally all-white Central High School, was that, for the first time since Reconstruction, federal troops protected black civil rights in the South. Moreover, the incident taught white southerners that the federal executive branch, though reluctantly, had now joined forces with the judicial branch in order to implement the *Brown* decisions in the South and to uphold the "American way of life" above the "southern way of life." To protect the black students' constitutional rights, President Eisenhower federalized almost ten thousand men and women of the Arkansas National Guard and dispatched some twelve hundred troops of the United States Army to Little Rock. When the president went on nationwide television to explain his actions, WLBT interjected a spot advertisement sponsored by the Citizens' Council that read: "Don't let this happen in Mississippi. Join the Citizens' Council today." The day after the president's address, the *Daily News* put its shortest editorial ever on the front page: "TO THE PRESIDENT: (an editorial) NUTS!"[123] In the meantime, Governor Orval E. Faubus of Arkansas, in his statewide television and radio address, issued a mournful statement informing the state's citizens that they "are now in occupied territory." "In the name of God whom we all revere, in the name of liberty we hold so dear, in the name of decency which we all cherish," the governor asked, "what is happening in America?"[124]

As soon as the 1958 regular session of the Mississippi legislature commenced in early January, the legislators, instead of wasting their time on pondering the question posed by Governor Faubus, hurriedly began to strengthen the state's fortress to keep "Mississippi's way of life" intact. Among the measures introduced into and passed by the 1958 state legislature was Senate Concurrent Resolution No. 127 offered by Senator George M. Yarbrough of Red Banks, Marshall County, on February 12. Intending to cripple the potentially formidable foe of the state—the NAACP—the resolution requested the Sovereignty Commission to investigate the activities of the civil rights organization in Mississippi. During the floor debate in the Senate, however, an amendment to the bill was offered, changing the investigative authority from the Sovereignty Commission to the State General Legislative Investigating Committee. This sudden change was a tacit expression of the suspicions held by some senators as to the Commission's vigorousness in carrying out this important task. In addition, rumors circulated among the legislators that Mississippi's "State Surrender Commission," as the *Daily News* had called it over the VA hospital controversy, might be dissolved at the end of the 1956–58 biennium. The Senate subsequently passed the amended version of the resolution on March 3 by a vote of forty-five to zero, and the House concurred on the following day.[125]

Then, true to the rumors, Senator William B. Lucas of Macon, Noxubee County, and three other senators, all of whom were members of the Legislative Tax Study Committee, introduced a bill to abolish the Sovereignty Commission. Senator Lucas was a Citizens' Council stalwart who once derogatorily referred to the black residents in his home county as "cornfield Negroes." "[W]ith the Citizens' Councils [*sic*], the Legislative Investigating Committee and the attitude of the people," the senator explained, "I don't think there's any need for the Commission." Lucas also complained that the Commission had not "carried out its overall mission." Though his measure was referred to the Senate Judiciary Committee, no decisive action was taken.[126] Other Council sympathizers in the legislature were also determined that it was time for their pro-segregation group to benefit from public funds to carry out its great cause and specifically to supplement financially its newly initiated *Forum* program. Led by Senator Campbell, an active member of the Jackson Citizens' Council who headed the subcommittee to draft the interposition resolution two years earlier, twenty-nine senators introduced Senate Bill No. 1776 into the upper chamber on February 10. The bill would authorize Mississippi's cities and counties to donate, at "their discretion," state funds to "any association or organization having as its purpose the perpetuation and preservation of constitutional government and the division of powers thereunder and as guaranteed thereby."[127] From the time the bill was intro-duced, Campbell had made it clear that it was intended to benefit the Coun-cil, without which, in the senator's opinion, "Mississippi would have lawlessness in its racial relations." At one point, asked by a newspaper re-porter if he thought that the Citizens' Council should replace the Sovereignty Commission, Senator Campbell, echoing the *Daily News*, sarcastically replied: "I don't think there's anything to replace. The commission hasn't done any-thing."[128] At a subsequent hearing held by the Senate Judiciary Committee, to which the bill had been referred, a Council leader testified that the Sover-eignty Commission under Governor Coleman had been a "miserable failure" in preserving the state's sovereignty and racial integrity.[129] The Memphis-based *Southern School News* observed that an estimated total of $225,000 could be made available to the Council each year if the Campbell bill was enacted. This estimated "revenue" for the Council was actually almost twice as large as the Sovereignty Commission's annual state appropriation.[130]

On March 17, the Senate passed the Campbell bill by a vote of thirty-eight to two. The *Delta Democrat-Times* noted trenchantly in its editorial that the bill, which was "aimed at swelling the treasury of the Citizens Councils [*sic*]," was "[o]ne of the most insipid prospects for a large number of Mississippi taxpayers." "It's another example of the old saying about the tail wagging the dog," the editorial concluded. Conversely, the *Daily News* wrote in its front-page editorial: "Some arm of government—or some organization—needs to conduct an educational campaign in behalf of Dixie." Approving the intended purpose of the Campbell bill, it further declared: "About the only organization in Mississippi to show its colors in the pinch has been the Citizens['] Council. There seems to be a movement in some quarters to squelch the organization. . . . But who will do the job of preaching segregation?"[131] Still disgruntled with the Sovereignty Commission's decision in the VA hospital matter, Senator Evans asserted that "the job of preaching segregation" should be taken over by the "private" group.[132] Following the upper House's actions, seventy-six representatives introduced a substitute bill for the Senate-approved Campbell bill. That bill was approved by a vote of ninety-one to thirty-two, with Representative Wroten voting no. In his explanation in the *Journal of the House* as to why he cast a negative vote, Wroten indicted the entire state House for its insanity:

> The authorization of such donations commits a vicious assault on freedom of the mind. Anyone who is acquainted with our complex social problems in Mississippi is aware of the fact that in the exercise of their freedom of mind a large majority of our citizens, of whom I am one, have chosen not to affiliate with or to donate to [the Citizens' Council]. What these people have elected not to do in the exercise of constitutional freedoms would be required of them under this unconstitutional House Bill. . . .[133]

With an air of finality, Wroten then concluded: "I cannot witness in silence the passage of this coercive measure, which would shackle the minds of a free people, destroy their democratic rights to differences of opinion and pillage their constitutional freedoms."[134]

The legislative maneuver on the Campbell bill dragged on, and on April 17, exactly a month after it first passed in the Senate, the Senate again approved an amended version of the original Campbell bill by a vote of twenty-nine to nineteen. This time the amended bill included several additional features: the Sovereignty Commission must approve use of all funds, the Citizens' Council must account to the local governmental bodies for use of the funds under state audit, and the Council must not use the funds for any political purposes.[135] In the midst of the legislature's struggle with the final wording of the bill, Governor Coleman was busy defending the Sovereignty Commission, while the *Tupelo Daily Journal* inadvertently editorialized that the Commission had already been "abolished."[136] "[T]he commission has been a complete success," the governor asserted at one point, "[and] we have no integrated schools in Mississippi and have had no Tuscaloosas, no Montgomerys or Little Rocks." Reminding Mississippians that he was opposed to the Campbell measure and was ready to veto it when it reached his desk, Coleman continued: "I am opposed to any group purporting to perform the duties of state government." Though he was careful not to be construed by the general public as overtly declaring war on the Citizens' Council, Governor Coleman nevertheless referred to the substance of the Campbell bill as "a raw grab for political power to be financed out of the taxpayers' pockets" when he appeared before the Senate Judiciary Committee.[137]

Dozens of letters commending Coleman for his stand against the Campbell bill poured into the governor's office. "If our people continue to panic themselves into such excesses in the name of segregation," wrote LeRoy P. Percy of Greenville, one of the most prominent planters in the Mississippi Delta, "we may find ourselves loosing [*sic*] many of our basic rights to the self-appointed arbiters of the race question." "They may cure the disease, but kill the patient," Percy concluded. Included in those offering support were some rank-and-file members of the white supremacist organization. "I am a 'dyed in the wool' segregationist," one Council member wrote to the governor, "but I have no sympathy with tax money being put in the Citizens['] Council." Another member even conveyed his belief that the enactment of the Campbell measure "could lead to a most unfavorable political control by the Citizens['] Council" in both state and local affairs. Obviously, not every white Mississippian was gratified with the governor. Calling Coleman a "deceiver," one Brookhaven resident asked the governor if he realized "why so many people are afraid to risk our all in the hands of the Sovereignty Commission." "It is because you dominate it and your words and action[s] do not indicate that you seriously oppose the type and kind of government we have in Washington, D.C." Meanwhile, having been "disturbed to learn" of Coleman's attitude toward the Citizens' Council, "a common old every day farmer" of Dumas, Tippah County, boldly demanded an explanation from the governor: "If your Sovereignty Commission has been working and have [*sic*] done anything worthwhile, I will highly appreciate at least some knowledge of WHAT."[138]

The Campbell bill, in the end, failed to reach the governor's desk when the House refused to concur in the Senate amendment that required that the Sovereignty Commission first approve any expenditures by the Citizens' Council. The bill died on the House calendar at the adjournment of the 1958 legislative session on May 10, but the Council's thirst for the state funds did not go away.[139] Though the life of the Sovereignty Commission was spared, its 1958–60 biennial appropriation was drastically slashed. The State Budget Commission initially recommended $250,000 for the biennium, but the House Appropriations Committee reduced it to $150,000. Nor was this the last attempt to do away with the agency. Representative John R. Junkin of Natchez, Adams County, who chaired the Appropriations Committee, commented that there was "a good deal of sentiment in our committee not to give the Sovereignty Commission an appropriation."[140]

The Lucas and Campbell measures and their relative popularity among lawmakers were direct manifestations of the dissatisfaction many legislators possessed with the Sovereignty Commission which, they thought, "hasn't done anything" to aid Mississippi's segregationist cause. There were, to be sure, some factors that warranted the lawmakers' resentment. During its first two years under the Coleman administration, the Sovereignty Commission, along with its general secrecy, had "been little more than a high-powered public relations group," as the *Daily News* observed with indignation. The agency's public relations work, "originally intended as a sideline," was given a great deal of attention. As early as February 1957, a United Press correspondent in Jackson took note of the Commission's less-than-expected activities, reporting that Mississippi's "segregation watchdog agency" had "turned out to be chiefly a stand-by force with most of its powers and resources unused."[141] At the end of the 1956–58 fiscal biennium, the state agency actually turned back to the state treasury $158,192.29 out of the original appropriation of $250,000, and more than half of the expended amount— about $92,000—was used for the salaries of its staff members.[142] The instability of its office personnel, particularly the absence of a director for almost a year, contributed to the Commission's ineffectiveness as well. Since Gore's resignation in November 1957, the agency had operated without a director until Malone took office on October 1, 1958, at a salary of $7,200 per year. Malone, a lawyer and one-time automobile dealer, resigned as a state representative to become the Commission's director. When Malone assumed the directorship, the Commission's long-expected second investigator, Van Landingham, a former FBI special agent for twenty-seven years, was finally added to the investigative department.[143]

After the failed attempts by Senators Lucas and Campbell to abolish the Sovereignty Commission and to fill the Citizens' Council's treasury with state funds, the state agency and its chair felt the need to alleviate the legislature's disaffection toward them. The belated appointment of Malone and Van Landingham was one way to show their accountability to the state, and another move was the Commission's August 1958 decision to begin to hold regular monthly meetings for the first time since the agency's inception. However, the meetings began to lack quorums in the early spring of 1959. Two weeks before the planned April 23 meeting, Malone contacted all the members to determine if they "should continue to try to have monthly meetings or . . . change to quarterly meetings." As a result of a mail vote, with only three members—Sillers, Johnson, and Hopkins—favoring monthly meetings, the Commission decided to hold quarterly meetings "in the months of January, April, July and October."[144] To be sure, this decision was made over Sillers's apparent dissatisfaction. He "favor[ed] continuation of monthly meetings" even without quorums and expressed his irritation that the Commission members did not "show more interest in attending" its meetings.[145] After Sillers urged the Sovereignty Commission to "get busy and get out to the public at large over the state" at its February 1959 meeting, the agency launched several programs in an effort to acquaint "Mississippians with various personnel of the Sovereignty Commission and the work it is carrying on." From early 1959 to the spring of 1960, for instance, the Commission dispatched Investigator Van Landingham to twenty speaking engagements held at the state's Parent-Teacher Association (PTA) organizations, church groups, and other civic meetings of concerned citizens. The former FBI agent's favorite topic was on "juvenile delinquency and school truancy." Previously, in the early summer of 1957, the State Board of Welfare revealed a 44 percent increase in juvenile delinquency cases following the February 1956 repeal of the state's compulsory school attendance law. The measure was part of the LEAC-recommended program for maintaining racial segregation in Mississippi, and ironically, the Sovereignty Commission ended up bearing the consequences of its predecessor's deeds. Van Landingham's appearances were well received, and one invitation was even extended from Louisiana College in Pineville, Louisiana.[146]

Having gone through its uneasy beginning troubled with a few controversies and internal problems, the Sovereignty Commission survived as Mississippi's "stand-by force with most of its powers and resources unused." But unknown to the majority of the state's lawmakers as well as its general public, the Commission was quietly deploying its "eyes and ears" throughout Mississippi to squash the civil rights crusades.

Chapter 2

FEAR OF THE UNKNOWN

Mobilizing Black Informants

True to the Supreme Court's 1955 implementation decree in *Brown*, public school desegregation in the South proceeded "with all deliberate speed" in the latter half of the 1950s, and the Court's words hardly affected the defiant posture adopted by Mississippi's political leaders. While attending the National Governors' Conference held in Williamsburg, Virginia, on June 23, 1957, James Coleman appeared on NBC's *Meet the Press* and was asked whether the public schools in his native state would "ever" be integrated. "Well, ever is a long time," the Mississippi governor replied, "[but] I would say that a baby born in Mississippi today will never live long enough to see an integrated school."[1] To enforce the governor's solemn inaugural pledge—"the separation of the races in Mississippi will be left intact"—the Coleman-chaired Sovereignty Commission was "very anxious to know" who the state's "enemies" were. By 1959, the Commission had "gone into every county in Mississippi to determine just where NAACP chapters are located, who the negro agitators might be, and where the potential trouble spots in the state might be." It endeavored to establish its "eyes and ears" in each county to inform the agency of "just what is going on in the matter of race relations." The Commission's "eyes and ears" in the state's white communities included sheriffs, other local law enforcement officials, state legislators, state judges, school officials, religious leaders, bankers, merchants, and members of the Citizens' Council. Regardless of Coleman's personally frigid relationships with the Citizens' Council, the Commission investigators frequently called upon Council stalwarts in various localities "to find out just what the racial situation" was in their respective communities and "to seek their guidance and help."[2]

In addition to employing Leonard Hicks as its full-time investigator, the Sovereignty Commission decided at its May 15, 1956, meeting that Governor Coleman, as chair of the agency, would be able to hire "Special Investigators" for the Commission who would be "known only to him" and would "work at his sole direction." Though the Commission was careful to make sure that its minutes did not "reflect any mention" of Coleman's "special investigators," the agency's other official documents and the governor's papers indicate that his chief retainer was William H. Liston, a student at the University of Mississippi Law School, who conducted "some confidential investigation[s]" and "reported directly" to Governor Coleman from July to August 1956. By the end of August, the governor had sent Liston to such Mississippi Delta towns as Yazoo City, Vicksburg, and Natchez to determine if there was "evidence of any movement at all to file [school desegregation] petitions" in those communities.[3] After all, with solid racial conformity reigning over Mississippi society, white students at the state's institutions of higher learning were neither immune to nor exempted from their sacred duties of defending their beloved state from racial "agitators."

While deploying white "eyes and ears" throughout the state, the Sovereignty Commission, as in the case of its public relations activities, vigorously cultivated the great potentialities possessed by "a large number of fine, level-headed negro citizens" who were "actively opposed to the NAACP" and were aware that "the best interest of the negro race lies along segregated paths." "They have played no small part in helping maintain the status quo of the races," a Commission document said of its black collaborators in the early summer of 1959, "[and] [t]his problem will never be resolved without the help and cooperation of the negroes in the State of Mississippi."[4] To be sure, though some of these black accomplices, for reasons best known only to themselves, were genuine in cooperating with the Commission, others simply tried to "curry favor with the authorities by appearing to be anti-

NAACP," seeking purely personal advantage, and they even dared to siphon off some monetary rewards from the state's "segregation watchdog."[5] One of those who qualified as what the Sovereignty Commission termed "fine, level-headed negro citizens" was James H. White, president of Mississippi Vocational College in Itta Bena, Leflore County, who was forced to climb out on a limb. Officially opened in 1950, Mississippi Vocational College was established as the third state-supported black college in Mississippi "for educating Negro citizens in all gainful occupations and trades," and White became its first president.[6] The Commission's ties with the black president began shortly after it was organized in 1956 when the agency distributed copies of a pamphlet entitled *A Noted Negro Educator Speaks for Mississippi*, a reprint of an address made by White. Strongly favoring racial segregation, the president pointed out in the nationally distributed pamphlet that what all black Mississippians really needed was equal opportunities and that they did not long for the right "to sit and eat next to a white person." But White was a shrewd college administrator as well. In the summer of 1956 he asked the Sovereignty Commission to help his office purchase typing equipment and to assist his college "in sending its band to Texas on Thanksgiving Day" in exchange for his works for the state agency.[7]

As in the case of White, many black educators in the state, particularly its black college presidents, were in a sense qualified to be the natural allies of the Sovereignty Commission. After all, they needed to reconcile themselves to serving two different "masters." While they were expected to serve their black constituencies—their students and communities at large—who were no longer willing to accept their second-class citizenship, black educators also needed to appease the state's white power structure, which would financially support their institutions but would not let their schools disrupt the cherished racial status quo.[8] The Sovereignty Commission's official records attest that its investigator invited Euclid R. "E. R." Jobe, executive secretary of the Board of Trustees of State Institutions of Higher Learning, to his Commission office for a conference, where they tried to determine the credibility of "certain negro educators in the State" as the agency's "[p]ossible negro informants." While he stated that "he had no use" for Presidents B. F. McLaurin of Coahoma Junior College and Al Johnson of the Prentiss Normal and Industrial Institute, the executive secretary "spoke highly" of such presidents as White, Jacob L. Reddix of Jackson State College, J. D.

Boyd of Alcorn Agricultural and Mechanical College, and L. C. Jones of the Piney Wood School. Though this does not necessarily mean that all of those whom Jobe approved did in fact work for the Sovereignty Commission, his suggestions were well taken by the state agency. "[W]e should go very slow in dealing with those negroes," Jobe cautioned the Commission investigator at the conclusion of their meeting.[9]

Although the Sovereignty Commission deployed its paid and unpaid black informants throughout the state, most were concentrated in the Mississippi Delta counties. The Mississippi Delta is a football-shaped expanse in the northwestern quadrant of the state, extending about two hundred miles from Memphis, Tennessee, to Vicksburg, Mississippi. With fertile alluvial soil abundantly available, the region became the center of cotton production. Historically, black people had constituted a majority of this region's population, and while it was a "source of great wealth for white landowners" such as Mississippi Senator James Eastland, the Delta was also "a place of appalling poverty for the blacks who tilled the land."[10] Aside from being a thriving cotton and plantation kingdom, the Delta exerted its disproportionally strong political power over state government, particularly the legislative branch. Delta residents committed themselves to various conservative agendas to perpetuate the region's peculiar social orders. With the area's historical, economic, political, and demographic characters as well as its traditionally paternalistic race relations, the Mississippi Delta was a natural hunting ground for the Sovereignty Commission to cultivate its black informants.

While the main function of the agency's "eyes and ears" in the state's black communities was to keep the NAACP and other civil rights organizations, such as the Mississippi Progressive Voters' League, under surveillance, these black informants also had a very important secondary function. From time to time the Sovereignty Commission secretly had one informant run a check on another informant for the purpose of ascertaining the latter's reliability. In so doing, the Commission gradually ended up in a quagmire of a chain of suspicions. Possessed by a siege mentality, the Commission's "fear of the unknown" ran deep through its investigative activities under the Coleman administration. Thus, it is no surprise to find that most of the agency's investigative reports contained a large amount of mind-numbing information filled with a hodgepodge of baseless rumors, imputations, and bizarre details, revealing the hysterical state of Mississippi's "thinking" white leaders.

The Sovereignty Commission's principal paid informants in the state's black communities during the Coleman years changed over time, though their respective employment periods often overlapped. The first principal informant was Rev. H. H. Humes.[11] The Commission's relations with the black Baptist minister were cultivated by its public relations director, Hal DeCell, who by the fall of 1957 had been fully mobilized by Director Ney Gore to participate in the agency's investigative activities as well. DeCell's involvement in its investigative matters, in a sense, signified that the Commission was no longer merely a "study and propaganda center." When Gore resigned from the Commission in November 1957, DeCell began to report on his investigations directly to the governor.[12] The primary mission assigned to Humes, who won DeCell's "complete faith in his truthfulness," was to attend various civil rights meetings held in his hometown of Greenville.[13] He occasionally had a black female stenographer take down in shorthand the complete proceedings of those meetings and reported them to DeCell. For instance, when the Regional Council of Negro Leadership held a meeting in Greenville in late April 1957, which the Commission's publicity officer later referred to as "a dismal flop," Humes paid the stenographer $20 out of his own pocket to do the work. "I think we owe a debt [of] gratitude to our negro friends who have been cooperating so fully," DeCell wrote in his April 29 memorandum to Gore, "because it was due to their work largely that this wildly ballyhoo meeting of agitators was such a grand flop." The Sovereignty Commission later paid Humes $35 as its "gratitude."[14]

By the time DeCell involved himself in the Commission's snooping activities as well as handling its publicity matters, Medgar W. Evers had become one of the most disturbing eyesores for the state agency. A native of Decatur, Mississippi, and a veteran of World War II, Evers returned to Mississippi from the war in 1946 with ambitions to do something to change what was the South's most segregated and oppressive society. After Evers's failed attempt to enroll at the University of Mississippi Law School, the national NAACP offered him a job as its first full-time field secretary in Mississippi seven months after the Supreme Court's *Brown* ruling.[15] In September 1957, due largely to the dramatic federal-state confrontation over the Central High School desegregation crisis in Little Rock, Arkansas, Evers "stepped [up] his tempo of [NAACP] meetings" in Mississippi. Whenever the field secretary held such meetings in Greenville or nearby Delta towns, Humes followed him to collect "full information" on those gatherings for the Sovereignty Commission. Having "requested [Investigator] Chief Hicks to obtain the license number and make of automobiles" used by Evers and other "Negro Agitators" in the state, DeCell reported to the Commission director in his memorandum dated September 25, 1957: "It is my suggestion that once this information is obtained that we request the highway patrol to begin a quiet harassment of these . . . negroes whenever they are seen on the highways." "It might also be of benefit," his viciousness continued, "to inform the legislators of the . . . counties in which these . . . negroes reside something of their activities so that they may take whatever undercover steps they might wish to."[16]

Motivated by Evers and the state NAACP, the germination of civil rights struggle also became evident on the black college campuses in the state. In March 1957 Clennon W. King Jr., a flamboyant black history professor at Alcorn College, wrote a series of anti-NAACP, pro-segregation articles. When the articles appeared in the *Jackson State Times*, a group of students at Alcorn began to boycott King's classes in protest and picketed with placards labeling the professor "an Uncle Tom." Unable to believe that Alcorn's black students were really taking the initiative in staging the boycott, DeCell wrote to Gore that it was "a fair assumption" that the boycott was organized by "outside pressure." But as the student boycott proliferated on the campus, the Sovereignty Commission arranged to send Humes to Alcorn "to talk to the students involved in an effort to determine exactly who sparked the incident." "[O]nce such information is at hand," DeCell reasoned, the Commission should "release news stories" on the boycott, "exploiting the use of publicity in protection of Professor King."[17] In the end, King was dismissed from the college, and the affair seemed to be over.

On May 11, 1958, however, King unexpectedly applied for admission to the graduate school of the all-white University of Mississippi, hoping to "become a candidate for the Ph.D. in Southern History."[18] His bold attempt took everyone by surprise, except for the Sovereignty Commission's publicity director and Governor Coleman. Previously, in late 1957, when King wrote a letter to Tom Waring, the conservative editor of the *Charleston News and Courier* in South Carolina, hinting that he would probably challenge Mississippi's racial norms in the near future, DeCell obtained a copy of the letter "on the sly." "[T]he general tone of the letter leaves me sorta uneasy with the premonition of something distasteful shaping up," he reported to Governor Coleman on December 30, 1957. "In any event, I am passing this copy . . . on to you for your information," the public relations director continued, "so that at least we will have an idea as to what our friend King is up to."[19]

DeCell's "premonition" proved true on June 5 when King appeared on the campus of the University of Mississippi. The governor, in consultation with Attorney General Joe Patterson, had deployed the highway patrol on and around the campus for "the enforcement of the laws of this State, and the maintenance of peace and good order." At Coleman's request, Commissioner of Public Safety Tom I. Scarbrough, a future Sovereignty Commission investigator, was on the scene while the governor and the attorney general drove to Oxford and parked off the university campus, where they "had two way communication" with Scarbrough. Coleman claimed he did not go to the university to block King's entrance personally; as he recalled later, he was inclined to let the former professor register "without any Federal Court proceedings or Court Orders" and to "see if he could do the work and stay in school." Though the governor might have believed that King "was not applying for admission in good faith" and was merely "doing some fancy publicity hunting," given his desperate future resistance to a desegregation attempt at all-white Mississippi Southern College, Coleman's own "good faith" in claiming that he was willing to let the former Alcorn professor register is questionable.[20]

Once he arrived at the campus, King, who was "courteously" offered the registration papers to fill out in the registrar's office, mistakenly thought that he had walked into a trap, and he "fell on the floor and went to hollering." Then, having refused to leave the campus for more than two hours, King was eventually arrested "for disturbing the peace on the University campus." The next day King was committed to Whitfield, the state mental institution, following a lunacy hearing in Jackson before Hinds County Chancery Judge Stokes V. Robertson Jr. At Whitfield, the former history professor went through a twelve-day observation period and was released with the doctors' unanimous opinion that he was "sane."[21] Thus, having betrayed the Sovereignty Commission, which once called him "our friend," King thereafter became a "distasteful" figure for the state agency.[22] "The

State of Mississippi," Governor Coleman proclaimed in a statement issued immediately after the incident, "has been unusually kind to Professor King."[23]

While Humes's liaison with the Commission continued, an Associated Press story in the middle of July 1957 disclosed that he, along with Percy Greene of the *Jackson Advocate*, had been paid approximately $400 by the state agency for making "investigations." This story prompted an attempt to oust Humes as president of the 387,000-member General Missionary Baptist State Convention of Mississippi, but he eventually survived. In fact, the Sovereignty Commission's first payment to the Baptist minister was made on August 28, 1956, with $29.76 for "investigations." Thereafter, in February 1957 the agency began to pay him on a regular basis, and by the end of June 1957 the Commission had paid Humes on six occasions a total of at least $839.76.[24] Following the public exposure of their unsavory relationships with the state's "segregation watchdog agency," Humes and Greene were criticized by the Ministerial Improvement Association of Mississippi, which the Sovereignty Commission had kept its tabs on since the association's inception in March 1957, fearing that it might be the Mississippi counterpart of Martin Luther King Jr.'s Montgomery Improvement Association in Alabama. Condemning both Humes and Greene, the association, which happened to be in session in Hattiesburg, adopted a resolution asserting that the two leaders were "unworthy of the fellowship of the ministers of the Protestant denominations in Mississippi" and could no longer "speak for Mississippi Negroes."[25] In the meantime, Executive Director Roy Wilkins of the national NAACP denounced Humes as a traitor who was "quick to get [his] hands in the till." Returning the fire, the Greenville minister fought back in his speech made before a jam-packed crowd of six hundred blacks at the Mount Bethel Baptist Church in Gulfport, charging that the NAACP "has fallen into bad hands, both nationally and locally."[26]

After this incident, Humes became "leery of coming to Jackson," which in turn obliged DeCell to take frequent "investigative trips" to Greenville to collect information from the black preacher.[27] The Sovereignty Commission's "Requisition on the Auditor of Public Accounts" forms and a series of Humes's receipts reveal that from August 1956 to December 1957 the Commission had paid him on fourteen different occasions a total of $1,865.76, and his monthly "salary" from the state agency averaged $150.[28] In addition to having Humes keep his watchful eyes on the state's civil rights activities, DeCell also began to use Fred H. Miller of Mound Bayou, an associate of Humes's and the future editor of the *Mound Bayou Weekly*, as another Commission informant in the fall of 1957. The state's and the South's first all-black town, Miller's hometown of Mound Bayou was founded in 1887 in the Mississippi Delta county of Bolivar, the same county that molded House Speaker Walter Sillers.[29]

On January 1, 1958, Humes suddenly died of a heart attack at the age of fifty-five. Two days later, DeCell drove to Greenville and visited the late minister's house for the first time and, unmindful of the mourning family, went through Humes's personal files "to remove all papers dealing with the Sovereignty Commission." When it was announced that the funeral service would be held on January 7, DeCell sent flowers "over [his] name without any title" for "the Negroes that worked with him expected it" of him. On the day of the funeral, the public relations director again drove to Greenville "just to be on hand." "As you probably realize," DeCell noted in reporting Humes's passing to Governor Coleman on January 6, "the death of Rev. Humes has cost us one of the most influential Negroes we have had working in our behalf." "His services to the State were such," he later wrote in another report, "that he should be allowed to rest in peace."[30]

Shortly after Humes died, DeCell promoted Miller from the deceased minister's assistant to the Commission's principal informant. Miller himself would be succeeded by a black minister in Leland, Washington County, in the spring of 1958.[31] In his January 21 memorandum to the governor, De-Cell reported that he had "obtained the services of a Negro to replace Rev. H. H. Humes" in his "flock." Whereas Humes had been placed on the Commission's "steady payroll," the publicity officer decided to "use this replacement as the occasion arises."[32] By the end of the month, DeCell had asked Miller "to begin compiling a list of all known NAACP members" in such Mississippi Delta towns as Clarksdale, Cleveland, Greenville, Vicksburg, Natchez, Yazoo City, and Greenwood. "The names [he] suppl[ies] with us," DeCell wrote to Coleman, "will be added to our master list of NAACP members which we have been getting largely from automobile license tags, spotted at Negro meetings."[33] A month later, the Commission's public relations director submitted to its chair "a partial list of NAACP members" in the state that had been assembled by his chief informant, notifying the governor that the agency was "constantly adding [new names] to [its] master list." While continuing to keep his list "as current and up-to-date as is humanly possible," DeCell believed "beyond a doubt" that the state NAACP had "absolutely no knowledge of the existence" of the Commission's "master list."[34] The state agency's records indicate that Miller, in exchange for his work, received a total of $300 from the Commission from October 1957 until March 1958.[35]

On October 1, 1958, the Sovereignty Commission's long-awaited second investigator, Zack Van Landingham, was added to its investigative department at a salary of $8,500 per year. Assisting the Commission's new investigator was his secretary, Barbara E. Perry.[36] Van Landingham's first task for his new employer was to consult with a white accountant who claimed that he had heard that law enforcement officers "were arresting white people who went into negro homes." The accountant had an old black friend, to whom he wanted to take some medicine, but he did not want to get arrested for doing this kind deed. In the end, the newly appointed investigator managed to assure the bewildered inquirer that "no one would object to . . . taking medicine to an 84[-]year[-]old negro who was ill."[37] The incident is indicative of a police-state mentality that not only crucified Mississippi's oppressed black citizens but also haunted the general white citizenry in the state.

Van Landingham, a former FBI agent who was at one time an administrative assistant to Director J. Edgar Hoover, soon began to contribute to and reinforce the proliferation of this peculiar mentality within the state by creating a filing system for the "watchdog" agency's accumulating investigative records. He eventually established and organized the Commission files by using a classification system that consisted of thirteen subject categories: "Race Agitators"; "Integration Organizations"; "School Integration"; "Civil Rights—Election"; "Civil Rights—Violence"; "Miscellaneous—Inquiry Concerning"; "Administrative—Office"; "Administrative—Personnel"; "Administrative—Informants"; "Publicity—General"; "Criminal Cases"; "Speeches"; and "Subversion." Having devised this classification system, he further suggested that the Commission make "a minimum of 2 copies" of all memorandums, investigative reports, and correspondence whenever their originals were created.[38] Only two weeks after he commenced working for the Commission, the new investigator proudly announced at the agency's October 16 meeting that his new filing system had just been "installed."[39]

By the early summer of 1959, the Sovereignty Commission, under Van Landingham's initiative, had also made "approximately 4,000 index cards cataloguing information in several hundred files." Those files contained a number of investigative reports identifying the "NAACP agitators" in Mississippi.[40]

Around the same time the Sovereignty Commission established its relations with Miller, the state agency also initiated a deal with Rev. J. H. Parker of Leland. As in the case of Miller, Parker, a Baptist minister, had been another close associate of Humes's in the latter's pet organization—the General Missionary Baptist State Convention.[41] Trusting that Parker "was the right hand man of the late Rev. H. H. Humes," DeCell, who was relieved of the Commission's investigative duties with the employment of Van Landingham, had stayed in contact with the black minister on a monthly basis. Though both Humes and Miller, as well as Greene and White, turned out to be the Commission's most reliable informants, the agency was not always blessed with such trustworthy sources, and its association with Parker was one of the cases where the Commission belatedly realized that it was handed, so to speak, a lemon. When DeCell sent a memorandum on October 2, 1958, to Maurice Malone, the newly appointed Commission director, indicating that he would take a "field trip" to Leland to pay Parker in cash for his information, Van Landingham decided to launch an inquiry to determine Parker's credibility as the agency's informant.[42] Van Landingham's series of reports on the Parker case, all dated November 6, are one of the best indications of the Commission's "fear of the unknown." In late October Van Landingham drove to Greenville to conduct some background checks on Parker and to determine if the Mississippi Delta town had "any known agitators for integration." After conferring with the chief of the Greenville Police Department, he proceeded to talk with W. M. Holmes, whom the police chief "regarded as reliable." While advising the Commission investigator that race relations in his community were "excellent at this time," Holmes, a sixty-three-year-old black grocery store owner, "threw off on" Parker. "Parker tried to take over the leadership when Dr. Humes died," the Commission's new contact told Van Landingham, "but was not intelligent enough and did not have enough influence to do so." In his report on this Greenville trip submitted to Director Malone, Van Landingham wrote that he would "maintain contact" with Holmes, but he hastened to add: "It might be well to keep in mind that other individuals have indicated Holmes is a member of the NAACP." "In this regard," the puzzled investigator concluded, "he could be acting as a 'double agent.' "[43]

Van Landingham then proceeded to interview Parker at the informant's residence in Leland. By the conclusion of the interview, the investigator had begun to have "the definite bad impression" that Parker was not " 'shooting straight' with us." "I am not at all 'sold' on Parker," he later reported.[44] Van Landingham eventually recommended to Malone that "no further money be paid" to Parker for his "influence among the negroes and his value to the State Sovereignty Commission would seem to be very little."[45] Malone in turn wrote to Governor Coleman on November 14, suggesting that the state agency "discontinue payments" to Parker "as his reputation does not seem to be good."[46] By then, the Commission had paid Parker on eight occasions from March to October 1958 a total of $725.[47] At the end of Coleman's term in office, Van Landingham left a memorandum in Parker's file in the hope of preventing the future Commission staff from making the same mistake. "It is believed that Parker is simply an opportunist and is in no position to be of aid or assistance to this office," he wrote on December 4, 1959, "[and] [t]his case is therefore being closed."[48]

As soon as the Commission's investigative department was relieved of the disconcerting Parker case, Governor Coleman, at the agency's November 20 meeting, suggested that "spot checks be made of the activities" of Evers, the state NAACP's field secretary, "both day and night, to determine whether he is violating any laws." Commission Investigator Hicks, who had previously asked the Jackson Police Department, the Hinds County Sheriff's Office, and the State Highway Patrol for their cooperation to keep tabs on Evers, was asked by the governor to renew his contacts with these law enforcement authorities to maintain "an adequate surveillance of Evers."[49] Two weeks later, Hicks distributed an information sheet that contained Evers's physical description, driver's license number, license plate number, and other personal data to "all interested parties" such as Chief of Detectives Meady Pierce at the capital city's police department. Besides Chief Pierce, Hicks also notified Andrew L. "Andy" Hopkins at the sheriff's office in Hinds County and Public Safety Commissioner Scarbrough at the State Highway Patrol, both of whom were future Sovereignty Commission investigators.[50] Reflecting the Commission's acceleration of its investigative activities on Evers, Van Landingham had compiled a six-page memorandum entitled "Medgar Evers—Integration Agitator" by the end of 1958. Having dismissed Parker, however, the Commission was in need of a replacement who would assist it in maintaining "an adequate surveillance of Evers" and of other civil rights activities in Mississippi. The state agency soon marked out a black educator in Bolivar County for the position.[51]

The Commission's new informant was B. L. Bell, the fifty-one-year-old principal of the all-black H. M. Nailor Elementary School in Cleveland, Mississippi, and former associate editor of Humes's *Delta Leader*.[52] The liaison between the Sovereignty Commission and Bell began with the black educator's November 13, 1958, letter to Governor Coleman. After introducing himself briefly, Bell stated that his "greatest ambition" was "to hold a job with the State Sovereignty Commission." "I believe I could be of a great help to them," he assured Coleman, "as well as helping to bring about the goals which . . . I can see through your manifestations." Referring to the late Humes, of whom he "was a long time close associate" and whose "spoken words were the words of B. L. Bell," the Commission's prospective chief informant hoped to win the governor's confidence. Explaining further that he was "prompted" by President White of the Mississippi Vocational College to write the letter and express his feelings to Coleman, Bell concluded: "[Y]ou should know me and . . . my ability to be able to help promote good will and understanding [between the races] in the State."[53] A month later, the governor's office referred Bell's "self explanatory" letter to Van Landingham, directing him to "go to Cleveland at [his] first convenience." Coleman wanted the investigator to talk to Bell personally and make his recommendations to the Sovereignty Commission as to the prospective informant's credibility.[54] At Governor Coleman's behest, Van Landingham drove to Cleveland on January 8, 1959. After consulting with Bolivar County's superintendent of education, who described Bell as a "white man's Negro," the Commission investigator met with the black principal at an unidentified location. At the prolonged conference, while providing Van Landingham with "considerable information and names of individuals in Bolivar County whom he stated were members of the NAACP," Bell boasted that he had obtained the information "through certain individuals" who belonged to the NAACP and "who have 'big mouths' and are unable to keep from talking." Bell also revealed his long-conceived plan to Van Landingham as to the possible organization of what he termed a "secret society," wherein he and like-minded black citizens "would let each other know of the [civil rights] activities in various sections of the state" to preserve "the present way of life in Mississippi."[55] His intended conspirators included White, Miller, Superintendent W. A. Higgins of Clarksdale's black public schools, President McLaurin of Coahoma Junior College, Principal O. M. McNair of the all-black McNair High School in Belzoni, Humphreys County, and a host of others.[56] In his January 12 memorandum to Governor Coleman, Van Landingham suggested that Bell's "secret society" plan be given further consideration. "It is my recommendation," he told the governor, "that we pay Bell $50 a month for a period of 3 months" to see if he would be successful "in organizing such a group and furnish any worthwhile information" to the Commission.[57] Three days later, at the Commission's January meeting, the members authorized Van Landingham to expend "up to $100 a month for a period of 3 months" for the purpose of helping Bell set up "a secret underground organization."[58]

Little more than a week after Van Landingham and Bell first met, Bell's "secret society," which Van Landingham would later refer to as a "secret underground organization," a "fraternity," or a "loose knit organization," held its organizational meeting in Greenville. Besides Bell, six other black leaders attended the gathering, including Miller and McLaurin. President White could not attend the meeting but sent his college's public relations director to represent him. All of the attendees, whom Bell described as "the nucleus" of the new organization, agreed that they should help the Sovereignty Commission by "preserving segregation" and "handling any incident or developments that might threaten segregation in the state of Mississippi."[59]

On January 21, Van Landingham drove back to Cleveland to confer with Bell in his office at the Nailor Elementary School. Informing the investigator of the positive outcome of his organization's first meeting, Bell suggested that his "secret society" hire a black person "as a Public Relations man" with a yearly salary of $6,000, who would "travel over the state and contact various Negroes for the purpose of blocking whatever the NAACP might have in mind" to break down the state's racial segregation. Perplexed by this sudden proposal, which would obviously involve a large amount of expenditures by the Sovereignty Commission, Van Landingham brushed off the idea. In his report to Director Malone, the investigator wrote that "at the present time, it would be necessary to get the organization going [first] and for [Bell]

to be able to show [us] what could be done." At the conclusion of the
meeting, it was decided that Bell would furnish Van Landingham with his
weekly reports, and Van Landingham gave him $50 in cash to get his "secret
society" started. It was the state agency's first payment to its newly acquired
"eyes and ears."[60] Thereafter, Bell "continue[d] to stress" that in order to
organize his "secret society" properly, it "would require a full-time Negro
employee" and "would necessitate paying him $5,000 to $6,000 a year."
Disgusted with Bell's repeated financial solicitations, in early March 1959
Van Landingham once again drove to Cleveland to meet with him and refused to discuss the matter with him further.[61] During this incipient stage of
Van Landingham's connection with Bell, the Sovereignty Commission lost
its other investigator, Hicks, who died on February 20, 1959, and Van Landingham became the Commission's sole investigator until the end of the Coleman administration.[62]

Bell's routine work for the Sovereignty Commission included informing
Van Landingham of the addresses, telephone numbers, birthdays, and physical descriptions of a number of real and suspected NAACP leaders and members in his hometown of Cleveland and the Mississippi Delta at large. Many
of Bell's reports to the Commission dealt with Amzie Moore, president of
the NAACP's Cleveland chapter, whom Van Landingham had once called in
one of his own reports "the biggest NAACP agitator in Bolivar County."[63]
In addition, through his long-distance calls to Cleveland and face-to-face
contacts with Bell, the investigator frequently tried to ascertain the credibility of the Commission's other and prospective informants. In this sense, Bell
played an important role as the agency's unofficial clearinghouse in its endless search for more "eyes and ears" to be deployed throughout the state.[64]

Whereas Humes, Miller, and Parker were reluctant to come to Jackson to
make their reports due largely to fears that their presence at the Sovereignty
Commission office would be "noticed by the newsmen," Bell was rather
nonchalant in this regard.[65] For instance, when the state NAACP held a
meeting in Jackson on April 1, 1959, to launch a membership drive, Bell
drove down to the capital city to "cover" the gathering, hoping that he could
"possibly get in with Evers and find out just what is going on."[66] Afterward,
Bell frequently visited Jackson under the auspices of the Sovereignty Commission.

In the following month, in anticipation of Roy Wilkins's planned visit to

Jackson on the fifth anniversary of the *Brown* decision, the Commission conceived an idea to have Bell organize the state's black citizens, "who would picket the NAACP meeting with placards." Earlier, during the Commission's April 23 meeting, State Senator Earl Evans had suggested that the agency consider mobilizing "a large group or delegation of Negroes" and having them picket the meeting "with placards bearing some inscription such as 'Go Home Roy Wilkins, We Don't Want You Stirring Up Trouble In Mississippi.' " However, Bell expressed his doubt as to "the value" of such a scheme, and this Evans-recommended plan was not carried out. "Roy Wilkins' speech," Bell later reported to the Commission, "was one of the old familiar ones[—]agitative and full of sarcasm aimed at the white people of Mississippi and at what he called the few negro 'stooges.' "[67] Meanwhile, at the Sovereignty Commission's July meeting, it was decided that Van Landingham would be allowed to expend "not exceeding $100.00 per month" for "securing information for the commission" from Bell with no time limit being set.[68]

In the middle of September the *Jackson Clarion-Ledger* reported that the Southern Christian Ministers Conference of Mississippi was organizing a meeting to be held at the black Masonic lodge in the capital city on September 23, with Martin Luther King Jr. being one of the guest speakers. By then, King's name had become synonymous with black southerners' struggle for civil rights and civil liberties. Having heard the news of King's planned visit to Jackson, the Sovereignty Commission was suddenly thrown into confusion. In a telephone conversation with Van Landingham on September 16, William Simmons of the Citizens' Council suggested that King "be harassed as much as possible" and even "be arrested by the Police, taken down and fingerprinted and photographed." The Commission investigator then talked to the chief of the Detective Division at the Jackson Police Department to see if the "procedure" Simmons recommended could possibly be carried out. Recollecting "a similar set-up" that was to be applied to Wilkins, the chief was not convinced of the effectiveness of the scheme. "[Since] any attempt to arrest [King] . . . would be played up by the northern press as denying free speech and as persecution on the negroes," the chief concluded that the suggested procedure "would possibly do us more harm than good."[69]

Unable to figure out how to deal with King's upcoming visit to Mississippi, Van Landingham asked the governor's office to call an emergency conference. At the meeting, where Governor Coleman, Attorney General Patterson, Senator Evans, and Van Landingham huddled together, it was decided that the Sovereignty Commission would "have a recording instrument present to take down everything [King] said" at the NAACP gathering. Since the Commission did not possess any recording instrument, Van Landingham's first problem was to secure the necessary device. To solve this problem, he obtained permission to borrow a voice recorder from the State Highway Patrol after conferring with Director Sam Ivy of its Identification Bureau. But the more important questions remained unanswered: Who was going to record the planned King speech, and how it could be done? "It will first be necessary," Van Landingham eventually figured out, "to get a negro to attend this meeting and have the microphone in his pocket." Naturally, Bell was called on for the Commission's project.[70]

On September 21, Van Landingham made an arrangement with Kirby Walker, superintendent of the Jackson city schools, who readily agreed to make available to the Commission investigator "an office in the Colored Teachers' Administration Building." The office, Van Landingham jubilantly reported, was "only two doors down from the Negro Masonic Lodge" on Lynch Street. Walker also made "the necessary arrangements" with an anonymous black person who would make sure that "no teacher [would] come in" the office and "surprise" the recording team "during the operation." In the meantime, Van Landingham called Bell and asked him to drive down to Jackson on September 23. The day before the planned meeting, however, the investigator encountered an unexpected problem. Director Ivy informed Van Landingham that the highway patrol's "recording machine was not functioning properly" and that a technician was trying to fix it. To the investigator's further dismay, Ivy told him that "he did not know of any other recording machine" similar to the highway patrol's "in the State of Mississippi."[71]

In fact, this was the second occasion that the Sovereignty Commission was troubled with the highway patrol's beat-up recording equipment when it tried to monitor civil rights meetings in the state. In March 1957, when the Ministerial Improvement Association of Mississippi held its organizational meeting at a black church in Hattiesburg, Commission Investigator Hicks, Ivy, and a highway patrol technician tried to record its proceedings. Unable to have any of the Commission's black informants attend the gathering, Hicks and the others struggled for over six hours to record the proceedings through a loudspeaker posted outside of the church, consuming five reel-to-reel audiotapes. But the result of their endeavor was nothing but miserable. "On Reel 2 and part of Reel 3 our recording machine shut off," Hicks later reported, "[and] [t]his was not discovered until the playback and a considerable amount of the argument and discussion was lost." Having given up on the recorder of the State Highway Patrol, they managed to borrow "another recording machine from a source in Hattiesburg to finish [recording] the afternoon session." "If a court reporter, or some person qualified to take verbatim notes on a meeting such as this, were present," the former chief of the highway patrol lamented in his report, "it would be much better . . . and the Commission could have a more complete report of the meetings."[72] The Commission's ill fortune was repeated two years later, and Van Landingham settled for a copy of a draft of King's sixteen-page speech distributed at the meeting, while Jackson Police Department personnel were busy taking down "numerous license tags" of the automobiles parked outside the Masonic lodge.[73]

Since the Sovereignty Commission has been referred to as the state's "segregation watchdog" or "spy agency," it is often believed that the agency was fully equipped with various state-of-the-art detective devices since its inception. But as the Commission's agency purchase order forms, its minutes, and other documents in its official records point out, such a notion is sheer fantasy. In the early days of the state agency under the Coleman administration, it in fact did not even have an electric typewriter to prepare its meeting minutes and investigative reports, probably due to a lack of administrative initiative. Through the good offices of Speaker Sillers, the Commission eventually borrowed one from the clerk's office of the House. Until the fall of 1957, when Director Gore was instructed to purchase two typewriters, the House-owned one was the sole "modern equipment" in the Commission office. A year later, a Dictaphone was finally added to the agency's office at the pleading request of Van Landingham.[74]

Secretly meeting with Bell sometimes in the Commission office and sometimes on the state capitol grounds at night, Van Landingham continued to gather information from the informant on the state's civil rights activities. But the Sovereignty Commission's "public enemy number one" in Mississippi—the state NAACP—was not obtuse in realizing what the "segregation watchdog" was up to. When the civil rights organization held its meeting in early November 1959, to which Van Landingham sent Bell to observe the proceedings, Evers condemned the activities of the Sovereignty Commission while warning the attendees that the Commission's investigator had been "receiving reports from Negro informants all over the State."[75]

Less than a month after he attended this meeting, for which he was rewarded with $75 by the Sovereignty Commission, Bell was invited by Cleveland NAACP President Moore to join the organization. Bewildered, Bell called Van Landingham to ask for his advice. Having heard Evers talk on the Commission's "Negro informants," Bell was fearful that "the NAACP might be trying to put him on the spot" and that "they might be suspicious of him and was just seeing if he would join." In a conference with Van Landingham, the Commission's chief informant suggested that he "give an affidavit to the Chancery Clerk of Bolivar County" that would "certify the fact that he was joining the NAACP to assist the State in investigations." Rebuffing the idea, the investigator reminded Bell that if "he should give any affidavit to the Chancery Clerk . . . it would become a public record." Van Landingham recommended in the end that it be "a good idea for [Bell] to join the NAACP" so that he would be able to provide the Commission with much more accurate information on "the broad policies of the NAACP in the State."[76] Regardless of the investigator's suggestion, Bell decided not to join the NAACP due to his concern for his self-protection. Instead, he cunningly attempted to have one of his close friends join the civil rights organization, hoping that he could get information from him and "furnish it to the State Sovereignty Commission."[77]

In filing his numerous memorandums and reports to the director and the governor, Van Landingham seldom expressed his personal emotions. His August 1959 report was a rare exception, where he opened the floodgates of his wrath when Bell slacked up on his duties. On August 3 the Mississippi Progressive Voters' League held a statewide meeting in Jackson, and Van Landingham had previously contacted Bell and ordered him to be at the Commission office by ten o'clock. The investigator waited for Bell all day at his office, but the informant "never put in an appearance." The next day, when Bell called the Commission investigator from Cleveland to try to make an inexcusable excuse, Van Landingham was filled with fury. "I told Bell in no uncertain terms," he later reported, "that I was very disappointed with him, that he had let me down and that I could not depend on him." "I told him that [his laxness] was . . . entirely erroneous," Van Landingham concluded, "and I did not do business that way."[78] Bell, who lost the investigator's confidence as well as a reward of $75 in this instance, had received monthly cash payments of at least $50 from the Sovereignty Commission for the eighteen-month period from January 1959 to June 1960, except for the two months of January and February 1960. On a few occasions, Van Landingham paid Bell $75 a month to cover the informant's travel expenses.[79] Toward the end of his undercover relationship with the Sovereignty Commission, Bell had become unabashed enough to request of Van Landingham that the state agency furnish him with a new car and $300 to be spent for his daughter's college tuition. Amazed by Bell's impudence, the investigator informed him that "there was no way [he] could let him have this money."[80] After Coleman left the governor's office in January 1960, the Sovereignty Commission's arrangement with Bell was continued briefly under the new administration, but with the agency's June 1960 payment to Bell, their relationship came to a halt.[81]

As Coleman pledged in his inaugural address, "the separation of the races in Mississippi" was "left intact" under his administration, but the governor had to deal with incidents, such as the Clennon King case, that involved desegregation attempts at the state's institutions of higher learning. In the immediate aftermath of the summer 1958 King incident, Governor Coleman expressed his desire to devote the remaining months of his administration to "preserving peace and quiet between the races" in the state.[82] However, his wishful thinking turned out to be hollow with the advent of Clyde Kennard's attempt to enroll at all-white Mississippi Southern College (later the University of Southern Mississippi) in Hattiesburg, Forrest County. Though the Kennard story would soon be overshadowed by the well-publicized 1962 desegregation attempt by James H. Meredith at the University of Mississippi, it nevertheless is too important, and too tragic, to be left out of the history of Mississippi's civil rights movement and its official resistance to black citizens' aspirations for freedom and equality.

Kennard, a native of Forrest County, enlisted in the United States Army in 1945. After serving with distinction for seven years as a paratrooper and receiving a Korean Service Medal, a United Nations Service Medal, and a Good Conduct Medal, he was honorably discharged with the rank of sergeant in October 1952. He then enrolled at the University of Chicago, but when his stepfather's health deteriorated in his senior year, Kennard returned to Mississippi to run his family's poultry farm in Eatonville, a small and predominantly black community near Hattiesburg. Though he was busy taking over the farm and having to care for his mother, Kennard did not surrender his hope to finish college. Located within a fifteen-minute drive from his Eatonville farm, Mississippi Southern was a logical choice as the place for him to continue his education. The only and the most knotty problem was that the college was an all-white institution. After returning to Mississippi, Kennard made two unsuccessful attempts to enter Mississippi Southern, but on both occasions his applications were denied on the grounds that he failed to submit the required five recommendations from alumni in his home county.[83] In early December 1958 Kennard, in a letter to the editor of the *Hattiesburg American*, indicated that he would make his third attempt to be enrolled at the Mississippi Southern for the quarter beginning on January 5, 1959.[84]

By the time Kennard's letter was printed in the newspaper, Van Landingham had already been assigned to investigate the Kennard case. When the Commission met on November 20, Governor Coleman warned the members that "he had received information that a Negro, Clyde Kinniard [*sic*] . . . intended to apply for admission to Mississippi Southern College next semester." The governor then requested that the Sovereignty Commission launch its investigation of Kennard immediately and that it be completed by December 20 "in order that whatever action deemed desirable might be taken prior to registration day." Thereafter, Kennard's name was added to the Commission's files categorized as "Race Agitators."[85]

Assisted by a confidential informant simply identified as "T-1," who also furnished the Commission with information on Medgar Evers, Van Landingham compiled an extensive thirty-seven-page profile of Kennard, and by the middle of December 1958 he had successfully recruited some black leaders in the Hattiesburg area to dissuade the "race agitator" from attempting to enroll at the white college.[86] Van Landingham's most willing recruit was Rev. R. W. Woullard, a pastor of black churches in Eatonville and Hattiesburg and an owner of an insurance company and a funeral home. Woullard was "recommended" to Van Landingham by both the Forrest County sheriff and the Hattiesburg chief of police as a reliable black leader, for he "had cooperated with them in the past and . . . had prevented a NAACP Chapter from being organized in his church at Eatonville." Woullard later furnished Van Landingham with names of several black civil rights activists in the Hattiesburg area who might be supportive of Kennard. Although many of those whom the Commission investigator contacted in the Eatonville and Hattiesburg communities—both black and white—described Kennard as a well-educated, intelligent, and courteous man, they also indicated that Kennard might be one of the NAACP activists in their areas.[87] In fact, though Kennard was a member of the NAACP and attended several meetings sponsored by the organization in the state, he was neither a civil rights crusader nor a beneficiary of any financial support from the NAACP.[88]

To be sure, not all white residents in the communities were favorably disposed toward Kennard since, after all, attempting to be enrolled at an all-white educational institution was regarded as a worse sin than being a sympathizer of the NAACP in the eyes of most white Mississippians. During one of several investigative trips to Forrest County, Van Landingham was advised by the head of the Hattiesburg Citizens' Council, Dudley Conner, that "if it was desired for Kennard to leave Hattiesburg and never return," the Council leader "could take care" of him. When the investigator asked Conner what he meant by to "take care" of Kennard, he replied that "Kennard's car could be hit by a train or he could have some accident on the highway and nobody would ever know the difference." Concerned about these disturbing remarks, Van Landingham later discussed the matter with an FBI agent in New Orleans.[89] Meanwhile, assuring Van Landingham that "he would be glad to cooperate" with the Commission "in ascertaining the activities of the NAACP" in Eatonville and Hattiesburg, Woullard indicated his willingness "to head up a committee of negroes to go visit Kennard and attempt to talk to him and persuade him against filing an application to enter Mississippi Southern." Agreeable to the black minister's scheme, Van Landingham soon recruited three black school principals to serve on the Woullard committee.[90] As a former special agent of the FBI, the Commission investigator also made good use of his connections throughout the nation, asking his former colleagues in Chicago as well as in North Carolina, where Kennard had briefly attended the Fayetteville State Teachers College, to provide him with information on Kennard's background.[91]

Governor Coleman, in discussing the status of the Kennard case with Van Landingham on December 16, further instructed the investigator to get in touch with the State Banking Board and "have them immediately send a bank examiner" to the Citizens Bank in Hattiesburg "for the purpose of examining the bank account of Clyde Kennard." The governor wanted to determine if the NAACP had financially supported Kennard in his desegregation efforts, and Attorney General Patterson concurred with Coleman in his plan. At first, Comptroller W. P. McMullan Jr. of the banking board expressed his willingness to cooperate with the Commission, but he later called Van Landingham and suggested that the investigator's authority under the Sovereignty Commission "extend[ed] to the examination" of Kennard's bank records because the Citizens Bank was "a state bank." At Van Landingham's request, McMullan subsequently called the president of the bank in Hattiesburg and told him that "the Governor's investigator" wanted to examine Kennard's account. The bank president, however, was reluctant to cooperate and eventually "declined to exhibit" the records.[92] Three days after he directed the Commission investigator to obtain Kennard's bank records, Governor Coleman received a report that the Eatonville black was not going to attempt to enter Mississippi Southern in January 1959. Accordingly, Attorney General Patterson suggested to Van Landingham that "no further effort be made at this time to examine the records" of Kennard's bank account. In the meantime, presuming that the Kennard affair was resolved and hoping that it would not resurface in the remaining months of his administration, Governor Coleman recommended that the Sovereignty Commission's investigative files on Kennard "be placed in an inactive status subject to being reopened should anything develop warranting further investigation." Kennard would soon betray the governor's expectation, for he merely postponed his third attempt to enter the all-white college until September 1959.[93]

Coleman's nightmare revisited him on August 27 when he received a hurriedly prepared memorandum from Van Landingham's office. Earlier in the day, President William D. McCain of Mississippi Southern College informed the Commission investigator that he had received a telephone call from Kennard, who requested an application to enter the college in September. The next day, Jobe, executive secretary of the Board of Trustees of State Institutions of Higher Learning, visited the Sovereignty Commission office to discuss the Kennard matter with Van Landingham. In search of any possible reasons to deny Kennard's application, Jobe even suggested that an authority at Mississippi Southern inform Kennard that "all the dormitories were full and their registration had reached the point where they could handle no more students." Van Landingham, in the meantime, asked President White of Mississippi Vocational College to go to Hattiesburg and do some "behind the scenes" work to dissuade Kennard from attempting to desegregate the college.[94]

While no one could shake Kennard's resolve to pursue his education at Mississippi Southern, economic pressures were exerted on him as the application deadline for the fall quarter neared. In early September, following the Forrest County Cooperative's foreclosure on his poultry farm, the Southern Farm Bureau Insurance Company suddenly canceled Kennard's liability coverage on his automobile due to its fear that "some foul play might take place."[95]

In his desperate efforts "to appeal to Kennard's inherent decency," President McCain invited Kennard to his office on September 7. At the conference, McCain "pointed out the dangers involved, both to Kennard and the tensions which would arise between the white and colored races should he go through with his plan." The president even threatened that Kennard "would get nowhere with his application as Gov. Coleman would close Mississippi Southern College." The following day, just a week before the beginning of the fall quarter, McCain and Van Landingham met with Governor Coleman in Jackson to determine the grounds for rejecting Kennard's third application.[96] As a result of this meeting, on September 14 Director of Admissions Aubrey K. Lucas, a future president of Mississippi Southern, prepared a letter to be presented to Kennard denying his application on the grounds of its "deficiencies and irregularities."[97] While Lucas was busy preparing the letter, McCain, Van Landingham, and Inspector W. G. Gray of the State Highway Patrol huddled in the college president's office. During the closed-door session, they made their plans. While McCain and Van Landingham would interview Kennard upon his appearance in the president's office on September 15, Chief of Highway Patrol B. S. Hood and Inspector Gray were to be in an office adjacent to McCain's room "in case anything happened which would warrant taking Kennard into custody." They also decided that "all individuals involved" would be "at their posts of duty" by 8 A.M. At approximately 9:20 A.M. on September 15, Kennard arrived on campus and was immediately ushered into McCain's office by the college's public relations clerk, where the president and Van Landingham awaited him. McCain once again asked Kennard if he would withdraw his application. In response, Kennard, a man of strong conviction, stated that "he believed what he was doing was right and that he was doing it for both the white and colored race[s]" of Mississippi. After the "friendly persuasion" that Coleman and McCain sought had failed, Lucas was called into the office, and he handed Kennard the letter formally denying his application.[98]

However, the real tragedy of the Kennard incident was yet to come. When Kennard returned to his car to leave the campus, he was suddenly arrested by Forrest County Constable Lee Daniels and his partner for "driving at an excessive rate of speed and recklessly" and "illegal possession of whiskey." The arrest was a result of two overzealous constables' acting on their own. Neither the Sovereignty Commission nor the State Highway Patrol "had anything to do with the arrest" and "knew nothing about it." Around 10 A.M., McCain and Van Landingham, who were still in the president's office, were notified that Kennard had been arrested on campus. Surprised, the Commission investigator immediately contacted the governor's office and talked with his administrative assistant, Ben Walley, reporting that the arrest "appeared to be a frame-up with the planting of evidence in Kennard's car." Later the same day, Forrest County Justice of the Peace T. C. Hobby recommended bond of $500 "for illegal possession of liquor" and $100 "for reckless driving," and Kennard made the bond. Two weeks later, Hobby found Kennard guilty on both charges after declaring that he had not known of any other case "where the state proved more clearly the guilt of a defendant."[99] In answering a newspaper reporter's question, Van Landingham asserted that though the Sovereignty Commission "had prepared itself to assist the Attorney General's office . . . in case Kennard filed suit to enter" Mississippi Southern College, the state agency "took no part in the arrest" of Kennard.[100] This statement might be accurate, but Van Landingham should have realized that the Commission's series of covert acts eventually helped create an atmosphere where local law enforcement officers would feel free to take the law into their own hands.

Determined, Kennard continued his efforts to enroll at Mississippi Southern, but his aspiration was brought to an abrupt end in late September 1960. On Sunday morning, September 25, the Forrest County Cooperative, which had foreclosed on Kennard's poultry farm, was burglarized, and five bags of chicken feed worth $25 were stolen from the warehouse. A nineteen-year-old black youth, Johnny Lee Roberts, was arrested for the crime, but Roberts claimed that Kennard had planned the theft. Kennard was arrested later that day and charged with accessory to burglary, a felony under Mississippi law. He was subsequently convicted by an all-white jury, which deliberated for only ten minutes before returning its guilty verdict. On November 21 Kennard was sentenced to seven years in state prison while Roberts, the "confessed thief," received a suspended sentence.[101]

The calamity of the Kennard case was also a product of the times when Mississippi prepared itself for the 1959 gubernatorial election, where the candidate "who could crack the loudest segregation whip" wound up the winner. Though racial segregation in the state's public schools had remained intact, emotions were high, and all three major candidates energetically supported segregation. Among them, the one who cracked "the loudest segregation whip" was Ross R. Barnett, a prominent lawyer in Jackson who was running for the third time to attain the governor's office.[102] In announcing his candidacy in early 1959, Barnett proclaimed: "I am a vigorous segregationist, [and] I will work to maintain our heritage, our customs, constitutional government, rights of the states, segregation of the races. . . . The next governor will be confronted with some of the most complicated problems since the era of Reconstruction following the War Between the States. I owe allegiance only to my God, my conscience, my family, and the good people of my native state."[103]

In the Democratic primaries held in August, Barnett defeated the two other major contenders—Lieutenant Governor Carroll Gartin and Charles L. Sullivan of Clarksdale, a state district attorney—with the strong backing of the ostensibly "nonpolitical" Citizens' Council.[104] Barnett himself had been an active member of the Jackson Citizens' Council since its inception. Without any Republican challenge, Barnett was easily elected governor, and the durable relationship between Barnett and the Council became evident when the governor-elect's first postelection public appearance occurred at a meeting sponsored by the Council. On the evening of September 8, Barnett appeared in the Victory Room at the Heidelberg Hotel in downtown Jackson. For the occasion, nearly a thousand attendees bought the $25-a-plate meals to help finance the public relations activities being carried out by the Citizens' Council.[105] "Friends," the elated governor-elect spoke to the appreciative audience, "I'm a Mississippi segregationist, and I am proud of it."[106]

Then, he had special words for the "fine organization": "I am proud that I have been a Citizens' Council member since the Council's early days. I hope that every white Mississippian will join with me in becoming a member of this fine organization." "The Citizens' Councils," Barnett assured the gathered crowd, "are fighting your fight [and] they deserve your support."[107] Having decided that Mississippi should not have "another Coleman" as the state's chief executive officer, the Council leadership ignored Gartin—Coleman's choice—during the election and lent their full support to Barnett, "a loyal Council member who left no doubt [as to] where he stood." While the Council's "well-oiled machinery" began to run "in high gear" and Barnett was successfully sailing into the governor's office, Coleman's "friendly persuasion" posture on the state's segregation-integration issues was soon to be drowned out in the roars of "Never!"[108]

In December 1959 the Sovereignty Commission under the Coleman administration issued its second official report to the state legislature, which covered its activities between October 1, 1958, and December 1, 1959. Whereas the Commission's first official report devoted most of its pages to the agency's public relations activities, this thirteen-page report mostly described its investigative activities, with fewer than two pages being spent for the explanation of the public relations programs. By then, thanks to Van Landingham, the Sovereignty Commission established its "complete card index and filing system," with which any "information in possession of the Commission can be located immediately." The Commission had compiled more than five thousand index cards, cataloging various sorts of information in some five hundred files. In addition, the masterpiece of the Commission's research activities under Governor Coleman was the compilation of "all the laws passed by each state . . . bearing on the integration-segregation issue" since the 1954 *Brown* decision.[109]

After Coleman left office in January 1960, many of the Commission's extensive arrangements with its black informants, who had been carefully cultivated by both DeCell and Van Landingham during the late 1950s, were discontinued under Barnett's administration. This situation partially stemmed from the new governor's variance with Van Landingham. During the 1959 gubernatorial campaign, when Barnett criticized the Commission under the Coleman administration for having "refused to make grants" to the Citizens' Council, Van Landingham came out to defend the agency's policy, implicitly denouncing the future governor.[110] Instead, with the expansion of its investigative department and with the help of some professional anti-Communist crusaders, the reorganized Sovereignty Commission under Barnett would soon launch a new enterprise to crack down on the state's broadly defined "subversive" activities.

Chapter 3

To Maintain Segregation in Mississippi at All Costs

Revitalizing the State Sovereignty Commission

From a humble beginning on a small farm in Leake County, Ross Barnett attended local public schools and went on to graduate from Mississippi College. After working for two years as principal of Pontotoc High School in north Mississippi, Barnett entered the University of Mississippi Law School. Upon graduation, he began his law practice in Jackson in 1926 and subsequently became the senior partner of a large law firm in the capital. A man with "a mixture of flamboyance and down-to-earth seriousness," Barnett seldom failed in attracting and fascinating people around him with his "energy, rhetoric, and antics."[1] On January 19, 1960, an extremely cold and windy day, Barnett took his oath of office as Mississippi's fifty-third governor. "You know and I know," he took a solemn pledge in his inaugural address, "that we will maintain segregation in Mississippi at all costs."[2] As his predecessor, James Coleman, had promised in his inaugural address four years earlier, when Barnett assumed his official oath "the separation of the races in Mississippi" was still "left intact." The new governor, who was destined to symbolize the South's harshest politics of defiance, was determined to keep it that way "at all costs." Paralleling Barnett's resolution, no sooner had the

1960 state legislature been convened than the lawmakers flooded the legislative body with scores of bills designed to further strengthen Mississippi's racial segregation policy. By the time the session adjourned on May 11, twenty-one new segregationist bills were approved by both Houses and signed into law by Governor Barnett, among which was House Bill No. 741, providing that "the board of trustees of institutions of higher learning may, at their discretion, determine who will be privileged to enter, remain in or graduate from the institutions of higher learning."[3] It was obviously designed to give the board authority to reject any applicant to state universities and colleges for virtually any reason but especially because of an applicant's race. Prodded by the governor, the legislature also built the state's massive fortresses against possible demonstrations, sit-ins, and economic boycotts by civil rights activists. House Bill No. 431, for instance, prohibited "any person or persons from obstructing public sidewalks, streets, highways and other avenues or passageways." Any violator could be punished with "a fine of not more than five hundred dollars or by confinement in the county jail not exceeding six months, or by both such fine and imprisonment."[4] The legislative blockbuster in the session, however, was a Senate bill that made it a felony if persons "who are prohibited from marrying by reason of race or blood, shall cohabit or be guilty of a single act of adultery or fornication."[5]

While these legal fortresses were added to the state's armament to maintain "Mississippi's way of life," the legislature appropriated a sum of $350,000 to the State Sovereignty Commission for the fiscal biennium beginning on July 1, 1960, and ending on June 30, 1962.[6] The new biennial appropriation was more than double the allocation in the preceding two-year period under the Coleman administration, and there was a story behind this sudden budgetary leap. In the closing days of the legislative session, the Senate rejected a House bill to appropriate $250,000 for "advertising Mississippi's position in the segregation and states['] rights battle" if at least two other southern states would join in such a "battle." After dismissing the bill, the Senate added $100,000 to the originally proposed $250,000 appropriation for the Sovereignty Commission without any specific restrictions on how the extra funds were to be used. The *Jackson Daily News* predicted that the extra monies "could be used to buy propaganda from the Citizens Councils [*sic*] and spread it throughout the nation." While the matter was being debated in the legislature, William Simmons, administrator of the Citizens'

Councils of America, remained on the House floor to watch the events develop. The $350,000 appropriation for the state's "segregation watchdog" was finally approved on May 11, the very last day of the session. At the conclusion of the eighteen-week-long political maneuvering in the capital, the *Daily News* observed that "segregation . . . and Gov. Ross Barnett were blue ribbon winners."[7]

With his first legislative session now behind him, Governor Barnett set about to reorganize and revitalize the Sovereignty Commission, which had been without a public relations director for several months. When the Coleman-chaired Commission issued its second official report in December 1959, it made several recommendations for the future administration to consider. While boasting that there had been "no integration of schools, parks or other public facilities in the State of Mississippi," the report emphasized that the state agency "should be reorganized" in the near future and left a blueprint for its reconstruction. The first suggestion dealt with the necessity of an "Assistant Director in charge of Public Relations" who "should be a newspaperman . . . to handle the job of selling Mississippi and its race relations to other sections of the country." The report added that the prospective publicity director should "also have the ability to promote amicable relations between the races at home." Furthermore, regarding the Commission's future investigative activities, the report recommended that the state agency employ another "Assistant Director in charge of Investigation" and three additional investigators, all of whom "should be well versed in the art of investigations." "If possible, these four investigators should be former FBI Agents," the report reasoned, "as these agents have all received special training in the matter of investigation of subversive activities." In conclusion, while calculating that the newly organized Commission would require an annual budget of $175,000, the report suggested that a sum of $50,000 be set aside for the agency's "informant investigations and informant expenses." "This would require a biennial appropriation of $350,000 for the State Sovereignty Commission," it concluded, "[but that] would be a small expenditure for maintaining successful segregation in the State of Mississippi."[8] Being of the same mind that the state's segregation should be perpetuated "at all costs," the new governor gave his careful consideration to these suggestions.

On May 19, just a week after the legislature approved the appropriation for the Commission, Barnett called the state agency's first meeting under his administration. The four ex officio members of the new Sovereignty Commission were the governor, Lieutenant Governor Paul B. Johnson Jr., House Speaker Walter Sillers, and Attorney General Joe Patterson. Johnson appointed Senators George Yarbrough and Earl Evans to the Commission. It was Evans's second appointment to the agency. Meanwhile, Speaker Sillers's choices were Representatives William Johnson, who had served as a Commission member under the Coleman administration; Joseph G. Moss of Raymond, Hinds County; and Edwin Wilburn Hooker Sr. of Lexington, Holmes County. As for the citizen members, Governor Barnett appointed three attorneys: Aubrey H. Bell of Greenwood, Leflore County; Jesse E. Stockstill of Picayune, Hancock County; and Thomas H. "Tom" Watkins of Jackson, Hinds County.[9] Less than a month after his appointment, Yarbrough resigned from the Commission after assuming the position of Senate president pro tempore. Evans also later resigned as a Commission member, and these two senators were subsequently replaced by Herman B. DeCell of Yazoo City, Yazoo County, and John C. McLaurin of Brandon, Rankin County.[10] Among these non–ex officio members, McLaurin, Moss, Hooker, and Bell were known to be hardliners. Representative Hooker, particularly, was one of the most vigorous sponsors of many segregationist bills on the House floor during the 1960 legislative session. Conversely, DeCell, Johnson, and Watkins were viewed as "cool-heads."[11]

Then, at the Barnett-chaired Commission's second meeting on May 24, Albert N. Jones was chosen as full-time director of the state agency with a handsome salary of $9,000 a year. A soldier in the United States Army during World War II, Jones was a man with rich experiences in the law enforcement field. He had served as a deputy sheriff and then chief deputy sheriff of Hinds County from 1932 until he entered the army in October 1943. Shortly after the war ended, Jones again had served as chief deputy sheriff in the same county until he was elected sheriff in 1947. Thereafter, he was reelected to the same position twice, serving until the end of 1959. In addition, during these twelve years he was president of the Mississippi Sheriff's Association. Jones's employment with the Sovereignty Commission became effective on May 25.[12]

In the meantime, Governor Barnett selected Erle E. Johnston Jr. as the agency's public relations director. Johnston took over the post that Hal DeCell, his cousin, had occupied under the Coleman administration. Johnston's part-time employment with the Commission also became effective on May 25 with a salary of $250 a month. As an experienced political publicist as well as a newspaper reporter, Johnston was the right person for the job. After graduating in 1935 from Grenada High School in Grenada County, Johnston went to work for the *Grenada Daily Star*. Two years later he joined the staff of the *Jackson Clarion-Ledger*, where he became state editor and then a political reporter. Just a month before the United States entered World War II, Johnston moved to Forest and bought the weekly *Scott County Times*.[13]

In 1942 Johnston had his first experience in a statewide political campaign when he traveled with young James Eastland as a publicity associate in Eastland's successful first bid for the United States Senate. Having been recognized as an able publicist, Johnston thereafter was invited to work in a number of statewide political races. In 1947 Johnston had his first assignment as a publicity director, handling Fielding Wright's successful campaign for governor. Later that year, he also managed the initial phase of the Senate campaign of State Circuit Judge John C. Stennis, who was elected in November. During the 1950s Johnston continued to work as a political publicist while he ran his own newspaper business. In 1954 he directed the publicity projects for Senator Eastland's successful campaign for reelection, and a year later, in handling the public relations duties for Barnett's gubernatorial candidacy, Johnston experienced his first and only loss in his career as a political publicist. But four years later, when Barnett decided to run for governor a third time, Johnston was asked again to serve as publicity director for the Barnett camp.[14]

With regard to the Sovereignty Commission's investigative department, before the agency was officially reorganized in the early spring of 1960, Barnett hand-picked Robert C. "Bob" Thomas as the Commission's "special investigator." Thomas, a thirty-nine-year-old former Hinds County deputy sheriff, was owner and operator of the Jackson Patrol Service, a private company that guarded several local business establishments. During the 1959 gubernatorial election, Thomas helped raise funds for the Barnett campaign while running unsuccessfully for sheriff of Hinds County. In announcing Thomas's appointment, whose employment at the agency commenced on March 1, the governor praised him for his dedication "in the work of investigation and the maintenance of our Southern Way of Life."[15] While welcoming Thomas as "his own," the new governor then "ousted" Zack Van

Landingham, who had criticized Barnett for attacking the state agency during his gubernatorial campaign.[16] The second Commission investigator, who was recommended by Attorney General Patterson, was Tom Scarbrough. Having served as Chickasaw County sheriff from 1944 to 1948, Scarbrough, before accepting the Commission's post, was appointed as commissioner of public safety to head the Mississippi State Highway Patrol in March 1956 by Governor Coleman.[17] In the middle of June 1960 Andy Hopkins, a graduate of the FBI Academy who had served for thirteen years as chief investigator for the State Highway Patrol, was added as the agency's third full-time investigator. Since 1956 Hopkins had also been chief of the criminal department at the Hinds County Sheriff's Office, working under Jones who was then the sheriff.[18] Thus, only a month after its first meeting, the Sovereignty Commission under the helm of Barnett was equipped with three highly experienced full-time investigators. However, Thomas's employment with the Commission was short-lived, for he resigned on July 31, 1960, to give his full attention to his own business. He was replaced by Virgil S. Downing, a former Hinds County constable, in December of the same year.[19] In addition to these full-time investigators, the Commission hired former Senator Hugh A. Boren of Tupelo, Lee County, as a part-time investigator in June 1960 with an initial monthly salary of $250; at the end of 1961, however, Boren resigned his position with the Commission to become an administrative assistant to Governor Barnett.[20]

As soon as the Sovereignty Commission under the chairmanship of Governor Barnett reached its full force, with its office personnel—including Mildred Curry continuing as secretary and bookkeeper, Marie Rayfield as secretary and filing clerk, and Naomi Scrivner as research clerk—being added, the Citizens' Council's leaders, as expected, began to make their steady move to cast its influence on the Barnett-led "segregation watchdog" and to enjoy the governor's "official blessings" on their "nonpolitical" segregationist enterprises.[21] One of the early manifestations of the political influence the Council exerted in forming the Barnett administration's racial policies was the legislature's adoption of Senate Concurrent Resolution No. 115 during the 1960 session. Supported by the governor and introduced by Senator Yarbrough, the resolution commended Simmons, the kingpin of the entire Council movement, for "his outstanding contribution to his native state and southland" in "its present struggle for a better national understanding of our position." It passed in the Senate by a vote of forty-three to four, and the House followed suit with only two dissenting votes, including the one cast by Representative Joseph Wroten.[22] However, for Simmons, who would soon be conferred "an office of prime minister for racial integrity" by Governor Barnett, a mere resolution was not sufficient.[23] No sooner had Barnett reorganized the Sovereignty Commission than Simmons set out to accomplish what he could not achieve under the Coleman administration—to obtain state funds to carry out the Council's cause.

In March 1960, for the first time since its organization, the Association of Citizens' Councils of Mississippi, which by then claimed eighty thousand members in the state's sixty-five counties, launched a statewide drive to solicit special contributions from its members and sympathizers to help finance the *Citizens' Council Forum* program.[24] During this fund-raising drive, Simmons began to prod the new governor into having the Sovereignty Commission contribute some of its state funds to the *Forum*. Barnett, who during his gubernatorial campaign the previous year had criticized the Coleman-chaired Commission for not offering financial aid to the state's segregationist groups, had no objection.[25] On June 16, at the third Sovereignty Commission meeting in just a month, its members approved Simmons's request to make an immediate donation in the amount of $20,000 to the *Forum*. During the same meeting, which Simmons was permitted to attend for the first time, the commissioners also adopted a resolution providing that the state agency would begin monthly donations of $5,000 to the Council's programs for an indefinite period. The lump-sum donation of $20,000 was made in June, and the monthly donations of $5,000 began the following month.[26] As of the late 1950s, the cost of producing the *Forum* program was estimated to be around $4,000 a month.[27] On July 7, announcing the $20,000 grant in public funds to the Citizens' Council, Commission Director Jones issued the following statement:

> After a thorough examination of the comparative facts, the Sovereignty Commission voted unanimously to make the grant because the members felt an expansion of the [*Forum* program's] facilities already established and developed over a period of three years offered the best possible means of presenting the case for State Sovereignty and Constitutional Government to the nation.
>
> We know of no other facility which offers so much for our cause. . . . It [the Citizens' Council] merits the active financial support of all patriotic Mississippians.[28]

Upon hearing Jones's announcement, John Oliver Emmerich editorialized on the donation in the *Jackson State Times*, calling the Commission's act a "grievous error." "Some people will reason that the Citizens['] Council will properly use this public fund," Emmerich noted, "[but] [o]thers . . . will be more concerned with the ever-growing, unofficial role the Citizens['] Council is playing in state affairs."[29] One of those "concerned" with the unsavory ties between the Commission and the white supremacist private group was Richard P. Ellerbrake, pastor of St. Paul's United Church of Christ in Biloxi and a member of the Mississippi Advisory Committee to the United States Commission on Civil Rights.[30] The day after Jones's statement was issued, the white pastor wrote to the Commission director protesting against the state agency's decision as "a flagrant violation of the democratic principle." Reminding Jones that "half of Mississippi's 'public' are colored citizens" and that "many intelligent white citizens, who see in it only the continued foment[ation] of discord and group hatreds upon the people of Mississippi," would not "approve such an expenditure," Ellerbrake asserted that it was "rather foolish" for the Sovereignty Commission, which was supposed to be a guardian of constitutional government, "to use extra-constitutional means to promote" its aims. "In my opinion," the Biloxi pastor went on, "this action is not only extra-constitutional, but immoral as well." "[I]n other words, [it is] wrong," he concluded.[31] While writing back to the pastor to promise him that his letter would "be presented to the Commission at the next meeting," Director Jones immediately ran a background check on Ellerbrake.[32] One member of St. Paul's United Church of Christ informed Jones that he had "very little respect for Ellerbrake's ideas regarding segregation." When the Commission director contacted the Biloxi mayor, the city's chief executive, who became overly self-protective, assured Jones that "he had nothing to do with Reverend Ellerbrake, in any manner" and flatly described the white pastor as "definitely an integrationist."[33]

As he continued his investigation of the pastor, Jones wrote to the agency's members, informing them of Ellerbrake's bold protest against the donation. Stockstill was quick to respond to Jones. Having been "urged to make a reply" to Ellerbrake's "outbursts," the attorney crafted "his intended reply" to the Biloxi pastor, where he condemned Ellerbrake for his "sentiment [toward] . . . and . . . leanings to nefarious Communistic Organizations."[34] "I withhold this letter," Stockstill wrote to Jones, "until it is submitted to and at least censured or approved" by the other Commission members.[35] Senator Evans, though he "agreed with the sentiments" expressed in Stockstill's "intended reply," dissuaded the attorney from sending the letter to the pastor, arguing that "no worthy objective can be attained other than self-satisfaction, through correspondence with men of the type which Rev. Ellerbrake appears to be."[36] Fearing a possible lawsuit, where the Sovereignty Commission's payments to the Citizens' Council would be contested, Senator DeCell concurred with Evans.[37]

In the end, Mississippi's "segregation watchdog" took no further action against the Biloxi pastor's protest. But Ellerbrake would eventually move out of the state in the summer of 1962 after he reluctantly relinquished his pastorate in the face of his congregation's dissention over his association with the United States Civil Rights Commission.[38] Placing the members of the state's civil rights advisory committee on a par with "scalawag southerner[s]," Simmons once bluntly predicted that any white Mississippians who "front[ed] for our mortal enemies" would "face the well-deserved distaste, contempt and ostracism" that "any proud people would feel for a traitor." This Council leader's curse was duly applied to the white pastor.[39]

The fate of four Jackson residents who also did not believe that the Citizens' Council "merits the active financial support of all patriotic Mississippians" was similar to Ellerbrake's. Shortly after the Sovereignty Commission belatedly acknowledged in December 1960, that it had also been donating $5,000 a month in public funds to the Council's *Forum* program since July, these four Jacksonians filed a lawsuit in the federal district court in the capital city, seeking an injunction against the payments. Objecting to the fact that their tax money was being used for "advocating and compelling resistance and subversion of the law of the land," they took legal action on January 7, 1961. They also sought that "the enforcement, operation, and execution of the Act creating the State Sovereignty Commission," which by then had contributed $50,000 to the Citizens' Council, should be "enjoined permanently." The four plaintiffs were William L. Higgs, a young Jackson attorney; C. E. Shaffer, a local official of the International Brotherhood of Electrical Workers; Lonnie B. Daniel, state director of the Communications Workers of America; and Robert L. T. Smith Jr., a grocer and civil rights activist along with his father. Smith was black, while the other three were white.[40] In the middle of January the United States Fifth Circuit Court of

Appeals in New Orleans appointed three judges—Ben F. Cameron of Meridian, a circuit judge; Sidney C. Mize of Gulfport, a district judge for the southern district of Mississippi; and Claude F. Clayton of Tupelo, a district judge for the northern district of the state—to hear the four Jacksonians' pleas for an injunction to halt the Commission's donations and to disband the agency altogether. On the same day, after Judge Mize announced that the three-judge court was scheduled to hear the case in Jackson on February 13, the Sovereignty Commission met in a special session, where Attorney General Patterson outlined the state's plans for defending the case.[41]

Less than a week after the hearing date was set, two of the plaintiffs—Shaffer and Daniel—suddenly withdrew from the suit under pressure exerted by their unions' rank-and-file. Daniel simply explained that his withdrawal was "in response to the expressed wishes of some of our [union] members."[42] In late January, acting as attorney for the Commission and Governor Barnett, Patterson asked the federal court to dismiss the suit on the grounds that "the federal court has no jurisdiction" over the case.[43] Thereafter, some twists and turns ensued, and the lawsuit was eventually dropped, but one of the four plaintiffs—Higgs—would have to pay dearly for his involvement in the case.

A native white Mississippian and avowed integrationist, Higgs graduated from the University of Mississippi and then from Harvard Law School. After receiving a law degree, he returned to Mississippi and began to get involved in several civil rights–related lawsuits in his native state. In late 1962 Higgs filed a federal lawsuit, asking the court to order the University of Mississippi to enroll Dewey Greene Jr., a black navy veteran and civil rights activist in Greenwood. But the attorney's career was suddenly jeopardized. A few hours after he filed the suit, Higgs was summarily arrested by the Jackson Police Department on a phony moral charge, accused of "contributing to the delinquency of a minor," a sixteen-year-old runaway from Pennsylvania, and further making "unnatural" advances on the teenage boy. Two months later, in February 1963, while Higgs was visiting New York, an all-white jury convicted him in absentia in a trial dutifully observed by Commission Investigator Hopkins. Though he continued to work as a civil rights attorney in Washington, D.C., after he was disbarred from practicing law in Mississippi, Higgs's life reflected one of the many tragedies incurred in Mississippi's "closed society."[44]

The ironic consequence of this incident was that just a few months after the lawsuit was dropped, the attorney general, who was the chief legal architect of the state's defense against racial integration, began to question the wisdom of the Commission's monthly donations to the Council. Although Patterson was a long-time Council member, he was a legalist as well and had hardly been a flag-waving racial bigot. At the March 1961 Sovereignty Commission meeting, the attorney general made a motion to discontinue the agency's monthly contributions to the private group "to devote state funds to the state's own program" being carried out by the Commission.[45] Though his motion received no second from other commissioners and the donations were continued, Simmons did not forget the attorney general's opposition to his baby—the *Forum* program. When Patterson ran for reelection in 1963, Simmons's organization failed to give its "endorsement" to his candidacy. Patterson, who nevertheless was reelected, resigned from the Council.[46]

While the Citizens' Council began to enjoy not only the governor's "official blessings" but also the state's generous subsidies, the Sovereignty Commission was getting ready to initiate its renewed public relations programs under Johnston's direction. On May 24, 1960, at the second Commission meeting since Governor Barnett became its chair, its newly appointed public relations director submitted a five-page proposal regarding the agency's future publicity programs. Entitled "Operation: The Message from Mississippi," it spelled out the grand objectives of the Commission's public relations activities:

> 1. To take the offensive in spreading to the nation the real story of race relations in Mississippi.
>
> 2. To show by available media that the two races in Mississippi enjoy a mutual respect and understanding even though socially and educationally segregated.
>
> 3. To prove that segregation is best for the dignity and progress of both races.
>
> 4. To change many existing attitudes about the attitude of white people toward Negroes.
>
> 5. To invite others in integrated states to join in our crusade and [have them] recognize that usurpation by the federal government over states' rights in administration of schools is just a forerunner of usurpation in other fields.[47]

In order to implement these objectives, Johnston suggested several concrete means to "sell" Mississippi. The most important scheme on his list was the creation of a speakers bureau, or what Johnston termed a "Message Bureau," within the public relations department by enlisting volunteer speakers who would travel to the North to "carry the message." As auxiliaries to the speakers bureau program, Johnston proposed two things. First, he suggested that the Commission publish "a mailing pamphlet" that "would be an invitation [to northern audiences] to hear THE MISSISSIPPI MESSAGE." His second proposal was to make a twenty-minute documentary film depicting the amicable race relations in Mississippi for presentation before civic clubs throughout the nation. Covering his flanks was a plan to buy a series of thirty-second or one-minute television spots all over the country in which a "carefully prepared statement by the Governor about why Mississippi prefers continued segregation" would be aired. Though this last proposal was subsequently dropped because it was too expensive, the Sovereignty Commission would eventually carry out the other projects with the governor's enthusiastic endorsement.[48]

In fact, in his January 1960 inaugural address, Barnett proposed the creation of a tax-supported speakers bureau program to "sell Mississippi" throughout the nation. "With the cooperation of all the people of Mississippi," he declared, "we will establish a foundation that will be responsible for an aggressive campaign that will alert the people in all walks of life in every section of this great nation to the dangers of centralized government."[49] Shortly after the Commission members agreed that Johnston should immediately draft a speech to be used for the bureau, he "wrote about fifty leaders, legislators, public officials, [and] college presidents" in the state and asked them "what [they] would tell the people up North about Mississippi segregation" in "about a hundred words." The new publicity director also compiled letters written by some forty college-educated black Mississippians whom the Sovereignty Commission had earlier asked to write "why they chose to remain in segregated Mississippi following [their] college graduation." Using the replies offered by these white leaders and "educated" blacks, Johnston soon completed a twenty-five-minute-long "civic-club speech."[50]

The primary purpose of the speakers bureau, according to Johnston, was two-fold: to "make personal contacts with civic club groups and participate in question-and-answer" interactions and to "get as much publicity as possible in newspapers, and on radio and television, in the area where an engagement was arranged." "Publicity sent to media from the [Commission's]

Jackson office would be ignored," Johnston reasoned, "but the media would not ignore local programs in their own back yard."[51] In order to lure these local media into listening to what white Mississippians had to say, Johnston believed that his speech, entitled "The Message from Mississippi," should be "reasonable and persuasive, without any reference, directly or indirectly, which could be construed as hatred or resentment" while containing Mississippi's reasons for supporting states' rights and racial segregation. "This is a selling job," he explained to the Commission members, "and it cannot be done by waving red flags or using emotional approaches which might create unfavorable impressions." "Facts, situations, and an appeal for understanding," Johnston went on, "will be more effective in gaining support for the South."[52] The introduction explained to prospective audiences that they were about to hear "the story of how whites and Negroes in our State work together, plan together, and make mutual progress together under segregation." After bragging about the economic and educational progress that black Mississippians had achieved under the state's segregated social system and white leadership, the "Message" went on to present the state's sanctified vindication of "states' rights" and "home rule"—the respectable mantles covering up Mississippi's inhumane treatment of its black citizens:

> We believe in the rights of the states to solve many of their internal problems. In Mississippi, we have made no attempt to solve the problems of the Mexicans in the Southwest, the Asiatics on the Pacific Coast, the Indians in the Midwest, or Puerto Ricans on the East Coast. We concede to the people who live closest to these problems the right to work out their own solutions with moral and ethical considerations. We ask for the same consideration— that we in the South be allowed to solve our own problems to the best of our abilities. We could do no more, and no less, regardless of legislation or orders from the courts.[53]

"We did not come here to make any converts," Johnston's draft pointed out on its concluding page: "If you are a segregationist, we won't try to change you. If you are an integrationist, we won't try to change you. That wasn't the purpose of this program." "But," it wound up, "we do hope that after hearing this Message from Mississippi . . . you will at least have a better understanding of our situation, our problems, and what we are trying to do."[54] The Sovereignty Commission finalized and approved Johnston's public relations programs, including the speakers bureau project, to "carry the message from Mississippi" at its July 21 meeting.[55] When the speakers bureau program was launched, Commission Director Jones proudly announced that Mississippi had "finally taken the offensive in describing racial situations" of the state: "We have found out that many of the attitudes in the North against Mississippi are due to lack of knowledge. Many northerners seem to have all the answers to our problem without having our problem. We don't try to convert anybody. We merely try to explain how our situation came about and how we are dealing with it the best we can."[56]

To advertise its fledgling speakers bureau program, the Commission's public relations department sent out hundreds of copies of a brochure that described the bureau's purposes, along with a personal message from Governor Barnett, to various civic clubs and other organizations in the North. Several members of the Mississippi Retail Merchants Association cooperated with the Commission to send the brochures to their northern suppliers.[57] In the pamphlet, entitled *A Message from Mississippi: Are You Curious?*, Governor Barnett "earnestly" asked northerners to "give Mississippi a hearing."[58] In order to solicit invitations from civic clubs in northern cities and towns, Johnston also mailed "letters to the editors" to some two hundred daily and weekly local newspapers, offering his expense-free programs to hear Mississippi's story. On some occasions, the speakers bureau's engagements were even arranged through Mississippians who had relatives or friends in the North.[59]

The first speaking engagement of the Commission's speakers bureau took place on August 9, 1960, before the two hundred members of the Kiwanis Club in Pipestone, Minnesota. The speaker was State Circuit Judge Oscar H. Barnett of Carthage, Leake County, who was the governor's cousin. His talk was also broadcast by a local radio station.[60] Just a month later, William McCain, president of Mississippi Southern College, made a speech before the Pro-American Forum in Chicago as the second speaker of the newly organized bureau.[61] Thereafter, the list of the Commission's volunteer speakers read like the state's who's who and included most of the agency's members. Representative Johnson, for example, made a speech in Charles City, Iowa, in late October 1960 as the fourth speaker.[62] When Representative Moss, another Commission member, appeared before the Rotary Club in Lorain, Ohio, on January 27, 1961, he asserted that black Mississippians preferred "racial separation." "We maintain that Negroes like segregation," Johnston, who accompanied Moss, elaborated before the audience, "[and] [t]here is no law in Mississippi requiring segregation of churches, but neither side is trying to force its way into worship with each other." "We believe the Negro is willing to leave the [state] government in white hands as long as we recognize our responsibility to them," the public relations director summed up.[63]

On most occasions, the volunteer speakers were received courteously in northern cities and towns regardless of what their speeches contained and what they represented. No physical confrontations between the Mississippi representatives and the audiences were reported, but as perhaps might be expected, there was some occasional "unpleasantness." On January 9, 1961, State Chancery Judge R. P. Sugg of Eupora, Webster County, was scheduled to appear before the Rotary Club in Port Jefferson, New York. The night before Sugg was to appear, Roy Wilkins, executive director of the national NAACP, issued a statement. He was "shocked" to know that any group in New York would actually receive "emissaries from a rotten, barbaric state" such as Mississippi. Unmindful, Sugg spoke before the civic club in Port Jefferson and went on to appear before a sociology class at New York University on the following day.[64]

Some black Mississippians also volunteered to become bureau speakers, including J. W. Jones of the *Community Citizen*, who had been receiving the Commission's monthly contributions since late 1957. "We Negroes who are enjoying the system of segregation here in the State of Mississippi should give every ounce of our support to the program," Jones wrote to the state agency a few days before the bureau's first speaking engagement took place. Claiming that no one "can express himself with any more enthusiasm on the subject" and that he could "consciously support segregation, at any time and at any place," Jones asked the Commission to consider his letter as an "application" so that his name would "be placed on the speaking staff" if and when "the program includes Negroes."[65] In the hope of being selected as a prospective candidate for the Commission's new program, the impatient black editor even sent Johnston his four-page speech entitled "Why We Should Keep Mississippi Segregated," which was filled with "enough facts to support the cause" of racial segregation. "I am proud to state those facts," Jones wrote to the public relations director, "because I know that they are true."[66] Though Jones was never assigned to any speaking engagement, his "enthusiasm on the subject" of racial segregation won Johnston's heart, and the Sovereignty Commission would soon call on him in making its propaganda film.

During its entire short life of less than three years, the speakers bureau used only one black speaker—Joseph F. Albright, a sixty-one-year-old native of El Paso, Texas, who was a former Chicago resident and a Jackson public relations professional.[67] Before he was sent by the Sovereignty Commission to the North as a speaker, Albright had worked for the agency as a part-time paid informant. On June 20, 1961, Commission Director Jones asked Mississippi Representative John Bell Williams in Washington to run a background check on Albright, who had "volunteered his services as . . . an informant to Governor Barnett . . . for the benefit of the Sovereignty Commission."[68] Assured by Williams that Albright had no connections with any "subversive" activities, the Commission decided to use his "services," and for the period of four months between June and September, the state agency paid Albright on eight occasions a total of $660.90 for his "travel and work in Negro organizations" and "public relations works."[69]

On October 18, 1961, appearing before some 250 students at Columbia University in New York and being "booed loudly" by them, Albright spoke in defense of Mississippi's segregation laws and practices and criticized the recent Freedom Ride campaign as "a needless, useless, unwarranted intrusion" into the state.[70] The *New York Times*, reporting that the audience had confronted Albright with "open hostility," wrote that one Columbia graduate student accused Albright of delivering a speech "obviously written by whites," in which he spoke as if a Jew would "praise the cleanliness of Hitler's concentration camps."[71]

In truth, Albright wrote his own speech, and the only thing that Johnston did was to approve the contents of his speech before Albright left for New York and to authorize his expense account for $75.[72] But the problem was that both Johnston and Jones authorized Albright's New York trip before obtaining the consent of all the Commission members. At the agency's August 17 meeting, the members had discussed the possibility of using Albright as one of the bureau's speakers. Governor Barnett, who was not satisfied with Albright's work as a Commission informant, presented a report to the Commission showing Albright's "thorough unfitness to represent" the state agency. In the end, a motion was made by Bell not to send him to Columbia

University, but before this motion was offered, the governor and Attorney General Patterson left the meeting, and technically the Commission lacked a quorum.[73] Meanwhile, Governor Barnett was later "convinced" by Senator McLaurin that the Sovereignty Commission was "overlooking a tremendous opportunity to have a member of the colored race speak to northerners on the progress of both races under segregation." Persuaded by his friend, Barnett endorsed Albright's speaking engagement, though the other Commission members were unaware of this.[74]

Unknown to the governor himself at this moment, his indecisiveness would soon create a source of discontent within the agency. "I was shocked last night when I heard an announcement over a television news broadcast that Joseph Albright had spoken at the Columbia University Forum on be-half of the State Sovereignty Commission," Bell wrote to Director Jones on October 19, demanding to know who sent Albright to New York.[75] On behalf of Jones, Johnston replied to Bell, revealing Senator McLaurin's involvement in persuading the governor to approve Albright's trip. "We even made reservations at an All Negro hotel in New York," Johnston added to ease Bell's fury, "in order that nobody could say that he was segregated in Mississippi and integrated in New York."[76] The unconvinced Commission member was then joined by another commissioner, Representative Hooker. "To put it mildly," Hooker wrote to Jones on October 21, "I was astonished to learn that the negro . . . was sent to Columbia University."[77]

Thereafter, the exchange of correspondence between Bell, Hooker, Jones, and Johnston continued until late October, when Bell finally wrote Johnston that it would "serve no good purpose to continue this correspondence." "[A]s a member of the State Sovereignty Commission," he added, "I disapprove of it [Albright's trip] and feel that the Commission has been ignored." Still disgruntled, the attorney concluded: "[A]nd the fact that Albright may have received favorable publicity does not rectify the error."[78] Wise enough, Governor Barnett remained silent throughout this entire controversy. In January 1962, when Cornell University asked the Sovereignty Commission to send Albright for another speaking engagement, Jones, having learned his lesson, politely advised the organizer that Albright was "not filling further speaking engagements for the State Sovereignty Commission."[79] Later, in the summer of 1963, Albright asked Johnston if he could be a part-time employee of the Sovereignty Commission. The matter was discussed at the agency's July meeting, but the members "rejected an application from Joe Albright to be retained" by the Commission for his "special services" because of some members' "considerable antagonism toward him."[80]

By early 1962 the speakers bureau had dispatched its volunteers to a total of thirty-two cities in thirteen northern and western states: one in Idaho; three in Illinois; one in Indiana; one in Iowa; two in Massachusetts; five in Michigan; one in Minnesota; three in Missouri; one in Nebraska; four in New York; four in Ohio; four in Pennsylvania; and two in Wisconsin.[81] On most occasions, Johnston, as public relations director, accompanied the speakers to handle publicity and the question-and-answer periods during each speaking engagement. After a few trips to the North, Johnston "formulated practical replies" and eventually compiled these into a five-page reference work entitled "Questions Asked, and Answers Given, by Sovereignty Commission Volunteer Speakers," which was distributed to all prospective speakers.[82]

The bureau's speakers included state officials, legislators, judges, attorneys, newspaper editors, and businesspeople, and the only compensation that they received was their actual expenses. "After all," Johnston reminisced later, "an expense-paid trip to Iowa or Maine was a pretty nice outing for them." "So, I was doing that politically," he added.[83] For the first one and a half years of its operation, the total cost of the speakers bureau had averaged $1,500 a month, which included the travel expenses for the speakers and the salary paid to Johnston.[84] The Commission's volunteers continued to make trips to the North and the West through 1962 and into the middle of 1963, producing some 120 speaking engagements.[85]

Noticeably, Johnston never invited Judge Tom Brady, author of *Black Monday* and a favorite son of the Citizens' Council movement, to speak on behalf of the Sovereignty Commission. Brady had made an astonishing total of almost seven hundred speeches on behalf of the segregationist private organization both inside and outside the state between the latter half of the 1950s and the early 1960s.[86] Actually, while the governor kept his close association with the Council, not only did Johnston fail to include Judge Brady, but he also tried to "dodge" those who were closely associated with the group, for he did not want to have anyone who would "wave the bloody shirt" in his program.[87] Besides, by the time the Commission launched its speakers bureau program, Simmons had already begun his speaking trips to the North as the Council's administrator, and rivalry had developed between the state agency and the private organization in terms of "who could better carry the state's message" to northern audiences.[88] Though Simmons's name, to be sure, was put on the roster of the Commission's potential speakers at Barnett's behest, Johnston adroitly "dodged" him, too. In April 1962, for instance, when Simmons was invited to speak at Carleton College in Northfield, Minnesota, and requested that he be sent as the Commission's speaker, Johnston declined the suggestion on account of "a limited budget."[89]

As an auxiliary to the speakers bureau, the Sovereignty Commission, under Johnston's initiative, also arranged for the production of a twenty-seven-minute film that "described in scenes and interviews the racial harmony that existed among the great majorities of both races" in Mississippi.[90] The making of the pro-segregation and pro–states' rights propaganda film, *The Message from Mississippi*, was approved at the July 21, 1960, Commission meeting.[91] In fact, the making of "a half-hour movie on conditions in Mississippi" was contemplated in the early days of the Commission, but Governor Coleman had not approved the project.[92] The editing of the film, which turned out to be the first and the only propaganda film that the Sovereignty Commission ever made, was completed in the middle of December.[93] The agency paid $29,979.64 to Dobbs-Maynard Advertising Company in Jackson to have it make the movie, which was three times as high as Johnston's initial estimate—somewhere between $7,000 and $10,000—made in May 1960.[94] Later, the Commission belatedly realized that it was "grossly overcharged" by Dobbs-Maynard.[95]

The film's basic theme was that both races could and in fact had progressed economically, socially, and culturally in a segregated society such as Mississippi. The film used a narrator, various interviews with the state's sympathetic black leaders as well as white officials, and several scenes from daily living in Johnston's hometown—Forest, Scott County—which was forty-five miles east of Jackson.[96] At the beginning of the film, while the narration boasted of the "business volume, industrial development, and job opportunities" that Mississippi enjoyed, it explained to viewers that "a situation" existed in the state that was "unlike the situation in most states in the nation." "This situation," which stemmed from the very fact that "forty-five percent of [the] population" of the state was "colored," had "brought problems" and "created challenges." The narrator continued: "But most important of all, it has inspired a social system to meet the challenge, a social system under which both races retain their identities and achieve their own destinies without either race forcing itself upon the other."[97]

Mayor J. E. Calhoun of Forest then explained that he was "indeed proud of the splendid racial relations" that he and the other citizens in Forest "enjoy." "Even though we are segregated in schools, churches, and other activities," the mayor continued, "I honestly believe that we have more contact with each other in business and community projects that the two races might have in the so-called 'integrated' areas." Other white officials who tried to convince viewers of the sanity of Mississippi's racial norms included Governor Barnett; Jack Tubb, state superintendent of public education; T. H. Naylor, director of the State Educational Finance Commission; and E. R. Jobe, executive secretary of the Board of Trustees of State Institutions of Higher Learning, all of whom had volunteered for the speakers bureau. J. W. Jones, who was eager to be recruited as one of the bureau's speakers, also put in a short appearance when the narrator accounted that "out of the statewide pattern of segregation, of mutual respect and cooperation among the races has arisen a productive law-abiding way of life" in the state. "We have far less crime in our race in Mississippi in proportion to the population than in any state in the nation," Jones spoke with pride, "[and] I believe this is because of the way of life in Mississippi." Echoing the contents of the speech Johnston prepared for the Commission's speakers, the film further asserted: "We, in Mississippi, know our social system works best for all of our citizens. But we will not therefore attempt to solve the problems of the Mexicans in the Southwest, the Indians in the Midwest, the Puerto Ricans in the East, or the Asiatics on the West Coast." The rationale of the state's policy not to "presume to solve" these racial "problems" in other parts of the nation, the movie explained, was based on "two basic reasons": "First, such problems are best solved by those closest to the situation, those who have an intimate and thorough knowledge of the facts. Second, Mississippi believes in the Constitution of the United States which reserves for the states those powers such as control of public education, not directly invested in the federal government."[98]

As the narrator explained the second "basic reason," the words "STATES' RIGHTS" were shown in huge letters across the screen. Concluding *The*

Message from Mississippi was a ninety-second appearance by Governor Barnett, who forcefully spoke of his determination to preserve the state's "segregated way of life": "You have heard a story of true progress, mutual respect . . . and understanding between the white and the colored races in Mississippi. . . . And I can truthfully say that this situation exists in all communities, towns, and cities throughout the entire state of Mississippi. It's true that we are segregated in our state. . . . [But] apparently, they [black Mississippians] prefer segregation in Mississippi to integration in some other states."[99]

On December 15, the completed film was shown to the Commission members, and five days later, a group of the state's businesspeople, bankers, and members of the press previewed it at the agency's office following Senator Evans's brief introduction.[100] The Commission later reported that all of those in the audience were "high in praise" of the "content and arrangement" of the propaganda movie, which was shot on 35-mm film, enabling the state agency to have it shown in theaters. For the regular showings at various civic clubs, the Commission also acquired twenty-four 16-mm copies of the film.[101] By early February 1961, the film had been booked at civic clubs in such cities as Oshkosh, Wisconsin; Salem, Oregon; Mobridge, South Dakota; Des Moines, Iowa; Milford, New Hampshire; and San Francisco, as well as having been sent to CBS News and New York University by request.[102] By early 1962, *The Message from Mississippi* had been circulated among civic clubs, service organizations, universities, and church groups in forty-three cities in twenty-seven states besides Mississippi, plus Washington, D.C. In New York, Ohio, and Pennsylvania alone, it was shown on twenty-two different occasions. The clubs and organizations that requested the film ranged from a Methodist church in Des Moines, Iowa; a Lutheran church in Greenville, Pennsylvania; the Farmer's Union in Denver, Colorado; and the Veterans of World War I of the U.S.A. in Brookline, New Hampshire, to the Defenders of States' Rights in Henderson, North Carolina; the Capital Citizens' Council in Little Rock, Arkansas; and the Louisiana State Sovereignty Commission in Baton Rouge.[103] In June 1962 the movie was even shown in London.[104]

Years later, when asked about his appraisal of the entire speakers bureau program, Johnston replied: "I think we enlightened a lot of people and corrected a lot of wrong impressions about Mississippi."[105] To be sure, not all white Mississippians shared his thoughts. While Curtis Mullen and Philip

Mullen of the *Madison County Herald* called the program a "popgun effort," Hodding Carter articulated that Mississippi had "more to hide" when the Sovereignty Commission was busy projecting a favorable image of the state's race relations.[106] In 1984 James W. Silver, a former history professor at the University of Mississippi, cynically equated the Commission's bureau project with a state-sanctioned program of "dispatching articulate natives to convince outlanders of the sanity of the state's culture."[107] Though the Sovereignty Commission's speakers strove to reflect "the sanity of the state's culture," its bureau program, in the end, failed in "making a dent [in] holding back integration or preserving segregation" in Mississippi.[108]

While the Sovereignty Commission occupied itself in carrying out its public relations programs by dispatching Mississippi's "articulated natives to convince outlanders" of the virtue of racial separation and inequality, some black Mississippians were also busy canvassing the state to make a little money under the pretense of working with the Commission's publicity efforts.[109] John E. Barksdale of Meridian, Lauderdale County, officially began his relations with the state agency on January 18, 1962, when he appeared before the Commission's regular monthly meeting. Explaining to the members that he was "in [the] process of publishing a magazine" that would depict the various accomplishments made by the black citizens in Meridian "under our way of life," Barksdale asked the agency for financial support. Favored by Senator Gillespie V. "Sonny" Montgomery of Meridian, a future Mississippi representative who "spoke many nice things" about the black solicitor, the Commission subsequently approved a handsome lump-sum donation of $1,000 to Barksdale's "ambitious project."[110] In March Barksdale began to send drafts of articles to be included in the proposed magazine to the Sovereignty Commission for Director Jones to censor. Discomfited by the fact that one of Barksdale's letters to the agency was inadvertently addressed to "Mr. Albert Johes, Mississippi Sovernity Commission," the director once wrote back: "I further suggest that before giving this [a draft article] to the printer that it should be carefully checked for proper spelling."[111] Barksdale's twenty-seven-page magazine entitled *Citizens of Color in Meridian, Mississippi* was finally published in the summer of 1962 with, at least, "proper spelling." "We have literally saturated Meridian with copies of *Citizens of Color*," Barksdale prided himself in his August 20 letter addressed to

Jones. "I have been hailed and feted locally," he added a postscript, "but [I now have] no money."[112]

Director Jones, in the meantime, was in a foul mood because, notwithstanding his assurance that he would "furnish the commission with several hundred copies" of his magazine, Barksdale did not carry out his promise. Later, when Barksdale boldly asked the Sovereignty Commission to help him again to begin a weekly newspaper for the purpose of "further propagat[ing] the cause" of the agency, Jones's patience ran out. "I do not feel," the director wrote to the habitual solicitor resentfully, "that the commission would be agreeable to give you further assistance in this matter." The Sovereignty Commission, in the end, had spent a sum of $1,100 for Barksdale's "ambitious"-turned-bogus project, including its petty cash payment of $100 to him.[113]

Even for some out-of-the-state blacks, the Mississippi agency was an easy mark. In late 1960 Rev. R. Fairley, founder of a dubiously named organization in Dallas, Texas, proposed that he appear on a radio program in Jackson that would be designed for "creat[ing] good will and better race relationship[s] between the races of the Southland." In "Humbly Submitt[ing]" his project to the Sovereignty Commission, the founder of the Goodwill Crusade Youth and Adult Council asked the agency to provide him with $500 to appear on Jackson radio station WOKJ. On November 30, Fairley was interviewed by some Commission members in Jackson and given $300 "to defray expenses . . . for [a] program against integration."[114] Nobody in the Mississippi agency, however, seems to have bothered to determine if Fairley actually gave a talk on the radio station. With these kinds of opportunists trying to pull the wool over the Commission's eyes, the Mississippi taxpayers' money sometimes went down the drain.

Shortly after Barnett became governor, along with administrating its speakers bureau program, the Sovereignty Commission began to take up the broadly defined "subversive hunt" as one of its most important functions.[115] Ironically, only after the *Brown* decision and the demise of Senator Joseph R. McCarthy's influence, both of which occurred in the spring of 1954, did many southern politicians and officials fully begin to merge the Cold War consensus with the segregationist cause into a peculiar ideology.[116] As Numan Bartley articulated in his 1969 book *The Rise of Massive Resistance*, southern white leadership "blatantly asserted that the quest for social justice and human dignity was nothing more than a foreign plot, a conspiracy dominated and directed by 'Communist subversives' " in confrontation with the full tide of black southerners' civil rights struggles.[117] With little doubt, the words and deeds of southern segregationists in Congress added some respectability to the efforts carried out by individual southern states to preserve the racial status quo by "cloaking [them] under the guise of resisting communist advances."[118] Though he may not be its original inventor, Mississippi Senator Eastland was "a logical custodian of the union of civil rights and communism," for he had sat on the Senate Internal Security Sub-Committee (SISS) since its inception in 1950 and became chair of the committee in 1955. In the following year, while still serving as chair of the SISS, Eastland was chosen to chair the powerful Senate Judiciary Committee over the objections of two northern Democratic senators who challenged his impartiality, as well as over the protest registered by the national NAACP—the most formidable "left-wing pressure group," to borrow the words of the senator.[119] "The Senate of the United States has just voted to put an accessory to murder and treason in its most powerful judicial position," the civil rights organization lamented in issuing a statement.[120] After becoming chair of the Judiciary Committee, Eastland did not fall short of the NAACP's expectations. As the senator himself once boasted, by the end of 1956 Eastland had "put a special pocket in [his] pants" in which he dutifully kept a number of civil rights–related bills in order to prevent their passage in Congress.[121]

While the rest of the nation was struggling to abandon the fanatical Red Scare of the 1950s, heartened by its own senator's persistent assertion of the "Communist conspiracy," "a homegrown McCarthyism" began to take hold in Mississippi.[122] By Mississippi's official definition given by its state legislature in the late 1950s, the term "subversive organization" meant any organization, association, or group that was listed or designated by "the United States Attorney General or a Congressional Committee on Un-American Activities" as a Communist or Communist-front organization. And "any officer or director or member" of such an organization, the state reasoned, was therefore a "subversive."[123] However, by the early 1960s, these terms had come to be understood more broadly by the state's white leadership. Thus, anyone or any organization that had anything to do with black Mississippians' civil rights struggles automatically qualified to be labeled as being either "subversive" or a "subversive organization." After all, the civil rights leaders, activists, and sympathizers in Mississippi could all be categorized as "subversives" in the sense that they willfully defied the state's white establishment and its long-cherished segregated "way of life." Under these circumstances, to call them Communist-influenced "subversives" was one of the most effective means for Mississippi's white leadership to undermine the credibility of the people who were involved in civil rights activities in the state.[124]

To be sure, the vast majority of the state's civil rights leaders and workers were not associated with any Communist or Communist-front organization at all. But "if you travel in the company of a skunk," a former Sovereignty Commission member later put it, "you're going to smell like a skunk."[125] This notably simplified view was also echoed by Governor Barnett. For instance, on July 12, 1963, the governor appeared before the United States Senate Commerce Committee to present his case against the civil rights legislation under consideration in Congress. Warning the committee members that "the passage of [the] Civil Rights legislation will positively provoke more violence, not just in the South, but throughout all areas of our nation," Barnett expressed his conviction with his "frightening kind of sincerity" that the civil rights movement and the probable passage of the legislation were all "part of the world Communist conspiracy to divide and conquer our country from within." "The decision is yours," the Mississippi governor concluded his solemn testimony, "[and] May God have mercy on your souls!"[126] "To the whites, anybody who wanted change had to be a communist," Edwin King, one of the state's prominent civil rights leaders recollected, "[a]nd, of course, the politicians who might have known better used that."[127] In addition, the fact that the majority of the state's civil rights crusaders were "born and bred" Mississippians mattered very little to the state's white politicians and officials because they almost unquestioningly presumed that any racial troubles in Mississippi were created by "outsiders."[128] "Negroes as a race," the Sovereignty Commission's publicity director once observed, "are very religious and [to them] anything Communist sounds like Godless atheism."[129] The underlying assumption of this view was that black Mississippians were deceived into participating in an improbable mission by self-serving "subversives," "outside agitators," and "atheists."

With this wrongful assumption on its way to becoming accepted, the Sovereignty Commission initiated a desperate search for any evidence that could possibly connect "the world Communist conspiracy" with the state's civil rights movement. In its "progress report" released at the agency's March 30, 1961, meeting, the Commission disclosed that it had been "engaged in a detailed investigati[ve] program" to compile a host of files on individuals whose "utterances or actions indicate they should be watched with suspicion on future racial attitudes." By then, the Commission had conducted some 230 "investigations" in all of the state's eighty-two counties.[130] In addition to its "commie hunt," for the purpose of educating white Mississippians on the danger of "recent alarming advances of the communist conspiracy" in the field of the civil rights struggle, the Sovereignty Commission also brought into the state some "carefully selected and usually well paid professional anti-Communist speakers." At the Commission's May 18, 1961, meeting, the state agency reported that it had obtained the services of speakers who were "of recognized authority on the subject of [the] communist threat."[131] One of these "authorities" was Myers G. Lowman, a self-styled anti-Communist fighter who was an "internationally recognized . . . top researcher and compiler of public records of individuals affiliated with Communist activities."[132] Lowman was executive secretary of an anti-Communist organization called the Circuit Riders, Inc., based in Cincinnati, Ohio, which was originally "formed by Methodist laymen for the purpose of oppressing Communism principally in the religious field."[133]

The details of Lowman's speaking tours in Mississippi were primarily taken care of by a women's group named the Paul Revere Ladies.[134] In December 1960 a host of conservative-minded women met at the War Memorial Building in downtown Jackson, with the initiative taken by Sara McCorkle of Grenada, who in January 1958 had been appointed as the women's activities director of the Association of Citizens' Councils of Mississippi.[135] Following a suggestion made by Naomi Scrivner, the Commission's research clerk, these women adopted the Paul Revere Ladies as their organization's name. Subsequently, Scrivner and Edna Alexander of Grenada were elected to serve as chair and vice chair, respectively.[136] While the Revolutionary War hero Paul Revere rode on horseback from Boston to Lexington in 1775 to warn his fellow Americans of an impending British military advance, these women were eager to alert Mississippians to the vice of Communism and to expose its exploitation of racial unrest in the state. Instead of riding on horseback, the Paul Revere Ladies turned to Lowman as their vehicle for spreading the alert. At the organizational meeting of the Paul Revere Ladies held on December 14, a petition was circulated to "request funds from the State Sovereignty Commission to finance the expenses" of Lowman's speaking engagements in the state. "The petition was signed by all ladies present," the meeting's minutes read, "and a list was attached of names that had been signed by a group of Grenada Citizen's [*sic*] Council ladies." On the following day, the Commission members were met by Scrivner, Alexander, and Mc-Corkle at the agency's office. Expressing "the importance of alerting Mississippi people . . . to [the] National threat" from Communism "by every means possible," the representatives of the Paul Revere Ladies presented to the Commission their request for the funds to organize Lowman's state tour. The Sovereignty Commission, in the end, decided to set aside $3,000 to invite the anti-Communist fighter.[137] Later, Lowman's planned two-week visit to Mississippi was divided into two separate tours—the first in January and the second in February 1960.

Under the sponsorship of the Sovereignty Commission and with the enthusiastic support offered by House Speaker Sillers, the Paul Revere Ladies meticulously organized Lowman's first speaking tour, which lasted from January 16 to 22.[138] The leadoff of this first tour was the $3-a-plate luncheon meeting to welcome Lowman, prepared by the Paul Revere Ladies and held at the King Edward Hotel in Jackson. The invited guests included Governor Barnett, Lieutenant Governor Johnson, Speaker Sillers, and Jackson Mayor Allen Thompson.[139] Following the luncheon, Lowman was featured at the "Operation Survival" patriotic rally held in the auditorium of the Woolfolk State Office Building with a jam-packed enthusiastic crowd of state legislators, departmental heads, and other state government personnel.[140] The tight schedule of Lowman's speaking tour, whose main theme was billed as "Subversion Challenges Sovereignty," included a number of mass meetings in Mississippi's major cities as well as campus lectures held at Mississippi Southern College and William Carey College, both in Hattiesburg, and Belhaven College in Jackson.[141] In her interim report to the Sovereignty Commission on Lowman's January speaking engagements, Scrivner commended the Commission for sponsoring the tour "to alert the people to our extremely dangerous situation" and "to advise them on ways to combat the enemy and protect our sovereignty." "[L]ittle time should be lost," the Commission's research clerk whipped up war spirit, "in fortifying the people with authorative [*sic*] information in their fight against Godless communism."[142]

Having flattered itself with Lowman's successfully organized first state tour, the Sovereignty Commission again invited the northern crusader to Mississippi from February 19 to 28 for his second series of speaking engagements. At the request of the Paul Revere Ladies' officials, who hoped that Lowman's program would reach every state institution of higher learning in Mississippi, most of his engagements were held at state universities and colleges as well as at several junior colleges.[143] Accompanied by Scrivner and Alexander and with Commission Investigator Downing as the driver, Lowman visited such institutions as the University of Mississippi in Oxford, Mississippi State University in Starkville, Mississippi State College for Women in Columbus, Hinds Junior College in Raymond, Decatur Junior College in Decatur, Meridian Junior College in Meridian, Sunflower Junior College in Moorhead, and Delta State College in Cleveland.[144] Following Speaker Sillers's advice, the Paul Revere Ladies also scheduled the "recognized authority" on Communism to appear before the student bodies at three black Mississippi colleges—Mississippi Vocational College in Itta Bena, Jackson State College in Jackson, and Alcorn Agricultural and Mechanical College in Alcorn—to "inform and alert" young black Mississippians "to the inroads being made by the international Communist conspiracy."[145]

While his message on "the Communist psychological warfare assualt [*sic*] upon American education, entertainment, church and journalism" and on "the cold war tactics and the prospects of American survival" was politely received by the black students without any incident, Lowman met with some hostile receptions at the all-white University of Mississippi.[146] On February 20, when Lowman spoke in Fulton Chapel on the picturesque university campus, James Silver of the history department, who had some students "grouped around him," "plunged into a vicious verbal attack" on Lowman and "continued to interrupt" the meeting until it was closed. "Here we had an incident," Scrivner reported the disturbance to the Sovereignty Commission, "where a College Professor who is an employee of the State of Mississippi was leading a demonstration against an authority whom a branch of the state government had brought in" for the purpose of alerting "the student body to the peril in which this nation stands."[147] Beginning with this incident, Silver's name was included in the Sovereignty Commission's investigative dossiers, and later, in the wake of the 1962 desegregation crisis at the university, Silver would become prey to the Commission's persecution.

To be sure, Lowman's misfortune did not end with his appearance at the University of Mississippi. A few days after Lowman left Mississippi for home, his credibility as a "recognized authority" on Communism came under suspicion. Representative Horace H. Harned Jr., a future Sovereignty Commission member, notified the state agency that there existed a rumor that Lowman himself had been "connected with a Communist front organization."[148] Disconcerted, Commission Director Jones had Representative John Bell Williams in Washington run a check on Lowman and obtained a telegram from a member of the House Un-American Activities Committee that denounced the rumor as "absolutely untrue."[149] Around the same time, the state auditor's office issued reports showing that the Sovereignty Commission had generously paid the northern anti-Communist crusader a total of $3,824—$2,470 for the January tour and $1,354 for the February speaking engagements.[150] As Wilson F. "Bill" Minor, Jackson correspondent for the *New Orleans Times-Picayune*, sarcastically observed, "self-styled experts on Communist subversion" apparently found Mississippi "a happy hunting ground to pick up nice fees for their services."[151] In the meantime, Sillers continued to defend Lowman's credibility as well as his tours' importance. "We've spent $80 billion in Europe since the war to fight Communism, and President Kennedy has asked Congress for $800 million to fight Communism in Latin America," the Speaker aired his dissatisfaction, "[b]ut when we put out a little money to alert our people here at home, people set up a howl."[152] The Sovereignty Commission's official records indicate that the agency thereafter contemplated organizing Lowman's third speaking tour for April 1961. However, the records do not indicate whether this planned third visit ever materialized.[153] Notwithstanding Sillers's support, the Commission eventually terminated its dealings with the northern crusader, and instead of importing "authorities" such as Lowman from the North, the agency began to direct its attention to Mississippi's own assets to further protect the state from "subversive" activities.

One of these assets was Scrivner, who led the state agency's "Education and Information Program." Organizationally, her program was put under the supervision of the Commission's public relations department, and during the period between July 1, 1960, and December 31, 1961, a total of $5,858.17 was earmarked for what the state agency termed "Mrs. Scrivner's project."[154] The project included gathering various pamphlets, magazines, and other materials "in the subversive field" as well as showing the film *Operation Abolition* before a number of "patriotic groups" in the state.[155] The forty-five-minute documentary, which depicted "student revolts" against a hearing held by the House Un-American Activities Committee (HUAC) in California, was put together from subpoenaed newsreels by the House committee and was narrated by Fulton Lewis Jr., a right-wing analyst.[156] In addition, for the purpose of "awakening . . . the people of the state as to the critical status of our state and of the nation," the Sovereignty Commission, through Scrivner, loaned such books as J. Edgar Hoover's *Masters of Deceit* and Carleton Putnam's *Race and Reason: A Yankee View* to the general public. Some audiotapes were also loaned to civic clubs and other "study groups" in the state. These tapes included the lectures entitled "Web of Subversion" and "America's Internal Security" given by Robert Morris, a former counsel for the SISS, and "Communism Psychiatry and Crime" and "Communism vs. Moral Power" given by former FBI Agent Cleon Shousen. However, the most frightening aspect of the Commission project's undertakings was its quasi-book-burning function. "[U]pon request," a number of books were "screened" by the Commission in order to "ascertain whether or not Communism is really treated in its true form" in those publications. To those books approved by the Commission, Scrivner attached small sheets of paper stating: "Clearly defines and points out the evils of Communism."[157] "In the beginning of this program, many people looked askance [at] it," the Commission reported on "Mrs. Scrivner's project," "but . . . as evidence of the truth of the information began unfolding in actual happenings over the state, the people have realized that such information is essential in combating the enemy that would destroy us . . . through our apathy." "It goes without question," the self-praising Mississippi agency concluded, "that the State Sovereignty Commission can take credit for [this] general awakening."[158] In April 1963, at Erle Johnston's request, Scrivner began to submit her monthly "activity report[s]" to the Commission members, but in less than two months, on attaining the age of seventy, the research clerk retired from the state agency.[159] "I am grateful," Scrivner once proudly wrote to the Sovereignty Commission members, "for the privilege of being one of your servants in this lofty undertaking."[160] As one Alabama journalist observed, the Sovereignty Commission was turning out to be "a sort of un-Mississippi activities Committee."[161]

In the final analysis, Mississippi's campaign to link the civil rights movement to "the world Communist conspiracy" was eventually destined to fail. However, it is important to note that anti-Communists who furthered McCarthyism and southern segregationists who tried to perpetuate their racial norms had much in common. After all, both camps heavily depended upon a social and political atmosphere of conformity, intolerance, and repression for their very existence. In this regard, the Citizens' Council in Mississippi, as well as the Sovereignty Commission, was no exception, and while it wielded its overwhelming political power in state government, the Council strove to achieve racial conformity at all costs. Any small deviation from "Mississippi's way of life" as they defined it naturally attracted their keen attention, and whenever they found violators who dared to challenge their cherished racial—and racist—views, they were eager and ready to strike back.

Chapter 4

THE GREATEST STATES' RIGHTS STATE

Helping Ross Keep Mississippi Sovereign

In the late spring of 1961 Mississippi came face to face with a possible constitutional crisis over black civil rights. On May 4, seven whites and six blacks boarded Greyhound and Trailways interstate buses in Washington, D.C., and began traveling through the South. The previous year, the United States Supreme Court ruled in *Boynton v. Virginia* that racial segregation in interstate travel facilities was unconstitutional, but the ruling had virtually been ignored in the South. Having been "aware of the Kennedy administration's unwillingness to enforce" the Court's decision, James Farmer, who became national director of the Congress of Racial Equality (CORE) in early 1961, decided to focus the nation's attention on the issue.[1] Conceived by Farmer, the project became known as the Freedom Ride, and it eventually involved hundreds of people and lasted into the fall of 1961. "We felt that we could then count upon the racists of the South to create a crisis, so that the federal government would be compelled to enforce the federal law," Farmer recollected years later, "[a]nd that was the rationale for the Freedom Ride." Carrying out a nonviolent and direct action test of the Court's ruling, the Freedom Riders headed for Mississippi, determined to make desegregation in interstate travel facilities a reality. But before they reached Mississippi, one bus was completely destroyed by a white mob in Anniston, Alabama. On May 24, as the Freedom Riders approached the suburbs of Mississippi's capital, one of the participants broke into a song. "I'm taking a ride on the Greyhound bus line. I'm riding the front seat to Jackson this time," his jubilant voice echoed in the bus, "Hallelujah, I'm traveling; Hallelujah, ain't it fine? Hallelujah, I'm traveling; Down Freedom's main line."[2]

However, when the bus wheeled into Jackson, the Freedom Riders realized that their "Freedom's main line" was directly connected to the "main line" to the Hinds County Jail. By the end of the day, twenty-seven Freedom Riders, including Farmer, were arrested for "breach of the peace." First held at the county jail, they were later transferred by vans to Parchman State Penitentiary.[3] Unknown to the Freedom Riders, by the time they arrived in Mississippi, Attorney General Robert F. Kennedy secretly made a deal with Mississippi authorities in handling the situation. When John F. Kennedy campaigned for president in 1960, he ran on a fairly strong civil rights platform, but once he occupied the White House, Kennedy sought to avoid the issue. The president was well aware that his other legislative agendas were in the hands of the southern senators and representatives, who then chaired more than half of the thirty-eight congressional standing committees. For this reason, President Kennedy believed that he simply could not afford to alienate such powerful politicians as Senators James Eastland and John Stennis from Mississippi, and he was thus "extremely reluctant" to take an affirmative stand in Mississippi's civil rights activities.[4] Acting as a mediator between the administrations of Governor Ross Barnett and the Kennedys, former Governor James Coleman once warned Burke Marshall, who had just become the assistant attorney general for the Justice Department's Civil Rights Division, that his successor—Barnett—could not be trusted.[5] Attorney General Kennedy then turned to Senator Eastland for help: "I talked to him [Eastland] . . . about what was going to happen when they [the Freedom Riders] got to Mississippi and what needed to be done. What was finally decided was that there wouldn't be any violence [and that] as they came over the [state] border, they'd lock them all up. . . . [Eastland] told us that they'd all be arrested. I said to him my primary interest was that they weren't beaten up. So I . . . concurred [with] the fact that they were going to be arrested. . . ."[6]

Though it was "a bizarre combination," the attorney general and the

Mississippi senator understood each other.[7] As a result of this veiled agreement, Kennedy decided that he would not enforce the Court's *Boynton* ruling, which would have given the Freedom Riders their constitutional rights to use any public facilities at the Jackson bus station. In return for the attorney general's concession, Governor Barnett promised that he would make sure there would be no violence. While the Kennedy administration barely avoided bloodshed in Mississippi, it ended up putting the Freedom Riders "at the mercy of the local police and local judges" by giving in to the state's segregation laws.[8] After the first group arrived on May 24, Freedom Riders continued to pour into Jackson, and by the end of the summer, approximately three hundred participants had been arrested and sentenced. Though Mississippi's honor and police power were both preserved at the sacrifice of those brave Freedom Riders, who were victimized by a political concession, the eventual confrontation between the Kennedy administration and Mississippi was merely temporarily spared. In late June, speaking before a Rotary Club gathering in Pocatello, Idaho, Public Relations Director Erle Johnston of the State Sovereignty Commission told the audience triumphantly that the "self-styled freedom riders" had failed "in their efforts to embarrass Mississippi or to provoke violence." "Instead," he went on, "they brought many representatives of news media into Mississippi who were able to learn firsthand how the two races work and live in harmony" in a segregated society. The Freedom Riders had "actually done the state a service," Johnston audaciously concluded.[9]

As the state legislature convened in January 1962, Barnett entered the second half of his term as governor. Though the state had briefly held at bay a constitutional predicament over the Freedom Riders' "invasion," Mississippi remained "sovereign and segregated" as the governor himself had avowed two years earlier. While the lawmakers were considering three new measures to strengthen voter qualifications, aiming at discouraging the foreseeable voter registration drives by civil rights activists in Mississippi, Johnston was busy drafting a speech in early May that he was to deliver at the Grenada High School commencement ceremony later in the month.[10] Though he was invited to make the speech as an alumnus by the graduating class, Johnston thought that it would not be inappropriate for him to talk about one of the state's most pressing issues—race relations. His commencement address, entitled "The Practical Way to Maintain a Separate School

System in Mississippi," was thus delivered to the graduates on May 25. "Since 1954—the year of the Supreme Court's desegregation decision—Mississippi has experienced periods of tenseness and uncertainty," Johnston began his speech. In sharing "a complicated subject" with the graduates, their families, and their teachers, the Commission official warned: "There are militant hot heads in both races. The colored people must restrain their own hot heads and we must restrain ours." Without mentioning the NAACP by name, he criticized the "five-letter group" of having misled black Mississippians. "We have one group of extremists," Johnston explained, "financed by outsiders, who have attempted to push the colored people too fast." Then, to the surprise of many in the audience, the Citizens' Council bore the sudden brunt of Johnston's castigation as well. "On the opposite side of the picture," the public relations director went on, "we have a group of extremists who still believe in threats and intimidations": "They mean well. They are dedicated to their cause. But they have agitated the friction and bitterness and there is some question as to whether this attitude is a help, a hindrance, or merely creates hysteria." Having said that, Johnston mentioned his "philosophy" of being a "practical segregationist," who acknowledged the importance of "the cooperation of [the] colored race" in dealing with the state's racial problems.[11]

The reactions to Johnston's address were swift. While Medgar Evers of the state NAACP condemned his speech and vowed that "nothing Johnston said will stop the NAACP from continuing to work for democracy in Mississippi," the Citizens' Council also did not waste its time and began to raise a dust.[12] William Simmons of the Council was in no mood to ignore Johnston's remarks, for the publicity director had recently disapproved Simmons's request bluntly to be sent to the North as a speaker of the Sovereignty Commission's speakers bureau program.[13] Asked to comment on Johnston's talk, Simmons told a United Press International reporter that "Johnston sounds like he is ready to surrender." "His approach," Simmons betrayed his anger, "is the sure way to integration."[14] Paralleling Simmons's outburst, Clarence W. McGowen, president of the Jackson County Citizens' Council in Pascagoula, wrote to the Sovereignty Commission to express his "consternation and alarm over certain stat[e]ments recently made" by Johnston. McGowen suggested that if the Commission was being "infiltrated by our enemies" such as Johnston, "the quicker it is abolished, the better."[15] "Does [*sic*] Mr.

Johnston's statements represent the present aims and policies of our State Sovereignty Commission?," another "loyal segregationist" in Pascagoula asked the state agency: "If not, why are such individuals carried on the commission's payrolls?" "Something is bad wrong somewhere," he concluded in disgust.[16] The most vociferous condemnation, however, came from R. K. Daniel, a white resident in Long Beach, Harrison County. "I wish that those in charge would immediately get rid of the self-styled 'practical segregation-ist' on your committee," Daniel began his protest letter. Reminding the commissioners that white Mississippians "have no place" in their beloved state "for anyone who makes 'goo-goo' eyes at the mongrelizing race mixers, while trying to make patriotic Mississippians believe that he believes in our segregation laws and customs," Daniel urged them to "find some way to get that misfit out of the Mississippi Sovereignty Commission without delay."[17]

In the midst of the general atmosphere of surprise, confusion, and disbelief created by Johnston's address, the only elected official in the state's adminis-trative branch who publicly endorsed the Commission official's remarks was State Tax Collector William Winter, whom the *Memphis Press-Scimitar* once called one of Mississippi's "rising young political figures." Applauding the address "as a very realistic and frank analysis of our situation," Winter, a graduate of Grenada High as well, regarded Johnston's words as representing "the only approach which will save us from serious trouble."[18] On June 6, in an editorial entitled "Racial Harmony in Forest Indicted by Council Head" that appeared in his *Scott County Times*, Johnston made a frontal attack on Simmons and his "respectable" organization, opening the already serious wounds further: "Its [the Council's] chief objective in Mississippi now ap-pears to be making white people hate other white people. . . . Mr. Simmons doesn't want [racial] harmony. He wants strife, confusion, and violence. He still believes in the swinging club and the cracking whip." While paying deference to "many dedicated and public spirited men" who had served on the Council's state executive committee, Johnston nonetheless criticized that "the present setup of the Citizens Councils [*sic*] . . . reminds us of a pep squad at a football game." "They make noises of encouragement from the sidelines and shout 'we-must-win' phrases," he continued, "but they have nothing to do with the outcome of the struggle on the playing field."[19] Turning an undeclared war into a declared one, Johnston wrote to Governor Barnett on the same day that the Sovereignty Commission should initiate to "educate" white Mississippians while enlightening northerners on the state's race relations. "Now, I firmly believe the public relations department is in a position to do an effective job right here in Mississippi," the publicity director wrote.[20] A week later, in writing to Lieutenant Governor Paul Johnson, Johnston suggested that the Sovereignty Commission spell out a new policy that would "include a reaffirmation that we give the colored race, in the interest of harmony, a square deal in education, job opportunities, courts, and recreational facilities" and would "deplore accusations of white people against each other":

> My opinion is a very logical appraisal of our situation, an appeal for cooper-
> ation and harmony, and [it expresses my] regrets that there have been threats
> and intimidations which do not help racial relations.
>
> There would have been no controversy had Mr. Simmons not rushed to the
> newspapers and said I had surrendered and was inviting integration. I do not
> believe that any of you fine gentlemen, had you been so unjustly accused,
> would have done any different[ly] than I. Certainly it is harmful in our overall
> program [in racial matters] for any one man to assume self-ordained powers
> to cast reflections on other individuals or groups.[21]

After the publication of his editorial, Johnston told a *Delta Democrat-Times* reporter that a "tragic fact" in the state was "Mississippi can hardly make a move or say a word without approval of the rajah of race, William J. Simmons, who is Mr. Citizens['] Council."[22] The day after the newspaper ran the article, Robert Patterson, executive secretary of the Association of Citizens' Councils of Mississippi, began to fire his covering shots to defend Simmons. In writing to the editor of another Delta newspaper on June 18, Patterson branded Johnston as an advocate of "compromise," who had "stated that [our] white organization was useless." He went on: "As a result of Bill's comment on Erle Johnston's speech Erle launched a vicious, ridiculous and utterly false attack on the entire Citizens' Council movement [which] contains many of the finest people in the South." Thus, with these two powerful leaders of the Council movement, who had launched their concerted attack on the Sovereignty Commission's public relations director on behalf of "the finest white people in the South," the controversy was drawn deeper into a quagmire. In the meantime, even some Commission members began to reveal their displeasure at Johnston's feud with Simmons and his Council, and they suggested to Governor Barnett that Johnston be fired as the agency's publicity officer. When the Johnston-Simmons controversy arose, there were three Commission members who were serving on the State Executive Committee of the Association of Citizens' Councils of Mississippi, and among them, Representative Wilburn Hooker took up the fight.[23] On June 11, Hooker sent a Western Union telegram to Barnett from his hometown of Lexington, complaining that he was "receiving many inquiries and objections" regarding "Johnston's position and attack on [the] Citizens' Council." Urging the governor to take action, the Council backer asserted: "WE WHO HAVE WORKED UNTIRINGLY IN THE COUNCIL MOVEMENT RESENT UNWARRANTED ATTACKS. BELIEVE ENTIRE DEPARTMENT ERLE HEADS SHOULD BE ABOLISHED."[24]

Prompted by Hooker's wrath and placed in a fix between the loudest Council supporter among the Commission members and Johnston, who was his long-time associate and loyal publicist, Barnett hastily decided to postpone the June 21 meeting of the Sovereignty Commission. At the governor's request, Commission Director Albert Jones sent letters to the agency's members, notifying them that the scheduled monthly meeting had been canceled. Hooker was enraged. "It certainly came to me as a great surprise to receive your letter," the Lexington representative wrote to the Commission director. "[W]ith the embarrassing position that Erle Johnston has put the Commission in," he vented his anger, "it seems inconceivable to me that a majority of the members of the Sovereignty Commission would request that this scheduled meeting be cancelled." Discontented with the circumstances under which the Commission members could only "idly sit by and do nothing" about the Johnston-Simmons feud, the lawmaker demanded further explanation from Jones.[25] Unable to quell his fury, Hooker then wrote to the governor on the same day. Reminding Barnett that it was his "duty as Governor and Chairman of the Sovereignty Commission to see" to it that proper action would be taken, Hooker reiterated his desire that Johnston "either should resign himself or be fired." "I beg of you to do something about this matter," he urged the governor, "and do it now."[26] With Johnston lying on a bed of thorns, the postponed regular meeting of the Sovereignty Commission was finally held on July 19. During the three-hour meeting, Tom Watkins asked Johnston several questions concerning his "ideas that segregation could be maintained only by cooperation between the races." Aubrey Bell and some others expressed their feelings that the publicity director's racial views "were not altogether in accord" with the agency's purposes. The Commission, at long last, suggested that Johnston submit his resignation on or before November 1, 1962, and he agreed to do so.[27] After the meeting, no mention was made to the press regarding this "deal" made between the agency and Johnston, and the reporters naturally assumed and reported that the public relations director managed to retain his position.[28] At the same time, the members secretly adopted a resolution on the Johnston-Simmons controversy, which would be later discovered by the press in October. While the resolution, offered by House Speaker Walter Sillers, made it clear that the Sovereignty Commission "declines to participate in any personal controversy" between its publicity director and the Council leader, it resolved that the state agency "approves a policy of cooperation with Negroes in an effort to maintain segregation in Mississippi."[29] The resolution was approved unconditionally by all attending members but Bell. In approving the resolution under protest, Bell requested that "it not be given to the press and remain . . . absolutely confidential," for he abhorred the probability that the resolution might be construed "as a complete adoption of the policy [advocated] by Erle Johnston." Explaining in unmistakable terms that he approved the resolution "out of respect for Walter Sillers" as an "exception," Bell further instructed Jones to record his vote as "disapproving" the resolution if and when it got in the papers. "That does not mean that I am not in accord with it," he added, "but only that it comes at a time when it could be construed as [my] adopting Johnston's policy." "[A]nd that shall never do," Bell flatly concluded.[30]

While the controversy over Johnston's Grenada High speech was blazing, the state legislature appropriated $250,000 to the Sovereignty Commission for the fiscal biennium beginning on July 1, 1962. Emotion was high in the legislative body due largely to the grim prospect of a federal court decision on the desegregation case at the University of Mississippi. Representative Ray H. Thames of Brookhaven, Lincoln County, spoke for the state's segregationists when the House debated the appropriation bill for the Sovereignty Commission: "We are going to find out how many people in this House are for integration. . . . Every vote against the bill is a vote for integration. You are in Mississippi now. You ain't in New York or some other place."[31] Just before the final vote was taken on the bill, the House members voted down an amendment offered by Representative Joseph Wroten, who vainly tried to prohibit the state agency from continuing its donations to the Citizens' Council. Reminding House members that they should vote according to their conscience and were obligated to vote for whatever was the best for the people they represented, Wroten took the floor after offering his amendment: "I refuse to be brainwashed with this [Thames's] approach." "If the day has come when we must vote under that kind of intimidation," the Methodist minister's son contended, "then the Lord God in heaven help us." The appropriation bill was approved by a vote of 112 to 4, with Wroten, George Rogers, Karl Wiesenburg, and Phillip D. Bryant of Oxford, Lafayette County, voting against the bill.[32] With these thin dissenting voices drowned out in the roars of defiance, the continuity of the Sovereignty Commission's life was assured.

As Mississippi's political circles were being flustered by the protracted feud between Johnston and Simmons, the United States Fifth Circuit Court of Appeals in New Orleans struck a blow at the state that would soon invite an all-out constitutional crisis over civil rights. On June 25, 1962, reversing the lower federal court's rulings, the Fifth Circuit affirmed that James H. Meredith, a black veteran of the United States Air Force and a native of Attalla County, had been denied admittance to the all-white University of Mississippi, better known as Ole Miss, solely because of his race. It directed Federal District Judge Sidney Mize of Mississippi to order the university to accept Meredith.[33] In the court's majority opinion, Judge John Minor Wisdom, a native of New Orleans, sharply criticized the lower court's mishandling of the case and declared: "A full review of the record leads the Court inescapably to the conclusion that from the moment the defendants discovered Meredith was a Negro they engaged in a carefully calculated campaign of delay, harassment, and masterly inactivity."[34] The day of the appeals court's judgment happened to be Meredith's twenty-ninth birthday.[35]

Though the Fifth Circuit ruled that Ole Miss must accept Meredith as its first black student, as in the case of the 1957 Little Rock crisis, one grave question remained unanswered: who would enforce the federal court order? Earlier in May 1954, standing on the floor of the United States Senate, Eastland proclaimed in the immediate aftermath of the Supreme Court's *Brown* decree that "people [in the South] will not change [their racial] views which have been instilled into them for generations, merely on the strength of a few words by a court." "It will take force to bring compliance with the decision of the Supreme Court. [But] [w]here is that force? The Court cannot supply it," the Mississippi senator remarked.[36] The Court truly could not "supply" the force, but in Little Rock, President Dwight Eisenhower, with much reluctance, eventually took on the task, and his popular campaign slogan, "I Like Ike," was replaced overnight by the chants of "I Hate Ike."

Both President Kennedy and Attorney General Kennedy were also reluctant participants in the Mississippi desegregation ordeal of 1962. After his brother's death, Robert Kennedy recollected in a December 1964 interview: "What I was trying to avoid basically was having to send troops and trying to avoid having a federal presence in Mississippi."[37] "His consuming fear," Arthur M. Schlesinger Jr. remembered, "was a mini-civil war with GIs and Mississippians shooting each other down."[38] President Kennedy shared the same thoughts with his younger brother. Nicholas Katzenbach, who served as a United States assistant attorney general and then as deputy attorney general under the Kennedy administration, once reflected that "the Kennedys thought that the one bad mistake Ike made was to send troops into Little Rock."[39] Meanwhile, Meredith, the central figure in the desegregation controversy, had a different perspective. "I knew that the Kennedys would do nothing on my agenda [if] they were not forced in[to] a position to do [something]," Meredith recalled three decades after his ordeal:

> It was my experience in the military that made [the desegregation of] the University of Mississippi possible. Most people don't know what I really did at the University of Mississippi. What I really did at the University of Mississippi was to force the federal government to employ its troops on my side against the Mississippi troops. That's what I did, and that's what I set out to do—to force the Kennedy administration in[to] the position where they [had] to use the armed force[s] for my purpose. . . .
>
> I knew that that had to happen in order for me to be successful [in desegregating the university].[40]

On the evening of September 13, just a few hours after Federal District Judge Mize ordered Ole Miss to admit Meredith immediately, Governor Barnett went on statewide television and radio to speak to Mississippians on the state's "greatest crisis since the War between the States." "We must either submit to the unlawful dictates of the Federal Government," the governor reminded the people, "or stand up like men and tell them 'NEVER!' " "I have made my position in this matter crystal clear," he went on, "[and] I have said in every county in Mississippi that no school in our state will be integrated while I am your Governor. I repeat to you tonight—NO SCHOOL WILL BE INTEGRATED IN MISSISSIPPI WHILE I AM YOUR GOVERNOR." Then, "in obedience to [the] legislative and constitutional sanction" of the state, Barnett interposed "the rights of the Sovereign State of Mississippi to enforce its laws and to regulate its own internal affairs without interference on the part of the Federal government." "Let us meet this crisis with dignity, courage and fortitude," the governor concluded, "and show to the world that we are people of honor, that we do not, we will not surrender to the evil and illegal forces of tyranny."[41]

Having invited the nightmarish repetition of the Little Rock crisis, Barnett marked a fatal point of no return. Wiping sweat from his brow following the broadcast, the governor realized that better than anyone else. Five days later, Barnett called the state legislature into its first special session of the year. Summoned by the governor, four representatives, led by Speaker Sillers, introduced House Concurrent Resolution No. 2, which pledged the legislature's "full support in the staunch stand" taken by Barnett.[42] There was no dissension in the Senate, but as expected, Representative Wroten voted against the resolution in the House. He was joined by Representative Wiesenburg, who vainly tried to convince his colleagues on the House floor that "the actions of the governor and the actions of our leaders would inevitably lead to bloodshed and riot."[43] Personifying Wroten and Wiesenburg as "Two Lonely Red Flashes," the *Jackson Daily News* castigated the two "traitors," whose lone nay votes had two red lights flash on the legislative scoreboard in the House chamber.[44]

The nature of the federal-state conflict over Meredith's attempt to desegregate Ole Miss was relatively clear, but the politics was not. In Washington, while President Kennedy and his advisers were determined that Meredith should eventually attend Ole Miss, they were also desperate to find a way to avoid direct military involvement in Mississippi by the federal government, which would certainly cost the president southern Democratic support that he needed in Congress and might even ruin his bid to be renominated as the party's presidential candidate in 1964. Thus, Kennedy preferred a political solution. Meanwhile, Governor Barnett in Jackson, more than anyone else, did not wish to invite the same federal intervention that had unfolded in Little Rock just five years earlier, with a possible bloody federal-state military confrontation. But at the same time, the governor could not simply retreat from the battlefield without a fight and let Meredith attend Ole Miss. Barnett wanted a political solution, too, and he turned to his advisers for any feasible suggestions to break the impasse. Among those counselors, Watkins, a Jackson attorney and one of the citizen members of the Sovereignty Commission who also was the chief legal adviser to the governor, played an important role as a conduit between Barnett and the Kennedy administration. This secret arrangement was made through the influence of Senator Eastland.[45] "[H]e was [someone] at least you could talk to [reasonably] who could understand you," Assistant Attorney General Marshall once remembered of Watkins.[46]

In truth, the Sovereignty Commission did not have much to do with dictating the course of events in the Ole Miss affair. The state agency, to be sure, had Investigator Andy Hopkins attend at least one federal court hearing held in Jackson in August 1961, and it dispatched both Hopkins and Virgil Downing to Attala County "to obtain all information on J. H. Meredith" and his parents on a few occasions in February and July 1962. But from the onset of the crisis, Governor Barnett realized, admittedly or otherwise, that if the state's defiance went all the way, the result would be the presence of federal troops to enforce the court order, and he sensed that the mobilization of the Sovereignty Commission would not be a great help in the end.[47] In fact, the inner sanctum of the governor's advisers, which consisted of Simmons and a host of others, did not include either Director Jones of the Sovereignty Commission or its publicity director, Johnston. Jones, who was an ardent supporter of the Council movement, was represented by Simmons in a sense. As for Johnston, the governor realized that the publicity director's presence was not expedient because of the lingering emotional disputes created by Johnston's recent Grenada High commencement address.[48] Aside from Watkins's direct involvement in the Ole Miss affair, the Sovereignty Commission as a state executive agency thus played a role as a stagehand and undertook a few inconspicuous projects. Among them was its ordering of some ten thousand bumper stickers for $732 in the early summer of 1962 that read: "Help Ross Keep Mississippi Sovereign."[49]

On the afternoon of September 20, Meredith was brought to the University of Mississippi campus by Attorney John Doar from the Civil Rights Division of the Justice Department and James P. McShane, chief of the executive office of United States Marshals. Earlier on that same day, the Board of Trustees of State Institutions of Higher Learning voted to invest Governor Barnett "with the full power, authority, right and discretion" of the board "to act upon all matters pertaining to or concerned with the registration or non-registration, admission or non-admission, and/or attendance of James H. Meredith" at Ole Miss, designating the governor as the official successor of Robert Ellis, registrar at the University of Mississippi. Inside the University Continuation Center building on campus, Meredith appeared before Registrar Ellis and Governor Barnett and quietly told the two men what his intended business was: "I want to be admitted to the University." Ellis, who did not waste his time, began to read the board's decision to transfer its authority to the governor. Following the registrar, Barnett then read his brief proclamation, refusing the admission of Meredith to Ole Miss.[50]

Three days after this first confrontation took place, President Kennedy called Barnett to express his apprehension over the Meredith matter. "I am concerned," the president said on the phone, "about this situation down there." "Oh, I should say I am concerned about it, Mr. President. It's . . . a horrible situation," the governor answered. By then, Watkins had already become a crucial link between the two administrations. He had even suggested to Attorney General Kennedy that they play a farcical drama where the marshals would escort Meredith to Ole Miss and, upon the lead marshal's drawing his gun, Barnett and other state officials would step aside to let Meredith register. Informed by President Kennedy that Watkins and the attorney general were not making as much progress as he had expected to break the deadlock, Barnett began to make a plea for the president's understanding on the phone: "[Y]ou know what I am up against, Mr. President. I took an oath . . . to abide by the laws of this state. . . . I'm on the spot here." "[T]he problem is, Governor," Kennedy also gave vent to his sentiments, "that I['ve] got my responsibility just like you have yours." At the end of their five-minute conversation, as if to try to put away the grave problem that he had just talked about with the president, Barnett abruptly, but sincerely, added: "I appreciate your interest in our poultry program and all those things." Laughing softly but wryly, the president simply replied: "Okay, Governor. Thank you."[51]

On September 25, Doar and McShane escorted Meredith to the office of the Board of Trustees of State Institutions of Higher Learning located on the tenth floor of the Woolfolk State Office Building in downtown Jackson. As the three men approached the board's office, Governor Barnett stood in the doorway. After studying Meredith and the two white federal officials seriously for a few seconds, Barnett mischievously asked them: "Which one of you gentlemen is Mr. Meredith?" While Meredith flashed a little grin, the two white men showed no amusement. Then, Doar vainly tried to hand the governor an order from the Fifth Circuit Court to prohibit him from interfering with Meredith's enrollment at Ole Miss. In response, Barnett began to read a proclamation directed to Meredith that, in essence, confirmed his previous position. "I, Ross R. Barnett, Governor of the State of Mississippi," the governor concluded, "do hereby finally deny you admission to the University of Mississippi."[52] When Doar once again asked the governor to permit them to enter the board's office, Barnett launched into an extemporaneous speech, citing the Tenth Amendment to the United States Constitution: "I took an oath when I was inaugurated governor of this state to uphold and try to maintain and perpetuate the laws of Mississippi. . . . Gentlemen, my conscience is clear."[53] In the meantime, Assistant Attorney General Marshall called Watkins at the governor's mansion in Jackson. "[I]f there [is] to be any school integration in Mississippi," the Sovereignty Commission member painfully told the assistant attorney general, "it would have to be done forcibly."[54]

The next morning, Marshall again placed a call to Watkins in New York, who had flown from Jackson on the previous evening as the governor's emissary. Consenting to Marshall's general appraisal of the situation, Watkins told the Justice Department official that "the matter had gone too far" and suggested that federal officials " 'gently' attempt to push the Governor aside" on their "next effort to escort Meredith into the University," which was to be carried out later that afternoon. Watkins reiterated, however, that these officials "should use 'the mildest kind of force.' " "This would make the Governor's point," he further explained to Marshall, "and give him an out because the Federal Government would have forcibly brought about desegregation." The assistant attorney general immediately passed Watkins's suggestion on to Doar and McShane and instructed them "to make an effort physically to force their way onto the campus."[55] Thus, the plan for a farcical play was set at last, but both Watkins and Marshall had no idea that the play's leading actor—Governor Barnett—would not be able to show up on the stage that afternoon.

In accordance with the Watkins-Marshall plan, Doar and McShane brought Meredith to the Ole Miss campus for his third attempt to register. But this time, the party was met by Lieutenant Governor Johnson. "We're going in," McShane told the lieutenant governor, wasting no time, but Johnson simply replied: "You aren't." Then, the chief marshal unsuccessfully tried to elbow the lieutenant governor aside, and at one point, even shook his fist at him. Notwithstanding this "show of force" on the part of the Kennedy administration, Johnson, who was not privy to the plan devised by Watkins and Marshall that same morning, "refused to be budged." Governor Barnett, who arrived late at the university due to mechanical trouble with his airplane, congratulated Johnson for having "stood tall" against the federal "tyranny."[56] In a sense, the lieutenant governor was a thoroughly unprepared stand-in who was suddenly drawn into the center of a very important scene without having been told in advance that there was a major change in the script. After this third confrontation, Marshall called Watkins once again and asked him what went wrong. The Sovereignty Commission member wryly explained that the federal officials did not use "a large enough show of force." Perplexed, Marshall asked Watkins, "What show of force would be enough?"[57]

While the lieutenant governor's defiant stand would later assure his ascent to the governor's office, Barnett began to lose his nerve. On September 28, the Fifth Circuit Court convicted Barnett of contempt of court and levied a fine of $10,000 a day. Having "stood tall" on the Ole Miss campus, Lieutenant Governor Johnson was also fined $5,000 a day. When the appeals court found both Barnett and Johnson guilty of contempt of court, the state legislature adopted a resolution protesting against "the tyrannical effort of the federal government." Sensing an imminent possibility of the use of federal force by the Kennedys and "speaking for peace-loving, law-abiding citizens of the State of Mississippi," the resolution, introduced by five senators, including John McLaurin who was a Sovereignty Commission member, declared: "We do hereby deplore and condemn the use of Federal force in any form and in an unconstitutional and illegal attempt to subjugate free American citizens and to subordinate constitutional government to the dictates of an organized, militant, and self-serving minority." Both Houses of the state legislature hurriedly voted for the resolution, with the only two dissenting votes cast by Representatives Wroten and Wiesenburg. After its adoption, certified copies of the resolution were immediately sent to the Kennedy brothers.[58]

The resolution was not the only thing that the state mailed to President Kennedy during the Meredith crisis. In late September, with the help of the Hederman brothers—Thomas and Robert—who controlled both the *Jackson Daily News* and the *Jackson Clarion-Ledger*, the Sovereignty Commission printed the astonishing number of 1,015,000 postcards addressed to the president for $3,118, protesting the federal actions regarding the Ole Miss affair. They were to be distributed to segregationist and other "patriotic" groups and at college football games in various major southern cities such as Nashville, Tennessee; Columbia, South Carolina; Birmingham, Alabama; Baton Rouge, Louisiana; and Dallas, Texas.[59] Under the command of Senator McLaurin and utilizing Citizens' Council networks, the Sovereignty Commission began to distribute the postcards on September 29, when Jones and Downing drove to Memphis, Tennessee, to deliver 75,000 postcards to Jack Aday, an official of the Citizens' Council of Memphis. The following day, they delivered another set of 75,000 postcards to a member of Little Rock Citizens' Council, Malcolm Taylor.[60] Preaddressed to "President John F. Kennedy, White House, Washington, D.C.," on one side, the other side of the card read:

> Please take notice that I respectfully resent the unnatural warfare being waged against the sovereign state of Mississippi and urge that you give more serious attention to facing up to the Communist menace and our Cuban problem.
> Signed: _____[61]

Just how many of the postcards actually arrived at the White House is sheer speculation, but the *Nashville Tennessean* took note that many of them were passed out at a college football game in Nashville on the night of September 29.[62]

Still hoping to resolve the Meredith crisis without employing federal

forces, President Kennedy called Barnett on Saturday, September 29, to discuss a new behind-the-scenes proposal, which Watkins had just suggested to
Attorney General Kennedy. According to the scheme, the Kennedy administration would announce that Meredith was going to the Ole Miss campus to
be registered on Monday, October 1. On the basis of this announcement,
Barnett and Johnson would be at the university to block Meredith's admission. While the governor and the lieutenant governor would await the arrival
of the Meredith party, federal officials were going to bring Meredith secretly
to the state office building in Jackson to get him registered there. The theory
behind this "hidden ball trick" proposal was simple, because it would enable
Barnett to claim that the Kennedys misled him, which in turn would allow
him to save face.[63]

Enthusiastic about this new proposal, throughout Saturday afternoon and
well into the early evening, the governor spent most of his time trying to
talk some of his intransigent advisers into accepting the plan. However, by
the time he left the Veterans Memorial Stadium in Jackson later in the evening after attending the Ole Miss–Kentucky football game, Barnett "had
lost his own resolve to honor" the trick plan.[64] Just before kickoff, as Governor Barnett and his wife appeared at their spectator box and waved to the
crowd, over forty thousand people who packed the stadium began to cheer,
waving their Confederate flags. At halftime, in response to the endless chants
of "We Want Ross" coming from the spectators, Barnett dutifully went
down to the middle of the field. There, in the glare of a spotlight, the governor spoke into a microphone with his right fist clenched and held high above
his head: "I love Mississippi! I love her people [and] our customs! I love
and respect our heritage!"[65] The governor did not utter a single word of
"segregation," "integration," "states' rights," or "federal encroachment," but
his message was clear. Moreover, Barnett was more than just the governor
of the state of Mississippi on that evening, becoming a symbol of the white
South—a personification of the cherished "southern way of life." In place of
the rendition of "Dixie," the Ole Miss band began to introduce the new state
song, "Go Mississippi," which was designated as the official state song during
the 1962 regular legislative session on May 17—the eighth anniversary of
the Supreme Court's *Brown* ruling. "Go, Mississippi, you cannot go wrong,
. . . Go, Mississippi, let the world know, That our Mississippi is leading the
show"—the words reverberated through the stadium.[66]

It was undoubtedly true that the nation's eyes were fixed on Mississippi and that the state was "leading the show." But contrary to the words of the newly introduced state song, Mississippi was definitely "going wrong." Shortly after the enthusiastic crowd at the stadium was driven into a frenzy by his appearance, Barnett placed a call to the Justice Department in Washington. The attorney general had gone home, but the governor's call was forwarded to his residence. Castigated by young Kennedy that he was breaking his word to the president, Barnett told the attorney general that he would have to call off the earlier proposal. President Kennedy was then phoned at the White House and informed by his brother that the deal was off. Upon hearing this, the president reluctantly signed the already prepared proclamation documents, federalizing the Mississippi National Guard and authorizing Secretary of the Army Cyrus Vance to call out troops for sending them to Ole Miss if it became necessary. A few seconds before signing the documents, President Kennedy looked up at one of his White House aides and asked: "Is this pretty much what Ike signed in 1957 with the Little Rock thing?" Assured that it was, the president went on to subscribe his name to the documents.[67]

While the Pentagon was busy notifying the Mississippi National Guard that it was now under the command of the federal government, Robert Kennedy and Barnett resumed their desperate search for a peaceful solution before the situation got any worse. At 10:45 A.M., on Sunday, September 30, the governor called the attorney general from his mansion in Jackson. The only person who accompanied him at this time was Watkins, and it was one of the rare moments during the previous few days when Barnett was not surrounded by a dozen of his advisers. In that quietness, the attorney general exploded a bombshell, informing the governor that the president might reveal the existence of their secret negotiations on national television. "The President is going on TV tonight," Kennedy broke the news, "[and] [h]e will have to say why he called up the National Guard; that you had an agreement to permit Meredith to go to Jackson to register, and your lawyer, Mr. Watkins, said this was satisfactory." Barnett was horrified at the ramifications of the president's possible revelation of their secret conversations and started begging for the attorney general's mercy: "Don't say that. Please don't mention it." At long last, almost thirty minutes after the conversation began, Governor Barnett agreed with Attorney General Kennedy that Meredith would be brought to the Ole Miss campus later that afternoon and that

Barnett would make a statement to the effect that he would "recognize the authority" of the federal government. The attorney general made sure that Barnett would issue his statement to "alleviate the situation" before his elder brother's appearance on television.[68]

Barnett and Watkins hurriedly set to write a draft of the governor's statement, but it was already 12:00 noon, and time was running short. An hour later, Barnett called Marshall at the Justice Department and "dictated the statement he intended to make." Around 6:00 P.M., Mississippi time, Attorney General Kennedy called the governor "to inform him that Meredith had arrived on the campus" of Ole Miss. The attorney general also asked Barnett to make some minor changes in his statement, but the perturbed governor answered that "he didn't have a pencil or . . . a secretary."[69] At 7:30 P.M., Governor Barnett, looking tired and strained, went on statewide television and announced that Meredith had already been placed on the campus of Ole Miss:

> Surrounded on all sides by the armed forces and oppressive power of the United States of America, my courage and my convictions do not waiver. My heart still says "never," but my calm judgement abhors the bloodshed that will follow. I love Mississippi. I love her people. I love those 10,000 good Mississippians in the National Guard who have now been federalized and requested to oppose me and their own people. . . . I know that our principles remain true, but we must at all odds preserve the peace and avoid bloodshed.[70]

"To the officials of the federal government," Barnett added, "I say: 'Gentlemen, you are tramping on the sovereignty of this great State and depriving it of every vestige of honor and respect as a member of the union of states. You are destroying the Constitution of this great Nation. May God have mercy on your souls.' "[71]

In the meantime, President Kennedy went on the air to deliver his address to the nation shortly after Barnett finished his statewide speech. While reminding American people at large that "our Nation is founded on the principle that observance of the law is the eternal safeguard of liberty and defiance of the law is the surest road to tyranny" and stressing that "the law which we obey includes the final rulings of the courts," Kennedy conveyed his special appeal to "white Mississippi's sense of honor": "You have a great tradition to uphold, a tradition of honor and courage won on the field of battle and on the gridiron as well as the University [of Mississippi] campus. You have a new opportunity to show that you are men of patriotism and integrity. . . . It lies in your courage to accept those laws with which you disagree as well as those with which you agree."[72] "The eyes of the Nation and of all the world are upon you and upon all of us," the president concluded, "and the honor of your University and State are in the balance."[73]

On the campus of Ole Miss, unknown to both Barnett and Kennedy, a large crowd gathered around the Lyceum—the university's administrative building—had already begun to throw bricks, bottles, and Molotov cocktails at the federal marshals. As President Kennedy began his nationwide address to appeal to white Mississippians' "sense of honor," the marshals, whom Tom Scarbrough, one of the Sovereignty Commission's investigators, described as being "dressed like frog men from Mars," started to fight back by firing tear gas.[74] When Jones and Downing returned to Jackson after their trips to distribute a total of 150,000 "Kennedy postcards," the campus riots had already broken out in Oxford.[75] "[T]he avalanche had been started," Judge Tom Brady, author of *Black Monday*, remembered, "and there wasn't anything to stop it, until it got to the bottom of the mountain."[76] By the time the "avalanche" reached "the bottom of the mountain," the campus riots and the Kennedy administration's efforts to subdue the night of terror brought two deaths. In addition, some two hundred rioters were arrested, only twenty-four of whom were identified as Ole Miss students.[77] The overwhelming military presence of some twenty-three thousand troops dispatched by the Kennedys had restored order to the campus by the dawn of Monday, October 1. At 8:00 A.M., escorted by a group of exhausted federal marshals, Meredith was finally registered, and he thus officially became the first black student to enroll at the University of Mississippi. President Kennedy made sure that Meredith would be accompanied by plainclothes marshals, not by army troops, to the registrar's office in an apparent attempt not to incite white Mississippians to further rebellion.[78] In Jackson, having just witnessed "the enormous usurpation of power by the federal government," Simmons of the Citizens' Council grudgingly realized that "things would never be the same":

> After it was all over, the next day [October 1] was a beautiful fall day,
> [with] bright sunshine [and] blue sky. I looked out the window of our office

overlooking the governor's mansion. We were on the third floor, and my wife was standing there beside me. We looked at people walking down the street, normally going about their everyday affairs, and I turned to her and I said, "These people have just been deprived of the power of self-government, and they don't know it." That's the shock [to me].[79]

Before Meredith's eventual success in desegregating Ole Miss, no public school in Mississippi—neither its elementary and secondary schools, colleges, nor universities—had been racially integrated. But now the absolute racial barrier in the state's educational system was finally broken. The Meredith crisis was what Willie Morris, a Mississippi writer, aptly called "Echoes of a Civil War's Last Battle."[80] Subscribing to Morris's observation, Constance Baker Motley, who had represented Meredith in his long legal battle, once looked back: "What really happened in the Meredith case when the state [of Mississippi] decided to resist was that they were playing out the last chapter of the Civil War."[81] Be that as it may, just as the Old South did after the bloody Civil War, "Old Mississippi," too, refused to go away gently. Though Meredith was enrolled by the overwhelming force of the federal armory, Governor Barnett felt that he had only lost a battle, not the entire war. From October 2, which was the day after Meredith's enrollment at Ole Miss, to October 18, the Sovereignty Commission, through investigator Downing, had continued to deliver a total of sixty-eight thousand "Kennedy postcards" to the "custodians" of the Vicksburg and Natchez Bridges over the Mississippi River, who then passed those cards out to various segregationist organizations in Louisiana.[82] In addition, Jones sent fifty thousand postcards by a freight truck to George W. Singelmann of the Greater New Orleans Citizens' Council, who had earlier offered his services to distribute the cards "among the loyal citizens" in the Louisiana port city.[83]

In the immediate aftermath of the Ole Miss incident, the Sovereignty Commission, which had kept a relatively low profile for the previous few months, resurfaced. On October 18, at the Commission's first meeting after the Meredith crisis, Johnston "proposed an acceleration" of the agency's speakers bureau program "with a change in policy to emphasize the rights of the states." Before the commissioners approved the reactivation of its speakers bureau program, however, the publicity director once again led the state agency into a dispute. The day after the October 18 meeting, Johnston wrote a letter to Barnett, asking the governor to let him continue to work for the Commission as its public relations director notwithstanding the decision previously made by the agency at its July 19 meeting. Bell, a Citizens' Council sympathizer, grew furious at Johnston's backdoor approach and began to protest vehemently, insisting that the publicity director's letter to the governor should not "supersede" the decision made at the July meeting. The final decision was left to Barnett as chair of the Commission, and Barnett eventually gave his nod to the public relations director. Though Johnston was spared by the governor this time, Bell's antagonism toward the publicity officer would continue.[84]

Shortly after this incident, Governor Barnett instructed Johnston to "accelerate" the Commission's speakers bureau program. "We must continue to try," Barnett wrote to Johnston, "to mould the hearts and minds of the people on Constitutional Government and States' Rights, local self-government and segregation of the races."[85] In response, Johnston set to revise his 1960 speech draft for the reactivated speakers bureau. One of the notable differences between the 1960 version and the new version of "The Message from Mississippi" was the complete omission of such words as "Negro" and "Negroes," which Johnston replaced with "colored" and "colored people." However, a more substantial change occurred in the context itself. Whereas the earlier draft read more or less like an information sheet on the state's racial situation and devoted only one and a half pages to the advocacy of the states' rights principle, the new version consumed almost eight pages out of a total of thirteen pages for issues surrounding constitutional government and states' rights. Lamenting "the continued centralization" of the federal government and its "usurpation" of powers reserved to the states of the Union, Johnston's new draft contained some harsh words for the Kennedy administration, criticizing it for mishandling the Meredith crisis.[86] Prior to the Ole Miss riots, instances of racial harmony in Mississippi were stressed in speeches made by the Commission's speakers. However, after the fall of 1962, as Johnston once told a newspaper reporter, the state agency's program began to devote "a great portion of the presentations" to "the legality of Mississippi's stand" in the Meredith incident.[87] Explaining the vindication of the course of actions taken by Governor Barnett in the face of the Ole Miss crisis, the new version of "The Message from Mississippi" reminded northern audiences that asserting Mississippi's "sovereignty right between the court's decree and its people" was the state's "only recourse." "This is not an act of rebellion or defiance," it read, "but is the only lawful means by which a sovereign state may assert its constitutional rights." Terming the Meredith crisis "one of the most tragic events in the history of our country," the speech draft further went on:

> We regret and do not in any sense of the word condone the violence and rioting at the University of Mississippi. That day at Oxford, all Americans witnessed one of the most tragic events in the history of our country—Federal force against a sovereign state, brother against brother, education at bayonet point, violence at its worst, the loss of two lives, injuries to many persons, extreme property destruction, damage to the reputation of a great University, and deep wounds that will be long in passing.[88]

Ample words that aspersed the Kennedys abounded in the text as well. The Kennedy administration exerted "pressures, name calling and intimidations" in their handling of the Meredith affair. Their pressure tactics, it asserted, should "cause one to wonder whether or not government by intimidation" was "taking the place of liberty under the law." The "Message" in its final words, reminded the Kennedy brothers that "armed forces are not going to solve our problems."[89]

With this new speech draft at hand, the Sovereignty Commission sent its first speaker to the North since the Meredith crisis. The engagement was carried out in early December 1962 by State District Attorney Michael L. Carr Jr. of Brookhaven, who spoke before a local Rotary Club in North Hampton, Massachusetts.[90] By the end of the year, Johnston secured three "firm" speaking engagements for January 1963 in Indiana, Iowa, and South Dakota; four for February in Colorado, Idaho, Illinois, and Iowa; and four for March in Massachusetts and Washington. State Senator Sonny Montgomery was among the speakers for the March engagements.[91] In early 1963, while asking the governor to "take another look at the approved budget for the speakers bureau," Johnston asked for support for the Commission's program in a speech before a civic club in Greenwood, a Mississippi Delta town.[92] However, the enthusiasm for the speakers bureau program that the state's elected officials and business leaders had entertained since the summer of 1960 was gradually dwindling, due mainly to the wretched consequences of the Ole Miss crisis.

In addition, the Sovereignty Commission invited disaster when the agency sent State Circuit Judge Sebe Dale to Brandeis University in Waltham, Massachusetts, as its speaker in the late spring of 1962.[93] Three years earlier, Judge Dale had presided over the nationally publicized trial of a young black named Mack Charles Parker, who was charged with raping a white woman in Pearl River County. But just three days before he was to stand trial, several local white men abducted Parker from the county jail in Poplarville and lynched him.[94] At Brandeis, when the judge finished his talk, one member of the audience asked him if he thought Parker's murderers would ever be apprehended. Johnston, who accompanied Dale, flashed at the judge his previously prepared answer to that specific question, which simply read: "We consider it an unsolved crime, just as other states have unsolved crimes." But Dale, who was "one of Mississippi's less gifted judges," unmindfully replied that "three of them [who lynched Parker] are already dead."[95] Dismayed, the public relations director turned pale and tried to let Dale come to his own rescue, but it was too late. With the judge's nonchalantly uttered comment, a travesty of justice in Mississippi, which was sometimes referred to as "the land of the tree and the home of the grave" with a tinge of irony, was exposed to the light of day.[96] Moreover, Judge Dale's appearance, for which the Sovereignty Commission spent a sum of $117.99, was a fatal blow to the speakers bureau's credibility, and coupled with the agency's budgetary squeeze, the bureau program was virtually terminated in May 1963.[97] By then, the Sovereignty Commission had dispatched nearly a hundred volunteer speakers to the North and the West since the summer of 1960.[98]

In the summer of 1963 House Speaker Sillers suggested that the Commission again revive its speakers bureau program by enlisting the services of the "heads of important departments and institutions of the state" as speakers, and the public relations director at one point hoped that the first set of trips by the bureau's speakers would "begin again during the month of October" 1963.[99] But to the disappointment of Johnston as well as Sillers and the governor, the plan never materialized. As if to fill the void created by the absence of the Sovereignty Commission's speakers bureau program, the Citizens' Council launched its own public relations project, "Operation Information," in the summer of 1963 "to present Southern views to Northern audiences."[100]

While Johnston's efforts to reactivate the Sovereignty Commission's speakers bureau program continued, Jones informed Governor Barnett and other Commission members of his decision to resign from the state agency in order to devote his full time to running for sheriff of Hinds County—the position he had previously held. His resignation date was set for March 22, 1963, the day after the scheduled March meeting of the Commission.[101] A few days before the meeting, Kenneth Toler of the *Memphis Commercial Appeal* predicted that the meeting would be a "showdown" between Johnston and the powerful Citizens' Council and its sympathizers over whom the "segregation watchdog" would choose as its new director.[102] When the Commission met on March 21, Johnston in fact was the only official candidate for the directorship, but once the meeting began, four members abruptly voted for Hopkins, who neither wanted nor would have accepted the position. Those who voted for Hopkins—Senator McLaurin, Representatives Hooker and Joseph Moss, and Bell—were all Citizens' Council officials or its strong supporters. The six members who placed their confidence in Johnston were Lieutenant Governor Johnson, Attorney General Joe Patterson, Senator Herman DeCell, Representative William Johnson, Jesse Stockstill, and Watkins. House Speaker Sillers was absent from the meeting, and Governor Barnett, following custom, did not cast his vote, though he explicitly approved of Johnston's promotion during the meeting.[103] At the end of this ninety-minute closed-door session, a group of a dozen determined women, most of whom were members of an organization called the Women for Constitutional Government, arrived outside of the meeting room to register their protest against Johnston's appointment as the Commission's new director. "[Johnston's] writings in the past had indicated . . . that he was not a dedicated segregationist," asserted the gathered women. Meanwhile, Simmons, who had been waiting just outside of the room to make a report to the Commission on the Citizens' Council expenditures, quietly left the building when Hooker angrily told him: "You won't get the report today, as we have adjourned."[104]

With the divided meeting behind him, Johnston thanked Barnett for the governor's confidence in him. "Nothing has ever made me more proud of any man than what you did at the Commission meeting [on] Thursday," the newly appointed director expressed his appreciation to Barnett the day after the meeting.[105] A few days later, DeCell wrote to Johnston to buck him up: "I regret that our decision was not unanimous but hope that we can now close ranks and give you full support in carrying out the responsibilities of the Commission." DeCell, whom Johnston would soon grow to respect and later depend upon to keep the state agency intact, was the only Commission member who dared to congratulate the new director on his appointment in writing.[106] On April 1, Johnston, who had been serving the Commission as its part-time public relations director with a compensation of $4,800 a year, began to assume the duties of both director and public relations director of the state agency at a salary of $9,500 a year.[107]

The following month, after spending seven months in preparation, the Mississippi State General Legislative Investigating Committee released its thirty-six-page report on the Meredith crisis, charging that the "political ambitions of the Kennedys" were to be blamed for the Ole Miss riots.[108] When the report came out, Mississippi's two senators in Washington— Eastland and Stennis—commended the committee for its efforts to present the "splendid factual" report that "reveals a heretofore untold chapter in the tragic events" at the University of Mississippi. The United States Justice Department conversely branded the report as being "untruthful, distorted, [and] shocking."[109] At Barnett's behest, in May the Sovereignty Commission approved an expenditure of $2,000 for the purpose of printing copies of the committee's report on the "occupation of Ole Miss." By the summer of the year, the Commission had the Hederman brothers print a total of twenty thousand copies of the state's "official" report; more than eight thousand copies of these were mailed to the legislators of every state in the nation.[110]

At the May meeting the Commission also agreed to purchase three prints of the 16-mm film entitled *Oxford, U.S.A.*, produced by Patrick M. Sims of Sims Associates in Dallas, Texas, for the purpose of "point[ing] out and accentuat[ing] Mississippi's point of views, moral code and political standing in connection with" the Ole Miss desegregation crisis and further propagating "the true facts in answer to erroneous charges and misconceptions heretofore conveyed to the public."[111] Replete with the newscast films depicting "the night of terror" and "comments about the various sections of the United States Constitution which were violated by the federal government" during the "forced integration," the forty-three-minute documentary included interviews with Governor Barnett, Lieutenant Governor Johnson, and other state officials and legislators.[112] The total cost of the three prints of *Oxford, U.S.A.*, which was enthusiastically endorsed by both Barnett and Alabama Governor

George C. Wallace, was $6,943. To order these rather expensive prints, the
Commission adjusted its contingent expenditure by reducing the budget allocated to the agency's moribund speakers bureau program. Due largely to
the purchase of the films, the original speakers bureau budget for the 1962
fiscal year ending on June 30, 1963, fell $4,315.88 into the red.[113] In the
middle of July the Commission received two "firm bookings" for the documentary to be shown in Iowa and Illinois, and by the end of August in the
following year it had been viewed by a number of civic groups in such northern and western states as Massachusetts, New Hampshire, New York, California, Ohio, Indiana, and Montana.[114]

For the 1963 fiscal year beginning on July 1, the Sovereignty Commission
allocated a nominal budget of $2,500 to its obsolete speakers bureau pro-
gram, $6,500 less than the previous year's $9,000 appropriation. By the end
of November, the agency had expended only $163.15, mostly for mailing
the newly acquired films on the Ole Miss riots to the North and the West.[115]
The general reduction of the Commission's budget for its public relations
activities in the middle of 1963 was also a consequence of the agency's
involvement in a nationwide campaign to defeat the proposed civil rights bill
in Washington.

On June 19, Medgar Evers, field secretary of the Mississippi NAACP who
had been gunned down in Jackson eight days earlier by Byron De La Beckwith, was buried in the Arlington National Cemetery, while the crowd of
more than two thousand sang "We Shall Overcome." President Kennedy
sent a package of civil rights legislation to Congress on the very same day
that included "a provision to guarantee all citizens equal access to the services
and facilities of hotels, restaurants, places of amusement, and retail establishments." By then, the civil rights movement had become the most pressing
domestic issue for the Kennedy administration, particularly after the extensive media coverage of the violence-stricken civil rights demonstrations in
Birmingham, Alabama, brought the southern black struggle for equality and
justice into each American home. The president could no longer escape from
the imperative issue. In concluding his message on the civil rights legislation
sent to Congress, Kennedy had special words for the lawmakers from the
South. "I . . . ask every member of Congress to set aside sectional and
political ties, and to look at this issue from the viewpoint of the nation," the
president made a plea, "[and] I ask you to look into your hearts—not in

search of charity, for the Negro neither wants nor needs condescension—but for the one plain, proud, and priceless quality that unites us all as Americans: a sense of justice."[116]

Despite the president's appeal, southern politicians were far from ready to "set aside" their "sectional ties" and to abandon their cherished "southern way of life." Mississippi, too, was eager to wage another battle against the Kennedy brothers. In late June 1963 Johnston, along with attorney John C. Satterfield of Yazoo City, attended a series of conferences in Washington "to lay plans for an organized effort to defeat the new Kennedy civil rights program." "It was apparent from these meetings," Johnston later reported to Governor Barnett and the other Commission members, "that we in the South now have new and important allies, who never before seemed seriously concerned with states['] rights or the federal government's determination to take over private enterprise."[117] Notwithstanding the Commission director's slightly exaggerated reportage, the attendees at these conferences, who "suddenly had become concerned about the vicious federal powers embodied" in the Kennedy civil rights program, were in fact impressive.[118] For instance, at one unpublicized conference arranged by Satterfield, those who attended included: William B. Barton, general counsel, Chamber of Commerce of the United States; Harvey M. Crow, associate general counsel, National Association of Manufacturers; Harding D. Williams, assistant director, Department of Governmental Relations, National Association of Real Estate Boards; Henry M. Shine Jr., legislative director, National Association of Home Builders; and Page L. Ingraham, director of research, Council of State Government. Johnston and Satterfield also met with Senator Eastland and Hugh White Jr. of Richmond, Virginia, who was former executive director of the Virginia Commission on Constitutional Government. As a result of these meetings and conferences held in Washington, one of the suggestions made for the Mississippi agency was that it would "trace back" its contacts with the people outside the South who had arranged the Commission's speaking engagements during the previous three years and "get from them a list of the conservative leaders in their own states." "It was a thrill for me," Johnston concluded the report on his Washington trip submitted to the Sovereignty Commission, "to see how the gentlemen at these meetings looked to Mississippi for leadership and expressed such confidence in Mr. Satterfield."[119]

The root of Satterfield's idea to launch an organized nationwide campaign to defend the South from the NAACP's "vicious and false propaganda" and to defeat the Civil Rights Bill of 1963 in Congress goes back to 1955 when the Supreme Court issued the implementation decree of its 1954 *Brown* decision. In November 1955 Satterfield, who was then the president of the Mississippi State Bar Association, declared before the audience of the Jackson Exchange Club: "We are upholding the Supreme Court in the opinion [the 1896 *Plessy v. Ferguson* ruling] which it held for more than 70 years, and respectfully disagree with that court in a recent unsound opinion [of *Brown II*]." With this premise, the president of the state bar went on to reveal his grand idea to form "a national organization" to fight "judicial tyranny." "The ultimate decision depends not on what a single court may do," he further elaborated, "but on whether the people of the South will rally to jointly act in forming a national organization with sufficient money and sufficient personnel to get the truth to the people of the United States."[120] Elected president of the American Bar Association in August 1961, during the 1962 Meredith crisis Satterfield became one of Governor Barnett's legal advisers and later served as attorney for the General Legislative Investigating Committee when it prepared the state's "official" report on the Ole Miss riots.[121] For Satterfield, the Kennedy-proposed civil rights program was nothing but "an extension of Federal control . . . over individuals, business[es] and the States." "What purports to be an act to 'equalize' civil rights," the Yazoo City attorney contended, "is in fact, but 10 per cent civil rights; *the rest is a grasp for Federal executive power*." Arguing that the Kennedy-sponsored bill, if enacted, would create unavoidable conflict with property rights and proclaiming that the bill's passage would presage "dictatorial control" over ordinary citizens, business establishments, and states' rights by the federal government, Satterfield centered his opposition on the bill's public accommodation provisions.[122]

In July 1963 Satterfield set out to organize a group in Washington, which would soon become known as the Coordinating Committee for Fundamental American Freedoms. As an educational and lobbying organization, the Coordinating Committee's sole purpose was to prevent the passage of "the Kennedy bill" in Congress. William Loeb, conservative publisher of the *Union Leader* in Manchester, New Hampshire, was elected chair of the committee, and James J. Kilpatrick, editor of the *Richmond News-Leader* in Virginia and author of *The Sovereign States: Notes of a Citizen of Virginia*, was chosen as its vice chair. John J. Synon, founder of a Richmond-based conservative organization called the Patrick Henry Club, was elected full-time director, and Satterfield himself became secretary-treasurer. The committee soon set up its headquarters in a luxurious $637-a-month suite at the Carroll Arms Hotel, located only a block away from the Capitol.[123]

From its inception, Satterfield and other officials of the Coordinating Committee hoped that their organization would help create a genuine nationwide movement to oppose the civil rights bill. But in reality, as in the case of the Citizens' Councils of America, Satterfield's committee derived most of its personnel and financial resources from southern states, and Mississippi became the most vigorous supporter of the movement. At the Sovereignty Commission's July 18 meeting, the civil rights bill inevitably became the main topic. With Governor Barnett presiding, the commissioners received Satterfield, who gave a detailed report on his plans for the nationwide campaign to defeat the bill. At the conclusion of the meeting, with Barnett's enthusiastic endorsement, the members "approved earmarking $10,000" for Satterfield's program, "with $5,000 to be paid immediately and another $5,000 later." To compensate Satterfield for his work as coordinator of the newly organized group, the agency agreed to pay him up to $2,000 per month for the upcoming four-month period.[124] Thus, as Wilson Minor, a political reporter of the *New Orleans Times-Picayune*, observed, the Sovereignty Commission committed itself to take part in "one of the highest priced and shortest lived Washington lobbies ever to arise on the Potomac," representing the South's "last-ditch efforts to block the federal civil rights bill."[125]

Immediately after the July meeting, Johnston issued a press release on the Sovereignty Commission's financial involvement in the Coordinating Committee's efforts against the civil rights bill. The release was prepared by the director and was approved by Governor Barnett, the other members of the Commission, and Satterfield. But in Washington, it infuriated Senator Eastland, who thought that the Commission's involvement in the new project should be "off-the-record" and "handled without publicity." Thereafter, the Commission refrained from making any public statements concerning the Satterfield program unless they were "cleared" by the Mississippi senator in advance.[126] In the following month the agency voted to spend $500 to disseminate ten thousand copies of a pamphlet authored by Satterfield.[127] Johnston later reported to the Commission members that the Satterfield pamphlet, *Due Process of Law or Government by Intimidation?*, was "one of our best mailing pieces as far as interest is concerned."[128] Two months later, on October 17, the Sovereignty Commission members received a personal report from Synon on the Coordinating Committee's activities to persuade senators and representatives in Congress into realizing that "the so-called Civil Rights Bill was a Civil Wrongs Bill." At Senator Eastland's request, the Commission also authorized the extension of its contract with Satterfield as coordinator of the Washington group, whereby Satterfield was again retained by the Mississippi agency at the same salary of $2,000 a month.[129] For the five-month period from July to the end of November 1963, the Sovereignty Commission had allocated a total of $24,888.03 to the Satterfield committee.[130]

As well as pledging to take vengeance upon the Kennedys in Washington, as the commencement ceremony at Ole Miss neared in the early summer of 1963, Governor Barnett concocted a scheme to settle an old score with Meredith by prodding the Sovereignty Commission and the Board of Trustees of State Institutions of Higher Learning into attempting to expel Meredith from the University of Mississippi. The governor's opportunity to carry out his scheme arrived when Meredith issued a public statement on June 12 concerning the assassination of Evers, where he charged that "Governors Barnett of Mississippi and Wallace of Alabama have proven without a doubt that a white man can do anything he wishes to a Negro and go unhampered."[131] Earlier, on January 31, Chancellor John D. Williams of the University of Mississippi issued a directive prohibiting any issuance of statements by both university personnel and students that were "likely to create disorder or impair the effectiveness of the educational programs of the university." In the eyes of Barnett, Meredith's statement was an apparent violation of the chancellor's order.[132] During the Sovereignty Commission's June meeting, "[c]onsiderable discussion was devoted to procedures for recommending punitive action" against Meredith. The Commission then adopted a resolution recommending that the Board of Trustees investigate Meredith's remarks. While both Attorney General Patterson and House Speaker Sillers warned that adopting and preparing the resolution "might give 'our enemies' in Washington 'more ammunition' for passing civil rights bills" and "would require careful wording," Governor Barnett dictated the resolution himself, paying little regard to what Patterson and Sillers had to say. In asking for the investigation, the Commission made it clear that once the chancellor and the Board of Trustees determined that Meredith's statements violated Williams's directive and were "harmful" to the university, the Commission would strongly suggest that "punitive action be taken immediately."[133] The next day, at the governor's urging, Johnston transmitted the resolution by hand to the board members, who were then meeting at the Woolfolk State Office Building.[134] Waging his last-ditch attempt to block Meredith's graduation, Barnett hoped to gain his revenge before his term as the state's chief executive expired.

In responding to the Sovereignty Commission's request, the chair of the Board of Trustees, Thomas J. Tubb, promised Governor Barnett on July 9 that a special four-person subcommittee would investigate Meredith's statement. The special subcommittee was composed of Tally D. Riddell, Malcomb Metts "M. M." Roberts, Charles Fair, and Tubb himself. Among the entire board members during the 1960s, Roberts, a Hattiesburg attorney and one of Governor Barnett's appointees on the board, was the most intransigent member, steadfastly refusing "to give up the defense of white supremacy and racial segregation."[135] On July 18, the subcommittee met in Biloxi to make an inquiry into Meredith's conduct. At Barnett's request, Charles Clark, a special counsel to Attorney General Patterson, appeared before the subcommittee to "advise with them as to the steps which may be taken legally to comply with the Sovereignty Commission's resolution." After "an extended session," the subcommittee could not reach a conclusion and voted to continue its inquiry at a later date.[136] However, to the governor's great disappointment, the subcommittee, meeting in Oxford, eventually voted three to one not to take any further action, with Roberts dissenting.[137] Then, Barnett suffered another blow on August 14 when the Ole Miss administration, siding with three of the subcommittee members, concluded that Meredith's statement could not justify his expulsion from the university. Finding that "there is no basis for properly and legally denying him . . . a diploma," the university administration hoped that "this vexatious problem can be met in a quiet and dignified manner."[138] On the following day, just three days before Meredith's planned graduation, the eleven-member full board voted six to five affirming that there existed no basis for expelling Meredith from the university. All five members appointed by Barnett voted in favor of expelling Meredith; the other six members, who were the appointees of former Governor Coleman, cast their votes in favor of conferring a diploma on Meredith. Defeated, the Sovereignty Commission dropped its charge against Meredith, and Governor Barnett lost another battle.[139]

On the last day of final examinations at the University of Mississippi, Meredith wore the same clothes—dark suit, white shirt, red necktie, and black shoes—that he wore on October 1, 1962, the day he became the first black student at the educational institution. However, there was one notable difference in his appearance. Meredith wore a button on his lapel that had become popular among some white Mississippians as well as Ole Miss students during the few weeks prior to his admission to the university. On the button, there was one word printed in white against a black background: "NEVER." It was a symbol of Mississippi's defiance in the fall of 1962; nine months later the graduating student put the button on upside down on purpose.[140] "I was making sure they [white Mississippians who fought against my admission to Ole Miss] knew who was the victor," Meredith recollected years later, "[and] [i]f you make that plain enough, you don't have to worry about another fight." "It was a symbol of defeat [for my enemy]," the air force veteran added, "[so] I wore it with total deliberation, [and] I planned it [wearing the button upside down] for nine months."[141]

While the Mississippi governor was busy waging his last-ditch attempt to retrieve his honor by trying to block Meredith's graduation, Clyde Kennard, who had unsuccessfully attempted to enter Mississippi Southern College in Hattiesburg under the Coleman administration, was lying on his deathbed at a Chicago hospital. After he was sentenced to seven years in prison at the state penitentiary in November 1960 for accessory to burglary, where five bags of chicken feed worth $25 were stolen from the Forrest County Cooperative, Kennard did not give up his fight and continued to seek admission to the university. Though he initially refused any legal assistance offered by the NAACP, the civil rights organization eventually began fighting to obtain a reversal of his conviction. In early 1962 Kennard was taken to the University of Mississippi Hospital in Jackson, where doctors found that he had intestinal cancer and suggested that he be released on parole. Governor Barnett, however, ignored the recommendation, and Kennard was soon put back in the penitentiary. While his health was further deteriorating, the NAACP kept up its pressure on Mississippi.[142] In addition to the NAACP, Martin Luther King Jr.; Dick Gregory, a nationally renowned black comedian and activist; and John Howard Griffin, a white native Texan who had journeyed through the South in the late 1950s disguised as a black man and who had written of his experiences in a book entitled *Black Like Me*, began to accuse Mississippi of denying Kennard proper medical care and to put pressure upon Governor Barnett to release him immediately. Finally, in the spring of 1963, having realized that some unfavorable publicity would ensue if Kennard died in the state institution, Governor Barnett ordered his release. Kennard soon left the state for Chicago and was hospitalized there.[143] When Griffin visited Kennard at the Chicago hospital just a few weeks before his death, the unsung civil rights hero was, in Griffin's words, "a tiny little dwarf." Griffin recollected later: "He lay with a sheet pulled on up over his face so no one could see the grimace of pain on that face. . . . He said, 'Mr. Griffin, I'd be glad it happened if only it would show this country where racism finally leads. But the people aren't going to know it, are they?' "[144] On the day the entire nation was celebrating the 187th anniversary of the official adoption of the Declaration of Independence, where the founders had penned the noble principle that "all men are created equal," Kennard's short life ended, leaving the mournful question behind him: "But the people aren't going to know it, are they?" It was the Fourth of July, 1963, and he was only thirty-six years old.

By the time Meredith left Ole Miss in August 1963, at least thirty-seven professors, including most of those who belonged to the chemistry department and the entire faculty of the philosophy department, had resigned from the institution in protest against both the state's and the university's handling of the desegregation crisis.[145] When forty-seven faculty members offered a resolution condemning the state for its attempts "to blame U.S. Marshals" for the school riots, the Sovereignty Commission compiled a list of these Ole Miss dissenters and the departments to which they belonged.[146]

Among those who remained at the university, the most vocal critic of the Barnett administration's defiant posture was James Silver of the history department, who would soon author a best-selling book entitled *Mississippi: The Closed Society*, where he relentlessly criticized the cultural, mental, and intellectual restrictiveness of Mississippi society and described how the state's reckless commitment to the doctrine of white supremacy had inevitably led to the Ole Miss riots. On November 7, 1963, Silver delivered his presidential address entitled "Mississippi: The Closed Society" at the annual meeting of the Southern Historical Association in Asheville, North Carolina.[147] Asked for his comments on the Ole Miss professor's speech, Governor Barnett castigated Silver: "[O]ld Silver's liable to say anything. I wouldn't waste words on that man."[148] While the governor did not waste his words on him, both the Barnett-chaired Sovereignty Commission and the Board of Trustees of State Institutions of Higher Learning invested ample time and energy on Silver in the hope of getting rid of him from the state. Less than a month after Silver's presidential address infuriated many white Mississippians, Johnston wrote a letter to Tubb of the Board of Trustees, questioning "the propriety or wisdom of retaining" the history professor on the state's payrolls, "who so flagrantly demonstrates disloyalty" to both the University of Mississippi and the state of Mississippi. Expressing his indignation that Silver's recent remarks and behavior were "not in accord with one of the programs of the Sovereignty Commission," which "points to the progress made by both races in our system of racial separation," Johnston asked the board's chair to find a way to "relieve" Silver of his duties at Ole Miss.[149]

"Nothing would please me better than to fire Dr. Silver," Tubb wrote back four days later, "but on the other hand, I will not do anything that will cause any of the institutions under the jurisdiction of the Board to lose accreditation. . . . You can rest assured that the Board of Trustees will do the best it can without jeopardizing the accreditation." Tubb closed his letter by thanking Johnston for his "continued co-operation" with the Board of Trustees in handling its "many headaches and problems."[150] Shortly afterward, Tubb reported to the Sovereignty Commission that his board had been "alert to Dr. Silver's activities" and expressed his "personal feeling" to Johnston that the Ole Miss professor "should be fired." By then, Tubb had appointed a special three-person committee within the board to "assemble information of Dr. Silver's attitude and recommend a decision to the full board."[151] The committee was composed of Roberts as its chair, Riddell, and Harry G. Carpenter. Both Roberts and Riddell had served on the board's special committee to investigate Meredith's remarks just five months earlier. "We all want to do the right thing," Roberts assured Johnston, "and I am sure that every Mississippian would be greatly relieved if Dr. Silver would cease 'biting the hand that feeds him.' "[152] In order to "do the right thing," the board subsequently hired some private detectives to follow Silver to his speaking engagements throughout the nation.[153] In the meantime, when the 1964 state legislature convened on January 7, Silver, as anticipated, became the prey of some disgruntled lawmakers. In the Senate, Corbet L. Patridge of Schlater, Leflore County, sounded the charge. Lambasting the history professor who "is opposed to everything we stand for in this state," Senator Patridge took the Senate floor in March 1964. "I am outraged that the taxpayers have to pay the salary of a man like this," the senator vented his anger, "[and] I am outraged that the legislature allows an idiot like Dr. Silver to teach at our university." "I think something should be done immediately to get rid of him," Patridge rallied his supporters, "and that responsibility lies on our shoulders."[154]

Three months later, Silver's book, based on an expanded version of the address that he delivered the previous winter, was published. The publication date of *Mississippi: The Closed Society* happened to coincide with the nationally publicized disappearance of three civil rights workers in Philadelphia, Neshoba County, and the book quickly became a bestseller.[155] Silver then requested and was granted a leave of absence from the university to accept a visiting professorship at the University of Notre Dame before the Board of Trustees made any final resolution against him.[156] In the late summer of 1964 Silver left Ole Miss, where he had taught for the previous twenty-eight years, and he never returned to the institution.[157] Even with the history professor self-exiled from Mississippi, the Sovereignty Commission kept its interest in him. In early 1965, for example, when Silver appeared on a two-hour radio program at WBBM, a CBS-affiliated station in Chicago, discussing his experiences in Mississippi, the Commission requested a tape of the program from the director of public affairs at the station.[158]

In addition to Silver, political science professor Russell H. Barrett at Ole Miss also became a target of the state agency's investigative department, even before the 1965 publication of his book entitled *Integration at Ole Miss*, where the professor condemned Mississippi's white leadership for having created a calamity on the Ole Miss campus over the Meredith affair. In early 1964, at Representative Hooker's request, the Commission became involved in "check[ing] some information" on Barrett, who was suspected of having published articles in a publication issued by "a communist-front organization."[159] When *Integration at Ole Miss* was published, the state agency purchased the book in order to inspect it.[160]

Apart from its fanatical preoccupation with defending "Mississippi's way of life" in the immediate post-Meredith crisis year of 1963, the Sovereignty Commission was involved in a number of bizarre incidents during the final two years of Governor Barnett's administration, manifesting both the state agency's heyday and its hypersensitivity to the Barnett-prescribed rigid racial norms. As an illustration, for the Mississippi "segregation watchdog agency," keeping outdoor toilets segregated at a construction site was as vital as dealing with the constitutional crisis embodied in integrating Ole Miss. Characterizing the agency's hysterical state of mind, Hopkins spent more than two weeks investigating the "alleged integration of outdoor toilet facilities" at the Standard Oil Company construction site located in Pascagoula. Earlier, Clarence McGowen, president of the Jackson County Citizens' Council, had asked Jones to look over this "delicate situation." Hopkins drove to Pascagoula in March 1962 to confer with the local Council leaders. After receiving some background information from them at the city's courthouse, the Commission investigator proceeded to the construction site, accompanied by two Citizens' Council stalwarts. When the outdoor toilets were first brought into the site, they initially bore "white" and "colored" signs on them. However, the project manager for the oil company ordered his subordinates to either "remove" or "tape over" those signs, asserting that "the Standard Oil Corporation adopted no attitudes . . . on racial matters" in Mississippi. As a result of their "toilet inspection tour," which covered the sixteen hundred–acre site "thoroughly by travelling . . . all of the roads," Hopkins and his companions spotted five outdoor toilets, and one of them had a "white" sign pasted on the door. "The wind or rain had almost blown this sign off . . . and only about half of it was hanging on the door while the remainder was hanging loose," the investigator gave a bizarrely detailed description. "After spending quite some time observing the activities at the construction site and the 'white' sign on at least one of the toilets," Hopkins concluded, "[the two Council members] appeared to be satisfied with the existing conditions."[161] Thus, the Citizens' Council leaders in Pascagoula, who had raised a stink about the "integrated" toilet facilities, were content. While in retrospect the incident might seem almost laughable, for both the Citizens' Council and the Sovereignty Commission, it was a serious business.

As the vanguard of the state's "closed society," the Sovereignty Commission naturally functioned as the state's "thought-control watchdog" as well. The Commission's surveillance extended not only to the state's noted civil rights activists and some moderate university professors but also to the general citizenry. Ordinary Mississippians, both black and white, who dared to write a few lines to the state's white leadership to express their thoughts on race relations could easily offend these leaders. Simple expression of thoughts as well as deeds, which was contrary to the state's "sovereign and segregated" policies, would not go unsuspected by the state agency. In May 1962 Jones instructed Downing to make "a complete run-down" on Billy Engram, a twenty-three-year-old black resident of Bay Springs, Jasper County. In late February Engram wrote a letter to Governor Barnett to complain of his plight because he was "a Negro" and was "not free" in his "own home state." Reminding Barnett that black Mississippians did not "have a state governor" and that God was "so displeased at the way we are living here in Mississippi," the young black wished that God would someday "send a good[-]hearted leader" to his native state "just as he sent Moses to lead his people out from the land of Egypt." "I wonder," Engram asked the governor, "have you ever thought about [how] God has bless[ed] you to still be living, or do you believe there is [a] God?" Expressing his belief that "most of the white people of Mississippi is [*sic*] afraid to face up the true word of God," the black youth concluded his letter: "Are you afraid?"[162] Engram's letter was eventually forwarded to the Sovereignty Commission by the governor's office. Having determined that the letter "showed contempts [*sic*] and insults to the honor and dignity" of "the Governor of the State of Mississippi," the Commission dispatched Downing to Bay Springs. There, accompanied by Deputy Sheriff Waites McNeill, the investigator visited Engram's foster father and then Engram himself. After talking with the author of the letter for a little while, whom Downing described as being "about one-half white," the Commission investigator concluded that Engram was simply "a smart aleck" and that the state agency should not meddle with him any further.[163]

In the meantime, Senator Eastland in Washington also bore a part in the Commission's "thought control" probing. In the early summer of 1963, when southern lawmakers in the nation's capital were uneasy at the prospect of the Kennedy administration's proposed civil rights legislation, a letter addressed from a white Mississippian attracted the senator's attention. The writer of the letter was Dennis Hale, the young pastor of the Harmony Baptist Church in Hancock County. Hale, who had always believed that it was "his duty as a citizen to write his senators and congressmen expressing his favor or disfavor of the passage of any legislation that might affect the future," addressed his letters to both senators from Mississippi, letting them know that he was "in favor of the passage of the civil rights legislation."[164] The senator's office immediately communicated Eastland's concern to the Sovereignty Commission, suggesting that the state agency launch a probe to ascertain if Hale was "white or colored" and why he wrote the letters "in favor of civil rights bills." Hopkins, who was chosen for the task, drove to Picayune, Pearl River County, on July 8. Assisted by a member of the Sovereignty Commission, Stockstill, who resided in Picayune, Hopkins managed to locate Hale's residence and his church in neighboring Hancock County in a rainstorm.[165] About a week later, with Stockstill's consent, Hopkins, this time accompanied by Scarbrough, showed up at the pastor's house, where Hale acknowledged without any hesitation that he and his wife had written the letters. Agape with the pastor's forthrightness, the two Commission investigators asked Hale some questions on his personal views regarding integration of churches and public schools. After the interview with Hale, Hopkins and Scarbrough went back to Stockstill in Picayune. Having heard their report, Stockstill recommended that the Commission "let the matter drop" until it obtained a copy of Hale's letter from Senator Eastland. Meanwhile, the Commission member promised that he would try to "ascertain the names of some of the deacons" of the Harmony Baptist Church, indicating that when the letter became available, it "could be shown to the deacons and members of the congregation."[166] In the end, notwithstanding its director's request, the Sovereignty Commission never received the copy from Washington. As the saying goes, fortune favored the brave this time.[167]

Aside from busying itself in keeping Mississippi "sovereign and segregated," the Sovereignty Commission undertook the responsibility for being the state's "moral watchdog" agency. Any hearsay that suggested moral lapses did not go unnoticed by the state agency. Among these indiscretions, racial miscegenation was the most abominable offense, as the *Jackson Daily News* editorialized the day after the *Brown* decision: "White and Negro children in the same schools will lead to miscegenation. Miscegenation leads to mixed marriages and mixed marriages lead to mongrelization of the human race."[168] Just a few months before Mississippi became deeply involved in the crisis over Meredith's attempt to be enrolled at Ole Miss, a Yalobusha County woman wrote to the governor's office expressing her profound dismay and embarrassment that her sister-in-law was a "mother of a child by a Negro man" and was "still consorting with another Negro man." A week later the governor's office referred her letter to the Sovereignty Commission, and Scarbrough was subsequently assigned to conduct a probe into this "disgraceful situation." On June 21, Scarbrough drove to Tallahatchie County to visit the woman in question, who lived with her father "in a dilapidated house." "My observation of the home in which they lived was that it was more filthy than the average Negro home," the Commission investigator reported, "[and they] are what most people would classify as being poor white trash." "Poverty and filth, as well as ignorance, can be observed at a glance, . . . however," Scarbrough added, "[they] are not feeble[-]minded people in my thinking." Upon his arrival at their house, he also observed a little girl on the front porch whose skin was a dark brown and hair was "kinky." To his mind, there was no doubt that the girl had "all of the characteristics of any half breed Negro." Scarbrough proceeded to talk with the child's mother. When he told her what his "business" was, the woman, whom the investigator described as "a very fat unattractive person" and who "appeared to be shook up by a state investigator talking with her concerning her activities," denied that her child was "half Negro" and that she had "gone with a Negro." Despite her statement, the unconvinced investigator concluded in his report that the father of the "kinky"-haired child was "a Negro." "I do not know if my investigation of [the white woman] and [her] family . . . will change their way of living," Scarbrough noted, "but I do believe she will discontinue going with Negro men as she appeared to be rather scared about her conduct being well known." "[H]owever from her appearance and the impression I got of her," the officious investigator interjected, "I do not believe that any self[-]respecting Negro would likely go with her anyway." Before preparing his final report on the incident, Scarbrough visited the original complainant in Yalobusha County and advised her that if he were her and her husband, he would move his family "along way away from the family environment under which they now are living."[169]

Though it concerned racial miscegenation as well, the case of the Knight family of Jasper County was much more complicated, and it eventually turned out that the Sovereignty Commission's involvement in the incident had extended over five years. The case originated in August 1960 when the Jasper County Board of Education requested the Commission to investigate Louvenia Knight "as to her status of race and that of her children."[170] Louvenia, whose birth certificate showed that she was "colored," had two illegitimate sons, and these children's birth certificates identified them as "white." In the early summer she submitted an application to the West Jasper County School Board to enter her older child into the all-white Stringer School. Having obtained "photostatic copies of the birth certificates" of Louvenia and her children from the State Board of Health, Scarbrough and Hopkins drove to Bay Springs on August 18 to hold a meeting with the members of the school board and several concerned Jasper County citizens. After being briefed on the controversy and informed by the board members that Louvenia's parents—Otho and Addie Knight—"had always been considered members of the Negro race by the people in Jasper County," the investigators returned to Jackson to confer with Director Jones and Attorney General Patterson on how to deal with the matter. Four days later, accompanied by the Jasper County chief deputy sheriff, Scarbrough and Hopkins visited Louvenia and her parents, where all of the Knight family stated that "they definitely would not send" the boy to a black school and that "they had done their duty" as white citizens "in making application" to the all-white school. However, confronted by the investigators, who presented them with Louvenia's birth certificate identifying her as "colored," and fearful of the repercussions of the investigation they were now under, the Knights conceded that "they would make no further attempt" to register the child at the white school. Some school board members were skeptical of the Knights' decision and conveyed their concern to the Commission investigators that there was "a good possibility" that the family would make another attempt. "Of course, there is a possibility," Hopkins interjected his feelings in preparing a report on the matter, "but it is the honest opinion of the writer that they were sincere."[171]

If Hopkins's observation had proven right, the whole controversy would have ended. But unknown to the investigator as well as to the Sovereignty Commission director, the agony that the Knight family had endured had a long history. Louvenia's white great-grandfather, Newton Knight, was a legendary Jasper County farmer and shoemaker. During the Civil War, Newton, then a resident of Jones County who saw the war as "a rich man's [slaveholders'] war and a poor man's fight," refused to join the Confederate army until he was conscripted and served as a hospital orderly. However, after witnessing a number of depredations committed by the Confederate cavalry, Newton deserted from the army. In October 1863 he then organized a militia with six "officers" and seventy-three "privates" to "fight for our rights . . . and protect our families and . . . property" in Jones County from the atrocities committed by both the Union and Confederate armies. Newton and his followers declared that Jones County to be "The Free State of Jones."[172]

Superficially, the Newton Knight story sounds like a legendary Civil War folktale in Mississippi. But Newton, a married man, had an extramarital affair with a young slave woman named Rachel. Newton and his wife had a daughter named Molly, who eventually married Rachel's son, Jeff, whose father was white (the father was not Newton Knight). Molly and Jeff had a son, Otho, who was Louvenia's father.[173]

In April 1946 a major crisis struck the Knight family when Louvenia's brother, Davis, married a white woman. After learning of her husband's family background, she filed for a divorce, asserting that Davis "was actually a Negro." This consequently led to Davis's arrest as an alleged violator of the Mississippi statute that prohibited "the marriage of a white person with a Negro Mulatto, or person who shall have 1/8 or more of Negro blood." On the assumption that Newton's mistress, Rachel, was a "full-blooded Negro," the prosecution contended that Davis, who possessed more than one-eighth of "black blood," was in violation of the state's antimiscegenation law. Davis was convicted and sentenced to five years in prison. But the case was appealed to the Mississippi State Supreme Court, which held that there was not sufficient evidence to sustain the state's assertion that Rachel was in fact a "full-blooded Negro." After the lower court's verdict was thus reversed and remanded, the case against Davis was nol-prossed.[174] Though Davis was set free, his case clearly manifested the rigidity of the state's "operating definition" of black. Meanwhile, the "social definition" of black, which was often referred to as "the one-drop rule," had prevailed in Mississippi "in case of doubt."[175]

In the late fall of 1963 the school board members' concern, which was

raised three years earlier, materialized when Louvenia decided to make another attempt to enroll her sons, who were then nine and eight years old,
into the Stringer School.[176] Having inherited the case from his predecessor,
Commission Director Johnston reported to the members at the state agency's
November 21 meeting that the Sovereignty Commission was "again [being]
involved in an investigation into a situation in Jasper County."[177] At this
time, State Superintendent of Public Education Jack Tubb was also drawn
into the case, when Louvenia and her sons visited Tubb to implore him for
his assistance in solving their problem.[178] In the meantime, Johnston, who
was not familiar with the Knight family controversy, set out to conduct
extensive research in order "to have a more complete picture of what the
actual blood lineage is on the Knights available." As a rare instance, all of
the three Commission investigators were assigned to the case to assist the
director.[179] After spending "considerable time studying" the Knight geneal-
ogy, Johnston reported that if "the slave girl Rachel" was "pure Negro,"
Louvenia's two sons should be "1/16 Negro," and that if Rachel was "a
Mulatto," the children should be "1/32 Negro." "In either case," Johnston
concluded, "under Mississippi law, they are white." The director's calculation
notwithstanding, "the one-drop rule" was in force in Jasper County, where
"deep resentment" existed "against any of the Knights going to school with
the white students."[180] While the members of the Jasper County School
Board also realized that "according to Mississippi law . . . the children in
question were, without a doubt, classed as white children," they asserted that
the boys were black "in the eyes of the people" of their locality.[181]

Having been caught in what Johnston himself termed the state's racial
"twilight zone," the Sovereignty Commission was on the horns of a dilemma.
If the Commission went along with Jasper County's demand and had the
children in question attend a black school, the state would have public school
desegregation, which the agency had been committed to prevent "at all
costs." "[I]f they [are] enrolled in a Negro school, because they are legally
white," the director pondered, "Jasper County would have an integrated
public school—the first integration of a public school in Mississippi history."
Louvenia's two sons, therefore, "cannot attend a Negro school without violating the state's segregation laws."[182] As a last resort, Johnston asked the
Jasper County School Board if it would be willing to "provide transportation
for Louvenia Knight's two boys to any other school beside[s] Stringer." As-

sured that it was, he then sought to get the two children into the Shady Grove School in Jones County, a neighboring country, which agreed to accept them. "As far as the Sovereignty Commission is concerned," Johnston wrote in his January 6, 1964, memorandum on his seemingly successful mission, "this case is closed."[183]

Within two weeks, however, his conclusion turned out to be premature, for the Jones County School Board, which had jurisdiction over the Shady Grove School, rejected the two boys' transfer. On January 23, just two days after Barnett left the governor's office, Johnston met with the Jones County School Board members in Laurel. While stressing that they had "no legal or moral obligation to accept" the transfer, Johnston asked the members to reconsider their previous decision, reminding them that "they were in a position to do a real service to the State of Mississippi." But the board members turned a cold shoulder to the Commission director, stating that they "were firm" in refusing to accept Louvenia's sons. "We still hope that something may be worked out whereby these boys may secure an education," the disheartened Commission director wrote in preparing a report to the concerned parties, showing his human side, which was rarely revealed in his official correspondence.[184] Responding to Johnston, Tubb concurred: "Those two boys are the people who are going to suffer if something is not done for them."[185] In early 1964, within a month after Barnett's successor took the governor's chair, Johnston sent a memorandum to both the governor's and lieutenant governor's offices to inform them that the Knight case had become deadlocked, appealing to them for help. "Unless the influence of the Governor's office and/or the Lieutenant Governor's office can be of some assistance in solving this problem," Johnston implored, "the Sovereignty Commission must close its files with the situation remaining status quo."[186] In the end, Johnston's appeal was of little avail, and both the Knight family and the Sovereignty Commission would have to wait one and a half more years before their problem was finally resolved.

On January 8, 1964, Governor Barnett delivered his farewell address to the joint assembly of the state legislature. No mention was made of the 1962 Ole Miss desegregation, but at the very end of his address, the outgoing governor dutifully cited "the so-called Civil Rights Legislation now before the Congress" that was "very vital to the people of Mississippi." "This vicious, un-American and completely un-Constitutional legislation," Barnett warned, "would rob you and other legislative bodies of those Constitutional powers heretofore exercised by sovereign states." Asking the state's citizens not to desist from having "confidence in our way of life," the unreconstructed governor declared that Mississippi was still "the greatest States' rights state in the American Union."[187] Eight days later, Barnett attended the last Sovereignty Commission meeting held under his administration. There, the members unanimously adopted a resolution to "express [the Commission's] highest commendation" to the governor, who had "furnished courageous leadership and guidance in fulfilling [the] mission" of the state agency. In response, while appreciating the members' "zeal and fidelity to duty," Barnett praised them for their "specific contribution toward perpetuation of local self-government, state[s'] rights, and racial segregation."[188] No one dared to talk about the dishonorable outcome of the Meredith crisis at this final meeting. Aside from the Ole Miss incident as a humiliating exception, racial segregation in Mississippi—the last citadel of racial injustice—remained intact. However, as Barnett rightly predicted in his farewell address, a series of storms on the civil rights front would soon bear down on Mississippi, forcing the state to realize belatedly that it could no longer shield its old way of life from the changing world. The lull before the storm was about to be over.

Chapter 5

FEELINGS RUN DEEP AND BLOOD RUNS HOT

Submerging the State Sovereignty Commission

During the summer of 1963, with the furor created by the Meredith crisis having not cooled down, Mississippi's gubernatorial election inevitably revolved around racial segregation as the most pressing issue. In the Democratic primary, there were three major candidates: Lieutenant Governor Paul Johnson; former Governor James Coleman, who had defeated Johnson in the 1955 gubernatorial election; and Charles Sullivan, a former state district attorney who ran third in the 1959 governor's race. The 1963 election also marked an important turning point in Mississippi politics because the state Republican Party, for the first time since the Reconstruction period, fielded a formidable candidate for the governorship. The Grand Old Party's choice was Rubel L. Phillips, a native of Kossuth in Alcorn County, who had chaired the State Public Service Commission. Asserting that the Ole Miss crisis clearly demonstrated the inadequacy of the one-party system for the preservation of the state's white supremacy, Phillips explained during his campaign that "the one-party system to which Mississippi has been shackled for these many years has failed miserably in preserving our customs and traditions and segregated way of life" and that the same political system to which the

Democrats "adhere [to] so strongly gave us John and Bobby Kennedy and the integration of our state university." "Mississippi, under a two-party system," the Republican contender reasoned, "would have a much better chance of maintaining segregation because each party would act as a watch dog over the other."[1]

From the gubernatorial race's earliest stages, Johnson was considered the strongest Democratic candidate. Having been painted in glowing colors by Governor Ross Barnett for "standing tall" against James Meredith and the Kennedy administration during the 1962 desegregation crisis, "Stand Tall with Paul" became the theme of the lieutenant governor's campaign.[2] Backed by this campaign theme, Johnson told the gathered Jackson Citizens' Council audience on May 17, 1963—the ninth anniversary of the Supreme Court's *Brown* decision—that he was "proud to have been part of the resistance" to Meredith's entrance to Ole Miss and that "Mississippi stirred the admiration of the world by her spirited stand against the Federal invaders." While stressing that his "prime objective during 1964 . . . will be to spearhead an all-out effort to secure cooperation from other state Governors and leaders to get the Kennedys out of the White House," the candidate promised, if elected as governor, that "the activities of the Sovereignty Commission" would "be expanded and enlarged," pledging himself to "offer suggestions for more effective programs [of the Commission] to the Legislature early in the 1964 session."[3] In the first Democratic primary held on August 6, Lieutenant Governor Johnson led the field, and three weeks later he won the second primary over Coleman by a margin of 261,493 to 194,958.[4] However, during the period between the second Democratic primary and the November general election, the validity of Johnson's campaign slogan was seriously damaged, for *Newsweek* magazine, in its October 14 issue, published a full-page article revealing the existence of the secret telephone conversations between the Kennedys, Barnett, and Johnson over desegregating Ole Miss.[5] Forced to divert the state voters' attention away from the Kennedy issues, the lieutenant governor began to arouse white Mississippians to a possible resurgence of vexing Republican rule:

> A scalawag of 1863 was a white Southerner who acted as a Republican during the Reconstruction period after the Civil War, when the South was an occup[i]ed territory, and federal bayonets forced the will of the minority on our people. A scalawag of 1963 is a white Southerner who acts as a Republican

in an attempt to divide our white conservatives, at a time when the South needs to stand united against its enemies. . . .[6]

As well as appealing to a longtime suspicion that had been historically harbored by white Mississippians about the Republican political advance in the state, Johnson reiterated his pledge to "expand and enlarge" the activities of the Sovereignty Commission to further protect his beloved state from the "Federal invaders." Just ten days before the general election, the Democratic nominee stood before the cheering audience of the Citizens' Councils of America Leadership Conference:

> As a member of the Mississippi State Sovereignty Commission during the past four years, I have been able to assist in furthering the very worthwhile program[s] carried on by this group. Much has been and is being accomplished to carry out our story throughout the Nation. But there is, of course, much still to be done before victory is won. . . . We must not wait to be invaded, but we must take positive counter-action in this all-out battle which others have launched to destroy our state and Nation.[7]

Despite the highly emotional and almost fatal controversy created by the *Newsweek* article, Johnson defeated Phillips in the November 5 general election by a vote of 225,456 to 138,515.[8] On January 21, 1964, Johnson stood on the state capitol's south steps to be sworn in as the fifty-fourth governor of Mississippi. Since he had been elected on a strong racist platform, many of the twenty-five hundred well-wishers gathered in front of the capitol on that inaugural day naturally anticipated that the new governor would continue his predecessor's hard-line approach toward the state's racial issues and the vexatious federal government. Appropriate for the occasion, the oath of office was administered by State Supreme Court Associate Justice Tom Brady, author of *Black Monday* and one of the chief philosophers of the Citizens' Council movement, who had previously been appointed to Mississippi's highest court by Governor Barnett. The stage was all set for another segregationist preachment.

But once Johnson began to deliver his inaugural address, he literally confounded the state's arch-segregationists because his speech not only was "devoid of both the white supremacist and Dixiecrat preachments heard frequently" during his campaign but also lacked Mississippi's hostile posture toward the national government.[9] Instead, pledging to strengthen the state's ties with the rest of the Union and to eradicate the "[h]ate, or prejudice or ignorance" prevalent in Mississippi, Johnson vowed: "I will say to you that you and I are part of this world, whether we like it or not. . . . Too, we are Americans as well as Mississippians." Projecting a stark contrast with the words uttered by Barnett in his farewell address just two weeks earlier, the new Mississippi governor went on:

> I want our people to know that Paul Johnson is fully aware of the forces, the conflicts that fashion our environment. Hate, or prejudice or ignorance will not lead Mississippi while I sit in the Governor's chair. I will oppose with every fiber of my being, and with every resource at my command, any man, any faction, any party, or any authority which I feel is morally wrong or constitutionally in error . . . but, if I must fight, it will not be a rear-guard defense of yesterday . . . [but] it will be an all[-]out assault for our share of tomorrow.[10]

Johnson's conciliatory posture, while bewildering the die-hard segregationists at home, drew national attention as well. The *New York Times* ran a front-page article on the Mississippi governor's inaugural address, and *Life* magazine, in an editorial entitled "Words Make News in Mississippi," even noted that Johnson's address had carried "[n]ot strong words, perhaps, but refreshing—possibly brave and important—ones."[11] To a great degree, Johnson's character was molded by his father, Paul B. Johnson Sr., who had started from a humble beginning on a small farm in Hillsboro, Scott County, in the 1880s. After unsuccessful runs for governor in 1931 and 1935, Johnson Sr. finally became the state's forty-sixth chief executive on January 16, 1940. His 1940–43 administration was characterized by its general progressivism and social welfare programs, which included increased welfare benefits for the elderly, better salaries for public school teachers, and eight-month school terms for children. One of his most important and controversial achievements was the enactment of a state statute providing free textbooks for every schoolchild in Mississippi. Opponents of this legislation bitterly accused him of socializing the state and undermining the free enterprise system. Nevertheless, he did not lose his concern for the common citizen, and he particularly held a deep feeling for those in the state who were underprivileged.[12]

Having been influenced by his father's political and social philosophy, as a young man Johnson held "an affectionate reverence" for Democratic President Franklin Roosevelt, and he later even supported President Harry Truman against the Dixiecrats in the 1948 presidential election. Though Johnson, to be sure, believed in and practiced racial segregation as his father had done, he was neither a rabid segregationist nor a racial demagogue. But over time, he had belatedly come to realize that as long as he held the political ambition to follow his father's footsteps and continued to cast his moderate posture on the state's racial matters, his political career in Mississippi was almost "hopeless." Thus, after unsuccessful attempts to win the governorship in 1947, 1951, and 1955, Johnson dared to campaign "on a platform of segregation and race hatred so inflexibly extreme as to satisfy the most violent white segregationists," exploiting his accidental role played in the Ole Miss desegregation ordeal.[13] Segregation issues became his political expediency.

After making a tacit declaration in his inaugural address that Mississippi could not forever stem the tide of the changing world, Johnson began to identify himself with a growing number of the state's business and civic leaders who "recoiled from violence and recognized the futility of bitter-end resistance" to the social and political advancement of black Mississippians.[14] The new governor's resolve for implementation of a strong "law and order" policy in the state was first reflected in his address delivered to a joint session of the legislature on March 3. Foreseeing a further increase of civil rights activities in Mississippi, Johnson told the lawmakers: "The situation we face is loaded with the most powerful emotions. Feelings run deep and blood runs hot. Thinking clearly is not easy amid the pressures which we all will have to endure in the months ahead." Having said that, the governor then plighted his troth that "law and order will be maintained within the State of Mississippi, at all times and under all circumstances" and that "no person, no organization, no group—whether from within Mississippi or from outside our borders—will be allowed to breach the peace, to incite strife, to commit violence." He further warned the legislators to keep their watchful eyes on the activities of the Ku Klux Klan–type "paramilitary or vigilante groups." "Conditions which spawn the night-riders and the hushed attack will exist," Johnson reminded the lawmakers, "only if we fail to act now [and] only if we fail to justify the confidence of the people in the adequacy of their duly-authorized law enforcement agencies."[15] True to his own vows made before the legislature, once he assumed the governor's office, Johnson also began to distance himself from the Citizens' Council, which had offered him the most important forums to satisfy Mississippi's segregationists during his gubernatorial campaign. Although he "did not openly break with the Council" and sent his administrative assistants to represent him at the organization's meeting from time to time, after December 1963 Johnson discontinued appearing before these gatherings.[16]

Markedly, in spite of his repeated preelection assurances, Governor Johnson did not fully activate the Sovereignty Commission and kept the state agency in rather low profile under his administration. The governor not only failed to "offer suggestions for more effective programs" of the Mississippi "watchdog" to the 1964 state legislature but also refused to make his appointments to the Commission until the spring of 1965, when two attorneys were belatedly added to the agency as its citizen members. More important, until the summer of 1966, Johnson had never called a meeting of the Sovereignty Commission during his first two and a half years in the governor's office.[17] These facts certainly did not mean that the governor abandoned or lost interest in the Sovereignty Commission, but since the official policy of his administration was that "Mississippi, even though reluctantly, is reconciled to obedience to law," Johnson did not want his position on this delicate matter to be jeopardized by defiant Commission members, who believed that the agency should play an active role in continuing a more vigorous fight for preserving the state's racial norms.[18]

Though it was submerged and kept out of the limelight without any regular meetings being held until August 1966, the Commission never became defunct during the first two years under the Johnson administration. More precisely, while preventing the Commission board from being fully constituted, the governor nevertheless kept the agency's staff both intact and active, with its day-to-day operations overseen by Director Erle Johnston. Governor Johnson received all of the Commission memoranda and reports prepared by Johnston either directly or through Herman C. Glazier Jr., who was the governor's top administrative assistant.[19] In early 1964, following the governor's suggestion, the Sovereignty Commission asked the House Appropriations Committee for its biennium budget of $500,000, which included $200,000 for general operation, $100,000 for "special projects," and $200,000 for "an emergency fund."[20] Subsequently, on June 11, the legislature agreed to set aside the handsome $500,000 appropriation for the state agency for the fiscal biennium beginning on July 1, 1964.[21] This was the largest sum that the Sovereignty Commission had ever received for a two-year period.

During the Johnson administration, the Sovereignty Commission underwent drastic changes in terms of its membership. Until the spring of 1965, the Commission consisted of only nine members and was without the three citizen members, who had to be appointed by the governor. The four ex officio members of the new Sovereignty Commission were the governor himself, who served as chair; Lieutenant Governor Carroll Gartin as its vice chair; House Speaker Walter Sillers; and Attorney General Joe Patterson. Gartin, as president of the Senate, reappointed Senator Herman DeCell and appointed Senator Bland Hayden Campbell of Jackson, one of the chief architects of the capital city's Citizens' Council movement, to the state agency. Sillers reappointed Representative Joseph Moss, and in addition to the Raymond lawmaker, the House Speaker chose Representatives Horace H. Harned Jr. of Starkville, Oktibbeha County, and Kenneth O. Williams of Clarksdale, Coahoma County, as the Commission's new members. Harned had been a very active supporter of the Council movement since its inception in 1954 and served on the organization's state executive committee, while Williams had been the president of the Coahoma County Citizens' Council in Clarksdale.[22] In April and May 1965 Governor Johnson tardily appointed attorneys Edward J. Currie Sr. of Hattiesburg, Forrest County, and Semmes Luckett of Clarksdale to the Commission. The governor's last appointment to the agency was finally completed in August 1966 with attorney Dan H. Shell of Jackson, a former special agent of the FBI, being named to fill the post.[23] Moreover, between January 1966 and the middle of 1967, five Commission members—Gartin, Sillers, Campbell, Williams, and Currie—were replaced for various reasons, ranging from unexpected deaths and taking up other state positions to overt dissatisfaction with the agency's performance. They were eventually succeeded by Senator George Yarbrough, president pro tempore of the Senate; Representative John Junkin of Natchez, Adams County; Senator Perrin H. Purvis of Tupelo, Lee County; Representative James Francis Geoghegan of Fayette, Jefferson County; and attorney Karl W. Kepper of Hattiesburg.[24]

As for the Sovereignty Commission's directorship, about one month after Johnson became governor, Albert Jones, the agency's director under the Barnett administration for three years, wrote to Kenneth Stewart, an administrative assistant to the governor, expressing his desire to be reappointed director of the Commission. With little doubt, the Citizens' Council officials were eager to get Jones back on the Commission since they well realized that he was "more pliable" to the Council than was Johnston. Two weeks later, Stewart wrote back to Jones to thank him for his interest in applying for the position and assured him that his application would receive the governor's "most sincere consideration." Regardless of Stewart's courteous assurance, Governor Johnson avoided reappointing Jones to the directorship, recognizing from his firsthand experience that the white supremacist organization had virtually "controlled" Jones during the Barnett era.[25] Johnston was thus retained by the governor as the Sovereignty Commission director with a salary of $10,000 per year. All three Commission investigators who had been hired under the Barnett administration—Tom Scarbrough, Andy Hopkins, and Virgil Downing—were also retained, and each received $7,100 per year.[26] Chief Investigator Scarbrough won Johnston's confidence and was entrusted with the Commission's day-to-day tasks when the director was out of state. "[M]y main investigator was Tom Scarbrough," Johnston recollected years later. Scarbrough was an able and proven law enforcement officer and investigator, but other factors also contributed to Johnston's dependence upon him. For one thing, soon after Johnston became director in the spring of 1963, Hopkins became ill with Hodgkin's disease and began his repeated hospitalizations. Downing simply was not efficient enough to satisfy the director's expectations in carrying out his duties, and Johnston consequently "did not send him out on very many [investigative] trips."[27]

In the early spring of 1964 the Sovereignty Commission began to fully mobilize its investigative department in anticipation of intensified civil rights activities in Mississippi. For the fiscal year July 1, 1964, to June 30, 1965, for example, the total expenditure for the Commission's investigative activities well exceeded that for its public relations programs for the first time since the beginning of the Barnett administration in 1960.[28] Ever since the Sovereignty Commission's creation under the Coleman administration in 1956, the agency's members and investigators had included several former FBI agents, but the surveillance techniques and equipment possessed by Mississippi's snooping agency could not bear comparison with those of J. Edgar Hoover's prized bureau. As an illustration, under the Barnett administration, the Sovereignty Commission purchased four units of Motorola's 1960 model two-way car radios for $1,996. However, by September 1963 the Commission had sold its two unused units, which "had been in [the agency's] store-room for three years," to the State Highway Patrol. Although the remaining two units were eventually installed in the Commission investigators' personal automobiles, "[n]one of the investigators were using the units," and by the end of June 1964 these units had also been sold.[29] Though Director Johnston at one point contemplated purchasing "a special electronic device for police and intelligence application" for his agency, he was dissuaded by Hopkins. "One person places a small microphone on his person which transmits conversation to a receiver which can be plugged into a tape recorder or listened to by earphones," the investigator explained to Johnston in his May 1963 memorandum how the "special electronic device" would work. "While I was a member of the Highway Patrol, I had many occasion[s] to use similar equipment," Hopkins continued, "[but] I never felt that the information gained by the use of this equipment justified the expense and time involved in attempting to gain information in this manner."[30] In addition to the fact that the Sovereignty Commission never possessed any "equipment to 'bug' a place and record what is said without knowledge of the participants" during its entire existence, the state agency did not equip its investigators with cameras either.[31] Hopkins once implored Johnston to purchase two Kodak cameras for Scarbrough and himself, which were "reasonably priced" and required "no settings or manipulations." "There has [sic] been many occasions in the past," he lamented in his June 1966 memorandum, "when situations arose that we could have taken pictures that would have been very beneficial to this organization if we had been equipped with cameras." Notwithstanding the investigator's plea, the agency never possessed any cameras.[32] Moreover, the Sovereignty Commission investigators were not furnished with firearms, and they were actually prohibited from bringing their personal weapons into the Commission office. When in May 1963 Hopkins flashed his pistol in the office, he was severely reprimanded by Director Johnston and was ordered "to keep the pistol in his car and never have it on his person" when he was in the office.[33]

Under these circumstances, instead of employing sophisticated surveillance devices for wiretapping and bugging phones, the Sovereignty Commission under the Johnson administration heavily relied upon several private detective agencies and informants. Since at least the time Johnston became the Commission director in 1963, the state agency had dealt with five detective agencies: Day Detectives, Inc., of Jackson, owned by Ralph D. Day; Pendleton Detectives, Inc., of also Jackson, whose president was Robert H. Pendleton; Delta Detective Agency of Vicksburg, whose owner was former FBI Agent John D. Sullivan; Risk Detective and Tracer Agency of Hattiesburg, which was directed by Louie Risk; and Jerry Harrison's Harrison Security Agency. The Sovereignty Commission particularly depended upon the Day Detectives, and all of the informants who were employed by the agency were identified as "Informant X," "Mr. X," or simply "X."[34] In early May 1964 Johnston was approached by a representative of the Pendleton Detectives, who informed the director that his agency "had developed an informant who could be of real service to the Sovereignty Commission." Having determined that the information furnished by this informant was "not available through other sources," Johnston agreed to retain the anonymous informant with a salary of $350 per month. "Reports from this informant," the director recorded on May 18, "will be filed under Informant 'Y.' "[35] In addition, Commission informants, who used identification symbols such as "Z" and "F," were hired by the other detective agencies, and they usually worked for the state agency for a short period of time when occasions arose.[36] The use of letters to identify the Commission informants began under the Barnett administration. The rules of the "Organization and Administration of the State Sovereignty Commission," which were adopted at the first Commission meeting that Barnett chaired, provided that when confidential informants were required in obtaining information, "the reports should indicate the source by a suitable symbol."[37] Following the procedure set by former Director Jones, Johnston never paid these informants directly. Instead, he paid bills submitted by the detective agencies, and these agencies in turn paid their respective "contacts" for their compensations."[W]e didn't want any informant's name to be on a state warrant," Johnston recalled later.[38] In March 1965 the director reported that the average fees the Commission had paid for the services rendered by each detective agency ranged from $50 to $75 per day.[39]

Though 1964 started out on a somewhat soft tone with Governor Johnson's conciliatory posture, Mississippi would soon be engulfed in a series of rapid-fire events on the civil rights front. Never before had the entire nation's eyes been so intensely focused on the state for such an extended period of time, and many white Mississippians were not yet ready to give up their "rear-guard defense of yesterday." Furthermore, by the time the new governor pledged in his inaugural address that he would wage "an all[-]out assault" for Mississippi's "share of tomorrow," the Sovereignty Commission had already involved itself deeply in waging its own "all-out assault" against President John F. Kennedy's legacy—the civil rights bill then pending in Congress. On November 22, 1963, President Kennedy was gunned down in Dallas, Texas, in the most controversial assassination in United States history. The remarks that the president intended to deliver to the dinner party for Texas Democrats in Austin echoed his previous resolve that he would continue "to make a commitment . . . to the proposition that race has no place in American life or law."[40] To the dismay of the southern legislative leaders in Washington, Lyndon B. Johnson, who had become the thirty-sixth president, was quick to express his vigorous support for the Kennedy civil rights program. Only five days after the assassination, in his very first address as president delivered before Congress on November 27, Johnson strongly urged the "earliest possible passage of the civil rights bill." Appearing before the joint session of Congress, the new president spoke to many of his former colleagues: "We have talked long enough in this country about civil rights. It is now time to write the next chapter and to write it in books of law." "No eulogy could more eloquently honor President Kennedy's memory," the Texan concluded, "[than the] earliest possible passage of the civil rights bill for which he fought so long."[41] Sometime later, when Commission Director Johnston went to Washington with John Satterfield to attend a meeting of the Coordinating Committee for Fundamental American Freedoms, he had a chance to confer with Senator James Eastland. Asked about the legislative status of the civil rights bill in Congress by Johnston, the all-powerful Mississippi senator gloomily shook his head and answered: "We had Kennedy stopped. But I'm afraid we can't stop Johnson."[42]

According to Satterfield's estimate, the Coordinating Committee had spent almost $260,000 to try to block the passage of the civil rights bill by the spring of 1964, and out of this amount, a total of approximately $250,000 had been funneled through the Mississippi State Sovereignty Commission.[43] Earlier in the same year, the Sovereignty Commission had received two large donations of $108,612.60 and $105,398.79, respectively, from an anonymous contributor. These donations were apparently made possible by the sale of certain securities handled by the Morgan Guaranty Bank in New York City, and they were transmitted to the Commission's bank account at the First National Bank in Jackson. The anonymous contributor turned out to be Wickliffe Preston Draper, a wealthy New Yorker. In 1937 Draper organized a nonprofit foundation named the Pioneer Fund, Inc., in New York, whose purpose was to "conduct or aid in conducting study and research into the problems of heredity and eugenics in the human race" with "special reference to the people of the United States." The northern millionaire's donations and some other private contributions were handled by Thomas Wright, vice president of the Jackson bank, and they were eventually chan-neled through the Sovereignty Commission to the Coordinating Commit-tee.[44] The bulk of the Satterfield committee's expenditures was used for distributing various "writings and [making] speeches in opposition to the [civil rights] bill" around the nation. Among these, the blockbuster of the committee's public relations efforts was a full-page newspaper advertisement entitled "$100 Billion Blackjack: The Civil Rights Bill," where the Coordi-nating Committee asserted that the proposed civil rights measure was noth-ing but a "socialists' omnibus bill." The advertisement appeared in early March 1964 in 215 northern and western daily newspapers.[45] Envisaging, albeit grudgingly, the eventual passage of the Civil Rights Act of 1964 with the vigorous support of President Johnson, Satterfield proposed to Governor Johnson in early March that his Coordinating Committee turn itself into a "permanent nation-wide organizations [*sic*] in the field of [advocating] race differences and [studying] race relations." "The time is ripe to form the proper national organizations [*sic*]," the Yazoo City lawyer wrote to the gov-ernor, "[and] I hope that Mississippi may take the lead." Within a month, Satterfield made his second proposal to Johnson that Mississippi take part in organizing a nationwide group that would study the relations between "state sovereignty and civil rights" on a two-year basis.[46] However, after the early summer of 1964, the influence of the Satterfield committee was on the wane, and in the end Governor Johnson ignored these ambitious proposals.

Imitating the ill-fated Federation for Constitutional Government of the 1950s in style, the Coordinating Committee had entertained high hopes to garner nationwide support for its programs since its creation.[47] But in reality, the committee, whose programs Satterfield once referred to as "the greatest unified project[s] ever undertaken in the South," failed even to receive regional support.[48] In truth, Mississippi was the only major financial contributor to the cause espoused by the Coordinating Committee. The counterparts of the Mississippi State Sovereignty Commission in other southern states—the Louisiana State Sovereignty Commission, the Virginia Commission on Constitutional Government, the Florida Constitutional Commission, and the newly organized Alabama State Sovereignty Commission—did not actively participate in the committee's programs, and they only made nominal financial contributions to its cause.[49]

In the final analysis, since its formation in July 1963 until April 1, 1964, the Coordinating Committee had spent a total of $343,191, and out of this amount, the contributions made by or funneled through the Mississippi State Sovereignty Commission was $262,581.[50] As the committee faded away in late 1964, Mississippi's tax money was also frittered away. In participating in the Coordinating Committee's efforts, the Mississippi agency once looked forward to region-wide cooperation and envisioned the establishment of its own "department" for the purpose of collaborating with the sovereignty commissions and other similar state agencies in Louisiana and Alabama to crack down on "subversive activities." By then, the Mississippi State Sovereignty Commission had become the template for both the Louisiana and Alabama State Sovereignty Commissions, and it was natural for Mississippi to take the lead in launching such an ambitious project. But this "three-way program of mutual assistance on subversive activities" did not materialize without the governor's blessing, and the Commission would have to wait four more years to establish a nominal "Interstate Sovereignty Commission" among the three states under the administration of Governor Johnson's successor.[51]

At the time the Sovereignty Commission was busy pouring Mississippi's state funds into the Coordinating Committee's activities in Washington in the spring of 1964, the state agency also began to engage in an "extensive research" on one of the most formidable citadels of "inside agitators" for the civil rights movement in the state—Tougaloo College.[52] The American Missionary Association founded the college in 1869 on a cotton plantation eight miles north of downtown Jackson. Until the early 1960s, Tougaloo had been an all-black institution, but in the spring of 1964, it had nine white students among its total enrollment of about five hundred.[53] In 1959 A. D.

Beittel, a white educator, became president of the college. From the outset of his presidency, he had refused to discourage the political and civil rights activities staged by its students both on campus and outside the institution. When in March 1961 nine black students from the college were arrested in the wake of their "study-in" at the Jackson Municipal Library, Beittel visited the "Tougaloo Nine" in jail to console them. Later, at the risk of his life, he even joined sociology professor John R. Salter Jr., Chaplain Edwin King, and a number of Tougaloo students in carrying out the 1963 Jackson movement, which included the sit-in demonstrations at the Woolworth's segregated lunch counter in Jackson.[54]

Since the state's first sit-in staged by the "Tougaloo Nine," the Jackson Citizens' Council and a growing number of state legislators had kept their watchful eyes on the black educational institution. After it became evident that Tougaloo was the base for the well-publicized Jackson movement, their dissatisfaction with the college and its white president had increased.[55] Beginning in late 1963 a few state lawmakers started to visit the Sovereignty Commission office to seek advice from its director on how they could possibly "shut down" Tougaloo, which Lieutenant Governor Gartin referred to as "a cancerous growth" and a haven for "queers, quirks, political agitators and possibly some communists."[56]

By the end of January 1964, a rumor had begun to circulate in the state capitol that the State General Legislative Investigating Committee might be called "to investigate Tougaloo." "I explained [to the legislators] that we have done everything we know to try to find something at Tougaloo which would justify some kind of action," Johnston once grumbled, "but so far we have not been able to accumulate the kind of evidence needed for a [legislative committee] hearing."[57] Having been pressured and become restless, the Commission director set out to investigate the black institution. On March 2, Lieutenant Governor Gartin, Assistant Attorney General Dugas Shands, Senator Yarbrough, and Johnston met in Gartin's office "to discuss possible plans against Tougaloo College." As a result, the Commission director was instructed "to make a detailed report on everything concerning Tougaloo activities."[58] In submitting his "first of a series of reports" on the black college, Johnston wrote to Governor Johnson on March 10 that the Sovereignty Commission had been "engaged in extensive research . . . to assemble evidence which might be used as valid reasons for revoking the charter of

Tougaloo and/or cancelling its accreditation by the Mississippi Accrediting Commission." He further informed the governor that the main targets of the agency's investigation were President Beittel and Chaplain King, who were suspected by the Commission as "veteran supporters of communist causes and communist enterprises."[59] On March 26, in preparing the second part of the Tougaloo investigative report forwarded to the governor's office, Johnston expressed his frustration of not having been able to "link" the white chaplain "with any communist front organization," though it was a well-known fact that King had "been active in sit-ins and demonstrations, etc."[60] Two weeks earlier, Johnston, accompanied by Sullivan of the Delta Detective Agency, had "made a surprise call in Memphis, Tennessee" on King's mother. "I believe both you and I have an entrée to Mrs. King," the former FBI agent wrote in his lengthy report on King submitted to Johnston, "and if followed up [we] might develop better cooperation from her." "I also believe that because of her emotional state future conversations with her should be on tape," Sullivan suggested.[61]

The Sovereignty Commission's "extensive research" in the Tougaloo case also included its investigation of Joan Baez's concert held on the campus on April 5. In late March one of the Commission's informants reported to Johnston that "there would be a Folk Musical . . . which would be completely integrated," featuring Baez as "[t]he star of the program," who reportedly had "stated that she would not appear unless the program audience is integrated." While the informant purchased two admission tickets to observe the concert of the "Queen of Folk Music," who was also a known espouser of the civil rights cause, the Commission director scribbled down his directions on the informant's report: "Andy: Be out in that area to see if many whites show up."[62] Instructed by Johnston, Hopkins drove up to Tougaloo and determined that Baez's concert "was well attended by an integrated audience." In the midst of thunder and lightening, the investigator vainly tried to write down the license plate numbers of "several out-of-state automobiles . . . entering the campus," but his efforts were of little avail. "Due to the weather and darkness," Hopkins reported later, "it was impossible to record these tag numbers with any degree of accuracy."[63]

When the Sovereignty Commission's surveillance on the "cancerous growth" was in progress, John Held, a white professor of philosophy and religion at Tougaloo, visited the Commission office with his wife on April 13 in response to Johnston's invitation and informed the director that there had been "dissension among faculty and students" at the college "because of the policies of the President, Dr. A. D. Beittel, and the chaplain, Rev. Edwin King, Jr." The confidential visitor also informed Johnston that Wesley A. Hotchkiss, executive secretary of the United Church of Christ in New York City and a member of the Board of Trustees of Tougaloo College, and other board members would meet on the college campus later in the month. Upon hearing this, Johnston hurriedly formulated a "plan to make a personal visit" to Hotchkiss and other trustees in New York "to show them the documents in our files linking Dr. Beittel with a communist front organization" and "to make a report on the campus and faculty dissension." "It is our plan . . . to offer a trade with Mr. Hotchkiss and those in authority," Johnston wrote in his April 13 memorandum. "We will suggest Dr. Beittel and Rev. King be removed from Tougaloo," he elaborated, "and in return we can pledge that the legislature will take no action on revocation of the charter [and] that the Mississippi Accrediting Commission will not take Tougaloo off the accredited list."[64]

Four days later, Johnston carried out his planned "trade" with the tacit approval of the governor's office. In writing, the Commission director informed Hotchkiss that Tougaloo College had "become more of a school for agitation than a school for education." "The present atmosphere [at Tougaloo] has created tension and bitterness," he went on, "and inspired the Mississippi Legislature to consider punitive action against the institution." Then, Johnston got down to brass tacks: "We are in position to guarantee to the trustees that if Dr. Beittel and Rev. King [are] removed and education takes the place of agitation under a new administration [then] no punitive action will be taken by the Mississippi legislature or its officials against the institution." In concluding his memorandum to Hotchkiss, the director suggested that the trustees launch an all-out investigation on the Tougaloo matter. "It is recommended very sincerely," Johnston added, "that the trustees of Tougaloo thoroughly investigate the administration of Dr. Beittel and the activities of Rev. King." "We have documents, letters and other material to prove the points mentioned [here]," he concluded. On the same day, the impatient director placed a long distance call to Hotchkiss, who then was on a trip in Tampa, Florida, and asked for an audience before the trustees. As a result of this telephone conversation, a meeting was set up for April 21 in New York City.[65]

As planned, Johnston flew to New York to confer with three members of the Tougaloo Board of Trustees, accompanied by Shelby R. Rogers, a Jackson attorney who was affiliated with Tom Watkins's law farm. To make their trip "a secret mission," Johnston did not inform Rogers of "the nature of the trip" until "the departure of the plane." Though the gathered trustees—Robert O. Wilder of Warren, Pennsylvania; Lawrence L. Durgin of New York City; and Hotchkiss—"did not appear to be thoroughly convinced that communist fronts were having any influence in what they described as the 'Negro revolution,' " the Commission director observed at the conclusion of the three-hour meeting that they "seemed impressed with [our] presentation," which "made us cautiously optimistic."[66] On April 27 the board abruptly announced that Beittel would retire as president of Tougaloo effective on September 1, 1964. The following day, Johnston proudly informed the governor's office that "this announcement occurred about a week after [our] trip to New York."[67] As a sequel to this story, on December 29 Johnston had a surprise visit from Beittel, who said that "he had received word" that the director "had a part in his dismissal from Tougaloo College." "I had nothing to do with the action of the trustees," Johnston replied to the former president, "but I was delighted to see [that you had been] dismissed and had I known of any way to bring this about, I would certainly have done it."[68]

However, the January and April 1964 minutes of the executive sessions of Tougaloo College's Board of Trustees reflect a different version of the story. In 1963 Tougaloo began "a cooperative relationship" with Brown University in Providence, Rhode Island. Barnaby Keeney, president of Brown, soon took an interest in the southern black college and promised to contact several northern foundations, such as the Ford Foundation, on Tougaloo's behalf. But there was one major precondition. Keeney wanted the Tougaloo board to discourage the college's active involvement in the black struggle in Mississippi. For many of the predominantly black colleges in the South, the financial support provided by major foundations was one of the most crucial factors for their future survival, and Tougaloo was no exception.[69] Keeney's influence on the Mississippi black college can also be determined from Johnston's April 17 memorandum to Hotchkiss, where the Commission director informed the trustee that "Dr. Beittel [had] attempted to abolish the entire religion department" at his institution, to which the Commission's confidential informer—Dr. Held—belonged, but the president was subsequently "dissuaded from this project by one of the trustees, who is at Brown University."[70] At the January 16 executive session of the Board of Trustees held in New York City, a board member advised other members that the northern foundations were "concerned and hesitant about giving money" to the black college "with presidents [*sic*] who may not carry through with the program" that the foundations desired. "Much discussion followed," the minutes read, but in the end the board members voted that Hotchkiss would "approach" President Beittel and inform him of the board's desire to replace him with "a younger man," who would "be able to carry the load for Tougaloo College."[71] On the same day, three board members, including Hotchkiss, who had just been "appointed to approach Dr. Beittel," met with the president in Hotchkiss's office in New York. "Dr. Beittel had expressed his personal disappointment as he had hope[d] to continue past his 65th birthday," the minutes of the April executive session noted, but Beittel eventually accepted the board's wish with much reluctance. A few days after the Commission director conferred with the three board members in New York, the entire board met at Tougaloo College to decide Beittel's fate. Hotchkiss explained to the joyless president that "a new program requires a new type of leadership" at Tougaloo, and the full board subsequently voted that it would "accept President Beittel's decision to retire on September 1."[72]

The minutes of the executive session thus indicate that the Tougaloo board had already decided that President Beittel should retire months before the Sovereignty Commission's involvement in the matter. It is unclear whether Johnston's personal appearance before the board members had any effect on their decision.[73] "It cannot be said, with conviction, whether the decision of the trustees, who fired Dr. Beittel, had anything to do with the information that he had collaborated with subversives," Johnston himself later admitted in his report sent to Senator Eastland in Washington.[74] Be that as it may, President Beittel's contract with Tougaloo was terminated as of September 1, and the Sovereignty Commission's original aim was achieved. But before the retirement of the Tougaloo president, who was regarded as both the representative of the state's "inside agitators" and the personifying symbol of "communist" influence at a "cancer[ous] college" by Mississippi's white officials, the state was destined to confront the most traumatic summer in its recent history—the "long, hot summer" of 1964—with an influx of a thousand "outside agitators."

A new wave of Mississippi's civil rights movement began in 1962 when a statewide coalition of several civil rights organizations—the Council of Federated Organizations (COFO)—was founded with Robert Moses of the Student Nonviolent Coordinating Committee (SNCC) and David Dennis of the Congress of Racial Equality (CORE) as the coalition's principal organizers. Realizing that black Mississippians could not enjoy "freedom" in a true sense as long as their political participation was suppressed, the COFO organizers had concentrated their activities in conducting several voter registration campaigns in the state. With the formation of COFO and its primary objective of voter registration drives, the contrasts between the 1950s and the 1960s, in terms of the posture taken by Mississippi's civil rights leaders, became striking. While the civil rights movement in the 1950s was "based in the cities, dominated by the NAACP, and centered around the small black middle class," the movement's leaders in the 1960s began to see "the rural poor" in the state "as their natural constituency."[75] In late 1963 COFO leaders formulated a statewide summer project for 1964—the Mississippi Freedom Summer Project—where approximately a thousand northern, predominantly white college students, who "represented the 'best and the brightest' of early Sixties youthful idealism," would join a cadre of black freedom fighters in Mississippi.[76]

As COFO's staff, three-fourth's of whom were from SNCC, was getting ready for the Freedom Summer Project, the Sovereignty Commission was busy preparing to defend the state from the upcoming "invasion" by the project's "outside agitators." Beginning in January 1964, the three Commission investigators—Scarbrough, Hopkins, and Downing—set out to make "a personal visit to each sheriff" in all eighty-two counties in an attempt to acquaint these sheriffs with various state laws. The state agency subsequently prepared and distributed "a digest of various laws" to the sheriffs, so that they "could use [it] in dealing with [civil rights] agitators," particularly with "the anticipated invasion of students from other states."[77] The Commission's two-page digest contained brief descriptions of fifteen state laws.[78] In the middle of April the agency again circulated to the state's law enforcement officers a revised three-page list of nineteen state laws that was "designed to be helpful as well as protective" to those officers in carrying out their duties in anticipation of the Freedom Summer Project.[79] In addition, in April and May the Commission investigators held a series of meetings with law enforcement officers in many municipalities and counties throughout the state. By holding these meetings, which the Commission referred to as "night clinics," the investigators hoped to familiarize these officers with "provisions of state laws applicable to practically every incident which might occur" in the coming summer.[80] During a two-hour conference with the law enforcement and other elected officials of Lafayette County held in Oxford on May 1, for instance, Scarbrough observed that "city and county officials are very much concerned about what is in store for their city, county, and state this summer." "The purpose of these meetings," he reported, "has been to organize the city and county officials to work in a coordinated unit to handle the racial agitators who have promised to invade Mississippi this summer." Scarbrough pointed out to the meeting's participants that Mississippi officials had "been telling the rest of the country for five or six years" that the Communists were "the main force behind all of the racial unrest and civil rights agitation." He then advised the group that those who would participate in the Freedom Summer Project were most likely "communists, sex perverts, odd balls, and do-gooders."[81]

In the middle of February 1964 an anonymous investigative report, whose basis was derived "from information given by a confidential informant," reached Johnston's desk at the Sovereignty Commission office. "A new program of voter registration attempts is under consideration [by COFO]," the report read, "and some preliminary plans have been formulated for this activity."[82] Wasting no time, the Commission began to place several black informants in the COFO office in downtown Jackson and in its gatherings. When a statewide meeting of the members of the NAACP, SNCC, and CORE was held at the Masonic Temple in the capital city on March 15, a black informant reported back to Johnston that COFO would sponsor the "Mississippi Freedom Summer" with "2,000 [northern] students coming to Mississippi this summer to participate in" the project.[83] "After a few interviews, I was offered a position with COFO," wrote another Commission informant in a "special report," covering his investigative activities from April 23 to May 9. "It was easy to mix with them," the writer identified only as "Operator #79" glorified himself.[84] Soon afterward, Operator #79, who was hired by the Pendleton Detectives, became one of the main pipelines between the

Sovereignty Commission and the COFO office. On the night of May 13 the informant secretly removed a file from the COFO office that contained the accepted applications of about a hundred prospective student summer workers. Twenty-seven applications, which had photos attached to them, were photocopied, and the applicants' names, schools, and hometowns were reported to the Commission through the detective agency.[85] Subsequently, in late August 1964 Operator #79 was replaced by Operator #68. Operator #68 was also employed directly by the Pendleton Detectives, and both informants were identified by the Commission as "Informant Y." Operator #68 continued to keep the COFO headquarters under surveillance, and the Commission heavily relied upon Informant Y until it terminated its arrangement with the Jackson detective agency on October 15.[86]

As well as deploying its informants in the COFO structure, the Sovereignty Commission, in preparation for the upcoming summer "invasion," also began to reactivate its "subversive hunt" programs. For the purpose of exposing "Communists among racial agitators," the state agency made arrangements with a Jackson resident by the name of John S. Kochtitzky Jr. in late March 1964 and had him subscribe to various "publications of communist front organizations" and deliver them to the Commission office each week. "We wanted a name which sounded 'Russianish,' " Johnston wrote in an activity report of the Commission.[87] The director agreed to pay Kochtitzky "the expenses involved" and "$20.00 per month for his time in . . . delivering the publications" to the state agency, and the first payment to him—a total of $120—was made on March 27. In order to keep Kochtitzky's name from appearing on any public records, it was also decided that all warrants would be made out "in the name of John Shidler," a fictitious name.[88] Shortly afterward, the Commission's conspirator rented a box at the Jackson post office in his own name and started to subscribe to a vast array of publications, ranging from the *Communist Viewpoint* published in New York City and the *Inter-Racial Review* of the Catholic Inter-Racial Council to academic journals such as the *Journal of Negro History*.[89] Thanks to the "Russianish"-named collaborator, who "rendered a great service in helping the Sovereignty Commission to build a file on subversives," the state's "un-American activities committee" had accumulated files on thirty-nine individuals by the end of the summer. These files, which were all specifically indexed as "subversives," were separated from other files for "a ready reference on those individuals engaged in racial agitation" in the state, who also had "connections with communist front organizations."[90]

Around the same time the Sovereignty Commission secured Kochtitzky's services, it also began its dubious relations with a self-proclaimed black crusader for anti–civil rights and anti-Communism in Richmond, California. Rev. C. Fain Kyle, a sixty-three-year-old native Tennessean, was the director of an organization called the Dedicated Independent Society Committee Against Racial Demonstrations (DISCARD). DISCARD was officially chartered as a "charitable and educational non-profit corporation" in California in November 1963. With its purpose being "[t]o seek to discourage and bring to an end all racial demonstrations throughout the State of California and the entire United States of American," DISCARD contended that these racial demonstrations were "a very definite part of the Communist Conspiracy to provoke a . . . frightening 'race war' in the nation."[91]

The relationship between the Richmond organization and the Mississippi agency began in early May 1964 when Johnston sent a letter to Kyle, appreciating his "convictions and . . . courage to speak out." "When this office can be of any service to you in your campaign," the Commission director added as a matter of formalities, "please let us know."[92] But Kyle did not take Johnston's words as mere formalities. Instead, he had just found a future financial source. "It was a wonderful, glad surprise to receive your letter which I shall always keep and cherish," Kyle wrote back immediately. While castigating Martin Luther King Jr., who had been used by the "Communist Conspiracy" to "head this so-called civil rights movement," DISCARD's director announced his conviction: "Since it was a Negro preacher that started this mess I sincerely believe that it will take another Negro preacher . . . to counteract and to curtail the work of this wolf in sheep's clothing."[93] Before long, DISCARD asked the Sovereignty Commission "for some financial assistance in connection with" the organization's "radio campaign" to propagate its "message of TRUTH and AMERICANISM" over two radio stations in Alabama and Georgia. For this project, the Mississippi agency sent Kyle a donation of $100, but nobody in the Commission office seemed to care to know if his program was in fact broadcast. The only certain things that the credulous Commission received in return for its investment were DISCARD's three "Contributing Membership" cards issued to "the great State of Mississippi," "His Excellency, Governor Paul B. Johnson," and "the Honorable Erle Johnston, Jr."[94]

By the early part of June, through its investigators and "other sources of information," the Sovereignty Commission had been "fully informed about COFO plans" in the state. "We know the names of the people working at the [COFO] headquarters," Johnston revealed in his address delivered before the Mississippi Economic Council on June 4, "and we already have obtained background information on many of the volunteer students."[95] Later in the same month, two-week orientation sessions for the summer project's volunteers began at Western College for Women in Oxford, Ohio. The sessions, whose busy schedule included various lectures given by COFO leaders, were "crammed with more history, more role-playing, more warnings about the dangers that lay ahead than the volunteers could begin to absorb." In addition to these regular programs, John Doar of the United States Justice Department, who was then the deputy assistant attorney general in charge of the department's civil rights division, flew from Washington on Friday of each week to discuss with the volunteers "the limited role the federal government could be expected to take in Mississippi over the summer."[96]

The peaceful campus of Western College for Women was not free from the Sovereignty Commission's infiltration either. "I had communicants not only in the school up in Ohio where they were being trained," Johnston recalled years later, "but also all along . . . when they were traveling, and when they reassembled in Mississippi."[97] The deployment of the Commission informants on the campus of the women's college was carried out with the approval of Governor Johnson, who also admitted the state's infiltration into COFO program a few years after he left the governor's office: "As a matter of fact, when we heard that they [the COFO staff and its volunteers] were going to set up the Freedom Houses, start the program, I sent some Negroes from Mississippi up to Oxford, Ohio. . . . I had these people to act as informants and to get the entire story, to go through the training and to return to Mississippi."[98]

One of the two informants, who were placed on the Western College for Women campus by the Day Detectives, reported to the Commission director that "during the entire orientation session" he had "been trying to determine if there [was] any communist activity or any sign of communist infiltration." Having not been able to detect such incidents, however, he plausibly concluded that "the officials [of COFO] seem to have been on the alert to keep any such activities out of the meetings." After his eleven-day stay at Western College, the Commission informant drove back to Jackson on June 27, accompanied by three other volunteer students who had just been trained to "agitate" Mississippi. Once they entered Mississippi, a state highway patrol car followed the group from Tupelo to Jackson, approximately 170 miles. "The other occupants of my car," the informant wrote in concluding his report, "were impressed by this and thought it was a good thing for the State to be doing." For this campus infiltration operation in Ohio, the Sovereignty Commission paid the Day Detectives a total of $334.84—$165.60 for "travel expense," $149.24 for "meals [and] lodging," and $30.00 for "long distance telephone"—excluding the fees for the informants' personal "services."[99]

In the meantime, white Mississippians' resentment toward the Freedom Summer Project was at its boiling point. Summing up their emotional reactions, the *Meridian Star*, in an editorial entitled "God Help the USA," warned its readers to prepare themselves for an ordeal to be created by "outside agitators": "The student volunteers—the beatniks, the wild-eyed left wing nuts, the unshaven and unwashed trash, and the just plain stupid or ignorant or misled—go on meddling and muddling with things about which they know nothing and which concern them not."[100] Some whites intensified their use of violence in order to defend their state's cherished "way of life." Reflecting the revival of Ku Klux Klan activities in Mississippi, cross burnings on weekends had been reported in such cities as Natchez, McComb, and Brookhaven since the spring, and on the night of April 5, twelve crosses were burned simultaneously in Neshoba County alone.[101] On June 16 the Mount Zion Methodist Church, a black church located in Longdale in the eastern part of Neshoba County, received the Klan-inspired baptism in kerosene and was burned to the ground. The church had previously been designated as a "Freedom School" site by COFO.

Three days after the Mount Zion Church had been destroyed, the first wave of volunteers began arriving in Mississippi from Western College for Women. Three young civil rights workers from CORE's Meridian office— Michael H. Schwerner and Andrew Goodman, white males from New York, and James E. Chaney, a black male from Meridian—drove to Philadelphia in Neshoba County to investigate the burning of the Mount Zion Church.

Around 4:00 P.M., Chaney, who was driving a Ford station wagon, was stopped and then arrested by Deputy Sheriff Cecil Price of Neshoba County, ostensibly for speeding. Schwerner and Goodman were placed in custody for investigation. The three young men were immediately taken to the county jail in Philadelphia, and they were released late in the evening. Outside the jail, however, a group of Lauderdale and Neshoba County Klansmen were waiting to fulfill their dreams of getting rid of the "nigger-lovers." Within an hour, after a heated car chase, Schwerner, Goodman, and Chaney were forever gone.[102]

On June 22, the day after the three men disappeared, Johnston dispatched Hopkins to Philadelphia. "Several rumors were being circulated in Philadelphia that these subjects had met with foul play either while in custody of the sheriff or shortly after their release," Hopkins reported back to the director on the following day, "[and] this cannot be excluded as a possibility due to the present racial situation in Mississippi."[103] A week later the investigator wrote in another report that "there are rumors that there is a K.K.K. in Philadelphia and that some prominent citizens are members of the Klan."[104] Hopkins soon cultivated a reliable informant in Philadelphia, who was identified only as "M. G.," and shared his investigative reports on the three missing civil rights workers with Gwen Cole, assistant director of the Identification Bureau at the State Highway Patrol.[105] Meanwhile, Johnston relied upon Jack Long Tannehill, editor and publisher of the *Neshoba Democrat* who was related to Louisiana's famous Long family and who had "deplore[d] the burning of the crosses" in his recent editorials, to receive information on the Klan activities in Philadelphia.[106]

As a matter of fact, Schwerner's name was not new to the Sovereignty Commission. Earlier, responding to a verbal inquiry made by Representative Betty Jane Long of Meridian in March, the Commission had conducted a surveillance of Schwerner and his wife, Rita, for a short period of time. The Schwerners first came to Mississippi from New York in January 1964 to participate in voter registration drives at CORE's Meridian office. "We have been informed that a representative of CORE has been engaging in [civil rights] activities in and around Meridian," Johnston noted in a memorandum on March 17, "[and] [a]s of now he has not been identified, but an investigation will be made." In his March 23 report entitled "Investigation of Unknown White Male CORE Worker at Meridian," Hopkins identified the "captioned subject" as Schwerner. In cooperation with Chief O. A. Booker and Detective G. L. Butler at the Meridian Police Department as well as the Lauderdale County's sheriff's office, the state agency kept the Schwerners "under surveillance." On March 24, Johnston provided Representative Long with a copy of the Hopkins's investigative report, which included a physical description of Schwerner and his automobile's license plate number. Informing the Meridian lawmaker that "this subject had not previously appeared in our files," the director thanked Long for bringing Schwerner to the Commission's attention.[107]

The very fact that two young middle-class whites from the North had disappeared in Mississippi also brought the White House into action. In Washington, while confiding his inner feelings to a political comrade that "this Mississippi thing is awful mean," President Johnson was concerned that he might "have to walk a tight wire" between the civil rights forces and Mississippi segregationists. As the nation's chief executive as well as a white southerner, the president was careful not "to be appearing to be directing this thing [the search for the three missing workers] and . . . invading the state and taking the rights of the Governor or Mayor." "I'm doing what I can to carry out my oath of office," Johnson once conveyed his predicament to Louisiana Senator Russell Long, "[but] at the same time [I can]not be ugly and vicious and mean [to my native South]." But in anticipation of a resurgence of the white supremacist activities in the state in the wake of the expected passage of the Civil Rights Act, President Johnson instructed J. Edgar Hoover to "fill Mississippi . . . with FBI men and put 'em in every place . . . as informers and put 'em in the Klan and infiltrate it." Accordingly, on June 23, FBI Inspector Joseph Sullivan, one of Hoover's top executives, flew to Meridian with five other agents to take charge of the search for the three missing men.[108]

At the same time, responding to Mississippi Governor Johnson's plea that the White House should send "an impartial observer" to his state, President Johnson decided to dispatch Allen W. Dulles, former director of the Central Intelligence Agency (CIA), to Mississippi to consult with state officials on the search for Schwerner, Goodman, and Chaney and on other related racial matters.[109] After a ninety-minute meeting with the governor on June 24, the former CIA director made it clear that he personally was opposed to federal protection for civil rights workers in Mississippi. But when he flew back to

Washington, he recommended to Johnson that the president authorize an increase of the FBI presence in Mississippi.[110] While in Jackson, Dulles also consulted with Johnston for an hour, where the president's emissary expressed his concern about the increasing activities of the Ku Klux Klan and other quasi-vigilante organizations such as the Americans for the Preservation of the White Race (APWR) in Mississippi.[111] As they left the Commission office, Dulles, who had just confirmed the growing influence of the violence-prone white supremacist organizations in Mississippi, advised an associate: "We have a little problem [here]." While Dulles was busy minding his own business during his two-day visit in Mississippi, Al Richburg, assistant director of the Safety Responsibility Bureau at the Mississippi Department of Public Safety, kept tabs on the former CIA director's minute-by-minute activities in Jackson and prepared a bizarrely detailed report.[112]

On July 10, J. Edgar Hoover visited Mississippi to attend the opening ceremony of the bureau's new office in Jackson. Hoover, who had earlier been instructed by President Johnson "to have the best intelligence system— better than . . . [the one] on the Communists" in Mississippi, emphasized that his bureau was "purely an investigative organization" and "not a police organization."[113] But the FBI director also privately warned Governor Johnson that the Klan activities had to be curtailed and secretly gave the governor and T. B. Birdsong, commissioner of public safety who headed the State Highway Patrol, "a nine[-]page list of Klan[-]type incidents" in Mississippi that had been reported to the FBI since October 31, 1963. In addition, Hoover presented the governor with a list of the state's "counties where the sheriff[s] had membership in or strong connection with the Klan," including some "eighty or ninety names" of the suspected members of the white supremacist groups. In return, to the surprise of the FBI director, Governor Johnson furnished Hoover with almost "eleven hundred names" of the state's Klan members.[114]

Three weeks after the opening of the FBI's largest field office in the nation, the three young men's whereabouts were still unknown. "If they were murdered," the *Jackson Clarion-Ledger* wrote on August 3, "it is by no means the first case of such disposition by Communists of their dupes to insure their silence." "However," the editorial went on, "the careful absence of clues makes it seem likely that they are quartered in Cuba or another Communist area awaiting their next task." The Jackson paper then concluded: "There is no reason to believe them seriously harmed by citizens of the most law-abiding state of the union."[115] In the meantime, Senator Eastland, in a telephone conversation with President Johnson, expressed his belief that the disappearance of the three men was "a publicity stunt" staged by the Communist-infiltrated civil rights forces.[116]

But on August 4, these self-serving observations were proven to be inaccurate when the FBI finally discovered the bodies of the three missing civil rights workers in an earthen dam in Neshoba County forty-four days after their disappearance.[117] Though James Chaney's brother, Ben, asserts that the Sovereignty Commission "was complicit in" and "participated in the murders" of Schwerner, Goodman, and his brother, the state agency most probably did not have any direct involvement in the slayings of the three civil rights workers.[118] But it certainly cannot be denied that the Commission's sharing of information on Schwerner with the law enforcement officers in Lauderdale and its neighboring counties created an atmosphere that encouraged Mississippi's citizens to take the law into their own hands. In addition to the fact that Schwerner's automobile "was one of 136 cars listed on a list" prepared by the Canton Citizens' Council in Madison County, Delmar D. Dennis, a onetime member of the White Knights of the Ku Klux Klan of Mississippi who worked for the FBI as an informant for three years during the 1960s, once reminisced that the Sovereignty Commission "gathered information that was passed along to the Ku Klux Klan and used against the civil rights workers." "Mr. Johnston denies this and he probably did not know how the information was passed along," Dennis looked back, "[b]ut in those days there were many in State Government who were allies or members of the KKK."[119] After all, collecting information on Schwerner's physical description, birthday, address, telephone number, and car license number might have been just one of the routine duties for the Commission investigators and many other state law enforcement officials. However, this information definitely had significant value for those who had calculated to harm Schwerner and his fellow "agitators." In this sense, it perhaps can be justifiably claimed that the Sovereignty Commission was "complicit" in the murders of Chaney, Schwerner, and Goodman.

While the search for the three civil rights workers was being conducted in the early phase of the Freedom Summer Project in Mississippi, the Civil Rights Act of 1964 passed Congress and was signed into law by President

Johnson on July 2. Despite the efforts made by the Coordinating Committee for Fundamental American Freedoms, which had been organized to oppose what John Satterfield termed "civil wrongs" under the guise of "civil rights," President Johnson's determination to "honor President Kennedy's memory" with the "passage of the civil rights bill" won the day. Mississippi's reaction to the law was swift but much calmer than had been expected. In issuing a brief statement, Governor Johnson simply called on Mississippians not to comply with the new law until it was tested in the courts.[120] Meanwhile, some black Mississippians immediately set out to test the act's public accommodation provisions. In Jackson, blacks checked in and ate at the city's two leading hotels and a motel without any incident. But the Robert E. Lee Hotel, the city's third largest hotel, chose not to comply with the act, which Senator Eastland had referred to as "a hydra-headed monster" during the congressional debate. In defiance of the nation's new law, Stewart Gammill, owner of the Robert E. Lee, furled the hotel's Confederate battle flag and put up a sign that read: "*CLOSED* IN DESPAIR. CIVIL RIGHTS BILL UNCONSTITUTIONAL."[121] Conversely, the Jackson Chamber of Commerce voiced the first genuine moderation within the state: "The citizens of Jackson have earned a reputation as a law-abiding community, and the business and professional leadership of the city, and our elected city officials, have always encouraged all of our people of both races to abide by the law of the land. We may not be in sympathy with all of the laws of the land, but we must maintain our standing as a community which abides by the law."[122]

In contrast with the calm posture taken by the city's Chamber of Commerce, the Jackson Citizens' Council, as expected, branded the Civil Rights Act as an unconstitutional "force bill" and urged white Jacksonians to refuse "to eat, swim or sleep under integrated conditions." Condemning the Chamber of Commerce for issuing its "surrender statement," the Council chapter further called for a massive economic boycott of all white business establishments that complied with the "civil wrongs" act.[123] On July 9, a major turning point in the city's history came about when Mayor Allen Thompson, who had steadfastly adopted his "no-retreat and no-surrender" posture against the demands raised by the city's civil rights leaders for many years, endorsed the statement issued by the Jackson Chamber of Commerce. Though he made it clear that he had not altered his personal belief that racial segregation was the best social condition for both races, Thompson praised the chamber's directors for their "courage" in speaking out. Realizing that his new position would be met with criticism and mark his official break with the Citizens' Council, the mayor explained further: "A public official is not in office to be popular. If your popularity is based on something that tomorrow can be undercut, it's not worth having [it]."[124] In the middle of December, the Supreme Court, in *Katzenbach v. McClung*, decreed that "racial minorities have full access to all public facilities by broadly defining a 'place of public accommodation' within the meaning of Title II" of the Civil Rights Act and thereby upheld the constitutionality of the law.[125]

But before the end of the year, Mississippi was thrown into one more crucible, which was a by-product of the newly enacted civil rights legislation. Title VI of the act provided that the federal government could deny funds to any state programs—including public school programs—where racial discrimination was practiced. When on July 7 Judge Sidney Mize of the United States District Court ordered that three Mississippi school districts be immediately desegregated in September, Mississippi was the only state that had not desegregated any of its public schools below college level, indicating that it had successfully lived up to the South's expectation that "it may well be the last major bastion of 'massive resistance' " in the region.[126] Both unable and unwilling to recognize the state's destiny, the defiant *Meridian Star* urged white Mississippians to "Carry On the Fight" in an editorial on August 26: "The horrors of school integration are upon us with a vengeance. We can find no words to adequately express our shock—our revulsion at this abominable crime of race mixing. . . . Some of us may be tempted in the agony of our oppression to give up hope—to yield the struggle. Yet this we can not—dare not—ever do. It is our sacred obligation to keep up the fight for our precious Southern way of life. We must never rest until this foul pollution of integration is forever banished from our soil."[127]

However "abominable" the "crime of race mixing" might be for the *Meridian Star*, Mississippi's segregation walls began tumbling down with great magnitude in the fall of 1964. In early October Jackson Mayor Thompson publicly began to attack William Simmons and other top officials of the Citizens' Councils of America for their uncompromising position on his city's program for orderly school desegregation. Daring to term the Council's policies as the ones that "would lead to anarchy," Thompson, a onetime Council stalwart, completed his break with the state's most powerful white supremacist organization.[128] Heedless of the mayor's indictment, the obdurate Jackson Citizens' Council launched its "Dial for Truth" telephone message campaign on October 12. By dialing the "Dial for Truth" hot line, callers could listen to a message "especially recorded for Mississippians" by Alabama Governor George Wallace, who warned them that "Federal bureaucrats and Federal judges are trampling upon our rights as free men and women."[129]

During the 1964–65 school year, only 56 of the state's 280,000 black schoolchildren attended traditionally all-white public schools.[130] Notwithstanding this rather grim figure, what happened during the fall of 1964 in the three Mississippi school districts cited by Judge Mize was a major breakthrough for the state's civil rights struggle. A breakthrough belatedly came to Louvenia Knight and her two sons in Jasper County as well. In the fall of 1965 her children were finally enrolled in the Stringer School without incident.[131] As Johnston observed in his memorandum to the governor's office, with "the Civil Rights Act and the desegregation orders," either Jasper County or the state no longer had "valid reason" to prevent the two children from attending the historically all-white school.[132] Louvenia eventually triumphed over years of frustration, agony, and most important, community prejudice. In the face of the 1957 Little Rock crisis, President Dwight Eisenhower used to reiterate that "people's hearts" could not be changed merely by laws and court orders.[133] But the 1964 Civil Rights Act and the subsequent school desegregation orders at least affected the people's practices in Jasper County.

The series of traumatic and rapid-fire incidents on Mississippi's civil rights front during the very first year of Governor Johnson's administration was more than the state could bear. All these events, which took place in a span of less than three months, resulted in severely crippling the governor's conciliatory posture. In spite of his inaugural vows to let the nation know that the state's citizens were indeed "Americans as well as Mississippians," these agonizing occurrences during the "long, hot summer" made Johnson's pledge look like an empty promise. To the nation as a whole, Mississippi seemed as if it could never change itself from within. By the end of 1964, the state had begun "to feel an economic pinch" due largely to the racial violence. The tourist business on the Gulf Coast, for instance, had dropped almost 50 percent since the summer's Neshoba County murders, and some factories in the southern part of the state had been moved across the Mississippi River to Louisiana to avoid using Mississippi mailing addresses.[134]

Even under these adverse circumstances, Governor Johnson refused to give in and tried to be true to his own inaugural pledges. In early 1965 he began to remake the public image of his native state before the nation in a series of speeches and addresses. The governor's most important testament came in February when the United States Commission on Civil Rights held public hearings at the Veterans Administration Center in Jackson for the purpose of examining the alleged instances of voter discrimination in twelve Mississippi counties and the general situation concerning the state's law enforcement practices. On the opening day of the hearings, Governor Johnson appeared before the commission and delivered a brief statement entitled "Mississippi: The State of Law and Order." Though "[m]ost Mississippians do not like" the Civil Rights Act of 1964 and "are convinced its passage was unwise," the governor told the commission, "[it] is the 'law of the land' and Mississippi knows it." Reassuring his "fellow Americans" that "Mississippi will continue to be the most law[-]abiding state in the nation," Johnson concluded his statement with the following plea to the nation: "What we need from our fellow Americans is good will, encouragement, understanding and assistance. Having accepted the will of the nation's majority, Mississippi now asks those who have criticized our former position and actions to 'get off our back and get on our side.' "[135] As well as asking the rest of the union for its patience, Governor Johnson also strove to promote a positive atmosphere within Mississippi in the hope that the transitions that the state's leadership and general white citizens had to endure could be made easier. On March 22, speaking before the annual conference of the Southern Association of Chamber of Commerce Executives, Johnson pledged that he, as governor, was going "to launch a ship of hope in troubled waters" and encouraged the audience: "Along with undesirable change comes desirable change. The former we have to endure; the latter we can facilitate to our advantage."[136]

Taking its cue from Governor Johnson's renewed resolve, the Sovereignty Commission also began to initiate its new public relations programs to project the state's favorable image, though in the end most of them were not adopted by the governor's office due mainly to their extravagant cost and Johnson's personal wish to keep the state agency in low profile. The day after the members of the United States Commission on Civil Rights gathered in Jackson, Johnston sent a memorandum to the governor's office and inquired if the governor would be interested in holding "a series of Mississippi press conferences" in some northern cities, suggesting that the state's prospective representatives to these conferences include Johnson, Attorney General Patterson, and even Mississippi's Miss Hospitality "as a greeter."[137] Johnston flew to Houston, Texas, late in the same month for a speaking engagement at Will Rice College at the invitation of the school's Speaker Committee. During this first out-of-state speaking engagement sponsored by the Sovereignty Commission since its speakers bureau became defunct in the middle of 1963, Johnston explained to the college's students and faculty members how his state had been struggling to deal with its difficult times while showing them the film *Oxford, U.S.A.*, which depicted the "savagery" of federal marshals in handling the 1962 Ole Miss riots.[138]

A week after his appearance at Will Rice, Johnston notified the governor's office of his decision to withdraw the film from future circulation "because the narration accompanying it is somewhat defiant and is out of step with Governor Johnson's 'new image' policies."[139] Johnston's subsequent proposal to make a new twenty-five-minute film, which would have been a "progressive version" of the Commission's 1960 propaganda movie entitled *Message from Mississippi*, went unanswered by the governor's office.[140] In place of his earlier proposal to hold "a series of Mississippi press conferences" in the North, the Commission director then recommended to the governor's office in late April that Johnson and other state officials consider participating in what he termed a "progress panel" in several northern cities.[141] In order to determine the effectiveness of this "progress panel" proposal, Johnston wrote to the *Kansas City Star* to see if its editors were interested in hearing Mississippi's new message. After their positive response, Johnston boarded a state-owned plane to take what he later termed "a pilot trip" to Kansas City, Missouri, on April 29 for an interview with the *Star*.[142] At the conclusion of the four-hour interview, where the Commission official presented "Mississippi as it actually is, and not as many liberal 'visitors' to the state view it in a biased fashion," Johnston compared his state's contemporary leaders and two Confederate leaders during the Civil War. "Some people consider Gen. Robert E. Lee and Jefferson Davis traitors to the Confederacy," he told the

Star, "[b]ut I feel that these two men knew when to stop destroying and start rebuilding [their beloved South]."[143]

While testing the validity of his new publicity schemes, Johnston gave considerable thought to launching what he called the BIG (Business, Industry, and Government) program:

> [T]he grand idea was that we could turn the Sovereignty Commission into a big public relations agency, with this money [funds donated by the state's business and industrial organizations] matching state money, in order to try to project Mississippi, outside the state, as a good place to be, as a good place to work, [and] as a good place to settle down. . . . [O]f course, we recognized that one civil rights[-related] murder was worse than a hundred blacks getting Ph.D. degrees. . . . But the idea was that we could try as much as we could to overcome the attitude outside Mississippi that we were a lawless state as far as race was concerned.[144]

The main features of the BIG program took shape in May 1965 when Johnston was appointed to the Public Relations Committee of the Mississippi Economic Council, though the program was never implemented. According to Johnston's proposal, the goal of BIG's grand public relations project was to coordinate "time, talent, and funds of state government, business and industrial groups" for the purpose of promoting "Mississippi's image," with the proposed participants including the Mississippi Economic Council, the Mississippi Manufacturers Association, the Mississippi Retailer's Association, the Mississippi Bankers Association, and the Sovereignty Commission. The estimated budget for the first three-year period of the program was $300,000, which would have been "shared by government, business and industry."[145]

In the course of developing the BIG program, Johnston gradually came to realize that the very state agency for which he had been serving was one of the prime contributors to projecting "a very questionable image" of Mississippi, because the word "Sovereignty" implied a "distasteful connotation of planned disobedience to the federal government" both at home and in the eyes of the nation.[146] "I must admit," the director wrote in his May 25 memorandum to the governor, reporting on a meeting with the state's business groups, "[that] it has not been easy convincing some of the business leaders that the Sovereignty Commission is not a super snooping agency trying to crack down on any Negro who raises his hand." "Sometimes it seems at these meetings that the image of the Sovereignty Commission must be clarified before the image of Mississippi can be discussed," Johnston lamented.[147] Shortly after that, as part of his BIG projects, Johnston officially suggested to the governor's office that the name of his agency be changed to the "Mississippi Public Relations Commission" or "any other identity deemed appropriate" because "[o]ur work in the Sovereignty Commission is shifting more and more into public relations.""[S]ince Governor Johnson has brought about a change of [Mississippi's] image," Johnston further reasoned, "it would . . . seem that a new name for the state agency would be in order." "We believe a better job could be done under a public relations title instead of under the name 'Sovereignty Commission,' " the director concluded.[148] About six months later, after the 1965 Voting Rights Act became law, Johnston once again recommended that "consideration be given to changing the name of the Sovereignty Commission to something like Mississippi Information Agency, or Mississippi Public Relations Commission, or a title similar." While asserting that the original purpose of the Sovereignty Commission had been greatly affected by the 1964 Civil Rights Act and the Voting Rights Act, Johnston reminded the governor, the Commission members, and the state legislators that the "only state agency which can continue an effective campaign against further federal encroachment" was the attorney general's office.[149] The director then turned to a Commission member, Senator DeCell, for help in drafting a bill to create the Mississippi Information Agency in place of the Sovereignty Commission and asked the senator to introduce the bill in the 1966 state legislature. One of the bill's provisions stated that the expected purpose of the new state agency "shall be . . . to engage in a general program of emphasizing Mississippi's assets through news media, pamphlets, special programs, or any other method determined by the agency . . . [and] to refute distortions or falsehoods written or told about Mississippi."[150]

Thus, while the Sovereignty Commission was not fully constituted organizationally during the first two years of Governor Johnson's administration, the state agency's functions underwent some shifts in the middle of the 1960s. It is somewhat ironic to note that while it continued to keep its watchful eyes on the state's civil rights activities—and after considerable white-perpetrated violence and even the murders of the civil rights workers in Neshoba County—the Mississippi "watchdog" began to realize the importance of a nonviolent accommodation to the new reality of the times and struggled to promote moderation and positive acceptance of change among the state's officials as well as its white citizenry. This, to be sure, did not indicate that the Commission was converted to a promoter of the advancement of black civil rights in the state. But its transformation was nevertheless an important occurrence for the state agency that was originally intended to defend white supremacy at all costs and to propagate the doctrine of states' rights. At the same time, having joined Governor Johnson in his conciliatory posture, Commission Director Johnston increasingly became another butt of criticism leveled by the state's die-hard segregationists, whose "feelings run deep and blood runs hot."

Chapter 6

OFFICIALLY BUT DISCREETLY

Dealing with Unreconstructed Forces

Having been influenced by Governor Paul Johnson's moderation and having realized, though reluctantly, that Mississippi would face inevitable change in its race relations sooner or later, Sovereignty Commission Director Erle Johnston set out to calm the state's troubled waters in the spring of 1964 while he dutifully kept his watchful eyes on the activities of the Council of Federated Organizations (COFO). On May 13, speaking before the Canton Rotary Club in Madison County, the director told his audience that the Sovereignty Commission had to bear the responsibility as the state's "troubleshooting" agency. "Many times when a situation [racial trouble] arises in a community, there are sound thinking people who know what should be done to ease their particular situation and to avoid something far worse," Johnston explained, "yet they hesitate to speak their mind through fear that a friend or neighbor would point a finger and accuse them of showing weakness in our overall efforts to preserve . . . our system of racial separation." "In such cases," he continued to reveal his agency's new function, "the Sovereignty Commission becomes the third party [and] make[s] our recommendation [to the community]." The director further elaborated that his agency's recommendation should not be based on "what extremists might think or what liberals might think" but should follow "only one formula": "Does it make sense, and does it have a chance of accomplishing something" that would improve the race relations in those particular communities? Johnston also warned the club members not to become affiliated with "any secret organization which might have well[-]meaning motives, but could get out of hand under emotional leadership" in the face of "the anticipated summer invasion." "If you are approached by a representative from any of these new undercover groups," he went on, "it is our recommendation that you politely decline and re-affirm your determination to cooperate with those legally constituted to enforce the law."[1]

Two weeks later, Johnston made another speech to the same effect before the Rotary Club in Tylertown, Walthall County, which was followed by his address delivered to the Mississippi Economic Council meeting held at the Robert E. Lee Hotel in Jackson on June 4.[2] In the latter address, whose speech draft bore the words "ABSOLUTELY RESTRICTED, NOT FOR PUBLICITY," the Commission director reminded the state's business leaders that "Mississippi's ability to maintain law and order will face its greatest challenge" during the approaching summer, for many "well-meaning, but misguided adults and students" from other sections of the nation were expected to "invade the state." While expressing confidence that "all of our peace officers will conduct themselves . . . with dignity in meeting the challenge of this invasion," Johnston cautioned the audience that Mississippi had its "citizens who ally themselves with secret undercover groups and may attempt to take the law into their own hands." "We have been very much disturbed with reports of some of the activities of these groups," the director concluded, "[and such] [o]rganizations . . . can do Mississippi great harm this summer."[3] Just seventeen days after this warning, Klan members took the law into their bloody hands in Neshoba County, and Michael Schwerner, Andrew Goodman, and James Chaney went on their last journey.

In the meantime, on June 19 the *Jackson Daily News*, under the byline of Associated Press reporter Ed McCusker, inadvertently quoted Johnston as having urged Mississippians to "steer clear of such groups as the Ku Klux Klan and Americans for the Preservation of the White Race," though Johnston had intentionally avoided naming these white supremacist organizations in his speeches. The day after McCusker's article appeared, Rowland N. Scott, president of the national chapter of the Americans for the Preservation of the White Race (APWR), and James M. Williams, who chaired the organization's Natchez chapter, sent a harsh protest letter to the Commission director. "[B]efore issuing derogatory remarks about AMERICANS FOR THE PRESERVATION OF THE WHITE RACE, INC., to a biased and unfriendly press," the two APWR officials admonished Johnston, "we believe you should become more familiar with the Charter and the purpose of this organization so that you will know then whereof you speak." "[I]t does seem that any organization dedicated as ours . . . should not be labeled as extremists or trouble makers, as you are so thoughtlessly doing," Scott and Williams concluded their letter, which was written just two days before the brutal murders in Neshoba County.[4] Thereafter, though Johnston began to refrain from mentioning the state's "secret undercover groups" in his subsequent speeches, the APWR would soon become a major quarry of the Sovereignty Commission's investigative activities.

The first organizational meeting of the APWR was held in the garage of a Conoco service station in Natchez, Adams County, on May 13, 1963, attended by nine white Natchez residents, including Scott.[5] It was then chartered by the state on June 25, 1963—exactly two weeks after the cold-blooded assassination of Medgar Evers, field secretary of the state NAACP—by Governor Ross Barnett through the office of Secretary of State Heber Ladner. Barnett soon became one of the most popular and frequent speakers before the organization's chapter meetings.[6] In 1964 and 1965 the intensity of the state's Klan activities, particularly those of the White Knights of the Ku Klux Klan of Mississippi, reached its peak, but when these Klan organizations gradually came under the scrutiny of the federal government, many in the Klan eventually turned to the APWR as their "shell organization" to continue their unsavory works. By the spring of 1968, the state's Ku Klux Klan had "taken firm control of most chapters of APWR in Mississippi" and started to use the organization "as an adjunct of the Klan."[7] In July 1965, for example, when the APWR held a "Conservative Rally" on the steps of the Rankin County courthouse in Brandon, flyers prepared by the United Klans of America and entitled "A Message from the Invisible Empire" were passed out. Distributed along with these flyers were handbills inviting the county's white residents to attend a movie night, where *The Birth of a Nation* was to be shown.[8] Meanwhile, in an article entitled "What We Stand For," which was printed in its organizational magazine, the APWR asserted: "We do not hate the negro, nor do we bear him any ill-will. We endorse the preservation of the negro race, as well as the white race, *separate* and *distinct*, THE WAY GOD MADE THEM! . . . Race-mixing is race murder, because it destroys both races."[9] By comparison with this seem-ingly suave propaganda, an APWR flyer soliciting new members abundantly revealed the organization's viciousness. Entitled "The Only Reason You Are White Is because Your Ancestors Believed In and Practiced Segregation," the flyer read: "Brother, if you are proud to be a member of the white race then join your friends and stand up and be counted, the Day of Reckoning is at hand. . . . Let[']s not let a crowd of screaming Negro[e]s beat us in this fight." "Come Join Us," it urged prospective members, "In This Crusade To Win."[10]

In fact, by the late spring of 1964, Johnston had become "increasingly concerned" about "reports of secret organizational meetings of white people" in Mississippi, "whose mission apparently is to take laws into their own hands." In a "special report" submitted to Governor Johnson on May 1, the director named two particular organizations—the APWR and the White Knights of the Ku Klux Klan of Mississippi. When the APWR organized a Hinds County chapter in Jackson and a Rankin County chapter in Brandon in late April, Johnston secretly sent Investigator Andy Hopkins to the orga-nizational meetings "to learn the identity of leaders in these local chapters" while instructing another Commission investigator, Virgil Downing, to "de-termine what kind of" meetings these were and "what organizations were involved in" these meetings.[11]

During the "long, hot summer," when Allen Dulles visited the Commis-sion director as President Lyndon Johnson's emissary on June 24, the former CIA director expressed his apprehension about the activities of the APWR in southwest Mississippi as well as those of the Ku Klux Klan in the state. Johnston informed Dulles that the Sovereignty Commission maintained "a few files on both of these organizations and some of their literature" but that the state agency "had no . . . policies toward these groups so long as the groups and their members observed Governor Johnson's policies of law and order."[12] However, contrary to its officials' statements that their organization would not "take any part in demonstrations" and "provoke any type of incidents," the APWR had in truth begun to lead demonstrations, stage economic boycotts, and take some coercive measures in the state by the early summer of 1964.[13] It did not take long for the Commission director to realize that the APWR, along with the state's Klan organizations, was not ready to "observe Governor Johnson's policies of law and order." Within a month after consulting with Dulles, Johnston was put in a position that would inevitably lead the director into confrontations with the white supremacist group.

In July, while anticipating the federal court–ordered public school desegregation in their community, the white business leaders in the rural town of Carthage were restless. Located fifty miles northeast of Jackson, Carthage had a population of twenty-four hundred in 1960. The town was also the county seat of Leake County, where Governor Barnett was born and raised. Shortly after Federal District Judge Sidney Mize ordered on July 7 that three Mississippi school districts, including the one in Carthage, be racially desegregated beginning in September, the APWR set out to plan an economic boycott against the town's white business establishments that were considered to be "too soft" in dealing with the "racial agitation" in their community. Some businesses, such as the Pepsi-Cola Bottling Company, were given "ultimatums" by the local APWR chapter. On July 24, the Commission director had a visit from three representatives of Carthage—J. M. Speed, mayor pro tempore; J. E. Smith, attorney for the town's school board; and George H. Keith, editor of the weekly *Carthaginian*—at his office in Jackson. "These gentlemen were very concerned," Johnston wrote in a memorandum, "about an attempt being made by APWR to instigate a boycott and divide the community at a time when the white residents should be united to face a real crisis this fall." At the end of the meeting, the Carthage delegates asked the director to recommend how they could possibly avoid the APWR boycott. As a result, another meeting was set for the evening of July 31 in Carthage.[14]

The day before the three representatives first conferred with Johnston, the Commission director sent a memorandum to Herman Glazier at Governor Johnson's office to express his apprehension, informing the governor's chief administrative assistant that "it may become necessary [for the Sovereignty Commission] to have an official policy on whether to become more directly involved" in local affairs in the state's communities that had been "infested by APWR." "[A]t a time when all the white people should be pulling together to face the crisis scheduled for the opening of school in the fall,"

Johnston observed, "APWR in Carthage . . . has stirred whites against whites and threaten[ed] boycott programs which would only punish innocent people." "We must be advised by the Governor if we should discourage APWR officially or discreetly or whether we . . . should refrain from any APWR controversies and by inference give them passive approval," the director asked, "[and] [w]e would like very much, if you can, to meet with us and discuss this APWR situation with the delegation from Carthage." Though Governor Johnson did not send Glazier to the July 24 meeting between Johnston and the Carthage representatives, he gave his tacit approval to the Commission director to discourage the APWR activities "officially" but "discreetly."[15]

A week later Johnston visited Carthage to make his recommendation to some fifty business and professional leaders in the town. "In view of the many crises now facing Mississippi, especially in Leake County where the federal courts have ordered school desegregation," the Commission director began his talk before the gathered white leaders, "it is more important than ever that we face these situations with a united determination that we will not allow emotionalism and radical thinking to interfere with judgement." While offering the Commission's recommendation to the business leaders "that if or when you are approached" by any organization that would resort to an economic boycott for the advancement of its cause, "you courteously but firmly declare your intention of continuing the operation of your business just as you have done in the past," Johnston made it clear that he was "perfectly willing to be the third party in this situation" to bring about an amicable solution. Then, without mentioning the APWR by name, the director criticized the white supremacist organization: "We are certainly in sympathy with the motives of any group which dedicates itself to opposing outside pressures and ultra-liberal policies that conflict with our own conservative viewpoints. Nevertheless, the thinking leadership of our cities and communities cannot ignore any group which in attempting to carry our its motives adopts a program that results in fear, hysteria or suspicious finger pointing."[16]

Three days after Johnston's visit to Carthage, the town's business group advised the Commission director that his recommendation was unanimously adopted, and it decided to print copies of the Johnston's recommendation and distribute them to each merchant in the town "to be used for reference or display."[17] However, no sooner had Johnston proudly written in a memo-randum that the attempted boycott in Carthage had been "nipped in the bud" than the APWR went after him.[18] Only a week after the Carthage leaders notified the Commission director that they would follow his recom-mendation, a meeting was held by the local chapter of the APWR. At the meeting, which was attended by Arcine Dick of Summit, Pike County, the state president of the white supremacist group, the APWR's Carthage chap-ter announced its "launching of a letter writing campaign" to Governor Johnson, "requesting that the present Director of the Sovereignty Commis-sion be dismissed and that he be replaced by the former director, Albert Jones." Some one hundred mimeographed letters, which had already been addressed to the governor, were distributed at the meeting. Each attendee was asked to sign the letter and send it to the governor's office immediately. Advised by some Carthage residents, Johnston soon learned about this APWR-initiated campaign against him, and in forwarding a memorandum to Glazier on August 24, the director warned the governor's office that it would be bombarded with the protest letters.[19] The mimeographed letters, which began to arrive at Johnson's office on August 21 and continued to pour into the office until late September 1964, read as follows:

> August 1964
> Honorable Governor Johnson:
> As a qualified voter and interested citizen of the sovereign state of Missis-sippi, I am very concerned about the public behavior of the leaders of the State Government.
> I am referring to the leader of our State Sovereignty Commission, Mr. Earl [*sic*] Johnston.
> The purpose of this letter is to request the dismissal of Mr. Johnston from this post because of his liberal views and recent public statement condemning the Americans for the Preservation of the White Race, Inc., which is a fine law-abiding organization chartered by the State of Mississippi.
> Careful consideration of Mr. Albert Jones for reappointment to this impor-tant position will be appreciated.
> Respectfully[20]

Approximately two hundred letters, all mimeographed with different sig-natures, eventually arrived at Johnson's office. After saving some, Glazier threw the rest into a wastebasket.[21] While the APWR protest letters were still being mailed to the governor's office, Scott wrote to Johnston to ask for a meeting with the Commission director and Governor Johnson. "I am continually getting rumors," the APWR's national president brusquely began his September 2 letter, "that you are fighting our organization." The director, in turn, wrote back a curt reply: "You said you have heard rumors and so have we." "Perhaps," Johnston suggested, "we could get together and straighten out rumors on both sides."[22] Accordingly, accompanied by both his attorney and Ray Owens of Jackson, who served as president of the Hinds County chapter of the APWR, Scott came to see Johnston on September 11 to "bring about amicable relations" between his organization and the state agency.[23]

At the conclusion of the meeting, part of which Glazier attended, Scott invited Johnston to give a talk before an APWR chapter. While implying that he would be willing to meet with the white supremacist group's board of directors, the Commission director politely declined the offer. Shortly afterward, Scott then invited Johnston to confer with his "headquarters staff" in Brookhaven on a Friday evening. "I mentioned at our meeting," the director replied properly but heartlessly, "that I attend all of the Forest High School football games on Friday nights." Thereafter, the Commission director and the president of the APWR exchanged some correspondence regarding Scott's request that Johnston contribute a statement that the APWR hoped to include in the first issue of its periodical entitled *American Patriot*. A series of Johnston's excuses ensued, and his statement never appeared in the periodical. As far as the Sovereignty Commission's official records attest, there was no more exchange of letters between the two after the early winter of 1964, and their relations would become far from "amicable."[24]

Five months after his appearance before the Canton Rotary Club, where he publicly denounced "secret undercover groups" in Mississippi, Johnston wrote to the governor on October 12, explaining that "for the past several months, the complexion of the Sovereignty Commission has been changed from 'watch dog' to 'trouble shooter.'" Though acknowledging that "the Commission originally was created to help preserve complete segregation" in the state, the Commission director admitted to Johnson that "the label of 'watch dog' is somehow moot" for "we have now experienced desegregation of some facilities in Mississippi."[25] Two months later, just a week after a shock wave ran through the state over the arrests of twenty-one suspects in the Neshoba County murder case, including the county sheriff and deputy sheriff, the Commission director stood before an assembly of Mississippi's sheriffs and deputies. In his speech to the Mississippi Sheriff's Association on December 12, Johnston stated that Mississippi was in "a period of transition . . . whether we like it or not." Emphasizing that Mississippians could not move forward by "longing futilely for yesterday," the director went on: "It behooves all of us to work together in salvaging a progressive future in spite of our adversities. We can disagree without being destructive, but we cannot go forward by backing up."[26] Recognizing that some state officials, including Governor Johnson, had been "under attack because nothing has been done to prevent or avoid desegregation" in the state, Johnston then told the law enforcement officers, as if to vent some of his frustration: "[I]f any person has a magic formula for returning Mississippi to the status of the past . . . we will gladly engage his services. He will have a red carpet welcome in the new capitol building and be assigned to the biggest chair and the biggest desk."[27] Thus, Johnston's speech, though it was short, indicated an important turning point in the history of the Sovereignty Commission. The Commission director unequivocally let it be known that his state agency could no longer properly perform its originally intended duties as Mississippi's "segregation watchdog." Thereafter, in addressing the state's youth, business organizations, and church-related gatherings, the Commission director's revamped theme persisted.

Into the fall and winter of 1964 the Sovereignty Commission continued to keep its eyes on the activities of APWR members, whom Hopkins once described as "rabble-rousing, trouble-making, undesirable individuals."[28] On November 16, when an APWR meeting was held in Freeny, Leake County, Johnston dispatched at least two informants to the meeting to determine "if there was any criticism" among the meeting's attendees directed at Governor Johnson's law-and-order policies. Johnston later noted in a memorandum immediately forwarded to the governor's office that "several men [at the meeting] made derogatory remarks about the Director of the Sovereignty Commission because the Director [had] 'offered to cooperate with Allen Dulles in exposing the membership of APWR and other groups.' "[29] The informants also reported to Johnston that one of the principal speakers at the meeting "declared it was time to 'clean house in Mississippi, including Governor, the senators and the congressmen [from Mississippi].' "[30]

The speakers on the program at this particular meeting included Elmore D. Greaves, editor of the *Southern Review* published in Jackson. A native of the capital city who had attended Millsaps College and then the University of Mississippi, Greaves was a Madison County cotton and cattle farmer by profession and also served as president of a segregationist conservative group called the Association of Christian Conservatives.[31] Since its beginning in late September 1964, the *Southern Review*, whose masthead proclaimed it to be "A Journal of Conservatives," had espoused reactionary ideas and encouraged its readers "to form . . . a climate of opinion favorable to maintaining White Christian civilization."[32] Through Greaves as the conduit, a close relationship was soon forged between the *Southern Review* and the APWR.[33] In January 1965 the *Review* maintained that it had more than twenty thousand subscribers, most of whom were Mississippi residents.[34]

In the aftermath of the Freedom Summer Project and the court-ordered public school desegregation, Governor Johnson naturally became one of the most vulnerable targets of criticism leveled by the *Review*. The reactionary sentiment in the state that was often reflected in the articles appeared in the publication did not easily die down. For the readers of the *Review* as well as its editor, by the end of 1964 the governor had become a vexing state figure who "sold out" Mississippi to the federal government by allowing the State Highway Patrol to cooperate with the FBI in its investigation into the Neshoba County murders of the civil rights "agitators" and who did not "stand tall enough" to prevent the most abominable sin of race mixing in the state's public schools. In addition, Commission Director Johnston, whom the *Southern Review* once called the "Governor['s] Intelligence Chief," could not escape from being pilloried by the publication. After all, for Greaves, the fact that "the head of an important State agency which is charged with the task of protecting the State's sovereignty" had furnished Dulles "with files on conservative groups and . . . patriots" in Mississippi was an unforgivable sin.[35] In early April 1965 the publisher of the *Review*, Meredith W. Tatum, visited Johnston at the Commission office, complaining that he had heard a rumor that "the Sovereignty Commission had investigated the *Southern Review*." During the two-hour conference, the director told Tatum that "during a period when state leadership was facing many new problems and trying to work them out for the best interest of Mississippi," it was "unfortunate" that "a publication such as *Southern Review* devoted itself to nothing but attack" on Mississippi's political leaders. "At this stage," Johnston reported to the governor, "it is not possible to determine whether anything was accomplished at the meeting with Mr. Tatum."[36] The Commission director's temperate observation was an accurate estimate.

On May 1, by invitation from the Department of Journalism at the University of Mississippi, Johnston delivered a speech on the very same campus where the bloody riots had occurred in the fall of 1962. Speaking before an audience of five hundred high school students and their teachers, who had gathered for a meeting of the Mississippi Scholastic Press Association, the Sovereignty Commission director urged the youngsters "to be ready to approach" various problems that their state would encounter in the near future, "with reason and respect for law rather than with emotionalism." Reminding the audience of the simple but hard-earned fact that Mississippi could not and should not be a "closed society" any longer, Johnston added:

> When you attend college or go into businesses . . . you will make many contacts with people who live in other states. You will be asked about Mississippi. Be prepared, not to excuse our vices, but to exploit our virtues. It takes more energy and courage to promote good, than to concur in evil. A pound of good is often required to offset an ounce of evil. . . .
>
> You also are aware . . . that Mississippi is undergoing a transition period that has broken down some of our cherished traditions. . . .
>
> You will face many of the same problems we have encountered. . . . I urge you to be ready to approach these problems with reason and respect for law rather than with emotionalism.[37]

As if to bring in an indictment against himself, the Commission director concluded his remarks: "Profit by some of the mistakes made by my generation."[38] Until this May 1965 address, the governor's office had seldom bothered with the contents of the speeches delivered by the Sovereignty Commission director. But realizing the potential importance that this particular speech might bear, the governor's office, in an unusual move, made some minor corrections of the speech before Johnston finalized the draft on April 27.[39] Three days after Johnston urged the state's high school journalists to learn from "some of the mistakes" his generation had made, the concern felt by the governor's office proved right when Tom Ethridge of the *Jackson Clarion-Ledger* raised quite an uproar. Entitling his column "A Subject Puzzling to Many People," Ethridge bombarded the Commission director:

> Many people . . . are wondering about out expensive Sovereignty Commis-
> sion. It not only has failed to work for [its] objectives . . . but actually propa-
> gandizes for compliance with federal usurpation. . . .
> The Commission has been inactive as a high-priced "watchdog" over our
> sovereignty, meanwhile, the agency's "moderate" director consistently
> preaches the futility of trying to preserve state sovereignty.[40]

"In other words," the unreconstructed columnist concluded with his unre-
strained bitterness, "even if this state-fed 'watchdog' is not actually running
with the federal pack, the noises he [Johnston] makes are remarkably similar
to those em[a]nating from the Washington kennels."[41] In answering the
charge brought by Ethridge, Johnston, who was invited to speak before the
members of the Public Relations Association of Mississippi on August 24,
discussed some of the recent activities of his state agency. "As Director of
the Sovereignty Commission," he began his address, "I am fully aware of
criticisms from those who seem to think that we can wave a magic wand and
bring about a complete halt to encroachment by the federal government on
what we like to define as 'states['] rights.' " Asking the audience for their
understanding that the Commission in 1965 could no longer be the same as
"what it was at the time of its establishment" in 1956 because there had
"been new laws and federal court decisions which have had a direct effect on
Mississippi," Johnston reasserted his stand: "We are making an honest attempt to use sound judgement during this troublesome period and help
salvage the best possible future for Mississippi regardless of adversities and
setbacks."[42] Soon thereafter, the director made a few more speeches in the
same vein before such groups as the Belzoni Rotary Club in Humphreys
County and the Exchange Club in Cleveland.[43]

While dealing with some "belligerent moves" being made by the APWR
and trying to reason the state's unreconstructed forces into "salvag[ing] the
best possible future for Mississippi" rather than fighting "a rear-guard defense of yesterday," the Sovereignty Commission director also began to consider severing his agency's monetary ties with the ostensibly "nonpolitical"
Citizens' Council and to remove the segregationist die-hards from official
entrée into the state government.[44] Ever since the rift between the Commission director and the Council officials became apparent in the wake of Johnston's Grenada High School commencement address in May 1962, relations

between the director and the white supremacist organization had been neigh-
borly at best, but far from cordial. When the Commission was under the
directorship of Jones, the agency at least maintained amicable relations with
the Council and carried out a few coordinated investigative activities and
public relations programs for a while.[45] Once Johnston assumed the directorship in the spring of 1963, however, he practically cut off the Commission's
cooperation with the private organization, although its monthly financial
contributions to the Council continued. By the time Barnett left the governor's office in January 1964, the Sovereignty Commission had given an incredible sum of $169,500 to the Citizens' Council's *Forum* program, whose
expenditures were never officially accounted for to the benefactor.[46] Two
weeks after Johnson was inaugurated, the Commission director sent a memorandum to the new governor on February 6, asking whether the state agency
should "suspend payments [to the Council] as of February until such time as
the new Commission is organized and can consider future payments or
whether we should continue to give them $2,000.00 a month pending action
by the new Commission." To Johnston's disappointment, Glazier informed
him that the governor "would like everything to remain 'status quo'" for a
while.[47]

However, Johnston soon obtained a formidable legal weapon in his efforts
to terminate the agency's stipends to the *Forum* when the 1964 state legislature "tacked a rider" on the Commission's appropriation bill. To Johnston's
advantage, the lawmakers inserted a provision in the appropriation act to
defray the expenses of the Sovereignty Commission for the fiscal biennium
years of 1964 to 1966 that specified that "no funds appropriated under the
provisions of this act shall be paid to any organization . . . without a full,
detailed accounting to the State Sovereignty Commission by such organization . . . of all State funds appropriated under this act." This "full, detailed
accounting," the added provision further read, "shall be available for inspection by the Commission of Budget and Accounting and the General Legislative Investigating Committee."[48] On the strength of these new words,
Johnston issued a statement regarding the relations of his agency with the
Council, explaining that unless the Commission had "a verified list by call
letters, city and town, of every radio and television station using the [*Forum*]
series," it could not "properly evaluate [its] investment" in the program.
"Such a list has never been made available to the Commission," the state-

ment went on, "[and] [i]t is possible the series may deserve more support from the Commission, or less support, or none at all." "I have no personal feelings either way except that we should be able to have this information for an accurate analysis," the director concluded.[49] Contrary to the words embodied in this public statement, however, Johnston did have his "personal feelings" toward the fate of William Simmons's pet project. In December the State Commission of Budget and Accounting formally questioned whether the Citizens' Council had been complying with the new provision, and it subsequently asked the Sovereignty Commission to halt allocations to the *Forum* program until a proper accounting form could be prescribed for use by the white supremacist organization. Behind the scenes, Johnston helped the budget commission with creating the new accounting form as well as a report form that would oblige Simmons to list all the television and radio stations carrying the *Forum* series.[50]

On February 23, 1965, Johnston mailed the report form to Simmons, asking for the *Forum* program's "full, detailed accounting" to the Sovereignty Commission.[51] In response, Simmons submitted to the state agency a list of the states where the television and radio stations using his program's broadcast tapes were located but declined to reveal the list of the individual stations in each of those states because he believed that the "publication of such a list would serve no useful purpose." He further reasoned that the revelation of such a detailed list "would guide the hands of those organizations and individuals who favor integration by making it easy for them to put pressure on stations to drop our programs." "We feel," the Council leader continued, "an obligation to stations cooperating with us not to subject them to such pressure and harassment as we have seen happen in the past in connection with other conservative programs." "Therefore, our best judgement is simply that it would be unwise to publicize this information," Simmons concluded.[52] Budget Commission Director Earl Evans, who was a former Sovereignty Commission member as well as a one-time member of the Association of Citizens' Councils of Mississippi's state executive committee, accepted Simmons's accounting report, stating that the list submitted by the *Forum* was "satisfactory," though he made it clear that his commission had no jurisdiction over "the format of the reporting form and the details required" and that "the decision as to the sufficiency or insufficiency of all reports covering grants to outside organizations should be made by the State Sovereignty Commission."[53]

Unimpressed with Simmons's shaky reasoning, Johnston decided to seek the state attorney general's opinion as a last resort. On March 23, the Commission director visited Joe Patterson in his office and asked the attorney general: "Joe, if I write you a letter and ask you if we should continue sending the Citizens' Council that $2,000 a month, how would you reply?" Patterson, who himself was no sympathizer for the Council movement and had earlier resigned from it after the organization's opposition to his reelection in 1963, looked up at Johnston and answered: "You're going to put me on the spot, aren't you, Erle?" Then, the attorney general finally gave the reply that the Commission director long looked for: "I would have to say that this decision was made by the previous Sovereignty Commission under the previous governor, and until and unless the present Sovereignty Commission and the present governor approve continuance of it, you cut it off."[54] Just three days later, Attorney General Patterson officially announced his ruling that the Sovereignty Commission should not make any further payments to the Council's *Forum* program until and unless the full Commission authorized such contributions.[55] After December 1964, no further payments were made to the Council by the Commission. But by the time of this suspension, the state agency had channeled a total of $193,500 in state funds to the "private" and "nonpolitical" organization over a four-year period.[56] Having lost financial support from the Sovereignty Commission, the *Forum* program survived just three more years and faded away in November 1967.[57]

By the end of 1965, while receiving "highly confidential" pieces of information on the state's violence-prone white supremacist organizations from Roy K. Moore, special agent in charge at the FBI's Jackson office, Governor Johnson had begun to utilize both the State Highway Patrol and the Sovereignty Commission in order to keep abreast of the activities of the two major Klan organizations in Mississippi—the White Knights of the Ku Klux Klan of Mississippi and the United Klans of America.[58] Those who functioned as the governor's eyes and ears in the State Highway Patrol were investigators from the Bureau of Identification and even from the Livestock Theft Bureau, who came to be called "Paul Johnson's niggers" by the state's Klansmen.[59] The Sovereignty Commission investigators also kept their watchful eyes on the Klan groups in Mississippi. For a week in July 1965, for example, Johnston assigned Hopkins to ascertain if any Klan activities existed in Hinds, Madison, Neshoba, Claiborne, Jefferson, or Adams Counties. Hopkins's investigation resulted in his three-page, single-spaced typed report, where he described the "dangerous explosive" development of the intense rivalry between the two major Klan organizations over recruiting new members.[60] Just two months before he was assigned to investigate the night riders' unsavory deeds, a shot was fired into Hopkins's house in Jackson. Though neither the Jackson Police Department nor the Commission investigator could identify the perpetrator, a mimeographed piece of Klan literature entitled the "Klan Ledger" was found in the Hopkins's yard. "If the Klan is of the opinion that they can change my mind about [its activities] by firing a few bullets into my home," the Commission investigator adamantly wrote in his report on this incident, "they are likely to waste many bullets."[61]

In the wake of the FBI's involvement in the search for the three civil rights workers in Neshoba County, Johnston's name was added to the bureau's investigative dossiers as an "informant." Captioned "MIBURN"—"Mississippi Burning"—by the federal agency, the dossiers included numerous investigative reports on the Neshoba County murders prepared by more than 250 agents. The FBI's first internal memorandum pertaining to Johnston indicated that the Commission director furnished a special agent from the bureau with information on Robert M. Shelton, imperial wizard of the United Klans of America, on June 25, 1964—the day after he conferred Dulles. Thereafter, Johnston's name continued to appear in a dozen of memorandums prepared by the FBI's Jackson office until he terminated his employment as director of the Sovereignty Commission in 1968. In notifying J. Edgar Hoover that the Johnston case "is being closed by the Jackson Office," a special agent in charge wrote on September 5, 1968, that the Commission director "has been most cooperative with this office" in the bureau's efforts to neutralize Klan activities in Mississippi.[62]

The Sovereignty Commission's unpublicized missions against the state's unreconstructed forces led Governor Johnson to proclaim by the summer of 1966 that the state agency's investigators were "perhaps one of the greatest helps I've had" in trying to maintain law and order in Mississippi.[63] In the spring of 1967 Johnson in fact considered, though it did not materialize, increasing the number of Commission investigators.[64] Notwithstanding the governor's assessment, the Sovereignty Commission's behind-the-scenes activities in dealing with the state's white reactionaries were not known to anyone but a few insiders. Precisely because many of its missions were secret and due to its ostensive inactivity, the Commission at the beginning of the 1966 state legislature faced possible extinction.

The 1966 legislative session opened with an avowed reaffirmation by Governor Johnson of his law-and-order policies. In his state of the state address delivered on the House floor on January 5, the governor reiterated his ever strong position on the vigilante activities in Mississippi: "The lawless men, negro and white, who don't believe hell is hot[,] better get their best hold, for the lives and property of all of Mississippi's citizens will be protected at all times from the ravages of civil disorder." "Throughout this time of trial and tribulation," Johnson concluded his message to the lawmakers, "the people of Mississippi have steadfastly refused to curse darkness; rather they have lighted a candle."[65] Even the *New York Times* noted the contents of the governor's address, reporting that Johnson "won applause . . . from the traditionally segregationist State Legislature in his war on nightriders and racial violence."[66] The "traditionally segregationist State Legislature," however, was not satisfied with the Sovereignty Commission's seeming inactivity during the previous two years, and two weeks after the legislative session convened, some dissatisfied lawmakers made an issue of the continuation of the state agency. After all, Governor Johnson had never called a Commission meeting since he took office in January 1964. In addition, only eight months earlier Johnson had at long last started appointing citizen members to the Commission when on April 23, 1965, he announced the first of his three appointments, Edward J. Currie Sr. A prominent attorney in Hattiesburg, the governor's hometown, Currie had served as president of the Mississippi State Bar Association from 1963 to 1964. Following this appointment, the governor named Semmes Luckett, a Clarksdale attorney, to the agency on May 7.[67] Then, contrary to the legislature's expectation, Governor Johnson stopped short of completing his appointments and did not name his third appointee to the Commission.

On June 30, 1965, the House requested the governor to complete his last appointment to the Sovereignty Commission and to activate the state agency immediately. Reminding his colleagues that the 1964 legislature had given a handsome appropriation of $500,000 to the Commission to "arm this state with a weapon to defend our good name against malicious falsehoods of degradation and assaults," Representative Horace Harned, a Commission member appointed by Speaker Walter Sillers more than a year before, offered a resolution calling for the activation of the agency.[68] Earlier, on January 25, 1965, disgruntled by the Commission's dormancy, Harned resignedly wrote a one-sentence letter to Governor Johnson that abruptly read: "Is Mississippi going to have a Sovereignty Commission?" "Because of certain reasons which will be given at a later date," Johnson wrote back a week later to try to quell Harned's passion, "I have felt the need to delay the matter [the reorganization of the Commission] for this period of time."[69] Unimpressed with the governor's explanation, however, the Commission member finally took his resolution to the House floor. Though it did not have any legal binding force, Harned's resolution was adopted in the House by a voice vote.[70]

In early January 1966 Governor Johnson's "de-activation" of the state agency resulted in the resignation of one commissioner. In his resignation letter submitted to Lieutenant Governor Carroll Gartin, Senator Bland Hayden Campbell, an active member of the Jackson Citizens' Council, complained that "not a single meeting has been called by the chairman during the two years of his administration" and that the governor "has yet to finish making his appointments" to the Commission. "This inactivity has greatly handicapped the department," the senator aired his dissatisfaction, "and I do not wish to remain a party of its inaction."[71]

Senator Campbell's sudden resignation from the Sovereignty Commission, which occurred the day before the commencement of the 1966 legislature, immediately created a stir among the lawmakers and propelled five House members to introduce a bill—House Bill No. 180—on January 18 that would abolish the state agency. Two of those who introduced the bill—Representatives Judson A. Thigpen Jr. of Cleveland, Bolivar County, and Thomas Z. Gipson of Columbia, Marion County—had proudly listed the Citizens' Council as one of their affiliated organizations in their respective biographical data printed in the 1964–68 edition of the *Mississippi Official and Statistical Register*. In introducing the bill, Thigpen stated that the Sovereignty Commission "has been mishandled during the past two years" and "[i]ts purpose is not being carried out." Echoing his colleague, Harned later told a newspaper reporter that "there were some jobs it could have done and it should be abolished because of inactivity."[72]

No sooner had House Bill No. 180 been referred to the House Judiciary

Committee than a bill to create the Mississippi Information Agency in place of the Sovereignty Commission was introduced in the Senate by Senator Herman DeCell, a Commission member, as a result of the joint venture carried out by the senator and Director Johnston. DeCell told his colleagues that his bill would convert the Sovereignty Commission into an information agency, whose new duties would include putting out "true stories" about Mississippi. Talking to his friends and foes alike on the Senate floor that the state had been going through "a period of transition" and emphasizing that the new agency would "provide fair information" on Mississippi and would "not be a propaganda mill," the senator went on: "If we have outrageous acts by hoodlums, we will want to have accurate information put out [and] [i]t [should] not be a fact-concealing agency."[73] At the same time, refuting the criticisms leveled against Governor Johnson by some legislative members, who claimed that the governor had allowed the Sovereignty Commission to depart from its original objectives, DeCell commended Johnson for having done "an outstanding job" in "his handling of the agency."[74] Some of the state's newspapers, most of which had shown an apparent segregationist inclination by the middle of the 1960s, reacted favorably to the DeCell-Johnston proposal. William L. Chaze of the *Clarion-Ledger* wrote that the "new legislation would simply put the commission into the proper perspective." "It would shed the dogmatic sovereignty tag," Chaze contended, "and assume the technically correct name of information agency."[75]

In the meantime, on the same day Senator DeCell introduced the bill to "shed the dogmatic sovereignty tag" by establishing the new state agency, ten House members visited the Sovereignty Commission office by invitation of Director Johnston to examine the files on the agency's recent activities. Two days later the lawmakers issued a unanimous joint statement, recording that the people of Mississippi "probably will never know the great debt they owe to the Sovereignty Commission for its achievements during the past two years" and commending the director and his staff "for an outstanding job under severe handicaps." "We pledge to Mr. Johnston," the statement assured, "our support for any legislation he considers necessary to make his work more effective." Two of the five sponsors of the House bill that had been introduced earlier for the abolition of the Sovereignty Commission—Representatives Gipson and Adrian Lee of Natchez—were among those lawmakers who "pledge[d]" their renewed "support."[76] Johnston's maneuver bore fruit, and the House bill did not come out of the House Judiciary Committee. But in spite of the encouragement offered by some House members, the chances that the DeCell-sponsored Senate bill would be enacted looked dim. Shortly after the bill was referred to the Senate Judiciary Committee, an anonymous open letter entitled "To the Members of the Mississippi State Legislature" was circulated among the lawmakers. Asserting that Mississippi would still need a state-financed Sovereignty Commission for the "restoration" of the state's "sovereignty," the open letter vilified Johnston for "his lack of interest in Mississippi's crucial problem":

> Instead of abolishing this commission, it should be put under the direction of a loyal Mississippian who believes in Mississippi's constitutional right to maintain her position as a sovereign state. . . .
>
> The present Director of the Sovereignty Commission has exposed his lack of interest in Mississippi's crucial problem; the restoration of our State's sovereignty. . . .[77]

"It is not necessary to burn a good servant house because the servant occupying it reverses the order of the duties for which he was hired," the anonymous letter further castigated the Commission director, "but rather to replace the arrogant servant with one who would not betray his employer."[78] Johnston later surmised that the distributor of this letter, who only identified himself as "Mississippians for Mississippi," was "somebody in the Citizens' Council, or the Americans for [the] Preservation of the White Race." After the letter's circulation, a few lawmakers who "were really on firm ground" came by the Sovereignty Commission office and told the director that he "might as well close up [the agency] . . . and go home."[79]

On March 1, DeCell's bill was deliberated in the Senate Judiciary Committee but did not pass. It lost in committee by a vote of seven to five, with nine committee members being absent and Chairman Elson K. Collins not voting. Thus, despite the senator's plea to his colleagues that the state would need a new agency to "improve Mississippi's image [and] to get our message across to other parts of the country," the Senate killed his bill to create the Mississippi Information Agency.[80] Three months later, the Mississippi legislature approved the new appropriation of $200,000 to the controversial Sovereignty Commission for the fiscal biennium beginning on July 1, 1966. Though the lawmakers finally decided to keep the state agency, the appropriation was drastically reduced from $500,000 that was allocated to the Commission for the 1964–66 fiscal years, mainly because the agency returned an unused sum of $319,583.88 to the state treasury at the end of the first biennium of Governor Johnson's administration.[81]

The legislature's final approval of financing the Sovereignty Commission for another two-year period, to be sure, came after a heated debate in the Senate. On May 25, Senator William Burgin, chair of the Senate Appropriations Committee and a former Commission member under the James Coleman administration, quietly called up the state agency's appropriation bill, but that was "the last calm moment for the next 15 minutes" in the Senate chamber. One of the participants in the debate was Senator Campbell, who had recently resigned from the agency because of Governor Johnson's failure to call any Commission meetings in two years. "[S]hout[ing] into the microphone," the senator told his colleagues: "I am sure that many [of you] expect me to vote against the appropriation bill. But I am going to vote for the appropriation. I think the state needs a sovereignty commission, more today than any time in the history of our nation." "The overpowering issue and threat," Campbell concluded, "are the forces in this country who are working day and night to change our form of government, to destroy the sovereignty of the states."[82]

In order to force Governor Johnson to call the Sovereignty Commission into session, the Burgin-guided measure provided that "no money hereby appropriated shall be expended by this commission unless such expenditure is first approved by a majority of the commission voting at a regularly called meeting."[83] In light of this new provision, State Auditor of Public Accounts William Hampton King eventually sent a notice to Johnston that until and unless the Sovereignty Commission held a meeting and adopted its budget, he would not be able to send paychecks to the Commission staff.[84] An Associated Press writer observed on August 1 that the state agency was facing its "extinction this month" unless Governor Johnson bowed to "pressures applied by the 1966 legislature."[85] Having been deprived of other choices, the governor hurriedly completed his third appointment to the Sovereignty Commission, choosing attorney Dan Shell for the post.

Shell's appointment came only a few days before Johnson finally called the Commission into session for the very first time under his administration.[86] Between August 1966 and January 1968, Johnson could have held a total of eighteen monthly meetings of the Sovereignty Commission, but he held only nine meetings before he left the governor's office. Moreover, for the last seven months under his administration, all of the monthly meetings were canceled, and markedly, though Johnson dutifully sent one of his administrative assistants—either Glazier or William Simpson—to most of those nine meetings as his representative, the governor himself attended only a part of just one meeting held on September 13, 1966. Thereafter, he never participated in the state agency's meetings.

The first Sovereignty Commission meeting under the Johnson administration was held on August 8, 1966, in the Senate Finance Committee Room adjoining the Commission office, which was located on the fourth floor of the New Capitol Building. The governor did not attend this first meeting but was represented by Glazier. In place of Johnson, Lieutenant Governor Gartin presided over the meeting, where several journalists were allowed to be present until the executive session began. Besides the lieutenant governor, those present included Attorney General Patterson; Senator DeCell; Senator Perrin Purvis, who had filled the vacancy created by Senator Campbell; Representative Harned; Representative Joseph Moss; Representative James Francis Geoghegan, who had previously been appointed in place of Representative Kenneth Williams; and Shell. House Speaker Sillers was being hospitalized, and Luckett and Currie were both absent.[87]

Johnston gave a lengthy report on the Commission's activities for the previous two and a half years, which was then followed by his suggestion that his six-point policy statement on the agency's future activities be considered. Johnston's policy statement did not officially renounce the agency's role as Mississippi's "watchdog" over the state's segregation-integration issues, but more important, placing the state's civil rights forces and its white supremacist forces in the same category as advocates of "civil disobedience," the statement recommended that the Commission's prime functions include taming the unreconstructed forces in the state:

> The Sovereignty Commission will continue in its roles as a "watch dog"
> over subversive individuals and organizations that advocate civil disobedience;
> as a public relations agency for the state; and as an advisor to local communities on problems resulting from federal laws or court orders. . . .
>
> It shall be the policy of the Commission to respond to any appeal from a
> local government for analyses and recommendations involving problems that
> affect its citizens.[88]

On a motion offered by Senator DeCell, the members adopted Johnston's policy statement, and Glazier made it clear that the governor had earlier endorsed the Commission's new policy. They then proceeded to decide that $70,000 would be allocated to the agency's investigative activities, while $72,000 was to be spent for its public relations department. For the first time since the Commission's creation in 1956, the investigative department received almost the same amount of the budget as that appropriated for the public relations department. At the conclusion of the meeting, the members voted unanimously to reappoint Johnston officially to the directorship and retain all of the three investigators.[89]

Ten days after the Sovereignty Commission adopted its new policies, House Speaker Sillers, writing from his deathbed at the University of Mississippi Medical Center in Jackson, proposed a revision of Johnston's statement. "I think the word 'watch dog' detracts from the dignity of the Sovereignty Commission," the fading Speaker explained. Attached to his August 17 letter addressed to the Commission director was a revised policy statement, which Sillers himself had drafted in his hospital bed:

> The State Sovereignty Commission, as a public relations agency of this State, will continue to perform the duties and discharge the responsibilities required of it as set out in Chapter 365, Laws of 1956 [the act creating the Sovereignty Commission]; and will watch over subversive individuals and organizations advocating civil disobedience; and as an advisor to local communities on problems resulting from federal laws or court orders.[90]

"I think the words 'and will watch over subversive individuals and organizations advocating civil disobedience' . . . are much more appropriate and dignified," Sillers wrote in his letter, "than for the Commission to designate itself as a 'watch dog.'" "If others apply that tag to us we might bear it," the Speaker explained in conclusion.[91]

Johnston wrote back to the House Speaker two days later to let him know that the matter would be discussed at the Commission's September meeting. "I am sure your points are well taken," the director noted, "and I will have your letter in my file at the next meeting of the Commission."[92] But despite Johnston's promise, the Speaker's proposal was not brought up at the September meeting. Nor do the minutes of the subsequent Commission meetings reflect that the matter was ever discussed, for Governor Johnson and the Commission director were in accord that the state agency could no longer "continue to perform the duties and discharge the responsibilities" prescribed for it in 1956 as spelled out by Sillers.

On August 18, ten days after the first Commission meeting was held during Johnson's administration, Johnston went to the resort city of Biloxi in southern Mississippi for a speaking engagement. Addressing the state's business leaders, who were attending the annual convention of the Mississippi Association of Chamber of Commerce Executives, the Commission director emphasized that "the white leadership of each community must be willing to face and discuss the problems that arise with the full support and confidence" of their black residents. Reminding the audience that Mississippians had "endured the disciples of discord, the advocates of anarchy, the harbingers of hate, and the prejudice of the national press" while "suffer[ing] the setbacks of deplorable deeds by our own people" during the previous few years, Johnston told the business leaders that they "have continued to go forward."[93] But the "harbingers of hate" in Mississippi were still holding their sway. In the middle of September Governor Johnson enforced public school desegregation in Grenada by having the State Highway Patrol escort several black children into the white schools in the town. Prompted by this incident, the *Southern Review* ran its most vicious attack yet on the governor in its October 1 issue. In an anonymous article entitled "Portrait of a Scalawag: The Governor of Mississippi," the *Review* wrote: "To a white southerner, there can be no lower form of life than a scalawag. . . . [And] Paul B. Johnson, Jr., Governor of Mississippi in 1966 is a scalawag." The front-page article, which was accompanied by a picture of Johnson, continued to vituperate against the governor: "Thirty years ago, Governor Johnson, the scalawag, would not have been allowed to sit in the Governor's chair in Jackson and perpetrate crime after crime against his State. The 'small bands' and 'toughs' and 'dividers' he vaguely and scornfully refers to were his supporters in 1963, only 3 years ago when he was elected as a 'segregationist.' "[94]

Following the appearance of the article in the *Southern Review*, the state's unreconstructed whites began to circulate a petition for the "impeachment of Paul B. Johnson" to try to get rid of their most detestable "scalawag" in Mississippi from state government. Calling themselves the "citizens of the Sovereign Republic of Mississippi," the petitioners asked the state House to "impeach . . . the present Governor of Mississippi" for "high crimes and misdemeanors" in neglecting his "paramount duty to preserve [the] most precious of all legacies—the purity of the bloodline of our Anglo-Saxon Race."[95] Johnston, having obtained a copy of the petition, had his investigators determine that the ringleader of this petition drive was Gordon A. Grogan, president of the APWR's Hinds County chapter and owner of a seat cover shop in Jackson.[96]

In the late fall of 1966, when Mississippi's die-hard segregationists were refusing to go away gently, it became apparent that the Sovereignty Commission was troubled with immanent discord among its own members over the scope of the agency's expected activities. The early indication of these splits surfaced at the Commission's October meeting, where two members let it be known that they disapproved of the agency's public relations programs to promote "Mississippi's image." On October 11, to the surprise of some Commission members, Harned and Luckett, both of whom had had ill feelings toward Johnston's BIG program since the summer of 1965, expressed their belief that the Sovereignty Commission should not engage in public relations projects at all and should instead "confine its policies and activities to the protection of state sovereignty."[97] Recalling the meeting, Harned reminisced years later: "I still believe we should have fought on constitutional grounds to the last ditch." "I felt it [the Commission's engagement in public relations activities] was a cop-out for those who were weak sisters," he added with chagrin, "and [the Commission] did not have the heart to stand [up] and fight."[98] Though the Commission minutes read that "there was no further discussion of this subject" at its October meeting, the matter would soon resurface in early 1967.[99]

At the February 14 Commission meeting, the "image" schemes once again became the butt of criticism leveled by Currie, who questioned the authority of the Sovereignty Commission to engage in public relations activities, citing the 1956 statute defining the duties of the state agency.[100] The question was resolved with a written opinion from Attorney General Patterson, who asserted that the statute did constitute such authority.[101]

The disagreements that came to the fore among the Commission members over the agency's proper roles were not confined to its public relations programs. At the Commission meeting on June 13, 1967, Johnston was sharply vilified by several members because of his recent involvement in soothing a community friction that had occurred between local white officials and black residents in Natchez. Earlier, Mayor John J. Nosser of the city had written to the director and asked for the Commission's "immediate council and help" concerning "a serious existing situation" in Natchez, which was in the midst of an effective economic boycott being staged against the city's white merchants by the local black residents. Several issues were at stake in the boycott, but the primary point of contention revolved around the black residents' dissatisfaction that no black had yet been appointed to the city's school board.[102] As a representative of the mayor and the involved white merchants, Paul Schilling, advertising manager of the daily *Natchez Democrat*, visited the Sovereignty Commission office and explained the city's plight to Johnston. In response to the appeal, the director then dispatched one of his investigators to Natchez for fact-finding. After the investigation, Johnston advised Schilling and Mayor Nosser that unless there was a resignation of a white member from the city's school board followed by the appointment of a black member, the economic boycott would most probably continue.[103]

On the day the Commission met in June, John Junkin of Natchez, the newly elected House Speaker after the death of Sillers in the fall of the previous year, and Luckett criticized Johnston for having made the recommendation to the city that a black person be placed on the school board in order to ease racial tensions. After the Speaker's tirade, which was joined by Luckett, the director told the members that if it was their wish, "they could adopt a motion prohibiting the Commission staff," including Johnston himself, "from making [further] recommendations even if requested by local governmental bodies." Representative Moss then made a motion that "hereafter if a political subdivision calls on the Sovereignty Commission for assistance," the agency's staff would "make an investigation only and report its findings to that political subdivision without recommendation" and "leave the responsibility for policy and decisions to the subdivision." Senator Purvis seconded Moss's motion, and "all members present," the meeting minutes read, "voted 'aye.' "[104] Senator DeCell, who happened to be absent from the meeting, might have voted differently. Years later, when asked his thoughts on the Sovereignty Commission's "troubleshooting" function carried out by Johnston, Harned, who cast an affirmative vote, remarked: "Every community has its own peculiar politics, and I didn't think that, as a state agency, we ought to be getting that far into some local politics. . . . I believe in the proposition of states' rights . . . to the degree that I think that people [in respective local communities] ought to handle their own problems, as much as they can, by themselves."[105]

As for Johnston, the fact that the motion carried unanimously did not come as a complete surprise, but he believed that the motion "was foolish on its face." "Officials of a subdivision knew already about their local situation [and] [t]hey did not need a Sovereignty Commission investigation to get the facts," Johnston once reminisced, "[but] [w]hat they really needed was some guidance or recommendations in bringing about solutions."[106]

At the same June 1967 meeting, Shell questioned the director about his March 1967 speech before the Mississippi Methodist Student Movement State Conference where Johnston, while praising Governor Johnson as being "a practical realist," told the gathered youth that "some of the biggest problems in the state" had "resulted from ignorance" of law and order. A few days after this speaking engagement, Johnston forwarded a copy of his speech to Glazier. "I thought the Governor might want to have it," he wrote to the governor's assistant, "in case he gets any calls from critics."[107]

Shortly after the disruptive June 1967 meeting, while Johnston began to contemplate resigning from the state agency at the end of Johnson's term, the governor canceled the Sovereignty Commission's upcoming July and August meetings. Following these cancellations, the governor's office advised members that there would be no Commission meeting in September because of Johnson's planned attendance at the Southern Governors' Conference.[108] In late October Governor Johnson personally wrote to each member of the Sovereignty Commission, informing them that he "do[es] not contemplate any more Commission meetings this year." "Unless an emergency develops or any of you know a particular reason for calling a special meeting," the governor closed his letter, "I hope you agree with me that no further regular meetings are necessary."[109] With this, the June 1967 meeting turned out to be the last Sovereignty Commission meeting under Governor Johnson's administration.

In the summer of 1967 another hotly contested political season came around in Mississippi—the governor's election. But Mississippians, who had been accustomed to race baiting in statewide campaigns led by James Eastland, Ross Barnett, and others over the previous thirteen years, saw in this election that the violent winds of past overt segregationist appeals were gradually dying down. Among the five major contestants in the Democratic camp—John Bell Williams, William Winter, William L. Waller, James E. "Jimmy" Swan, and Barnett—only Swan and Barnett drove their campaigns with strong segregationist postures. Though none of them publicly repudiated the virtue of racial segregation and openly sought to garner black votes, the very fact that the state's segregation walls, particularly in its public school system, had already collapsed inevitably contributed to the campaign strategies and atmospheres of each candidate. Less than three months before the first Democratic primary, all major candidates appeared before a Jackson Citizens' Council gathering to participate in a question-and-answer session. The capital city's Council had submitted six questions to each candidate in advance, which were to be discussed at the session. The contents of four of these six questions ranged from the 1962 Meredith crisis and the state's public school desegregation in 1964 to the 1965 Voting Rights Act and the forthcoming 1968 presidential election. One of the two other questions dealt with Mississippi's "image," and the last question, as if to show the Council's obvious dismay, was put in this way: "Why haven't our ideals of States['] Rights and Racial Integrity been featured in this campaign as in the past?"[110] In any event, this meeting turned out to be the last "political scrutiny" conducted by the Citizens' Council in Mississippi's statewide elections.

With the first Democratic primary being imminent, the Barnett camp launched a vigorous advertising campaign, putting out a twenty-page political advertisement entitled "The Barnett Record" as a supplement to the Sunday, July 30, combined issue of the *Clarion-Ledger/Daily News*. In the advertisement, the former governor pictured himself as the only candidate who "Still Stands Firm for Segregation." "While some of the candidates in this year's election for governor have either turned liberal or are middle-of-the-roaders," it boasted, "Ross Barnett has stood firm for the principles that have been the heritage of every true and proud Southerner."[111]

The candidate who campaigned as a "sensible conservative" was Representative Williams, who had been deprived of his seniority status in the House of Representatives by the national Democratic Party for having supported Barry Goldwater, Republican nominee, during the 1964 presidential election. In waging his campaign, though he firmly stood for "constitutional government and local self-rule" and made it clear to the state's voters that their choice would be between "the liberal philosophy of surrender" espoused by some other candidates and his "sound conservative philosophy," Williams minimized any overt racial baiting.[112]

State Treasurer Winter presented to the voters his meticulously crafted blueprints for salvaging the state's "underfinanced educational system, lack of job opportunities, and inadequate highway program" and promised to make Mississippi a state that all Mississippians, both black and white, would "be proud of" and would never "have to apologize for." Though he, too, expressed his opposition to "federal encroachment into state affairs" on principle, Winter spent less time denouncing the federal government than speaking about his solutions to the state's economic and educational problems, asserting that the Mississippi voters were tired of the "arm waving and bombast that excites emotion but fails to get the job done."[113]

"The most vociferous segregationist" candidate in the 1967 gubernatorial election was Swan, a country music singer and a radio broadcaster by profession, who once proclaimed during his campaign that white Mississippians could no longer "allow [their] children to be sacrificed on the filthy, atheistic altar of integration." Declaring that he was "the ONLY candidate in the Governor's race" who had promised "to DO SOMETHING about the integration" in the state's public school system, Swan pledged that "within twelve months from the day" he took the governor's office, "his plan for FREE, private, SEGREGATED SCHOOLS for every white child in the State of Mississippi" would be "in operation."[114]

On August 8, in the first Democratic primary, the Mississippi voters gave Winter 222,001 votes to Williams's 197,778 votes. Though a political amateur, Swan nonetheless placed third with 124,316 votes, winning the hearts of the members and sympathizers of the Citizens' Council, the APWR, and the state's Klan groups. As for Barnett, in spite of his vigorous appeal, his influence among Mississippi's militant segregationists had diminished by 1967, and "Ole Ross"—the former hero of the Ole Miss affair—finished fourth with 76,053 votes.[115] Reemphasizing his conservative approach and making some covert racist appeals to the white voters this time, Williams drew widespread support from the former Swan and Barnett backers in his campaign during the second primary election, and he eventually received 371,815 votes to win the Democratic nomination on August 29, while 310,527 votes were cast for Winter.[116]

Though victorious in the second Democratic primary, Williams still needed to face the Republican candidate Rubel Phillips, who had fought for the governorship four years earlier. In campaigning for the November general election, the Republican candidate renounced his strong segregationist posture in sharp contrast with his 1963 campaign. Appearing on a statewide television program, Phillips even told the state's voters that "the white cannot keep the Negro down without paying the awesome penalty of restricting his own advancement." This dramatically revised racial stand, however, did not help Phillips in the end, and the final result in the November 7 general election was 315,318 votes for Williams to 133,379 votes for Phillips.[117]

Governor Johnson, who was unable to succeed himself as governor by constitutional limitation, unsuccessfully ran for the lieutenant governorship, and during his campaign, the breach between Johnson and the APWR became definite. On September 17, the Jackson chapter of the white supremacist organization issued a press statement labeling the governor as "a turncoat from the day of his inauguration" and asserting that Johnson "must be seeking revenge against the voters who sent him down to defeat [in the lieutenant governor's election], or else he is attempting to secure for himself a federal judgeship."[118]

After the heat of the election summer subsided, while notifying each member of the Sovereignty Commission that there would be no more Commission meetings during the remaining few months of his administration, Governor Johnson made a rare appraisal of the state agency. "Regular reports from the Commission office have been invaluable to me and to other agencies in making decisions," the governor wrote, "[and] [t]he Commission office also has been working effectively with local communities on their problems." "I have been very proud of the diligence shown by the entire staff," Johnson commented.[119] Concurring in Johnson's decision not to hold any more Commission meetings in the coming months, Senator DeCell, who had been the most sympathetic member to the agency's director, wrote back to the governor:

> I want to take this opportunity to express again my sincere appreciation for your leadership during this administration and particularly the work of the Sovereignty Commission under your direction. Unfortunately, a great deal of our work goes without public notice or acclaim but is, nevertheless, of tremendous value to the State of Mississippi. I have been especially grateful to our director and his staff for their effort. I think they have done an admirable job in working with local people in local situations.[120]

Notwithstanding these encouraging words offered by both the governor and the senator, Johnston had already announced his wish to resign from the Sovereignty Commission. "I had really lost heart," Johnston later reminisced, "and there wasn't anything [I] could do."[121] "The Sovereignty Commission was a product of the time," he recalled on a different occasion, "[and it had] certainly outlived its usefulness [by 1968 and] was ready for its grave."[122] Four months after the new administration took shape, Albioun F. Summer, a confidant of Governor Williams and a future attorney general, asked Johnston to stay on as the Sovereignty Commission's director. But the offer did not shake the director's resolve, and he officially resigned from the state agency as of July 1, 1968.[123]

Two months before Johnston left the Commission, Wilson Minor, the correspondent for the *New Orleans Times-Picayune*, observed that the "once feared undercover investigating arm of segregationists" had "quietly moved into a racial reconciliation role." "What the Sovereignty Commission has achieved behind the scenes in the last three years in helping communities come to grips with the realities of the Civil Rights Act of 1964 and in bringing racial peace," he wrote, "has gone unsung and unknown to but a few."[124] On the other hand, in reporting on the director's resignation, the *New York Times* labeled Johnston as a "shrewd engaging man," who had "quietly left" the Sovereignty Commission "after eight tempestuous years in which he helped put velvet gloves on Mississippi's two-fisted racism." However, the northern paper did not fail to note that the "shrewd engaging man" had moved the Commission "from one of the South's most notorious foes of desegregation toward a force for racial compromise."[125]

Chapter 7

THE LAST HURRAH

Cracking Down on New Subversives

The significance of the 1967 gubernatorial election was that it represented the final gasp of overtly blatant racist appeal in the history of Mississippi's statewide elections, making John Bell Williams become the last beneficiary of the state's racial "hurrah." However, once he assumed the governorship, Williams took over his predecessor's law-and-order policies. "Because our State has been the focal point of a highly emotional issue in recent years, we are being examined more critically than other states," the new governor told Mississippians in his inaugural address on January 16, 1968: "[W]e have within our society certain elements who apparently consider themselves above the law; who perpetrate cowardly crimes and atrocities under the protective cover of darkness." "I want it known here and now," Williams resolved, "that lawless violence in any form will not be tolerated, nor can the perpetrators of these crimes find comfort in this Administration." Having said that, Mississippi's fifty-fifth governor pleaded with citizens "to lend their cooperation and support toward the end that we can stand here today and declare with assurance that Mississippi [had] witnessed its last street mob, its last rebellion against lawful authority, [and] its last bombing!"[1]

Despite Erle Johnston's observation that the Sovereignty Commission had "outlived its usefulness" and "was ready for its grave" by 1968, ten days before the Commission director formally resigned from the agency, the state legislature approved an appropriation for the Commission on June 21. For the fiscal biennium beginning July 1, 1968, the Sovereignty Commission received a sum of $200,000 from the state treasury.[2]

The new ex officio members of the Commission under the Williams administration were the governor; Lieutenant Governor Charles Sullivan; House Speaker John Junkin; and Attorney General Joe Patterson. On April 24, 1969, Albioun Summer was appointed attorney general to fill the unexpired term of Patterson, who had passed away.[3] Lieutenant Governor Sullivan asked Senators Herman DeCell and Perrin Purvis to stay on the Commission, and both of them agreed to do so. Speaker Junkin also asked Representatives Joseph Moss and Horace Harned to continue to serve on the state agency and appointed Representative J. Lonnie Smith of Poplarville, Pearl River County, as a new member. In early September 1968 Moss was succeeded by Representative Betty Jane Long of Meridian, Lauderdale County. Long became the first woman to serve on the Commission and would turn out to be the only female member during the agency's entire life. In February 1970, when Harned resigned from the Commission to accept an appointment on the State Building Commission, Representative Malcolm H. Mabry Jr. of Dublin, Coahoma County, took his place.[4] "I had probably lost a little bit of my enthusiasm in the Sovereignty Commission due to the foot dragging of Governor Johnson," Harned later recollected.[5] Mabry's membership on the Commission did not last either, and in the early spring of 1971 Speaker Junkin announced his appointment of Representative DeVan Dallas of Pontotoc, Pontotoc County, to fill the vacancy created by Mabry's resignation.[6] Eight months after he took the governor's office, Williams appointed three citizen members to the state agency on August 13: attorneys Karl Kepper who was reappointed; O. J. Bori of Vicksburg, Warren County; and William H. Jolly of Columbus, Lowndes County.[7] Two weeks later, the governor announced the appointment of William Webster "W. Webb" Burke to the directorship of the Sovereignty Commission, who assumed his new post on September 1, 1968. A native of Hattiesburg, Burke had an impressive law enforcement career. After receiving his law degree from the University of Mississippi, he was appointed to head the State Highway Patrol when it was organized in 1938. Three years later, Burke left the Highway Patrol to accept an appointment as a special agent for the FBI, and after working for the federal bureau for twenty years, he retired from the service in August 1960.[8]

Under Burke, as well as employing three office personnel—a secretary, a bookkeeper/stenographer, and a research/file clerk—the Commission possessed three investigators: Leland E. "Lee" Cole Jr. of Hattiesburg, who had been appointed to the agency under Governor Johnson's administration following the death of Investigator Virgil Downing, covering the south and southwest areas of the state; Fulton Tutor, a former sheriff of Pontotoc County, covering northern Mississippi; and James Malcolm "Mack" Mohead of Clarksdale, whose law enforcement experiences included five years of service with the District of Columbia Police Department and four years at the Clarksdale Police Department, covering the Mississippi Delta region.[9] In February 1969 Cole, who had worked for the Commission as a private investigator from Risk Detectives and Tracer Agency in Hattiesburg on a contractual basis before his appointment to the state agency, resigned as a Commission investigator. He was succeeded by Edgar C. Fortenberry, a former FBI resident-agent in Hattiesburg.[10] Though Cole had impressive records as both a private and public investigator, to the Commission's great distress he turned out to be chronically in debt, and by the time Cole resigned from the agency, Burke had been troubled by a county court that served a writ of garnishment on him due to Cole's indebtedness.[11] In striking contrast with Governor Johnson, Williams dutifully held the Sovereignty Commission's monthly meetings, and he attended most of them until the last year and a half of his administration, when Administrative Assistant Herman Glazier represented the governor at the meetings.[12]

In pursuing his law-and-order policies, Williams was much more interested in the Sovereignty Commission's investigative works than in its public relations programs. The state agency's investigative concerns included "activities of subversives operating in the state, campus unrest, use of narcotics on campuses, boycotts, and other matters which tend toward destruction of state institutions and traditions."[13] Among these, the "matters pertaining to campus student disturbances and use of drugs and sale of [the] same on campuses of state operated schools" were specific concerns for both the governor and the Sovereignty Commission.[14] In search of minimizing the drug trafficking on the state's university and college campuses, the Commission cooperated with the new Narcotics Unit of the Mississippi Department of Public Safety, which was organized in late 1968 as a result of Governor Williams's "growing concern over the many instances of drug abuse" in the state.[15] While using both the Sovereignty Commission and the Narcotics Unit, Williams also created the Law Enforcement Assistance Division attached to the governor's office, and Public Safety Commissioner Giles W. Crisler gave one of the governor's administrative assistants, Kenneth W. Fairly, "the responsibility of setting up an investigative unit to deal with" the problems regarding narcotics abuses as well as student activities.[16] Unlike the practice observed under the previous administrations, the Sovereignty Commission's three investigators ordinarily attended the agency's monthly meetings and were called upon for "reports of happenings" during the previous month.[17] Along with the investigative staff, Burke energetically involved himself in the Commission's investigative works, covering areas near Jackson "in all directions."[18]

In addition, the Sovereignty Commission continued to depend upon the Day Detectives, which employed "Informant X," and it also began its dealings with Security Consultants, Inc., another private investigative agency in Jackson.[19] As a matter of fact, under the previous administration, Governor Johnson's directive to the Commission in June 1965 prohibited the state agency from "engag[ing] the services of any detective agency for any purpose" and advised that "[a]ny service being utilized at the present time must be discontinued."[20] However, the services rendered by Informant X were eventually excepted from this restriction, and Governor Johnson later approved to pay "a flat amount of $500.00 per month" to the Day Detectives for the services of Informant X.[21] Under Governor Williams's administration, the Sovereignty Commission, for instance, sent Informant X to Chicago from August 16 to August 31, 1968, to monitor the violence-stricken Democratic National Convention.[22] The Commission's use of Informant X lasted at least until May 1973 under the administration of Governor William Waller, who succeeded Williams.[23] The agency's records attests that B. F. Sullivan of Hattiesburg was one of the black informants the Commission used during Williams's tenure. Sullivan, who was identified as "Informant X-1" in the agency's investigative reports, was a member of the NAACP's Forrest County chapter and periodically reported the "Negro activities and racial matters" in the Hattiesburg area to Commission Investigator Fortenberry. Moreover, once Governor Williams took the helm of the Sovereignty Commission, it expanded its cooperative posture with other investigative arms—both state and federal—such as the State Highway Patrol, the FBI, and the Internal Revenue Service. The Commission investigators fully utilized the Highway Patrol's "sub-stations," which were located in the nine geographic regions for its patrolling operation, to receive messages and traveling schedules from Director Burke.[24]

At the same time, Williams did not even bother to appoint a public relations director for the Sovereignty Commission, and as a natural consequence, the agency's publicity department became virtually defunct. One of the manifestations of the governor's new attitude toward the Commission was reflected in the agency's decision to terminate its monthly donations to J. W. Jones of the *Community Citizen* in New Albany. "While your attitude and your published editorials have been and are genuinely appreciated . . . the Commission has determined that a change in policy is an absolute necessity," Burke wrote on November 8, 1968 to Jones, to whom the state agency had been funneling its $75-a-month contributions since November 1959 under the administration of Governor James Coleman.[25] Jones, in his seventies, had earlier reminded the Commission that "there is no Negro, in the State, who more appreciate[s] and . . . respects the rights of white neighbors" than he did. "My stand has caused some of my people to dislike me," the black editor wrote, "[b]ut I thank God that I have no remorse of conscience for any thing that I have written." It is somewhat ironic to note that while the state's originally intended "segregation watchdog"—the black editor's financial benefactor—had grudgingly realized that it could no longer "continue to perform the duties and discharge the responsibilities" prescribed for it in the middle of the 1950s, Jones never desisted from advocating the righteousness of racial separation and playing the role of an unreconstructed black Mississippian to the very end.[26] In the late fall of 1968 Burke also contacted several newspaper clipping companies with which the Commission had dealt to inform them of the agency's decision to discontinue their services after November 1, explaining that "the Sovereignty Commission has ceased its function in the area of public relations."[27] But perhaps the most telling testimony of the demise of the Sovereignty Commission's public relations department was that the disbursement columns such as "Public Relations" and "Advertising" completely disappeared from the agency's auditing reports under the Williams administration. Instead, the state auditor's reports indicate that the Commission had spent a sum of $44,040.73 for either "Private Investigations" or "Private Investigators" for the four-year period between July 1, 1968, and June 30, 1972.[28]

By the time Williams was inaugurated as governor of Mississippi, as the United States' involvement in the Vietnam War deepened, the domestic struggle to end racism and the struggles by people of color throughout the world, particularly that of the Vietnamese people against American troops, had merged together. Led by SNCC, among others, the nation's major civil rights organizations and their leaders gradually began to argue that fighting for freedom in the United States was an alternative to fighting in Vietnam. Throughout the years of his involvement in the civil rights movement, Martin Luther King Jr. had been hesitant to identify himself with the anti–Vietnam War movement, but his decisive break with the past came about in the spring of 1967. In his historic address delivered at the Riverside Church in New York City on April 4, King denounced America's involvement in the growing quagmire. Though this address was not his first public expression in opposition to the war, it was the first time that he directly attacked the war policy of President Lyndon Johnson's administration while linking the war to the civil rights cause in the United States.[29]

Reflecting the anti–Vietnam War mood prevalent throughout much of the nation and propelled by the waning House Un-American Activities Committee's report on "communist infiltration" into the antiwar movement, the fears of racial change in the South were linked to the antiwar movement–driven domestic upheavals, inviting Mississippi segregationists to make their last desperate attempt to discredit the state's civil rights struggle and its leaders.[30] As an illustration, at the request of Executive Secretary E. R. Jobe of the Board of Trustees of State Institutions of Higher Learning, the Sovereignty Commission compiled "a tremendous file of literature, policy statements, and plans" of various "Leftist Student Organizations" that opposed the nation's involvement in the war in Vietnam. The student groups included, among others, the Students for a Democratic Society (SDS) and the Southern Student Organizing Committee (SSOC), whose "pamphlets," the Commission concluded, "closely link [them] with COFO, SNCC, and some subversives."[31]

While the nation's foreign policy in Vietnam was under intense scrutiny, hundreds of black urban ghettoes across the United States were plagued by unparalleled race riots. As many northern communities were forced to reveal their long-concealed de facto segregationist practices to the nation's eyes, the advocacy of "Black Power" began spreading throughout the country. Contending that American blacks could no longer afford to believe that their political, social, and economic "liberation" would come through existing political processes, a number of black revolutionary groups sought the establishment of a separate and independent black nation in the South. One of these radical separatist organizations was the Republic of New Africa (RNA), which the Williams-led Sovereignty Commission closely watched and called the "most violence[-]prone black extremist organization ever to seek a foothold in Mississippi."[32]

The RNA was organized in Detroit, Michigan, under the leadership of Milton R. Henry and Richard B. Henry on March 31, 1968. Robert F. Williams, a native of Monroe, North Carolina, who had been an avowed advocate of armed self-defense against white violence and was then living in exile in Beijing, China, became its first president. Adopting its own "Declaration of Independence," the RNA sought to establish an independent nation within the United States, which was to be composed of the five Deep South states. From its inception, the RNA dedicated itself to black independence and the concept of systematic armed revolution, organizing a military arm known as the Black Legion.[33] In the spring of 1970 the RNA leaders decided to move their headquarters from Detroit to Mississippi, where they hoped to establish the organization's "capital." After setting up its temporary base in New Orleans, the RNA purchased eighteen acres of pastureland in Bolton, Hinds County, in February 1971. Three months later, however, the Hinds County Chancery Court issued an injunction prohibiting the RNA from holding its meetings on the land, and they eventually moved their headquarters to Jackson.[34] By then, in cooperation with several special investigators from the Alcohol, Tobacco, and Firearms Division at the Internal Revenue Service, the Sovereignty Commission had deployed at least three black informants in the central part of the state to keep abreast of the RNA.[35] Though the group claimed that it had some twenty-five hundred followers in the early 1970s, the RNA's activities were severely curtailed after the August 1971 shoot-out between its members and local police in Jackson, resulting in the death of one police officer.[36]

Enfolded by the antiwar movement and the new awakening espoused by black radicals, campus life in Mississippi could no longer be incurious of the drastic social changes in the late 1960s. In November 1967, a mimeographed underground publication entitled the *Gadfly* began to appear on the campus of Jackson State College, a traditionally all-black institution. The *Gadfly*, whose masthead proclaimed "Agitation! Stimulation! Inspiration!," was highly critical of the college administration, contending that the students at Jackson State were "victims of [a] paternalistic system," where the "patricians (administrators) spend much of their time making petty regulations to control the plebeians (students)." Disparaging the "lily-white" Board of Trustees of State Institutions of Higher Learning and revering Malcolm X as "one of the greatest of all Negro leaders," the editorial staff of the *Gadfly* made a demand for "student power."[37] Later, in 1970, President Richard M. Nixon's announcement of the invasion of Cambodia by the United States forces provoked a massive antiwar protest on the campus of Kent State University in Ohio, where the state's National Guard killed four students on May 4. Then, just ten days after the Kent State killings, a similar incident took place at Jackson State. During a student protest on May 14, some city police officers and approximately seventy-five members of the state highway patrol fired automatic weapons into Alexander Hall, a women's dormitory on the campus, killing two black students and leaving more than three hundred bullet holes in the front of the building.[38]

The campus mood at Mississippi Valley State College—formerly Mississippi Vocational College—in Itta Bena was similar to that at Jackson State. In the early spring of 1969 it came to the Sovereignty Commission's attention that a foreign student from Trinidad by the name of Wilhelm Joseph was one of the leaders of "the radical student activity" that had taken place at Mississippi Valley during the previous few months. Through Mississippi Representative Charles H. Griffin, who was Williams's former legislative assistant in Washington, the governor made an inquiry as to "whether there existed a possibility that this foreign student could be deported" from the United States. Griffin in turn asked his friend, Garner J. Cline, who was a counsel to the Subcommittee on Immigration of the House Judiciary Committee, to look into the Joseph case. But to Governor Williams's disappointment, his Washington friends found that the Trinidad student was "a bona fide nonimmigrant complying with" the Immigration and Nationality Act.[39]

Prompted by the governor's action, the Sovereignty Commission members then unanimously passed a resolution instructing Burke to ask Senator James Eastland for the "promotion of legislation which would provide deportation proceeding in any case where a foreign student is found guilty of participation in this undesirable and unlawful activity" at any tax-supported university or college. The Mississippi senator, however, could not be of much help to the Commission.[40]

As the Sovereignty Commission kept its tabs on the "outside agitator" from Trinidad, the fury of the students at Mississippi Valley, which was specifically aimed at the administration of President James White, one of the Commission's longtime accomplices since 1956, came to a head. "You are a str[an]ge animal!," a mimeographed leaflet entitled "AN OPEN LETTER FROM CONCERNED STUDENTS AT MVSC TO PRESIDENT WHITE" made a series of sweeping condemnations. Accusing their own president of being "old J. H. White, a good 'nigra,' " the students vilified White: "It seems that you are constantly reminding students that if they don't like your way of managing 'your' 'snake-infested cotton patch' then they should leave." Asking White if it had "ever occurred" to him that the president's "ideas are those of one who lived 300 years ago," that he was "petty, vindictive and without any sense of direction other than kissing the feet of whitey," and that "the best solution" to the campus unrest would be his "leaving or retiring," the open letter insisted that the student body at Mississippi Valley would "need someone who is interested in advancing the cause of Blacks." Black college administrators such as White, who had been "constantly showing his remaining teeth to whitey whenever he is around," were no longer needed in Mississippi, at least by the Mississippi Valley students.[41] In February 1970 President White even received a death threat. Indicating that "SOMEONE WILL MURDER" him if the president did not voluntarily leave the campus, the threatening letter reminded White that he had been "NOTHING BUT A WHITE MAN FLUNKY, A WHITE MAN HOUSE NIGGER." Though President White's office duly furnished the Sovereignty Commission with the students' open letter and the death threat, the agency decided not to intervene in the unrest and to remain as a mere onlooker. By then, the tide of social events had definitely turned against the Commission, and it could no longer exercise enough authority or threat to row against the stream.[42] President White, a "friend" of the Sovereignty Commission since its creation, left the college in July 1971 and was succeeded by E. A. Boy-kins.[43]

As in the case of school administrators and the members of the Board of Trustees of State Institutions of Higher Learning, the Sovereignty Commission could not escape the wrath of student radicalism either, even on the campuses at the state's traditionally all-white educational institutions. In the December 6, 1968, issue of the *Reflector*, the student paper at Mississippi State University, David P. "Pat" Coughlin wrote an article entitled "Sovereignty Commission Promotes Bigotry." "I have known for some time that the Sovereignty Commission existed for the purpose of defending the Fascist, reactionary power structure which rules the State of Mississippi," Coughlin began his article, "but I was shocked to discover the depths to which this small group stoops on . . . its masters." Denouncing the activities of the Commission and its "police state tactics," he continued to assert that the state agency had been "undoubtedly the most dangerous anti-democratic bureau in our totally reactionary state government." "The mission of the Sovereignty Commission, in brief," the article reminded its readers, "is to promote and preserve the Mississippi tradition of bigotry and reaction, while harassing and intimidating those who are outspokenly opposed to the 'official viewpoints.' "[44] A few days later, the governor's office received Coughlin's article and immediately forwarded it to the Sovereignty Commission office. Disturbed by the "very derogatory article," Burke called the campus police chief at Mississippi State to determine whether Coughlin was "the type [of] individual who could be contacted and talked to." Assured by the chief that he was, the Commission director paid a surprise visit to Coughlin at the *Reflector*'s office on December 10, accompanied by Investigator Tutor. While explaining to Coughlin the responsibilities and the current activities of the Commission "[i]n a very tactful and firm manner," Burke and Tutor extended their invitation to the young student to visit the agency's office in Jackson, assuring him of "a genuinely courteous reception at the office." In answer to Coughlin's allegation that "there is reason to believe that certain students on this campus are picking up some extra coins by acting as informants" for the Sovereignty Commission, the director insisted that "the use of individual sources of information definitely is legal and ethical." Burke later reported that "there appeared to be genuine appreciation on the part of Mr. Coughlin" in their "free discussion" on the Commission's activities.

"[B]oth Mr. Tutor and the writer felt that the visit was well worth the time and effort," the self-contented Commission director concluded.[45]

In the course of dealing with the state's "new subversives," the Sovereignty Commission finally gave shape to its long-cherished dream, initiating a "three-way" cooperative program with the sovereignty commissions in its neighboring states, which was once envisioned by former Director Johnston in early 1964. On May 4, 1968, the state sovereignty commissions of Mississippi, Louisiana, and Alabama formed the Interstate Sovereignty Commission, which was soon to be officially named the Interstate Sovereignty Association. A total of seventeen people—nine from Alabama, four from Louisiana, three from Mississippi, and one from Georgia—got together at the Monteleone Hotel in New Orleans on that spring day to organize their new group. Mississippi sent two Commission members—Purvis and Kepper—and William Simmons of the Citizens' Councils of America to the meeting. Johnston, who was then expected to resign from the Commission shortly, did not participate in this gathering.[46]

The second conference was held in Jackson in June. The minutes listed the association's eight objectives, with its main purpose being to "promote the exercise of the constitutionally guaranteed sovereignty of the individual states" by "constructive activities designed to encourage and improve the exercise of the responsibilities which such sovereignty imposes." The organization also sought to "gather and exchange information concerning high school and college campus activities" in regard with "Communistic influences, narcotics traffic, subversive activities and pornographic literature."[47] At their November meeting, Mississippi's Sovereignty Commission members unanimously decided that the third "joint meeting of all State Sovereignty Commissions or similar groups" would be held in Jackson again, where they hoped "to formulate a permanent organization" among the southern states.[48]

At the third meeting convened at the Sun and Sand Motor Hotel on February 15, 1969, Governor Williams, Director Burke, and five other Commission members represented the Mississippi agency, while Representative Harned, a former Commission member, was also present as an observer. With Burke presiding at the meeting, much discussion revolved around the federal government's school desegregation efforts such as "force[d] bussing" of students. Though the attendees from three Deep South states unanimously decided to hold another meeting in Jackson "in the near future" to fortify the association's organizational structure, the Mississippi State Sovereignty Commission's records do not reflect any further genuine intercourse among the three state sovereignty agencies.[49] In fact, soon after the association's third meeting, the Louisiana State Sovereignty Commission lost its state funding. Moreover, Executive Secretary Eli H. Howell's resignation from the Alabama State Sovereignty Commission greatly contributed to the demise of the short-lived Interstate Sovereignty Association. Howell, who had been the most energetic supporter of the interstate organization, left the Alabama agency in late 1968 to accept a position in Washington on the staff of newly elected United States Senator James B. Allen.[50]

While the Interstate Sovereignty Association was fading away, on October 29, 1969, the Supreme Court unanimously declared in *Alexander v. Holmes County Board of Education* that public school desegregation at "all deliberate speed" as allowed in the Court's 1955 *Brown II* implementation decree was "no longer constitutionally permissible." Instead, it ordered that the dual school system that had operated in Mississippi's thirty school districts had to be terminated at once. The *Alexander* decision initiated a new era of the Court's "more rigorous judicial intervention" in public school desegregation cases, declaring that every school district in Mississippi had the obligation to achieve racial "integration" in its true sense and not mere nominal "desegregation."[51]

In early January 1970, just two days before the federal court–ordered massive integration was to take effect in many Mississippi school districts, Governor Williams made a thirty-minute talk on statewide radio and television. "The moment that we have resisted for 15 years—that we have fought hopefully to avoid, or at least delay—is finally at hand," the governor explained, "[and] [w]e have reached the moment of decision." "I am frank to tell you that our arsenal of legal and legislative weapons has been exhausted," he went on. After reminding his audience that there were only three choices that Mississippi could take in the wake of the *Alexander* ruling—to accept the order, to make a last-ditch effort to defy it, or to close the state's elementary and secondary public schools altogether—Williams added: "I am strongly of the opinion that we must preserve our public school system as an absolute necessity for the good of all." "[M]ake the best of a bad situation," the governor urged white Mississippians in concluding his speech, "with God's help."[52]

With this mournful statement, Mississippi's official resistance to public school desegregation was virtually over, resulting in the flourishing movement to establish all-white "academies" in the state.[53] Two months later, the state legislature appropriated $100,000 to the Sovereignty Commission for the fiscal year beginning on July 1, 1970, for the legislature began to convene its regular sessions annually after 1970. Almost 70 percent of the appropriation—or $69,109 to be precise—was set aside for "salaries, wages and fringe benefits" for the agency's staff members.[54] The state funding to the Commission for the next fiscal year was almost similar to that of the previous year both in terms of its total amount and breakdown of expenditure. For the fiscal year beginning July 1, 1971, the state agency was given a sum of $117,000, with approximately 70 percent of the total spent for "personal services" rendered by the Commission's personnel.[55]

One of the waning Sovereignty Commission's final plays, which featured its distrust of the unknown, came about in the early summer of 1971 when it was involved in the state's efforts to block the opening of a widely publicized rock festival. The concert, billed as "A Celebration of Life," was to be held in the rural community of Oloh, Lamar County, from June 21 to June 28, with some sixty rock musicians and an expected turnout of more than six thousand. The residents of Lamar County, a primarily agricultural area with a population of eighteen thousand, were suddenly thrown into confusion over the rock 'n' roll "mod scene" that was anticipated. On June 8, at the request of the county's Board of Supervisors, Lamar County Chancery Court Judge Howard H. Patterson Jr. issued an injunction prohibiting the sponsors from holding the rock concert on the grounds that the festival "would be contrary to [the state's] interest of public health and welfare" and would be "likely to promote . . . distribution of drugs and narcotics."[56]

While building a series of legal fortresses, the state was on war footing. On the same day Judge Patterson issued the court injunction, Commission Investigator Fortenberry huddled with several officers from the 138th Transportation Battalion of the Mississippi National Guard and the United States Third Army at the guard's armory in Columbia, Marion County, to prepare for the possible invasion of the state by the "mods."[57] At the same time, the governor's office sent Chief Investigator Rex P. Armistead of the Bureau of Identification at the Department of Public Safety to New Orleans and had him hold a series of "conferences with officials of the Celebration of Life rock festival" between June 11 and June 18. For his efforts, the Sovereignty Commission later paid Armistead $198.62 at the request of Governor Williams.[58] Due partially to Armistead's persuasion, the sponsors of the rock festival eventually gave up on Lamar County as their prospective concert site, setting the Commission's mind at rest.[59]

On November 19, 1971, the last Sovereignty Commission meeting under Governor Williams's administration was held in the Senate Appropriations Committee Room. "Please try to be with us," Director Burke pleaded with the Commission members in notifying them of the final meeting, "[because] [w]e would so much like to have a good attendance."[60] Regardless of the director's plea, however, all of the four ex officio members, including Williams, were absent from this last meeting, reflecting the marked wane of interest in the state agency held by the bulk of its members and even by the governor himself.[61]

During the same month, the state's voters elected William Waller as their new governor. A highly successful trial lawyer in Jackson, Waller was a gubernatorial aspirant in the 1967 election and was a former district attorney for Hinds County who had unsuccessfully prosecuted Byron De La Beckwith on two occasions for the murder of Mississippi NAACP Field Secretary Medgar Evers. Among the seven Democratic candidates who ran in the party's first primary held in August, Lieutenant Governor Sullivan led the group with 288,219 votes, followed by Waller who received 227,424 votes. But in the second primary contested three weeks later, Waller successfully obtained the Democratic nomination over the lieutenant governor by a vote of 389,952 to 329,236. Then, in the November 2 general election, without a Republican challenge at this time, he was elected governor over two independent candidates—Charles Evers, the older brother of Medgar Evers, and Mississippi Supreme Court Justice Tom Brady. Brady, the author of *Black Monday* who garnered only 6,653 votes, passed away fifteen months after the election.[62]

As for the lieutenant governorship, there were three Democratic contenders: William Winter, a future governor; Charles Clifton "Cliff" Finch, also a future governor; and Elmore Greaves, who had edited the *Southern Review* during the 1960s. In the first Democratic primary, Winter overwhelmingly led the two other candidates, and without any challenge from the Republican or independent candidates, he thus was elected lieutenant governor.[63]

In the absence of the long-lived dominance of overt segregationist rhetoric in statewide campaigns, even the *Jackson Daily News* welcomed the 1971 gubernatorial race as a "new look."[64] Throughout his campaign, while stressing Mississippi's need for vigorous "economic development" and "efficient operation of state government," Waller asserted that the Sovereignty Commission should be abolished and that its funds ought to be redirected to a state public relations office. In late September, speaking before the Mississippi chapter of Sigma Delta Chi, a professional journalist fraternity, the Democratic hopeful pledged that if he was elected governor he would call upon the state legislature to increase the public relations staff at the governor's office "to promote the Mississippi story to the nation." In order to launch this new publicity project, Waller also suggested that "the functions of the State Sovereignty Commission be incorporated into the executive office." Commission Director Burke disagreed with Waller's idea, though he admitted that the state agency's name should be altered.[65]

On January 18, 1972, Waller started off his inauguration day by attending a special prayer service held at the First Baptist Church in Jackson. After a brief silent prayer, the sanctuary choir rendered "The Battle Hymn of the Republic," which was followed by a spirited song entitled "I'm Thankful to Be an American" sung by the youth choir. "Dixie" was not heard on that day.[66] In delivering his inaugural address, the forty-five-year-old governor pledged to materialize the "visionary operation of state government and the implementation of modern public relations concepts" under his administration. "[I]t is my goal," Waller concluded, "that Mississippi will be as popular and respected as any state at the end of these four years."[67]

No sooner had he become governor than Waller began to fulfill one of his campaign promises by naming blacks to several prominent posts in state government, thus becoming the first Mississippi governor since Reconstruction to appoint the state's black citizens to public offices. Waller's first move in this direction was his appointment of Jim Rundles from Jackson as one of his administrative assistants. Rundles, who served as a liaison between the governor's office and black communities throughout the state, eventually helped Waller name many blacks to governmental posts at such agencies as the Board of Public Welfare, the Penitentiary Board, the Mississippi Authority for Educational Television, and the newly created Bureau of Drug Enforcement. In addition, three black troopers were added to the 379-member State Highway Patrol for the first time since its formation in the late 1930s.[68]

True to his administration's slogan, "Mississippi—the State of Change," the new governor also struggled to carry out another campaign pledge. During the 1972 legislative session, Waller proposed to terminate the Sovereignty Commission and to "redirect" its state funds to a "centralized public relations" office. But his move failed, and on May 1, the legislature approved the Commission's appropriation of $113,191 for the 1973 fiscal year.[69] While refraining from appointing any new citizen members to the Commission, Waller kept pursuing his idea to create a "centralized public relations" program to function under his office. During a cabinet meeting with forty department heads in August, the governor reiterated that the new publicity office "would not only provide information for state news media" but also "seek to improve Mississippi's image in other areas of the nation."[70]

Having inherited the Sovereignty Commission halfheartedly, Governor Waller kept the agency's staff intact, with Burke as its director, three investigators, and two office clerks.[71] The new ex officio members of the Commission were the governor, Lieutenant Governor Winter, House Speaker Junkin, and Attorney General Summer. On October 20, while reappointing Representative Dallas to the state agency, Speaker Junkin named Representatives Tommy A. Horne of Meridian and Jerry Wilburn of Mantachie, Itawamba County, as the Commission's new members.[72] Contrary to what some expected, however, Waller did not follow suit. "The Governor has not indicated in any manner, or to any degree, who he will appoint, nor has he even indicated that he intends to appoint anyone," Burke revealed his unpleasantness on November 1 to Senator Purvis. In fact, Waller had earlier inquired of Burke if the Commission "could get a quorum without his appointments," indicating his unwillingness to commit himself to the state agency that, after all, he had been trying to eliminate.[73] On December 22, eleven months after he took office, Waller finally named three citizen members to the Commission, appointing Dan Martin of Brandon, Rankin County; H. Ted Lambert of Monticello, Lawrence County; and J. R. Parker of Tupelo, Lee County.[74] Lieutenant Governor Winter, another halfhearted ex officio member who was no more enthusiastic about the continuing existence of the Sovereignty Commission than was the governor, also refrained from completing his appointment to the agency until late January 1973. At Burke's suggestion, on November 8, 1972, Winter reappointed Senator Purvis, who had served the Commission under the Johnson and Williams administrations. The lieutenant governor's other choice was Senator William Chester Butler of Eupora, Webster County, who was appointed on January 19, 1973. Furthermore, Winter did not even bother to notify Secretary of State Heber Ladner of Senator Purvis's November 1972 appointment until February 1973.[75]

With the governor's and lieutenant governor's lack of interest in and enthusiasm for the Sovereignty Commission being apparent, the agency's first meeting under the Waller administration was held on November 17, 1972. Three of the four ex officio members—the governor, the lieutenant governor, and the House Speaker—were absent from the meeting. Waller sent one of his administrative assistants, Katie Barter, to the meeting, and Jesse L. White Jr., secretary of the Senate, represented Winter. Speaker Junkin had to send Frances D. Burke, office supervisor of the House, to this first meeting so that the Commission could form a quorum to approve its expenditures of the 1972–73 budget. In Waller's absence the members selected Burke to preside over the meeting, where the director advised the attendees that his office had been operating "without the necessary Commission approval of expenditures" since July 1 and explained further that he had previously been warned by the State Budget Commission "to bring to Governor Waller's attention the need for immediate action in bringing together the Sovereignty Commission."[76] For the eight-month period between November 1972 and June 1973, the Sovereignty Commission held nine meetings in total, but Governor Waller never attended any of them, and, except for the June 1973 meeting, neither did Lieutenant Governor Winter, though both of them ordinarily sent their representatives.[77] In notifying Waller of an upcoming Commission meeting, Burke once wrote: "If your busy schedule will permit, we so much would like to have you with us." "Should you not be able to make it, would you please designate a member of your Administrative Staff to represent you," the director implored, "[but] [j]ust a brief visit with us would be so very much appreciated."[78]

Though its first meeting was finally held and its fiscal year budget was belatedly approved, the Sovereignty Commission did not have much to do except for extending its officious kindness to the state's other agencies and local communities, and Director Burke himself once told a newspaper reporter that the Commission was mainly working with local law enforcement officers "on minor problems." As an example of the Commission's involvement in those "minor problems," Burke spent considerable time in late 1972 "to check into a problem that existed" at an integrated public school in Kosciusko, Attala County. The issue developed when a white female teacher was accused of having "slapped" a "Negro girl who attended the seventh grade" at the school, followed by a school boycott staged by fifty black students in protest. Shortly after this incident, Burke drove to Kosciusko to talk with the school superintendent, who happened to be the husband of the accused teacher. The superintendent assured Burke that he "would go over the situation" with the local chief of police. Burke satisfied himself with "expressions of appreciation" offered by both the superintendent and the police chief.[79]

During the 1973 legislative session, grasping the governor's idea to consolidate the state's public relations functions under his wing, Representative Glenn E. Endris of Biloxi, Harrison County, sought to abolish the Sovereignty Commission. His bill to do so was referred to the House Appropriations Committee but did not go anywhere from there. Meanwhile, on the assumption that the Sovereignty Commission's life would continue, Representatives Edgar J. Stephens and Kenneth Williams, who served as chair and vice chair of the Appropriations Committee, respectively, introduced a bill to defray the expenses for the state agency for the fiscal year of 1974, providing for a total appropriation of $118,991 to the Commission for the period from July 1, 1973, to June 30, 1974.[80] On March 12, the bill passed the House by a vote of eighty-five to twenty-eight; ten days later the Senate concurred by a vote of forty-eight to three. Among those who voted against the appropriation bill in the upper chamber was Senator DeCell, the former Commission member who had introduced legislation to create the Mississippi Information Agency in place of the Sovereignty Commission in the 1966 legislature.[81] However, when the appropriation bill reached the governor's desk, Waller vetoed it. In his April 17 veto message, the governor wrote that the Sovereignty Commission no longer "performs . . . real indispensable services to the people" of Mississippi. "Its investigative work," he explained, "can and should be done by either the Department of Public Safety or the Attorney General's Office." "This veto will add economy in State government and dispose of one State agency which is no longer needed," Waller concluded his message to the state's lawmakers.[82]

Two months later, at the Sovereignty Commission meeting held on June 7, where Governor Waller was absent and did not even bother to send his representative, Attorney General Summer informed the members that the powers and authority of the Commission were "still as strong as prior to the vetoing of the funds."[83] After the closed-door session, while expressing that "chances are good" for overriding the governor's veto in the next legislature, Summer lamented that if the Commission was abolished, Mississippi would "not have any information gathering agency for its own protection against those who would seek to undermine the state's sovereignty."[84] During the same meeting, the attorney general also reminded other Commission members that they would still be able to continue to hold meetings even though there would be no funds available for the staff and other expenses of the agency. Unimpressed by Summer's suggestion, Director Burke, who was then making $1,362 per month, let it be known that he would close down the Commission office after July 1: "I don't think we could work for six months [until the opening of the 1974 legislative session] without pay."[85] Two weeks before the planned July 1 shutdown of the Sovereignty Commission, the *Memphis Commercial Appeal* observed that Mississippi's "Ole Watchdog Is Barking for Its Life."[86]

On June 22, several Commission members met for the second time in the month, with all of the four ex officio members being absent. After reminding the members that "even though the Sovereignty Commission will be without a paid staff, it is still a lawful existing State agency," Senator Purvis made a motion to lock the Commission's official files and to turn them over to the secretary of state "for safekeeping." His motion was unanimously adopted. In his desperate attempt to keep the state agency alive, Representative Wilburn then moved that the Commission approve payment of the $212-a-month rent for its office space in the State Executive Building in downtown Jackson for the period between July 1, 1973, and January 15, 1974. This motion was also unanimously passed. At the meeting's conclusion, Senator Purvis suggested that another Commission meeting be held on November 9 and that the "reminders of the meeting be made by the Attorney General's staff."[87] Shortly after the adjournment of the closed meeting, Representative Dallas expressed his hope that the 1974 state legislature would resurrect the agency, while Wilburn criticized Governor Waller, who had left the state for a trade mission to Japan on the previous day, for his "back-door approach" to killing the Sovereignty Commission.[88]

During the 1974 legislative session, no attempt was made to override Governor Waller's veto, and at the end of the fiscal year on June 30, 1973, the Sovereignty Commission office was closed and locked, and its staff disbanded. While the howling of Mississippi's "segregation watchdog" reverberated in vain, the state's organized defiance in its public sector came to an end. Though the Commission's phone number continued to be listed in South Central Bell's Jackson phone book until 1989 by a mere oversight, the calls no longer got answered.[89]

Conclusion

TO GRAPPLE WITH THE PAST

From "Mississippi Burning" to "Mississippi Learning"

By vetoing the annual appropriation for the Sovereignty Commission in 1973 with a stroke of a pen, Governor William Waller terminated the seventeen-year-old state agency. But the 1956 act that created the Commission in the first place remained on the state's law books until the spring of 1977. After the agency closed its doors on June 30, 1973, the six cabinets of the Commission's official files were placed in the custody of Secretary of State Heber Ladner. The files were then stored in an underground vault at the state's Vital Records Center located in Flora, Madison County.[1]

However, the "old times" that the Sovereignty Commission had lived through "were not forgotten." When the 1977 state legislature convened on January 4, House Bill No. 276 was introduced, which stipulated that the Commission's official files and equipment be transferred to the State Department of Public Safety, and it was referred to the House Judiciary "A" Committee. The House committee subsequently amended the bill, providing that the files would be turned over to the Mississippi Department of Archives and History in Jackson and be sealed for fifty years. When the bill came out of the committee and was submitted to the House floor for deliberation, a heated debate ensued over the fate of the Commission documents. Offering an amendment to the bill that would authorize the secretary of state to destroy the files, Representative John Sharp Holmes Jr. of Yazoo City told his House colleagues: "The way to close the book on this chapter [of Mississippi's turbulent civil rights years] is to destroy the files." Representative Richard L. "Dick" Livingston of Pulaski, Scott County, echoed Holmes's argument, insisting that even if the Commission's records were sealed for fifty years, they would reflect dishonor upon many Mississippians when they became public. "There are a very few of us that will be living then, but most of us will have a family left behind," Livingston spoke on the House floor, "[and] [i]t's going to affect people sitting right here in this chamber." Following Livingston, Representative John Walter Brown of Natchez took the floor and asserted that the Sovereignty Commission files should be burned to "forever erase them from Mississippi."[2]

Conversely, three black lawmakers, who had just joined Robert E. Clark— the lone black lawmaker in the Mississippi legislature for eight years—in the House, voiced their opposition. Representatives Horace L. Buckley, Douglas L. Anderson, and Fred L. Banks Jr., all of whom were from Jackson, fought for the preservation of the Commission records. "I thought all the book burning and manuscript burning ended in the 12th century," said Buckley. Then, Anderson followed: "By your vote to burn those files you are, in my opinion, condemning those people you have worked along with. . . . If there is evil in those files, we should keep them to learn a lesson." "You don't put anything behind you," Banks added, "by shoving it under the rug." "The Sovereignty Commission and these records are part of the history of this state. . . . I don't think we should be about the business of destroying any of the history," Banks, a future justice of the Mississippi State Supreme Court, stated. During the effervescent debate on the House floor, Representative Horace Harned, who had served on the Sovereignty Commission under Governors Paul Johnson and John Bell Williams, defended the defunct state agency. "During that time," he contended, "the Freedom Riders and a lot of subversive groups were sending money and coming in here to disrupt our local governments." "I'm glad those days have gone," Harned concluded, "[b]ut at the time, it was a necessary service."[3] On January 27, the lower chamber passed a further amended version of House Bill No. 276 by a vote of 103 to 16 to abolish the twenty-one-year-old Sovereignty Commission and to authorize the secretary of state to destroy the agency's files "in their entirety."[4] The day after the House approved the destruction of the Commission records, the state archives' Board of Trustees adopted a resolution, pleading with the legislature to preserve the files. "This may be an unpopular or unfortunate period of history," Elbert R. Hilliard, director of the archives, offered, "but historians in the future would find these records of value in documenting the history of the 50's and early 60's."[5]

The House bill was immediately forwarded to the Senate for its consideration, where it was referred to the Senate Judiciary "B" Committee chaired by Senator Herman DeCell, a former Commission member. On February 16, former Lieutenant Governor William Winter and State Secretary Ladner visited the committee and "implored" its members to amend the House bill to prevent the destruction of the Sovereignty Commission files "in their entirety." "I feel there is too much historical value in these records to destroy them without giving historians some way to interpret this era of our history," Winter told the Senate committee, "[and destroying the files] is inconsistent with the way we do things and smacks of totalitarianism." "As a man who loves this state and loves her traditions and her history," Ladner followed Winter, "I want to prevail upon you not to burn those records." Reminding DeCell and other lawmakers that "this legislature wouldn't want to be characterized as book burners," the secretary of state went on: "It was during a traumatic period that this legislature created the commission, and . . . I implore you to preserve those records."[6] Three days later, the Senate committee concurred with the House to do away with the Sovereignty Commission but rejected the House's proposal to destroy the agency's records. Instead, the committee voted that the files would be sealed for fifty years at the state archives while prescribing fines and imprisonment for making the records public before the opening date. Following the committee's decision, on March 22 the full Senate approved turning the Commission records over to the Department of Archives and History and to seal and place them in the vault of the archives until the year of 2027 by a vote of 35 to 9. The next day, the House gave its nod to the Senate amendments by a vote of 110 to 7.[7]

On March 4, Governor Cliff Finch signed House Bill No. 276 into law, repealing the 1956 act that created the Mississippi State Sovereignty Commission and set forth its powers and duties. In addition, the newly enacted law read in part that "the files and equipment of the State Sovereignty Commission are hereby placed in the custody of the Department of Archives and History." "Said files," it further provided, "shall be immediately sealed, impounded and maintained as confidential files" until July 1, 2027.[8] In compliance with this provision, the Commission records were sealed and placed in the vault of the state archives in Jackson on March 25. A few days after his committee voted to reject the House-proposed destruction of the Sovereignty Commission files, DeCell, his voice strained with emotion, stated that he "felt neither pride nor shame in having served" on the state agency: "We made mistakes, but I think it [the Commission] helped alleviate the anxiety of a lot of our citizens. It served a useful purpose, in its day." "[B]ut [i]t has outlived its usefulness," the senator observed, "[and] [i]t is a part of history we need to put behind us."[9] To be sure, not every former Commission member was in accord with DeCell, for during the 1978 legislative session Representative Harned introduced House Bill No. 1217 for the purpose of creating the Mississippi State Commission for Constitutional Government in place of the abolished Sovereignty Commission. Though the bill was referred to the House Rules Committee, no further action was taken.[10]

As the lawmakers were struggling to grapple with the state's past, Edwin King, a former chaplain at Tougaloo College, and John Salter, a former Tougaloo professor, along with the Mississippi branch of the American Civil Liberties Union (ACLU) and others, filed a lawsuit in the United States District Court in Jackson, asking the court to issue an injunction to prohibit the state from destroying the Sovereignty Commission files and to have the records opened to the public. One of the defendants named in the lawsuit was W. Webb Burke, the last Commission director.[11] The complaint was later dismissed by District Judge Harold Cox, no sympathizer for civil rights causes who had once referred to blacks as "chimpanzees" in his own court. However, his decision was subsequently reversed by the United States Fifth Circuit Court of Appeals in New Orleans.[12]

Until Cox's retirement from the bench, little progress had been made in the lawsuit, and the case was then bequeathed from him to District Judge William H. Barbour Jr., a native of Yazoo City. Barbour, whose father used to be Senator DeCell's law partner, was a conservative Republican and one of President Ronald Reagan's appointees.[13] In late 1987 Judge Barbour was informed by the plaintiffs' counsel that there were some differences among them concerning the methods by which the Sovereignty Commission files should be opened. To resolve the disagreement and "to assure . . . adequate representation," Barbour divided the plaintiffs into two groups. The first group was designated as the "access plaintiffs," who demanded "unlimited public access to the records of the Commission"; the second group, referred to as the "privacy plaintiffs," sought "access to the records for those named in the records" but advocated "no further access by other parties without the prior consent of each person or persons described in a particular record." The "access plaintiffs" consisted of the Mississippi ACLU and others, and King and Salter became the "privacy plaintiffs."[14] By then Salter had moved to Grand Forks, North Dakota, to teach at the University of North Dakota.[15] Thus, with the plaintiffs being divided, the complexity of the case increased.

While the fate of the Sovereignty Commission's official records was at the mercy of the federal judge, Ross Barnett, who while governor had served as chair of the Commission, drew his last breath and quietly passed away at a Jackson hospital. He was eighty-nine years old. After helping to make Mississippi a major civil rights battleground under his administration, Barnett went back to private law practice, but he was always in demand for speeches throughout the state. His favorite appearance was at the famed annual Neshoba County Fair every August, where people, not only from Mississippi but from all over the nation, got together and enjoyed various kinds of entertainment, southern cooking, and political orations. The former governor would deliver a short speech there, but what really made the crowd cheer was his out-of-tune singing. When he brought out his guitar and began to sing "Are You from Dixie?," Barnett never failed in eliciting more applause than that offered to other political orators. "How many of you are from Dixie? Hold up your hands," he would ask the audience. "Friends, I love Dixie! And I know you love Dixie! And I know your friends and relatives everywhere love Dixieland!"[16] Barnett loved the South, and as the words in the song "Dixie" go, he "live[d] and die[d] in Dixie." But much more than that, he loved Mississippi and liked to brag about his native state in every speaking engagement he accepted. "No man can make you prouder to be a Mississippian than Ross Barnett," he was often told.[17] At the same time, he never desisted from reiterating the vindictiveness of his handling of the 1962 Meredith crisis until his death. "I have no regrets, no apologies," Barnett flatly answered in a newspaper interview conducted just five years before his death.[18] Ross R. Barnett Jr., who attended his father's death, later reflected: "Things change, people change, times change, and Mississippi changes, too."[19] But his own father was a marked exception. Former Governor Barnett remained and died as a proud and unreconstructed "Mississippi segregationist."

No news had been heard from Judge Barbour's chambers during 1988 regarding the Sovereignty Commission files, and another hot and steamy summer revisited Mississippi the following year. While Neshoba County was getting busy to prepare for its celebrated county fair in the early summer of 1989, a significant event in modern Mississippi history was about to take place in the county's small community of Longdale. With the twenty-fifth anniversary of the 1964 Philadelphia murders approaching, the families of the late Michael Schwerner, Andrew Goodman, and James Chaney began organizing a commemorative ceremony in Neshoba County, where the three young men were brutally slain. On June 21, a memorial service was held on the lawn outside the Mount Zion United Methodist Church, whose burning brought the three civil rights workers to Neshoba County a quarter century before. All three major national television networks—ABC, CBS, and NBC—devoted considerable broadcasting time to cover the service, and what set the tone for much of the media attention was a speech made by Mississippi Secretary of State Dick Molpus, who was born and raised in Philadelphia. Previously, during the winter of 1988, Molpus was approached by the organizing committee for the twenty-fifth commemoration of the Philadelphia murders and was asked to serve as its honorary chair.[20] A young and popular secretary of state, Molpus was told by some of his closest advisers that his involvement in the commemorative ceremony would be politically unwise. But he decided that the committee's offer would be an appropriate opportunity for both himself and his community "to apologize to the parents, siblings and spouse of Messrs. Chaney, Schwerner and Goodman."[21]

On June 21, standing before the racially mixed audience of about a thousand people, Molpus began to deliver his short speech. No sooner had he completed his welcoming remarks, which were offered "[o]n behalf of the local steering committee and the citizens of Philadelphia and Neshoba County," than the state secretary announced that he had "a special word" for the families of the late Schwerner, Goodman, and Chaney: "We deeply regret what happened here 25 years ago. We wish we could undo it. We are profoundly sorry that they are gone. We wish we could bring them back. Every decent person in Philadelphia and Neshoba County and Mississippi feels that way." Molpus then began to unleash what his community had kept to itself for twenty-five years:

> My heart is full today.
>
> It is full because I know the overwhelming majority of the people in Neshoba County are good and decent folks.
>
> It is full because this is where I was born and raised and molded into who I am.
>
> My heart is full because I know that for a long time, many of us have been searching for a way to ease the burden that this community has carried for 25 years, but we have never known quite what to do or say.
>
> But today we know one way. Today we pay tribute to those who died. We acknowledge that dark corner of our past. . . .[22]

"Listen to the words that will be said today," the secretary of state continued, addressing his remarks to the families of the three men: "But most of all, see what is around you. Draw strength and solace from it. Know that it is real. . . . Fear has waned—fear of the unknown, fear of each other—and hope abides."[23] Coming to grips with one of the most sordid events in recent Mississippi history, Molpus did what no one was sure if any white elected official in Mississippi would ever do. In response, Chaney's mother, Fannie Chaney, made a brief but profound comment. "I'm so glad," she said peacefully, "that I lived long enough to see this day come."[24]

During the same month, the headquarters of the once all-powerful Citizens' Council in Jackson closed its door. Robert Patterson, one of the pulling vehicles of the Council movement since its inception, explained the reason for its closure: "Our program was based on legality. Every law supporting segregation has been struck down by the courts. . . . We had no program left."[25] It had taken a quarter of a century for the Citizens' Council to finally realize that racial segregation was legally defenseless since the 1964 Civil Rights Act. Thereafter, by the early summer of 1990, the defunct Citizens' Councils of America had been fully "merged" with the Council of Conservative Citizens in St. Louis, Missouri, under the leadership of Gordon Lee Baum, chief executive officer of the new white conservative movement.[26]

A month after Molpus's acknowledgement of the "dark corner" of Mississippi's recent past, Federal District Judge Barbour ruled on July 27, 1989, that the public should have access to the Sovereignty Commission documents under the condition that those who were referred to in the files be entitled to add any corrective information. "[T]o leave the files closed," the judge contended, "would perpetuate the attempt of the State to escape accountability." Making a strong imputation against his native state, Barbour's opinion read:

> This Court finds that the State of Mississippi acted directly through its State Sovereignty Commission and through conspiracy with private individuals to deprive the Plaintiffs of rights protected by the Constitution to free speech and association, to personal privacy, and to lawful search and seizure, and statutes of the United States. . . .
>
> The denial of access to the Commission files perpetuates this pattern of injury. . . . The State acted unconstitutionally in compiling these files, and this [state] statute [to seal the documents] merely perpetuates the unconstitutional acts.[27]

Upon hearing Barbour's decision, Raymond Edwin "Ray" Mabus Jr., the young and reform-minded sixtieth governor of Mississippi who had graduated magna cum laude from Harvard Law School, and Mike Moore, the ambitious state attorney general who "carried no baggage from the sixties," decided that the state would not appeal the district court ruling.[28] The attorney general's announcement that Mississippi would not seek an appeal would have been the end of this twelve-year-old Commission lawsuit only if the plaintiffs had not been divided into two groups. Unsatisfied with the district court's decision, the "privacy plaintiffs"—King and Salter—immediately requested a stay of the order pending an appeal to the Fifth Circuit Court.[29]

Though the stay was granted, an odd twist of fate awaited the Sovereignty Commission documents. Earlier, on December 7, 1981, former Governor Johnson donated his family papers, which also included most of his gubernatorial records, to the William D. McCain Library and Archives at the University of Southern Mississippi in his hometown of Hattiesburg. "No formal agreement of the donation was ever made" between the Johnson family and the archives, but there apparently was an oral agreement between the Johnsons and University Archivist Claude E. Fike that "the papers of Paul B. Johnson Jr., were to be closed to the public until his death."[30] Four years later, on October 14, 1985, the former governor passed away at the age of sixty-nine.[31] While the Johnson Family Papers were still being processed by the McCain Library personnel in preparation for their future opening to the public, Leesha Cooper, a staff writer from the *Jackson Clarion-Ledger*, visited the library in early spring of 1989 and became aware that the Johnson Papers contained a large number of documents relating to the Sovereignty Commission. In response to Cooper's request to examine the Commission documents, the library's special collections director, Terry S. Latour, decided not to show the records "until access to them was [legally] clarified."[32]

Shortly thereafter, the *Clarion-Ledger* made "a formal request" to the university "to examine and copy the files of the late Governor Paul B. Johnson," part of which were specifically classified as the Sovereignty Commission records. Reluctant to grant the Jackson paper access to the Commission documents, President Aubrey Lucas of the university wrote to Attorney General Moore on April 24, asking his opinion on the matter.[33] Subsequently, on the advice of the attorney general, President Lucas became the plaintiff in a lawsuit filed in the Hinds County Chancery Court seeking a declaratory judgment on the availability of the Sovereignty Commission files included in the Johnson Papers. On July 28, just one day after Judge Barbour ordered that the Commission files at the state archives be opened, Hinds County Chancery Judge Stuart Robinson declared that the agency's records at the University of Southern Mississippi were "public records" covered by the Mississippi Public Records Act of 1983. The chancery judge further ordered that "the Plaintiff shall immediately make these records available for inspection and/or copying by the Defendant and/or its employees."[34] Thus, unknown to King and Salter, who were then in the midst of preparing their legal documents to request the stay of Judge Barbour's ruling, the Mississippi chancery court ironically declared that the Sovereignty Commission records contained in the former governor's family papers should be considered as "public records" under a state statue.

On September 14, 1990, ruling in favor of the two civil rights activists, the Fifth Circuit Court held that the district court's decision did not give adequate consideration to the privacy interest of those who were named in the Sovereignty Commission files. Judge Barbour's order was vacated and the case remanded to his court.[35] Three more years passed until Barbour held another hearing in September 1993 to determine how to protect the privacy of "victims" mentioned in the Commission records. In a courtroom located on the fourth floor of the federal court building on Capitol Street in downtown Jackson, which was named after the late Mississippi Senator James Eastland, there is a huge white drapery hanging from the high ceiling and covering the front wall that faces the court's spectators. Behind the drapery is a brightly colored tableau measuring forty feet across and twenty feet high. The painting shows a black woman picking cotton at the left; to the right, it depicts a poorly dressed black man strumming a banjo, while the plantation master is dismounting with the help of another deferential black man. Beyond them is a white woman standing in front of the plantation house, welcoming her husband with their daughter. Dominating the foreground is a black-robed judge, holding a law book under his arm. This painting is not an antique from the antebellum period but was actually created by an artist commissioned by the Works Progress Administration (WPA) in 1939. For more than two decades, until it was covered by the drapery, the tableau had witnessed numerous courtroom dramas, whose players included the state's civil rights activists as both plaintiffs and defendants. For many of them, the painting was an appropriate symbol of Mississippi's racial oppression. Under the tableau, which the court's spectators could no longer see, Judge Barbour sat quietly on September 30, struggling to formulate an order to make the sealed files of the Sovereignty Commission, once the state's "segregation watchdog," accessible to the public. For King and others who sat in the courtroom on that day and knew what was under the drapery in front of them, the contrast between the covered painting and the judge, who was trying to decide on how Mississippi could atone for its past deeds, was somewhat overwhelming.[36]

On May 31, 1994, after due consideration of the testimony given at this hearing, the judge devised a method of opening the Commission records "while balancing the competing interests of the 'privacy Plaintiffs' and the 'access Plaintiffs.' " The formula that Barbour came up with was composed of a series of complicated and time-consuming procedures, by which the Department of Archives and History was directed to place a public notice in the *New York Times*, the *Wall Street Journal*, and *USA Today* to "sufficiently notify those who may have been victims of unlawful Commission activities as to their rights as set forth" in his decision. Those who responded to the notice and were found to have been named in the Commission records, except for persons who had acted for the state agency, would be given an opportunity to ask the state archives to seal their individual documents.[37]

However, to Judge Barbour's dismay, King once again appealed his decision to the Fifth Circuit, contending that the district court's plan was not sufficient enough in protecting the privacy of the innocent people named in the Commission files. No one was certain when the lawsuit would eventually be resolved.[38]

Meanwhile, for the Department of Archives and History, the federal judge's order was one thing, but securing the necessary funds to process the defunct agency's official records for their release was another matter. During the 1994 legislative session, an appropriation bill that would have provided approximately $300,000 for the state archives was killed in the House after it cleared the Senate. The funds were to be used for purchasing imaging equipment and hiring three additional archival staff members to process the Commission records. Discontented with the federal judge's order, the chair of the House Appropriations Committee, Charles W. Capps Jr. of Cleveland, opposed the state funding. "I think the opening of those files will achieve no purpose," he insisted, "but open old wounds that are 40 years old or over and have been forgotten." Later, when the state held a special legislative session in August, Republican Governor Daniel Kirkwood "Kirk" Fordice Jr. refused to put the funding matter on the legislative agenda.[39]

While the Sovereignty Commission lawsuit dragged on, the state agency's only living former director, Erle Johnston, died of complications from a heart attack at St. Dominic's Hospital in Jackson on September 26, 1995. He was seventy-seven years old.[40] Throughout the state's troubled days during the 1950s and the 1960s, which he appropriately called "Mississippi's defiant years," Johnston was neither a reactionary nor a full-fledged racist. Nor was he a moderate or a liberal. In the face of Mississippi's fanatical defense of its racial status quo, Johnston was both a realist and a pragmatist who recognized, albeit reluctantly, the importance of a nonviolent accommodation to the reality of the 1960s, searching for the least painful route for his native state to take in adjusting itself to the vast changes taking place everywhere in American society. After all, born and raised in what James Silver once termed the "closed society" of Mississippi, where his parents and grandparents believed in and practiced racial segregation, Johnston had never seriously doubted the righteousness of the segregated society until his middle forties. Ironically, however, after he assumed the directorship of the Sovereignty Commission, Johnston gradually began to see the injustice in legally prescribed and imposed racial segregation for the first time in his life. "If I had not been appointed to the Sovereignty Commission," he once looked back, "I could not have realized that the civil rights struggle in Mississippi was fought not only for the state's black folks, but for us white[s]. . . . It was for the redemption of our white souls."[41]

Late in 1991, when Tougaloo College, which during the 1960s Johnston used to call "a school for agitation [rather] than a school for education," decided to organize the Committee on the Preservation of Civil Rights Papers at the college, the former Sovereignty Commission director was invited to serve on the biracial group. The ten-member committee composed of five blacks and five whites chose a black woman and a white man as its co-chairpersons—Constance Slaughter-Harvey, who was a trustee of Tougaloo and a former Mississippi assistant secretary of state, and Johnston. In accepting his appointment to the committee and helping to preserve the black institution's "courage of the past," Johnston might have been in search of his own "redemption."[42]

The former director's soul-searching continued until his death. In 1993 Johnston conceived a plan to bring together the white football players from Jones County Junior College in Ellisville and the black players from Compton Community College in Compton, California, who played a game some forty years before.[43] In December 1955, in open defiance of Mississippi's segregation laws, Coach Jim Clark's all-white Jones County Junior College Bobcats took the field against Coach Tay Brown's integrated Compton Community College Tartars in the Junior Rose Bowl held in Pasadena, California. Until then, no athletic team of Mississippi's all-white universities and colleges had ever competed against a racially integrated opponent. As a result of this "sinful" act, Jones County Junior College suffered condemnations as well as overt threats of losing its biennial appropriation by the state legislature. "There is no escaping the cold fact," the *Jackson Daily News* editorialized on its front page, "that a game between Mississippi junior collegians and a California team having five Negroes in its organization would not only be a violation of the ban we have declared on social equality but would be an acceptance of social equality."[44] Determined, Jones's thirty-seven players and the school's 110-piece band left for Pasadena without taking the best wishes of their entire home state with them. "[I]f the Jones Junior College team meets with a stinging defeat it will not cause any mourning in their home state," the Jackson paper viciously remarked, "[and] [t]hat will be exactly what they ought to get." Indeed, Coach Clark and his Bobcats did lose the game to Compton before the 57,000 spectators by the final score of 22 to 13.[45]

Johnston, who saw this forty-year-old incident as an important moment in Mississippi's recent history, planned to invite the former players of both colleges to Ellisville to participate in the 1995 homecoming game of Jones County Junior College. However, in the midst of preparing for the reunion, Johnston, who was looking forward to serving as the master of ceremonies at the event, died. The day before the reunion, when the former black members of the Compton team arrived at the Jackson International Airport, they were warmly greeted by Governor Fordice, who was then campaigning for reelection. Above where he stood was a huge banner: "Welcome, COMPTON COLLEGE to the NEW Mississippi!"[46] On the following day, at the end of the reception in honor of the former players from both teams held on the campus of Jones County Junior College, all attendees stood up and sang "God Bless America." As they sang, the black hands and the white ones were tightly clasped.[47] "This was his last hurrah," Johnston's son, Bubby, contemplated, "[and] [h]e wanted to show the rest of the country that Mississippi had changed."[48]

But a question remains: had Johnston himself changed? "Erle's crime, if his critics choose to characterize it as such," Sid Salter, publisher of the *Scott County Times*, offered in the eulogy at the memorial service held for the late Commission director two days after his death, "was being a human being—capable of growing and changing and evolving."[49] It is perhaps impossible to measure the precise magnitude of the growth, change, and evolution of Johnston's inner soul. At the same time, it is an unequivocal fact that the Sovereignty Commission did considerable damage to Mississippi's civil rights struggle, and in the final analysis, it cannot be denied that Johnston, in his own right, was among those who shared in sustaining and contributing to the state agency's destructive nature.

In the early summer of 1996 the Fifth Circuit Court upheld Judge Barbour's 1994 decision on the Commission files. Though King promptly appealed the case to the Supreme Court, it refused to hear the argument on November 18. Following the Court's announcement, the Department of Archives and History ran a public notice twice in January 1997 in the three nationally circulated dailies as well as in twenty-three Mississippi newspapers for the purpose of informing those who might have been named in the Sovereignty Commission documents of their legal rights in dealing with their respective files.[50] A year later, in January 1998, Judge Barbour ordered "the State of Mississippi via the Mississippi Department of Archives and History" to "release into the public domain . . . the records of the defunct Mississippi State Sovereignty Commission," directing that the records, which the department's staff had been electronically prepared and put on CD-ROM, be opened on March 17.[51] In accordance with this order, out of a total of 132,000 pages composing the entire existing records, approximately 124,300 pages were to be released by the state archives, which had spent $677,213 to process these documents.[52] From its birth in 1956 to its death in 1973, the Sovereignty Commission had received a total appropriation of $2,230,191 from the state, of which $1,542,172.75 was expended in its efforts "to protect the sovereignty" of Mississippi. It is almost ironic to note that not counting the expenses involved in the twenty-one-year-old lawsuit, the state's taxpayers had to bear with expending some $678,000 more to preserve and protect the official records of the high-priced agency, which used to spy upon some of its own financial benefactors.[53]

On March 17, 1998, which Anne L. Webster, reference services librarian at the state archives, had once referred to as "the MAGIC DAY," the Sovereignty Commission's official records were opened.[54] It was a "magic day" in a sense because the viewers of the records, as if they were bound by a magic spell, were transported to a different age, where the state's "closed society" was kept intact. However, the scene that Mississippians and the rest of the world saw in those records on that day was far from a land of magic but was instead a land of fear, hysteria, and bigotry. More than three decades after her husband's death, Rita Schwerner finally had an opportunity to read some of the Sovereignty Commission records pertinent to Michael and herself. Among those documents was a surveillance report in which a Commission investigator accurately informed the state agency that Rita purchased a brand-new "Singer sewing machine" just three months before her husband was murdered. "When I first read it," she recollected in an interview, "I have to say [that] I laughed." But it did not take long for Rita to realize the "astounding" depth of the Commission's work: "Then I thought about it, and I was quite chilled by it because of the fact that we were being surveyed to such an extent."[55] One by one, people came by the state archives in search of the "ghosts of Mississippi." The "magic day" has come and gone, but for the liquidation of the dark journey that the state had taken during the 1950s and the 1960s, Mississippi still struggles.

The diverse changes that Mississippi underwent in its race relations and the eventual collapse of the state's officially sanctioned "massive resistance" have, to borrow the words of George B. Tindall, "produced the most vivid human drama in the recent South." Those changes have also continually entailed some emotionally straining issues, one of which has been reflected in the recent heated debates over the use of the state flag due to its incorporation of the Confederate battle flag design.[56] Nevertheless, for the last forty years it is beyond dispute that a tremendous amount of progress, though not without pain, has been made in the state's race relations, and all Mississippians of good will, both black and white, can certainly be proud of that.

In November 1999, as a new millennium was drawing near, the *Clarion-Ledger* asked its readers to name both the greatest and the lowest moments in Mississippi's recent history. For the greatest moment, the readers chose the end of racial segregation, and the 1964 Neshoba County killings were named as the second lowest moment in the state's history.[57] Be that as it may, what is less certain, but not less crucial, is not only the ability of the state and its people to continue to learn from their past crucibles but also their willingness to embrace and apply that insight to their future endeavors. "[O]ur trials and difficulties have given Mississippi a special understanding of the need for redemption and reconciliation," State Secretary Molpus related to those who were present at the twenty-fifth anniversary of the Neshoba County murders, "and [they] have empowered us to serve as a beacon for the nation."[58]

For too long Mississippi has been a symbol of shame, and it still has an enormous burden to carry. Yet for this very reason, the state is capable of serving as a model of racial justice and opportunity for the rest of the nation. By grappling with their state's past, which has been forged not only by some Magnolia State romances but also by tragedy and suffering, and, as Erle Johnston himself once uttered, by "profiting" from "the mistakes" made by his generation, both black and white Mississippians can support the future of Mississippi.

NOTES

Abbreviations and Shortened References

ASSC Records   Alabama State Sovereignty Commission Records, Alabama Department of Archives and History, Montgomery

CA   Memphis (Tenn.) Commercial Appeal

CC Collection   Citizens' Council Collection, Special Collections, Mitchell Memorial Library, Mississippi State University, Mississippi State

CC/CR Collection   Citizens' Council/Civil Rights Collection, Archives and Manuscript Department, William D. McCain Library and Archives, University of Southern Mississippi, Hattiesburg

CCFF   Citizens' Council Forum Films, Audio-Visual Records, Mississippi Department of Archives and History, Jackson

CL   Jackson (Miss.) Clarion-Ledger

CL/DN   Jackson (Miss.) Clarion-Ledger/Jackson Daily News (combined Sunday edition)

Coleman Library   L. Zenobia Coleman Library, Tougaloo College, Tougaloo, Mississippi

Coleman Papers   James P. Coleman Papers, Archives and Library Division, Mississippi Department of Archives and History, Jackson

Cox Collection   A. Eugene Cox Collection, Special Collections, Mitchell Memorial Library, Mississippi State University, Mississippi State

CR   Congressional Record

CSDI Collection   Center for the Study of Democratic Institutions Collection, Davidson Library, University of California at Santa Barbara, Santa Barbara

DDT   Greenville (Miss.) Delta Democrat-Times

DN   Jackson (Miss.) Daily News

Faulkner Collection   Leesha Faulkner Civil Rights Collection, Archives and Manuscript Department, William D. McCain Library and Archives, University of Southern Mississippi, Hattiesburg

FF   Facts on Film (microfilm), Southern Education Reporting Service, Nashville, Tennessee

FR Archives   Fund for the Republic Archives, Public Policy Papers, Department of Rare Books and Special Collections, Seeley G. Mudd Manuscript Library, Princeton University, Princeton, New Jersey

Godwin Collection   Godwin Advertising Agency Collection, Special Collections, Mitchell Memorial Library, Mississippi State University, Mississippi State

Holmes Collection   Verner S. Holmes Collection, Archives and Special Collections, John D. Williams Library, University of Mississippi, University

JH   Journal of the House of Representatives of the State of Mississippi

Johnston Papers   Erle E. Johnston Jr. Papers, Archives and Manuscript Department, William D. McCain Library and Archives, University of Southern Mississippi, Hattiesburg

JS   Journal of the Senate of the State of Mississippi

King Collection   Ed King Collection, Special Collections, L. Zenobia Coleman Library, Tougaloo College, Tougaloo, Mississippi

Ladner Papers   Heber Ladner Papers, Secretary of State (Record Group 28), Official Records, Archives and Library Division, Mississippi Department of Archives and History, Jackson

LBJ Library   Lyndon B. Johnson Presidential Library, Austin, Texas

LSM   Laws of the State of Mississippi

Marshall Papers   Burke Marshall Papers, John F. Kennedy Presidential Library, Boston

McCain Library   Archives and Manuscript Department, William D. McCain Library and Archives, University of Southern Mississippi, Hattiesburg

MDAH   Archives and Library Division, Mississippi Department of Archives and History, Jackson

Minor Papers   Wilson F. "Bill" Minor Papers, Special Collections, Mitchell Memorial Library, Mississippi State University, Mississippi State

Mississippiana Collection   Mississippiana Collection, William D. McCain Library and Archives, University of Southern Mississippi, Hattiesburg

MOHP   Mississippi Oral History Program, Center for Oral History and Cultural Heritage, University of Southern Mississippi, Hattiesburg

MOSR   Mississippi Official and Statistical Register

MSSC Records   Records of the Mississippi State Sovereignty Commission, Archives and Library Division, Mississippi Department of Archives and History, Jackson

NYT   New York Times

NYTM   New York Times Magazine

PBJ Papers   Paul B. Johnson Family Papers, Archives and Manuscript Department, William D. McCain Library and Archives, University of Southern Mississippi, Hattiesburg

PBJ (MDAH) Papers   Paul B. Johnson Jr. Papers, Governor's Office (Record Group 27), Official Records, Archives and Library Division, Mississippi Department of Archives and History, Jackson

Schutt Papers   Jane M. Schutt Papers, Special Collections, L. Zenobia Coleman Library, Tougaloo College, Tougaloo, Mississippi

SSN   *Southern School News*, Southern Education Reporting Service, Nashville, Tennessee

ST   *Jackson (Miss.) State Times*

Stennis Project   John C. Stennis Oral History Project, Mississippi State University, Mississippi State

Toler Papers   Kenneth Toler Papers, Special Collections, Mitchell Memorial Library, Mississippi State University, Mississippi State

TP   *New Orleans (La.) Times-Picayune*

Preface

1. W. J. Cash, *The Mind of the South* (New York: Knopf, 1941; reprint, New York: Vintage, 1991), 1.

2. Pete Daniel, *Standing at the Crossroads: Southern Life in the Twentieth Century* (Baltimore: Johns Hopkins University Press, 1996), 201.

3. Charles W. Eagles, "Toward New Histories of the Civil Rights Era," *Journal of Southern History* 66 (Nov. 2000): 842–43.

4. C. Vann Woodward, *The Burden of Southern History*, rev. ed. (Baton Rouge: Louisiana State University Press, 1968), 22.

5. C. Vann Woodward, "Teaching American History," *American Scholar* 67 (winter 1998): 105.

Introduction. For the Purity of White Blood: The Dixiecrat Revolt and the Creation of the Legal Educational Advisory Committee in Mississippi

1. John R. Skates, *Mississippi: A Bicentennial History* (New York: Norton, 1979), 151; Neil R. McMillen, "Fighting for What We Didn't Have: How Mississippi's Black Veterans Remember World War II," in *Remaking Dixie: The Impact of World War II on the American South*, ed. Neil R. McMillen (Jackson: University Press of Mississippi, 1997), 93.

2. John Hope Franklin and Alfred A. Moss Jr., *From Slavery to Freedom: A History of African Americans*, 7th ed. (New York: McGraw-Hill, 1994), 438–40, 461.

3. Skates, *Mississippi*, 150.

4. Ibid., 151, 155.
5. President's Committee on Civil Rights, *To Secure These Rights: The Report of the President's Committee on Civil Rights* (Washington, D.C.: GPO, 1947), 151–73.
6. *JH*, 1948, regular sess., 85.
7. Ibid.
8. William F. Winter, "New Directions in Politics, 1948–1956," in *A History of Mississippi*, vol. 2, ed. Richard A. McLemore (Jackson: University and College Press of Mississippi, 1973), 142.
9. *TP*, 13 Feb. 1948; *DN*, 20 Feb. 1948.
10. V. O. Key Jr., *Southern Politics in State and Nation* (New York: Knopf, 1949), 333.
→11. Kenneth H. Williams, *Mississippi and Civil Rights, 1945–1954* (Ann Arbor, Mich.: University Microfilms, 1985), 146–47.
12. Mississippi State Democratic Party, *Know All the Facts about Truman's So-Called "Civil Rights" Program and What It Means to You* (Jackson: Mississippi State Democratic Party, n.d.), 1, 8, MDAH.
13. Colleen McGuiness, ed., *National Party Conventions, 1831–1988* (Washington, D.C.: Congressional Quarterly, 1991), 99.
14. Nadine Cohodas, *Strom Thurmond and the Politics of Southern Change* (New York: Simon and Schuster, 1993), 167.
15. Key, *Southern Politics*, 329.
16. Numan V. Bartley, *The Rise of Massive Resistance: Race and Politics in the South during the 1950's* (Baton Rouge: Louisiana State University Press, 1969), 33.
17. Donald B. Johnson, comp., *National Party Platform*, vol. 1, rev. ed. (Urbana: University of Illinois Press, 1978), 466–68.
18. "The South of V. O. Key," in *The American South Comes of Age* series, prod. Alvin H. Goldstein, South Carolina Educational Television Network and Division of Continuing Education of the University of South Carolina, Columbia, 1985, videocassette.
19. Ibid.
20. Carolyn Goldinger, ed., *Presidential Elections since 1798*, 5th ed. (Washington, D.C.: Congressional Quarterly, 1991), 131, 204.
21. Bartley, *The Rise of Massive Resistance*, 36.
22. *JH*, 1952, regular sess., 105; Cecil L. Sumners, *The Governors of Mississippi* (Gretna, La.: Pelican, 1980), 114–17.
23. Winter, "New Directions in Politics," 147.
24. Williams, *Mississippi and Civil Rights*, 177–204; Charles C. Bolton, "Mississippi's School Equalization Program, 1945–1954: 'A Last Gasp to Try to Maintain a Segregated Educational System,' " *Journal of Southern History* 66 (Nov. 2000): 784–85.
25. *JH*, 1952, regular sess., 270, 534.
26. *LSM*, 1952, regular sess., 737–38.

27. James W. Loewen and Charles Sallis, eds., *Mississippi: Conflict and Change*, rev. ed. (New York: Pantheon, 1980), 247.

28. *DN*, 30 Jan. 1953.

29. *JS*, 1953, extraordinary sess., 970.

30. Erle Johnston Jr., *Mississippi's Defiant Years, 1953–1973: An Interpretive Documentary with Personal Experiences* (Forest, Miss: Lake Harbor, 1990), 3–4; Bolton, "Mississippi's School Equalization Program," 807.

31. Loewen and Sallis, *Mississippi*, 247; Bolton, "Mississippi's School Equalization Program," 808–9.

32. Neil R. McMillen, "Development of Civil Rights, 1956–1970," in McLemore, *A History of Mississippi*, 155; Winter, "New Direction in Politics," 152.

33. *JH*, 1954, regular sess., 596; William J. Simmons to Erle Johnston Jr., 25 Nov. 1987, folder 9, box 2, Johnston Papers.

34. *LSM*, 1954, regular sess., 585–87; *JS*, 1954, regular sess., 926–27.

35. *CL*, 18 May 1954.

36. *Brown v. Board of Education of Topeka*, 347 U.S. 483 (1954).

37. *DN*, 18 May 1954; *DDT*, 18 May 1954.

38. *CR*, 83d Cong., 2d sess., 19 May 1954, 6857; Hodding Carter, *The South Strikes Back* (Garden City, N.Y.: Doubleday, 1959), 26.

39. Thomas P. Brady, oral history, interviewed by Orley B. Caudill, 4 Mar. 1972, vol. 2, pt. 1, transcript, 24–25, MOHP.

40. Tom P. Brady, *Black Monday* (Brookhaven, Miss.: n.p., 1954), 13.

41. *NYT*, 18 May 1954; *CL*, 18 May 1954.

42. *CR*, 83d Cong., 2d sess., 27 May 1954, 7251–52; *DN*, 27 May 1954. See also Forrest McDonald, *States' Rights and the Union: Imperium in Imperio, 1776–1876* (Lawrence: University Press of Kansas, 2000), 229–30.

43. *Brown v. Board of Education of Topeka*.

44. *DN*, 15 June 1954.

45. William J. Simmons, oral history, interviewed by Orley B. Caudill, 26 June 1979, vol. 372, transcript, 44–46, MOHP; Robert B. Patterson, *The Citizens' Council: A History* (Greenwood, Miss.: Association of Citizens' Councils of Mississippi, n.d.), folder 10, CC Collection; W. F. Minor, "The Citizens' Councils [*sic*]: An Incredible Decade of Defiance," folder "Citizens' Council," box 2, Minor Papers; Neil R. McMillen, *The Citizens' Council: Organized Resistance to the Second Reconstruction, 1954–64* (Urbana: University of Illinois Press, 1971), 18–23.

46. Brady, oral history, 25.

47. Hodding Carter, "Citadel of the Citizens' Council," *NYTM*, 12 Nov. 1961, 23.

48. Gordon W. Lovejoy, "In Brotherhood Week: A Look at the South," *NYTM*, 17 Feb. 1957, 13.

49. *SSN*, 1 Oct. 1954.

50. McMillen, *The Citizens' Council*, 319.

51. Richard Kluger, *Simple Justice: The History of* Brown v. Board of Education *and Black America's Struggle for Equality* (New York: Knopf, 1976), 710.

52. Erle Johnston Jr., oral history, interviewed by Betsy Nash, 26 Mar. 1991, transcript, 20–21, Stennis Project.

53. "Sixth Annual Meeting, Regional Council of Negro Leadership," 2-2-0-6-1-1-1, MSSC Records; Jeff Roche, *Restructured Resistance: The Sibley Commission and the Politics of Desegregation in Georgia* (Athens: University of Georgia Press, 1998), 23–24.

54. *FF*, May 1954 to June 1958, roll no. 38, N38 3534–47.

55. Erle Johnston Jr., television interview, interviewed by Cal Adams, *Eyewitness News 16: Dateline*, WAPT, Jackson, Mississippi, n.d., videocassette, Special Collections, Coleman Library.

56. *FF*, May 1954 to June 1958, roll no. 38, N38 3534–47.

57. *JS*, 1954, extraordinary sess., 9; *CL*, 8 Sept. 1954.

58. *FF*, May 1954 to June 1958, roll no. 38, N38 3534–47.

59. *JH*, 1954, extraordinary sess., 6; *LSM*, 1954, extraordinary sess., 51–52.

60. *JH*, 1954, extraordinary sess., 40; *JS*, 1954 extraordinary sess., 67–68.

61. *FF*, May 1954 to June 1958, roll no. 38, N38 3548; *MOSR*, 1956–1960, 397.

62. *SSN*, 6 Jan. 1955.

63. Bartley, *The Rise of Massive Resistance*, 59. At the time of the *Brown* decision, seventeen states and the District of Columbia practiced racial segregation in public schools by virtue of their state constitutions and laws. The seventeen states were Alabama, Arkansas, Delaware, Florida, Georgia, Kentucky, Louisiana, Maryland, Mississippi, Missouri, North Carolina, Oklahoma, South Carolina, Tennessee, Texas, Virginia, and West Virginia. In addition, four other states—Arizona, Kansas, New Mexico, and Wyoming—permitted the practice without the sanction of law. See "To All on Equal Terms," *Time*, 24 May 1954, 9; William A. McClenaghan, rev., *Magruder's American Government*, 55th ed. (Boston: Allyn and Bacon, 1972), 120; Paul E. Wilson, *A Time to Lose: Representing Kansas in* Brown v. Board of Education (Lawrence: University Press of Kansas, 1995), 25–26.

64. Bartley, *The Rise of Massive Resistance*, 59, 75.

65. *Brown v. Board of Education of Topeka*, 349 U.S. 294 (1955).

66. Alfred H. Kelly and Winfred A. Harbison, *The American Constitution: Its Origins and Development*, 5th ed. (New York: Norton, 1976), 863–64.

67. To be sure, Chief Justice Warren realized that the *Brown* case was of such magnitude that only a unanimous opinion could convey the Court's resolve to the nation. To achieve this end, Warren vigorously tried to dissuade Justices Robert H. Jackson from Pennsylvania, Tom C. Clark from Texas, and particularly Stanley F. Reed from Kentucky from filing any dissenting or even concurrent opinions. See Kluger, *Simple Justice*, 694–98; *Separate but Equal*, prod. Stan

Margulies, dir. George Stevens Jr., New Liberty Production, 1991, videocassette.

68. William Liston, confidential report, n.d., folder 36, box 21, Coleman Papers; *SSN*, Aug. 1955; John Dittmer, "The Politics of Mississippi Movement, 1954–1964," in *The Civil Rights Movement in America*, ed. Charles W. Eagles (Jackson: University Press of Mississippi, 1986), 68–69; McMillen, *The Citizens' Council*, 29–31.

69. *MOSR*, 1956–1960, 411.

70. Charlotte Capers, ed., "Mississippi Bicentennial Celebration: The Address of Judge James Plemon Coleman," *Journal of Mississippi History* 39 (Feb. 1977): 52.

71. *SSN*, Oct. 1955; *CA*, 22 Sept. 1955.

72. *SSN*, Jan. 1956.

73. Ibid., Oct. 1955.

Chapter 1. To Protect the Sovereignty of the State of Mississippi: The Origins of the State Sovereignty Commission

1. *JH*, 1956, regular sess., 65; *Segregation and the South*, prod. George M. Martin Jr., Newsfilm Project, Fund for the Republic, Los Angeles, 1957, videocassette, CSDI Collection.

2. *JH*, 1956, regular sess., 67.

3. *SSN*, Mar. 1956.

4. *LSM*, 1956, regular sess., 366–67.

5. *JH*, 1956, regular sess., 107–8; *LSM*, 1956, regular sess., 716–17.

6. *CA*, 1 Mar. 1956; *DN*, 1 Mar. 1956.

7. *JS*, 1956, regular sess., 282–83.

8. *CA*, 1 Mar. 1956.

9. *LSM*, 1956, regular sess., 741.

10. Ibid., 742–44.

11. *JH*, 1956, regular sess., 358.

12. *CA*, 1 Mar. 1956.

13. *LSM*, 1956, regular sess., 744.

14. *JH*, 1956, regular sess., 616.

15. *LSM*, 1956, regular sess., 521.

16. "State Sovereignty Commission," 7-0-1-56-1-1-1 to 12-1-1, pp. 1-1-1 to 2-1-1, MSSC Records.

17. *LSM*, 1956, regular sess., 520–24.

18. *DN*, 22 Mar. 1956; *DDT*, 22 Mar. 1956.

19. *JH*, 1956, regular sess., 659, 678.

20. Joseph E. Wroten, oral history, interviewed by Yasuhiro Katagiri, 4 Nov. 1993,

vol. 476, transcript, 20–21, MOHP; *JH*, 1956, regular sess., 688; William J. Simmons to Erle Johnston Jr., 18 Nov. 1987, folder 9, box 2, Johnston Papers. The transcript of the author's oral history interview with Wroten can also be read on-line at <http://www.lib.usm.edu/~spcol/crda/oh/wrotentrans.htm> in *Oral Histories in the Civil Rights in Mississippi Digital Archives* series, William D. McCain Library and Archives, University of Southern Mississippi, Hattiesburg, consulted 1 Dec. 2000 <http://www.lib.usm.edu/~spcol/crda/oh/index.html>.

21. *JH*, 1956, regular sess., 726.

22. *JS*, 1956, regular sess., 564.

23. *LSM*, 1956, regular sess., 524; *JH*, 1956, regular sess., 886–87.

24. *LSM*, 1956, regular sess., 79; *SSN*, Apr. 1956.

25. "State Sovereignty Commission," 7-0-1-56-1-1-1 to 12-1-1, p. 3-1-1, MSSC Records; *DN*, 17 Apr. 1956.

26. Maurice L. Malone to H. V. Cooper, 25 Feb. 1959, 99-16-0-36-1-1-1; Cooper to Malone, 27 Feb. 1959, 99-16-0-37-1-1-1; *DN*, n.d, 7-0-1-33-1-1-1, all in MSSC Records; William Liston, confidential report, n.d., folder 36, box 21, Coleman Papers.

27. *CA*, 29 Apr. 1956; *MOSR*, 1949–1951, 49; *MOSR*, 1956–1960, 97.

28. *TP*, 3 May 1956; *DN*, 16 May 1956.

29. Ney M. Gore Jr. to Hugh Clayton, 7 Sept. 1956, 99-9-0-38-1-1-1; minutes, State Sovereignty Commission, 15 May 1956, 99-14-0-1-1-1-1; Earl Evans Jr. to Gore, 23 May 1956, 99-9-0-12-1-1-1; Hal DeCell to James Coleman, Joe Patterson, W. S. Henley, Evans, and Gore, memo, n.d., 99-9-0-12-2-1-1, all in MSSC Records; DeCell to Coleman, 18 Feb. 1956, folder 4, box 27, Coleman Papers; *LSM*, 1956, regular sess., 521, 523; *SSN*, June 1956; *DN*, 16 May 1956; *TP*, 3 May 1956.

30. *DN*, 16 May 1956.

31. Minutes, State Sovereignty Commission, 15 May 1956, 99-14-0-1-1-1-1, MSSC Records; *DN*, 16 May 1956; *SSN*, June 1956.

32. *CA*, 2 Oct. 1958.

33. Audit, State Sovereignty Commission, 97-1-0-1-1-1-1 to 11-1-1, p. 10-1-1, MSSC Records.

34. *DN*, 16 May 1956.

35. Erle Johnston Jr., *I Rolled with Ross: A Political Portrait* (Baton Rouge, La.: Moran, 1980).

36. Ney M. Gore Jr. to J. P. Coleman, 22 May 1956, folder 13, box 28, Coleman Papers.

37. *DN*, 10 Sept. 1956; *The Constitution of the State of Mississippi* (Jackson: Mississippi Secretary of State's Office, 1992), 7; *SSN*, Feb. 1957; *Scott County (Miss.) Times*, 12 July 1956; Ben H. Walley to Erle Johnston, 9 Apr. 1958; Johnston to Walley, 10 Apr. 1958, both in folder 2, box 31, Coleman Papers.

38. *DN*, 19 Sept. 1956, 21 Sept. 1956, 14 Oct. 1957.

39. Minutes, State Sovereignty Commission, 4 Nov. 1957, 99-14-0-9-1-1-1, MSSC Records; Ney M. Gore Jr. to J. P. Coleman, 4 Nov. 1957, folder 14, box 28, Coleman Papers; *Quitman County (Miss.) Democrat*, 7 Nov. 1957; *SSN*, Dec. 1957.

40. "Report to the Mississippi State Legislature on Activities of the State Sovereignty Commission," 7-3-0-5-1-1-1 to 13-1-1, p. 1-1-1, MSSC Records.

41. Hodding Carter, *The South Strikes Back* (Garden City, N.Y.: Doubleday, 1959), 64; *State Sovereignty Commission: Report to the Members of the Senate and House of Representatives of the State of Mississippi*, 99-111-0-1-1-1-1 to 9-1-1, p. 2-1-1, MSSC Records.

42. Carter, *The South Strikes Back*, 64; *SSN*, May 1956.

43. *SSN*, May 1956.

44. "State Sovereignty Commission," 7-0-1-56-1-1-1 to 12-1-1, p. 6-1-1, MSSC Records.

45. *State Sovereignty Commission*, 99-111-0-1-1-1-1 to 9-1-1, p. 4-1-1; activity report, State Sovereignty Commission, 1 June 1956 to 15 Oct. 1956, 7-0-1-27-1-1-1 to 3-1-1, pp. 1-1-1 to 2-1-1; Hal C. DeCell to state auditor, 6 Aug. 1957, 97-1-0-1-1-1-1 to 11-1-1, p. 2-1-1, all in MSSC Records; James Peck to J. P. Coleman, 30 Nov. 1956, folder 3, box 112, FR Archives; Stephen J. Whitfield, *A Death in the Delta: The Story of Emmett Till* (New York: Free Press, 1988).

46. Harry S. Ashmore, *Hearts and Minds: A Personal Chronicle of Race in America* (Cabin John, Md.: Seven Locks, 1988), 332–33; Paul M. Gaston [professor emeritus of history, University of Virginia], "Fund for the Republic," e-mail to the author, 21 Feb. 1999; Randall L. Patton, "Southern Regional Council," in *Encyclopedia of African-American Civil Rights: From Emancipation to the Present*, ed. Charles D. Lowery and John F. Marszalek (New York: Greenwood, 1992), 494–95; Donald Cunnigen, *Men and Women of Goodwill: Mississippi's White Liberals* (Ann Arbor, Mich.: University Microfilms, 1988), 76–78.

47. George Martin Jr. to W. H. Ferry, memo, 23 Oct. 1956, folder 4, box 111; Martin, "Production Outline," [1957], [p. 1], folder 3, box 112, both in FR Archives.

48. George M. Martin Jr., curriculum vitae, [1957], 1–2, folder 3, box 112; Martin to W. H. Ferry, memo, 23 Oct. 1956, folder 4, box 111, both in FR Archives.

49. Hal C. DeCell to Robert Hutchins, 15 Apr. 1957, folder 3, box 111, FR Archives.

50. James Peck to John Thompson, 23 Nov. 1956; Peck to J. P. Coleman, 30 Nov. 1956, both in folder 3, box 112, FR Archives.

51. George Martin Jr. to Frank K. Kelly, memo, 3 Jan. 1957; Hal C. DeCell to Robert Hutchins, 15 Apr. 1957; Hutchins to DeCell, 24 Apr. 1957, all in folder 3, box 111, FR Archives; DeCell to state auditor, 6 Aug. 1957, 97-1-0-1-1-1-1 to 11-1-1, pp. 2-1-1 to 3-1-1, MSSC Records.

52. *State Sovereignty Commission*, 99-111-0-1-1-1-1 to 9-1-1, p. 4-1-1; Hal C. De-Cell to Ney M. Gore Jr., memo, 12 Mar. 1957, 10-0-1-101-2-1-1; DeCell to Gore, memo, 20 May 1957, 10-0-1-106-1-1-1, all in MSSC Records; "Crisis in the South" [documentary film script], [1957]; "Segregation and the South" [documentary film script], 1957, both in folder 4, box 112, FR Archives.

53. George Martin Jr. to Robert M. Hutchins, memo, 24 May 1957, folder 3, box 112, FR Archives.

54. Ibid., 21 May 1957, folder 3; "Segregation and the South," 1, 8, folder 4, both in box 112, FR Archives; *Segregation and the South*.

55. Hal C. DeCell to Ney M. Gore, memo, 20 May 1957, 10-0-1-106-1-1-1, MSSC Records; "Segregation and the South," 3, 8–9, folder 4, box 112, FR Archives; *Segregation and the South*.

56. Edward Reed to Robert M. Hutchins, et al., memo, 23 May 1957; press release, American Broadcasting Company, 24 May 1957, both in folder 3, box 112, FR Archives.

57. "Fund for Republic Newsfilmery Axed," *Variety*, 5 June 1957, n.p.; Hallock Hoffman to G. H. Griffiths, 11 June 1957; Edward Reed to Thomas H. Wolf, 13 June 1957, all in folder 3, box 112, FR Archives.

58. Hal C. DeCell to Robert Hutchins, 15 Apr. 1957, folder 3, box 111, FR Archives.

59. Hal C. DeCell to Ney M. Gore, memo, "Subject: The Fund for the Republic," 12 June 1957, 2-131-0-9-1-1-1; DeCell to Gore, memo, "Subject: TV Film Entitled 'Segregation in [*sic*] the South,'" 12 June 1957, 10-0-1-108-1-1-1, both in MSSC Records.

60. Hal C. DeCell to Ney M. Gore, memo, 20 May 1957, 10-0-1-106-1-1-1, MSSC Records.

61. *State Sovereignty Commission*, 99-111-0-1-1-1-1 to 9-1-1, pp. 3-1-1, 5-1-1; *DN*, 13 June 1956.

62. *Report to the People: A Summary of Articles Written by New England Editors after Their Tour of Mississippi*, 1, FF, May 1954 to June 1958, roll no. 38, N38 3561–77.

63. "On the Spot," *Time*, 22 Oct. 1956, 54.

64. William Rotch, "Cotton, Cordiality and Conflict [part 1]," *New South* 12 (Feb. 1957): 9.

65. *CA*, 7 Oct. 1956.

66. "On the Spot," *Time*, 22 Oct. 1956, 54.

67. "Tour Comments in Answer to Direct Question on Segregation," 99-12-0-39-1-1-1 to 2-1-1, p. 1-1-1, MSSC Records; *SSN*, Nov. 1956.

68. "Tour Comments in Answer to Direct Question on Segregation," 99-12-0-39-1-1-1 to 2-1-1, p. 1-1-1, MSSC Records; William Rotch, "Cotton, Cordiality and Conflict [part 2]," *New South* 12 (Mar. 1957): 9.

69. *Report to the People*, 1, FF, May 1954 to June 1958, roll no. 38, N38 3561–77.

70. *CL/DN*, 28 Oct. 1956.

71. *Report to the People*, 2, *FF*, May 1954 to June 1958, roll no. 38, N38 3561–77.

72. "State Sovereignty Commission," 7-0-1-56-1-1-1 to 12-1-1, p. 9-1-1, MSSC Records.

73. "New England Tour Expense Report," 99-12-0-37-1-1-1; "Statement of Receipts and Expenditures from May 15, 1956, to June 30, 1957," 97-1-0-1-1-1-1 to 11-1-1, p. 9-1-1, both in MSSC Records.

74. Hal C. DeCell to Ney M. Gore, memo, 14 Mar. 1957, 10-0-1-103-1-1-1; "State Sovereignty Commission," 7-0-1-56-1-1-1 to 12-1-1, p. 8-1-1, both in MSSC Records.

75. *State Sovereignty Commission*, 99-111-0-1-1-1-1 to 9-1-1, p. 1-1-1.

76. *Don't Stone Her until You Hear Her Side: All Mississippi Asks Is Fairness and a Chance to Present Its Side of the Case*, *FF*, May 1954 to June 1958, roll no. 38, N38 3558–60; "State Sovereignty Commission," 7-0-1-56-1-1-1 to 12-1-1, p. 10-1-1; activity report, State Sovereignty Commission, 1 June 1956 to 15 Oct. 1956, 7-0-1-27-1-1-1 to 3-1-1, p. 1-1-1, both in MSSC Records; *DN*, 13 June 1956.

77. *Don't Stone Her until You Hear Her Side*, *FF*, May 1954 to June 1958, roll no. 38, N38 3558–60.

78. Minutes, State Sovereignty Commission, 20 June 1956, 99-14-0-4-1-1-1 to 4-1-1, pp. 1-1-1 to 2-1-1, MSSC Records; *DDT*, 2 Jan. 1958.

79. *Laurel (Miss.) Leader Call*, 2 Jan. 1958.

80. Hal C. DeCell to Ney M. Gore, memo, 20 May 1957, 10-0-1-106-1-1-1, MSSC Records; "Segregation and the South," 8, folder 4, box 112, FR Archives; *Segregation and the South*.

81. Julius E. Thompson, *Percy Greene and the* Jackson Advocate: *The Life and Times of a Radical Conservative Black Newspaperman, 1897–1977* (Jefferson, N.C.: McFarland, 1994); Thompson, *The Black Press in Mississippi, 1865–1985* (Gainesville, Fla.: University Press of Florida, 1993), 26; *DN*, 2 July 1954; *CL*, 16 Dec. 1964.

82. "State Sovereignty Commission," 7-0-1-56-1-1-1 to 12-1-1, p. 9-1-1; minutes, State Sovereignty Commission, 7 Aug. 1958, 99-14-0-10-1-1-1 to 2-1-1, p. 1-1-1; minutes, State Sovereignty Commission, 22 Oct. 1959, 99-14-0-18-1-1-1; "The Jackson Advocate (Percy Greene)," 99-95-0-37-1-1-1, all in MSSC Records.

83. Thompson, *The Black Press in Mississippi*, 68. The folder entitled "Governor's Subject Files—1" in oversized materials box 2, PBJ Papers, contains several original issues of the *Community Citizen*.

84. Hal C. DeCell to Ney M. Gore Jr., memo, 10 Apr. 1957, 2-2-0-5-1-1-1, MSSC Records.

85. Walter Sillers to J. P. Coleman, 29 June 1957, folder 8, box 36, Coleman Papers.

86. Minutes, State Sovereignty Commission, 9 Oct. 1957, 99-14-0-8-1-1-1 to 2-1-1, p. 1-1-1; Hal C. DeCell to J. P. Coleman, 5 Nov. 1957, 99-9-0-111-1-1-1; J. W. Jones to Coleman, 3 Dec. 1959, 9-16-0-45-1-1-1 to 2-1-1, p. 2-1-1, all in MSSC Records.

87. J. W. Jones to State Sovereignty Commission, 10 Aug. 1959, 9-16-0-21-1-1-1; Zack J. Van Landingham to whom it may concern, 12 Aug. 1959, 9-16-0-22-1-1-1, both in MSSC Records; *Community Citizen*, 11 Sept. 1959.

88. Tom Scarbrough to whom it may concern, 15 Sept. 1960, 9-16-0-80-1-1-1; J. W. Jones to Albert Jones, 6 Nov. 1962, 9-16-0-111-1-1-1 to 2-1-1, p. 2-1-1; Albert Jones to whom it may concern, 6 Nov. 1962, 9-16-0-112-1-1-1, all in MSSC Records; *Community Citizen*, 20 Oct. 1960.

89. Zack J. Van Landingham to Ross R. Barnett, memo, 15 Feb. 1960, 9-16-0-51-1-1-1; W. Webb Burke to J. W. Jones, 6 Nov. 1968, 9-16-0-118-1-1-1, both in MSSC Records.

90. *Mississippi Negro Progress Edition*, 6-6-0-3-1-1-1 to 40-1-1; Zack J. Van Landingham to Clyde Coker, 18 Mar. 1959, 6-6-0-7-1-1-1, both in MSSC Records.

91. Erle Johnston Jr. to Herman Glazier, memo, 17 Aug. 1965, 9-29-2-89-1-1-1, MSSC Records.

92. M. L. Young to Earl Johnson [*sic*], 14 Jan. 1961, 9-29-1-3-1-1-1, MSSC Records. As for the relations between the Sovereignty Commission and Young, consult the documents contained in the files 6-6: "Mutual Association of Colored People, South," and 9-29: "Rev. M. L. Young" of the Commission's official records.

93. "Meeting of September 5, 1956," 99-13-0-2-1-1-1 to 9-1-1, p. 8-1-1, MSSC Records.

94. Minutes, State Sovereignty Commission, 20 June 1956, 99-14-0-4-1-1-1 to 4-1-1, p. 2-1-1; "Meeting of September 5, 1956," 99-13-0-2-1-1-1 to 9-1-1, p. 9-1-1, both in MSSC Records.

95. Activity report, State Sovereignty Commission, 1 June 1956 to 15 Oct.1956, 7-0-1-27-1-1-1 to 3-1-1, p. 2-1-1; *State Sovereignty Commission*, 99-111-0-1-1-1-1 to 9-1-1, p. 5-1-1; Hal C. DeCell to state auditor, 6 Aug.1957, 97-1-0-1-1-1-1 to 11-1-1, p. 2-1-1; DeCell to Ney M. Gore, memo, 13 May 1957, 10-0-1-105-1-1-1, all in MSSC Records; George P. Cossar to DeCell, 29 May 1957, folder 37, box 21, Coleman Papers; *ST*, 9 Sept. 1956.

96. Audit, State Sovereignty Commission, 97-1-0-1-1-1-1 to 11-1-1, pp. 4-1-1, 10-1-1 to 11-1-1, MSSC Records.

97. Minutes, State Sovereignty Commission, 9 Oct. 1957, 99-14-0-8-1-1-1 to 2-1-1, p. 2-1-1, MSSC Records.

98. J. P. Coleman to Hal DeCell, memo, 31 May 1957, folder 7, box 27, Coleman Papers.

99. Audit, State Sovereignty Commission, 97-1-0-2-1-1-1 to 8-1-1, pp. 2-1-1 to 3-1-1, 8-1-1, MSSC Records.

100. "Voucher for Reimbursement of Expenses Incident to Official Travel," 97-105-0-53-1-1-1 to 4-1-1, pp. 2-1-1 to 3-1-1; minutes, State Sovereignty Commission, 9 Oct. 1957, 99-14-0-8-1-1-1 to 2-1-1, p. 1-1-1, both in MSSC Records.

101. Audit, State Sovereignty Commission, 97-1-0-2-1-1-1 to 8-1-1, p. 2-1-1, MSSC Records.

102. Ibid., p. 3-1-1.

103. "Conference of Employees, State Sovereignty Commission, October 13, 1958," 7-1-0-3-1-1-1 to 2-1-1, MSSC Records.

104. Maurice L. Malone to Hal C. DeCell, memo, 28 Oct. 1958, 99-95-0-6-1-1-1, MSSC Records.

105. Minutes, State Sovereignty Commission, 16 July 1959, 99-14-0-17-1-1-1 to 2-1-1, p. 2-1-1; resolution, State Sovereignty Commission, 16 July 1959, 99-95-0-34-1-1-1; "Report to the Mississippi State Legislature," 7-3-0-5-1-1-1 to 13-1-1, p. 1-1-1, all in MSSC Records; Hal C. DeCell to J. P. Coleman, 1 June 1959, folder 15, box 27, Coleman Papers; *ST*, 2 July 1959.

106. Carter, *The South Strikes Back*, 75.

107. James P. Coleman, oral history, interviewed by Orley B. Caudill, 6 Feb. 1982, vol. 203, pt. 2, transcript, 207–8, MOHP; Coleman and Verner S. Holmes, oral history, interviewed by David G. Sansing, 16 June 1979, transcript, 81–82, box 6, Holmes Collection; J. P. Coleman to Erle Johnston Jr., n.d., folder 18, box 9, Johnston Papers.

108. Earl Evans Jr. to Ney Gore, 2 Aug. 1956, 2-77-0-5-1-1-1 to 2-1-1, MSSC Records.

109. Ibid., p. 2-1-1.

110. "Meeting of September 5, 1956," 99-13-0-2-1-1-1 to 9-1-1, p. 6-1-1; minutes, State Sovereignty Commission, 5 Sept. 1956, 99-14-0-6-1-1-1, both in MSSC Records.

111. Ney M. Gore Jr. to William H. Johnson Jr., 15 Oct. 1956, 2-77-0-17-1-1-1; untitled list of representatives from veterans' organizations, 2-77-0-39-1-1-1, both in MSSC Records.

112. Carter, *The South Strikes Back*, 77.

113. *DN*, 8 May 1957.

114. "Motion Made by Hon. Hugh Clayton at Meeting of the State Sovereignty Commission, May 7, 1957," 99-8-0-49-2-1-1; minutes, State Sovereignty Commission, 7 May 1957, 99-14-0-7-1-1-1 to 3-1-1, both in MSSC Records.

115. *DDT*, 2 June 1957.

116. Hal C. DeCell to Eph Cresswell, memo, 31 May 1957, 7-0-1-28-1-1-1; Hugh N. Clayton to Ney M. Gore Jr., 30 May 1957, 99-9-0-71-1-1-1; Herschel H. Terrell to Clayton, 27 May 1957, 99-9-0-71-2-1-1, all in MSSC Records; *SSN*, June 1957.

117. *DN*, 8 May 1957.

118. Ibid.

119. Resolution, Association of Citizens' Councils of Mississippi, 16 May 1957, folder 6, box 12, Coleman Papers.

120. J. P. Coleman to M. C. Durr, 11 Apr. 1958; Coleman to C. C. Smith, 10 Apr. 1958, both in folder 5, box 12, Coleman Papers.

121. J. P. Coleman to C. C. Smith, 10 Apr. 1958, folder 5; Robert B. Patterson to Coleman, 25 July 1957, folder 6; Coleman to Patterson, 26 July 1957, folder 6, all in box 12, Coleman Papers.

122. William J. Simmons, oral history, interviewed by Orley B. Caudill, 26 June 1979, vol. 372, transcript, 65, MOHP; Simmons to Erle Johnston Jr., 18 Nov. 1987, folder 9, box 2, Johnston Papers; W. F. Minor, "The Citizens' Councils [*sic*]: An Incredible Decade of Defiance," 36, folder "Citizens' Council," box 2, Minor Papers; Carter, *The South Strikes Back*, 187–88.

123. Juan Williams, *Eyes on the Prize: America's Civil Rights Years, 1954–1965* (New York: Penguin, 1987), 107; Erle Johnston Jr., *Mississippi's Defiant Years, 1953–1973: An Interpretive Documentary with Personal Experiences* (Forest, Miss.: Lake Harbor, 1990), 71.

124. *NYT*, 27 Sept. 1957.

125. *JS*, 1958, regular sess., 174, 309; *JH*, 1958, regular sess., 420; *LSM*, 1958, regular sess., 1170; *DN*, 8 Mar. 1958.

126. Zack J. Van Landingham to director, State Sovereignty Commission, memo, 6 Apr. 1959, 2-113-0-1-1-1-1 to 2-1-1, p. 1-1-1, MSSC Records; *Vicksburg (Miss.) Evening Post*, 11 Feb. 1958; *DN*, 8 Mar. 1958; *SSN*, Feb. 1958.

127. *JS*, 1958, regular sess., 164.

128. Carter, *The South Strikes Back*, 88; *Vicksburg (Miss.) Evening Post*, 11 Feb. 1958.

129. John Herbers, "Council Fund up for Vote," newspaper unknown, 17 Apr. 1958, folder 16A, box 1, Cox Collection.

130. *SSN*, May 1958.

131. *JS*, 1958, regular sess., 419; *DDT*, 21 Mar. 1958; *DN*, 24 Mar. 1958.

132. *SSN*, May 1958.

133. *JH*, 1958, regular sess., 641–42, 679–84.

134. Ibid., 684.

135. *SSN*, May 1958.

136. *Tupelo (Miss.) Daily Journal*, 31 Mar. 1958.

137. Rufus Mock to J. P. Coleman, 11 Apr. 1958, folder 5, box 2, Coleman Papers; *SSN*, May 1958.

138. LeRoy P. Percy to J. P. Coleman, 10 Apr. 1958; C. L. Crawley to Coleman, 18 Apr. 1958; J. M. Rigby to Coleman, 8 Apr. 1958; M. C. Durr to Coleman, 9 Apr. 1958; C. C. Smith to Coleman, 9 Apr. 1958, all in folder 5, box 12, Coleman Papers.

139. *SSN*, June 1958.

140. "Report to the Mississippi State Legislature," 7-3-0-5-1-1-1 to 13-1-1, pp. 12-

1-1 to 13-1-1, MSSC Records; *LSM*, 1958, regular sess., 74–75; *DN*, 8 Mar. 1958.

141. *Tupelo (Miss.) Daily Journal*, 23–24 Feb. 1957.

142. Audit, State Sovereignty Commission, 97-1-0-2-1-1-1 to 8-1-1, p. 2-1-1; *State Sovereignty Commission*, 99-111-0-1-1-1-1 to 9-1-1, p. 9-1-1 both in MSSC Records.

143. Minutes, special meeting, State Sovereignty Commission, 10 Sept. 1958, 99-14-0-11-1-1-1 to 2-1-1, p. 1-1-1, MSSC Records; *CA*, 2 Oct. 1958; *MOSR*, 1956–1960, 138.

144. Minutes, State Sovereignty Commission, 7 Aug. 1958, 99-14-0-10-1-1-1 to 2-1-1, p. 1-1-1; J. P. Coleman to all Commission members, 8 Aug. 1958, 99-10-0-2-1-1-1; Maurice L. Malone to all Commission members, 10 July 1959, 99-10-0-38-1-1-1, all in MSSC Records.

145. Walter Sillers to M. L. Malone, 13 Apr. 1959, folder 38, box 21, Coleman Papers.

146. Zack J. Van Landingham to director, State Sovereignty Commission, memo, 24 Feb. 1959, folder 6, box 2, Faulkner Collection; "Report to the Mississippi State Legislature," 7-3-0-5-1-1-1 to 13-1-1, p. 4-1-1; Van Landingham to J. Edgar Hoover, 11 Apr. 1960, 12-24-0-8-1-1-1, both in MSSC Records; *CL/DN*, 17 Apr. 1960; *SSN*, July 1958.

Chapter 2. Fear of the Unknown: Mobilizing Black Informants

1. *SSN*, July 1957.

2. "State Sovereignty Commission," 7-0-1-56-1-1-1 to 12-1-1, p. 11-1-1; "Report to the Mississippi State Legislature on Activities of the State Sovereignty Commission," 7-3-0-5-1-1-1 to 13-1-1, p. 8-1-1, both in MSSC Records.

3. Minutes, State Sovereignty Commission, 15 May 1956, 99-14-0-1-1-1-1; "Meeting of September 5, 1956," 99-13-0-2-1-1-1 to 9-1-1, p. 8-1-1; Zack J. Van Landingham to file, memo, 30 June 1959, 7-0-1-51-1-1-1; Maurice L. Malone to William H. Liston, 1 July 1959, 99-16-0-56-1-1-1, all in MSSC Records; Liston, confidential report, n.d., folder 36, box 21, Coleman Papers.

4. "State Sovereignty Commission," 7-0-1-56-1-1-1 to 12-1-1, pp. 11-1-1 to 12-1-1, MSSC Records.

5. Zack J. Van Landingham to director, State Sovereignty Commission, memo, 5 Feb. 1959, 1-26-0-4-1-1-1, MSSC Records.

6. *MOSR*, 1949–1951, 126; "History of Mississippi Valley State University," Mississippi Valley State University, Itta Bena, consulted 19 Dec. 1998 <http://www.mvsu.edu/history.html>.

7. "State Sovereignty Commission," 7-0-1-56-1-1-1 to 12-1-1, p. 8-1-1; J. H. White to Ney Gore, 8 Aug. 1956, 99-40-0-119-1-1-1; Gore to White, 25

Sept. 1956, 99-40-0-101-1-1-1, all in MSSC Records; *Atlanta (Ga.) Journal-Constitution*, 10 Feb. 1957.

8. David G. Sansing, *Making Haste Slowly: The Troubled History of Higher Education in Mississippi* (Jackson: University Press of Mississippi, 1990), 211.

9. Zack J. Van Landingham to director, State Sovereignty Commission, memo, 28 Aug. 1959, 9-0-0-45-1-1-1, MSSC Records.

10. James F. Findlay Jr., *Church People in the Struggle: The National Council of Churches and the Black Freedom Movement, 1950–1970* (New York: Oxford University Press, 1993), 114.

11. *Laurel (Miss.) Leader Call*, 2 Jan. 1958.

12. See, for example, Hal C. DeCell to Ney M. Gore, memo, 29 Oct. 1957, 1-0-0-18-1-1-1 to 2-1-1; DeCell to J. P. Coleman, memo, 27 Jan. 1958, 9-4-0-1-1-1-1, both in MSSC Records.

13. Hal C. DeCell to Ben Walley, memo, 19 May 1958, 1-12-0-1-1-1-1 to 2-1-1, p. 1-1-1, MSSC Records.

14. Hal C. DeCell to Ney M. Gore Jr., memo, 29 Apr. 1957, 2-2-0-7-1-1-1; DeCell to Gore, memo, 30 Apr. 1957, 2-2-0-3-1-1-1, both in MSSC Records.

15. John Dittmer, *Local People: The Struggle for Civil Rights in Mississippi* (Urbana: University of Illinois Press, 1994), 48–49.

16. Hal C. DeCell to Ney M. Gore, memo, "Subject: Negro Agitators," 25 Sept. 1957, 1-18-0-1-1-1-1; DeCell to Gore, memo, "Subject: Medgar W. Evers," 25 Sept. 1957, 1-23-0-21-1-1-1, both in MSSC Records.

17. Hal C. DeCell to Ney M. Gore, report, 5 Mar. 1957, 1-28-0-67-1-1-1; DeCell to Gore, memo, 7 Mar. 1957, 1-28-0-1-1-1-1, both in MSSC Records; Sansing, *Making Haste Slowly*, 144–46.

18. Clennon King to registrar's office, University of Mississippi, 11 May 1958, 1-28-0-10-1-1-1, MSSC Records.

19. Hal C. DeCell to J. P. Coleman, memo, 30 Dec. 1957, 1-28-0-66-1-1-1, MSSC Records.

20. Ibid.; "Joint Statement of Governor J. P. Coleman and Attorney General Joe T. Patterson," 1-28-0-33-1-1-1 to 4-1-1, p. 1-1-1, both in MSSC Records; Coleman to Erle Johnston, 31 Aug. 1987, folder 12, box 5, Johnston Papers.

21. "Joint Statement of Governor J. P. Coleman and Attorney General Joe T. Patterson," 1-28-0-33-1-1-1 to 4-1-1, pp. 2-1-1 to 3-1-1, MSSC Records; Coleman to Erle Johnston, 31 Aug. 1987, folder 12, box 5, Johnston Papers; *SSN*, July 1958.

22. Hal C. DeCell to J. P. Coleman, memo, 30 Dec. 1957, 1-28-0-66-1-1-1, MSSC Records.

23. "Joint Statement of Governor J. P. Coleman and Attorney General Joe T. Patterson," 1-28-0-33-1-1-1 to 4-1-1, p. 3-1-1, MSSC Records.

24. Hal C. DeCell to Ney M. Gore, memo, 17 Sept. 1957, 2-5-1-11-1-1-1, MSSC Records; *DN*, 18 July 1957; *Montgomery (Ala.) Advertiser*, 19 July 1957; *Laurel*

(Miss.) Leader Call, 2 Jan. 1958; *Jackson (Miss.) Advocate*, 4 Aug. 1959. See also the following documents in MSSC Records: 97-104-0-211-1-1-1 to 3-1-1; 97-108-0-58-1-1-1; 9-0-0-41-1-1-1; 97-104-0-75-1-1-1; 99-11-0-62-1-1-1; 99-11-0-58-1-1-1; 99-11-0-56-1-1-1.

25. Hal C. DeCell to Ney Gore, memo, 28 Feb. 1957, 2-3-0-3-1-1-1; L. C. Hicks to Gore, memo, n.d., 2-3-0-6-1-1-1 to 6-1-1, both in MSSC Records; *SSN*, Aug. 1957.

26. "Negro Editor Blasts NAACP," newspaper unknown, 15 Aug. 1957, 2-5-1-45-1-1-1, MSSC Records; *Meridian (Miss.) Star*, 30 July 1957; *DN*, 31 July 1957.

27. Hal C. DeCell to J. P. Coleman, memo, 19 Dec. 1957, 9-0-0-39-1-1-1, MSSC Records.

28. See the following documents in MSSC Records: 97-104-0-211-1-1-1 to 3-1-1; 97-108-0-58-1-1-1; 9-0-0-41-1-1-1; 97-104-0-75-1-1-1; 99-11-0-62-1-1-1; 99-11-0-58-1-1-1; 99-11-0-56-1-1-1; 99-11-0-50-1-1-1; 99-11-0-49-1-1-1; 99-11-0-46-1-1-1; 99-11-0-51-1-1-1; 99-11-0-43-1-1-1; 99-11-0-52-1-1-1; 99-11-0-40-1-1-1; 99-11-0-37-1-1-1; 9-0-0-39-1-1-1.

29. Fred H. Miller, W. A. Higgins, and B. L. Bell to O. M. McNair, 11 Feb.1958, 9-9-0-27-1-1-1 to 3-1-1, p. 2-1-1, MSSC Records; Julius E. Thompson, *The Black Press in Mississippi, 1865–1985* (Gainesville: University Press of Florida, 1993), 61; James C. Cobb, *The Most Southern Place on Earth: The Mississippi Delta and the Roots of Regional Identity* (New York: Oxford University Press, 1992), 80–81.

30. Hal C. DeCell to J. P. Coleman, memo, 6 Jan. 1958, 9-0-0-40-1-1-1; DeCell to Ben Walley, memo, 19 May 1958, 1-12-0-1-1-1-1 to 2-1-1, p. 2-1-1, both in MSSC Records; *Laurel (Miss.) Leader Call*, 2 Jan. 1958.

31. Hal C. DeCell to J. P. Coleman, memo, 27 Jan. 1958, 9-4-0-1-1-1-1; DeCell to Coleman, memo, 28 Jan. 1958, 9-4-0-2-1-1-1, both in MSSC Records.

32. Hal C. DeCell to J. P. Coleman, memo, 21 Jan. 1958, 9-0-0-1-1-1-1, MSSC Records.

33. Ibid., 27 Jan. 1958, 9-4-0-1-1-1-1.

34. Ibid., 24 Feb. 1958, 2-5-1-15-1-1-1; DeCell, note, n.d., 2-42-0-3-1-1-1, both in MSSC Records.

35. See the following Fred Miller's receipts in MSSC Records: 14 Oct. 1957, 99-11-0-47-1-1-1; 31 Jan. 1958, 99-11-0-34-1-1-1; 1 Mar. 1958, 99-11-0-33-1-1-1.

36. Audit, State Sovereignty Commission, 97-1-0-4-1-1-1 to 7-1-1, p. 7-1-1; minutes, State Sovereignty Commission, 16 Oct. 1958, 99-14-0-12-1-1-1; Zack J. Van Landingham to director, State Sovereignty Commission, memo, 5 Nov. 1958, 8-4-0-1-1-1-1, all in MSSC Records.

37. Zack J. Van Landingham to file, memo, 1 Oct. 1958, 1-0-0-1-1-1-1, MSSC

Records; Van Landingham to James P. Coleman, 16 Sept. 1958, folder 19, box 38, Coleman Papers.

38. "Classification—Cases," 7-0-1-1-1-1-1; Zack J. Van Landingham to director, State Sovereignty Commission, memo, n.d., 7-0-1-2-1-1-1 to 2-1-1, both in MSSC Records.

39. Minutes, State Sovereignty Commission, 16 Oct. 1958, 99-14-0-12-1-1-1,MSSC Records.

40. "State Sovereignty Commission," 7-0-1-56-1-1-1 to 12-1-1, p. 12-1-1; Zack J. Van Landingham to director, State Sovereignty Commission, memo, n.d., 7-0-1-2-1-1-1 to 2-1-1, both in MSSC Records.

41. Hal C. DeCell to Maurice Malone, memo, 28 Oct. 1958, 99-95-0-9-1-1-1; "Official Program, Seventy-Second Annual Session of the General Missionary Baptist State Convention of Mississippi," 10-52-0-10-1-1-1 to 2-1-1, both in MSSC Records.

42. Hal C. DeCell to Director Malone, memo, 2 Oct. 1958, 99-95-0-13-1-1-1, MSSC Records.

43. Zack J. Van Landingham to director, State Sovereignty Commission, memo, "Subject: NAACP, Greenville, Mississippi—Integration Organizations," 6 Nov. 1958, 1-13-0-2-1-1-1 to 2-1-1; Van Landingham to director, memo, "Subject: NAACP—Leland, Miss.—Integration Organization," 6 Nov. 1958, 2-11-0-3-1-1-1 to 3-1-1, both in MSSC Records.

44. Zack J. Van Landingham to director, State Sovereignty Commission, memo, "Subject: Rev. J. H. Parker—Administrative—Informant," 6 Nov. 1958, 2-6-0-27-1-1-1 to 3-1-1, p. 3-1-1, MSSC Records.

45. Zack J. Van Landingham to director, State Sovereignty Commission, memo, "Subject: Rev. J. H. Parker—Administrative—Informant," 6 Nov. 1958 [on the same subject with the same date, but with different contents from the above memo], 9-4-0-6-1-1-1 to 3-1-1, p. 3-1-1, MSSC Records.

46. Maurice L. Malone to J. P. Coleman, 14 Nov. 1958, 99-95-0-38-1-1-1, MSSC Records.

47. Zack J. Van Landingham to director, State Sovereignty Commission, memo, "Subject: Rev. J. H. Parker—Administrative—Informant," 6 Nov. 1958, 9-4-0-6-1-1-1 to 3-1-1, p. 2-1-1; Van Landingham, "Report on Rev. J. H. Parker," 6 Nov. 1958, 9-4-0-4-1-1-1, both in MSSC Records.

48. Zack J. Van Landingham to file 9-4, memo, 4 Dec. 1959, 9-4-0-10-1-1-1, MSSC Records.

49. Memo, n.d., 1-23-0-12-1-1-1, MSSC Records.

50. L. C. Hicks, "Subject: Medgar Evers," 2 Dec. 1958, 1-23-0-14-1-1-1, MSSC Records.

51. Zack J. Van Landingham to file 1-23, memo, n.d., 1-23-0-22-1-1-1 to 6-1-1, MSSC Records.

52. Zack J. Van Landingham to J. P. Coleman, memo, 12 Jan. 1959, 2-10-0-6-1-

1-1 to 3-1-1, p. 2-1-1; Van Landingham to director, State Sovereignty Commission, memo, 10 Aug. 1959, 2-4-0-10-1-1-1 to 2-1-1, p. 1-1-1, both in MSSC Records.

53. B. L. Bell to J. P. Coleman, 13 Nov. 1958, 9-9-0-1-1-1-1 to 4-1-1, pp. 2-1-1 to 4-1-1, MSSC Records.

54. J. P. Coleman to Zack J. Van Landingham, 17 Dec. 1958, 9-9-0-1-1-1-1 to 4-1-1, p. 1-1-1, MSSC Records.

55. Zack J. Van Landingham to J. P. Coleman, memo, 12 Jan. 1959, 2-10-0-6-1-1-1 to 3-1-1, MSSC Records.

56. Zack J. Van Landingham to file 9-9, memo, 8 Apr. 1959, 9-9-0-27-1-1-1 to 3-1-1, MSSC Records.

57. Zack J. Van Landingham to J. P. Coleman, memo, 12 Jan. 1959, 2-10-0-6-1-1-1 to 3-1-1, p. 3-1-1, MSSC Records.

58. Zack J. Van Landingham to file 9-9, memo, 15 Jan. 1959, 9-9-0-10-1-1-1; Van Landingham to director, State Sovereignty Commission, memo, 27 Jan. 1959, 9-9-0-14-1-1-1, both in MSSC Records.

59. Zack J. Van Landingham to director, State Sovereignty Commission, memo, 26 Jan. 1959, 9-9-0-11-1-1-1 to 3-1-1, p. 1-1-1, MSSC Records.

60. Ibid., 9-9-0-11-1-1-1 to 3-1-1; Van Landingham to director, memo, 27 Jan. 1959, 9-9-0-14-1-1-1, both in MSSC Records.

61. Zack J. Van Landingham to director, State Sovereignty Commission, memo, 9 Mar. 1959, 9-9-0-20-1-1-1, MSSC Records.

62. "Report to the Mississippi State Legislature," 7-3-0-5-1-1-1 to 13-1-1, p. 1-1-1, MSSC Records.

63. Zack J. Van Landingham to director, State Sovereignty Commission, memo, 12 Jan. 1959, 1-17-0-6-1-1-1 to 2-1-1, p. 1-1-1; Van Landingham to director, memo, 13 Jan. 1959, 9-9-0-7-1-1-1 to 2-1-1, p. 1-1-1, both in MSSC Records. Regarding the Sovereignty Commission's series of investigations on Amzie Moore, see Van Landingham to file 1-17, memo, 24 Feb. 1959, 1-17-0-8-1-1-1 to 2-1-1, MSSC Records.

64. See, for instance, "Henry Cullen Watts," 9-9-0-15-1-1-1; "Garrett Eugene Gray," 9-9-0-16-1-1-1 to 2-1-1, both in MSSC Records.

65. Hal C. DeCell to J. P. Coleman, memo, 21 Jan. 1958, 9-0-0-1-1-1-1, MSSC Records.

66. Zack J. Van Landingham to director, State Sovereignty Commission, memo, 26 Mar. 1959, 1-23-0-34-1-1-1, MSSC Records.

67. Ibid., 30 Apr. 1959, 9-9-0-30-1-1-1 to 2-1-1, p. 1-1-1; Van Landingham to director, memo, 6 May 1959, 1-23-0-38-1-1-1; B. L. Bell to State Sovereignty Commission, 25 May 1959, 9-9-0-35-1-1-1 to 2-1-1, p. 1-1-1, all in MSSC Records.

68. Minutes, State Sovereignty Commission, 16 July 1959, 99-14-0-17-1-1-1 to

2-1-1, p. 1-1-1; Zack J. Van Landingham to file, memo, 20 July 1959, 7-0-1-64-1-1-1, both in MSSC Records.

69. Zack J. Van Landingham to director, State Sovereignty Commission, memo, 18 Sept. 1959, 1-15-0-7-1-1-1 to 3-1-1, MSSC Records.

70. Ibid., p. 3-1-1.

71. Ibid., 23 Sept. 1959, 9-1-1-71-1-1-1 to 3-1-1, p. 2-1-1; Van Landingham to director, memo, 24 Sept. 1959, 9-9-0-42-1-1-1, both in MSSC Records.

72. L. C. Hicks to Ney M. Gore Jr., memo, n.d., 2-3-0-6-1-1-1 to 6-1-1, pp. 1-1-1 to 4-1-1, MSSC Records.

73. Zack J. Van Landingham to director, State Sovereignty Commission, memo, 21 Oct. 1959, 2-72-1-30-1-1-1; Martin Luther King Jr., "Address by Dr. Martin Luther King Jr., at Public Meeting of the Southern Christian Ministers Conference of Mississippi, Wednesday, September 23, 1959," 2-126-1-30-1-1-1 to 16-1-1; Van Landingham to director, memo, 22 Oct. 1959, 2-72-1-34-1-1-1; "Tag Numbers of Cars Parked around the Negro Masonic Temple on Lynch Street," 23 Sept. 1959, 2-126-1-39-1-1-1 to 2-1-1, all in MSSC Records.

74. Minutes draft, State Sovereignty Commission, 20 June 1956, 99-13-0-4-1-1-1 to 4-1-1, p. 4-1-1; minutes, State Sovereignty Commission, 9 Oct. 1957, 99-14-0-8-1-1-1 to 2-1-1, p. 2-1-1; minutes, State Sovereignty Commission, 20 Nov. 1958, 99-14-0-13-1-1-1, all in MSSC Records.

75. Zack J. Van Landingham to director, State Sovereignty Commission, memo, 9 Nov. 1959, 1-4-0-25-1-1-1 to 2-1-1, MSSC Records.

76. Ibid., p. 2-1-1; Van Landingham to director, memo, 4 Dec. 1959, 1-17-0-12-1-1-1, both in MSSC Records.

77. Zack J. Van Landingham to file, memo, 24 May 1960, 1-17-0-22-1-1-1, MSSC Records.

78. Zack J. Van Landingham to director, State Sovereignty Commission, memo, 10 Aug. 1959, 2-4-0-10-1-1-1 to 2-1-1, MSSC Records.

79. Ibid., 11 Aug. 1959, 9-9-0-38-1-1-1; Van Landingham to Ross R. Barnett, memo, 25 Feb. 1960, 9-9-0-58-1-1-1; Van Landingham to Barnett, memo, 23 Mar. 1960, 9-9-0-62-1-1-1, all in MSSC Records.

80. Zack J. Van Landingham to file 9-9, memo, 12 May 1960, 9-9-0-70-1-1-1, MSSC Records.

81. "Requisition on the Auditor of Public Accounts," 30 June 1960, 97-107-0-3-1-1-1 to 2-1-1, MSSC Records.

82. *SSN*, July 1958.

83. Zack J. Van Landingham, investigative report, 17 Dec. 1958, 1-27-0-6-1-1-1 to 37-1-1, pp. 4-1-1, 6-1-1, 8-1-1, 12-1-1, 25-1-1, MSSC Records; Monte Piliawsky, *Exit 13: Oppression and Racism in Academia* (Boston: South End, 1982), 22. The same investigative report can also be located in folder 2, box 4, Holmes Collection.

84. *Hattiesburg (Miss.) American*, 5 Dec. 1958.
85. Zack J. Van Landingham to director, State Sovereignty Commission, memo, 24 Nov. 1958, 1-27-0-1-1-1-1 to 2-1-1, MSSC Records.
86. Zack J. Van Landingham, investigative report, 17 Dec. 1958, 1-27-0-6-1-1-1 to 37-1-1, pp. 11-1-1 to 12-1-1; Van Landingham to file 1-23, memo, 5 Jan. 1959, 1-23-0-23-1-1-1, both in MSSC Records. Van Landingham's thirty-seven-page report on the Kennard case can also be located in folder 38, box 21, Coleman Papers, and in folder 2, box 4, Holmes Collection.
87. Zack J. Van Landingham, investigative report, 17 Dec. 1958, 1-27-0-6-1-1-1 to 37-1-1, pp. 27-1-1 to 29-1-1, MSSC Records.
88. Allan K. Chalmers to dear friend, 3 Dec. 1962, folder 40, box 1, King Collection; Zack J. Van Landingham to file, memo, 6 July 1959, 2-5-2-77-1-1-1, MSSC Records; James Cohen, oral history, interviewed by Mike Garvey, 2 Feb. 1976, vol. 705, transcript, MOHP, <http://www.lib.usm.edu/~spcol/crda/oh/cohentrans.htm>; J. C. Fairley, Mamie Phillips, and Charles Phillips, oral history, interviewed by Charles C. Bolton, 24 June 1998, vol. 711, transcript, MOHP, <http://www.lib.usm.edu/~spcol/crda/oh/fairleytrans.htm>, both in *Oral Histories in the Civil Rights in Mississippi Digital Archive* series, William D. McCain Library and Archives, University of Southern Mississippi, Hattiesburg, consulted 1 Dec. 2000 <http://www.lib.usm.edu/~spcol/crda/oh/index.html>; Ronald A. Hollander, "One Mississippi Negro Who Didn't Go to College," *Reporter*, 8 Nov. 1962, 30; Sansing, *Making Haste Slowly,* 148; Charles M. Payne, *I've Got the Light of Freedom: The Organizing Tradition and the Mississippi Freedom Struggle* (Berkeley: University of California Press, 1995), 55.
89. Zack J. Van Landingham to director, State Sovereignty Commission, memo, 17 Dec. 1958, 2-66-0-2-1-1-1 to 4-1-1, p. 1-1-1; Van Landingham to director, memo, 4 May 1959, 5-3-1-19-1-1-1, both in MSSC Records.
90. Zack J. Van Landingham, investigative report, 17 Dec. 1958, 1-27-0-6-1-1-1 to 37-1-1, pp. 28-1-1 to 31-1-1, 34-1-1, MSSC Records.
91. Kline Weatherford to Zack J. Van Landingham, 12 Dec. 1958, 1-27-0-10-1-1-1 to 2-1-1; Van Landingham to Weatherford, 18 Dec. 1958, 1-27-0-8-1-1-1; "Voucher for Reimbursement of Expenses," 1-27-0-9-1-1-1 to 2-1-1; Robert W. Pope to Van Landingham, 12 Dec. 1958, 1-27-0-11-1-1-1; Van Landingham to Pope, 18 Dec. 1958, 1-27-0-12-1-1-1; Van Landingham to J. P. Coleman, memo, 18 Dec. 1958, 1-27-0-14-1-1-1 to 2-1-1, all in MSSC Records.
92. Zack J. Van Landingham to file 1-27, memo, 18 Dec. 1958, 1-27-0-15-1-1-1 to 2-1-1; Van Landingham, investigative report, 17 Dec. 1958, 1-27-0-6-1-1-1 to 37-1-1, p. 37-1-1, both in MSSC Records.
93. Zack J. Van Landingham to file 1-27, memo, 22 Dec. 1958, 1-27-0-16-1-1-1, MSSC Records.
94. Zack J. Van Landingham to J. P. Coleman, memo, 27 Aug. 1959, 1-27-0-26-

1-1-1; Van Landingham to director, State Sovereignty Commission, memo, 28 Aug. 1959, 1-27-0-27-1-1-1, both in MSSC Records; Van Landingham to director, memo, 3 Sept. 1959, folder 37, box 21, Coleman Papers.

95. Zack J. Van Landingham to J. P. Coleman, memo, 14 Sept. 1959, 1-27-0-36-1-1-1 to 6-1-1, pp. 5-1-1 to 6-1-1, MSSC Records.

96. James P. Coleman and Verner S. Holmes, oral history, interviewed by David G. Sansing, 16 June 1979, transcript, 68–69, box 6, Holmes Collection; Zack J. Van Landingham to director, State Sovereignty Commission, memo, 9 Sept. 1959, 1-27-0-31-1-1-1 to 3-1-1, pp. 1-1-1 to 2-1-1, MSSC Records.

97. Aubrey K. Lucas to Clyde Kennard, 14 Sept. 1959, 1-27-0-41-1-1-1, MSSC Records.

98. Zack J. Van Landingham to J. P. Coleman, memo, 21 Sept. 1959, 1-27-0-40-1-1-1 to 6-1-1, pp. 1-1-1 to 3-1-1, MSSC Records; *Tupelo (Miss.) Daily Journal*, 23–24 Feb. 1957.

99. Zack J. Van Landingham to J. P. Coleman, memo, 21 Sept. 1959, 1-27-0-40-1-1-1 to 6-1-1, pp. 3-1-1 to 6-1-1, MSSC Records; *Hattiesburg (Miss.) American*, 29 Sept. 1959.

100. "Negro's Arrest Surprise, Says Sovereignty Prober," newspaper unknown, n.d., folder 36, box 1, Cox Collection.

101. *DN*, 9 Oct. 1961.

102. Erle Johnston Jr., *Politics: Mississippi Style* (Forest, Miss.: Lake Harbor, 1993), x.

103. Erle Johnston Jr., *I Rolled with Ross: A Political Portrait* (Baton Rouge, La.: Moran, 1980), 73.

104. *MOSR*, 1960–1964, 363, 380.

105. William J. Simmons to dear member, 31 Aug. 1959, folder 1, CC Collection; "Barnett Praises Council Activity," *Citizens' Council*, Sept. 1959, folder 2, box 1, Cox Collection; *DN*, 9 Sept. 1959.

106. "Fighting Back, 1957–62," in *Eyes on the Prize: America's Civil Rights Years* series, Blackside, Boston, 1987, videocassette.

107. Neil R. McMillen, *The Citizens' Council: Organized Resistance to the Second Reconstruction, 1954–1964* (Urbana: University of Illinois Press, 1971), 326.

108. Walter Lord, *The Past That Would Not Die* (New York: Harper and Row, 1965), 77.

109. "Report to the Mississippi State Legislature," 7-3-0-5-1-1-1 to 13-1-1, pp. 1-1-1 to 2-1-1, MSSC Records.

110. Hugh N. Clayton to J. P. Coleman, 16 June 1959; Coleman to Clayton, 17 June 1959, both in folder 18, box 26, Coleman Papers; *CA*, 20 June 1960; *SSN*, Aug. 1960.

Chapter 3. To Maintain Segregation in Mississippi at All Costs: Revitalizing the State Sovereignty Commission

1. Cecil L. Sumners, *The Governors of Mississippi* (Gretna, La.: Pelican, 1980), 129–30.

2. *JH*, 1960, regular sess., 51.

3. *LSM*, 1960, regular sess., 413–14; *CL/DN*, 12 June 1960.

4. *LSM*, 1960, regular sess., 360.

5. Erle Johnston Jr., *Mississippi's Defiant Years, 1953–1973: An Interpretive Documentary with Personal Experiences* (Forest, Miss.: Lake Harbor, 1990), 100.

6. *LSM*, 1960, regular sess., 76.

7. *DN*, 6 May 1960.

8. "Report to the Mississippi State Legislature on Activities of the State Sovereignty Commission," 7-3-0-5-1-1-1 to 13-1-1, pp. 9-1-1 to 12-1-1, MSSC Records.

9. Minutes, State Sovereignty Commission, 19 May 1960, folder 2, box 135, PBJ Papers.

10. George M. Yarbrough to Paul B. Johnson Jr., 10 June 1960, folder 2, box 57, PBJ Papers; *MOSR*, 1960–1964, 131.

11. Erle Johnston Jr., letter to the author, 23 Dec. 1993; Herman B. DeCell, oral history, interviewed by Orley B. Caudill, 9 June 1977, vol. 207, transcript, 37, MOHP; *CL/DN*, 12 June 1960.

12. Minutes, State Sovereignty Commission, 24 May 1960; Albert Jones to Paul B. Johnson Jr., memo, 31 May 1960, both in folder 2, box 135, PBJ Papers; "Albert Jones" [biographical data], subject file: "Jones, Albert," MDAH; *DN*, 28 Dec. 1958.

13. Erle Johnston Jr., oral history, interviewed by Yasuhiro Katagiri, 13 Aug. 1993, vol. 276, pt. 2, transcript, 4, MOHP; minutes, State Sovereignty Commission, 24 May 1960, folder 2, box 135, PBJ Papers.

14. Erle Johnston Jr., oral history, interviewed by Orley B. Caudill, 16 July 1980 and 30 July 1980, vol. 276, transcript, 5–58, MOHP.

15. Ralph D. Ford to Zack Vanlandingham [*sic*], 1 Apr. 1960, 8-11-0-6-1-1-1; audit, State Sovereignty Commission, 97-1-0-5-1-1-1 to 7-1-1, p. 7-1-1, both in MSSC Records; *TP*, 23 Mar. 1960; *CL*, 26 Mar. 1960; Robert C. Thomas, investigative report, 19 July 1960, folder 6, box 5, Faulkner Collection.

16. Hugh N. Clayton to J. P. Coleman, 16 June 1959; Coleman to Clayton, 17 June 1959, both in folder 18, box 26, Coleman Papers; *CA*, 20 June 1960; *SSN*, Aug. 1960.

17. Minutes, State Sovereignty Commission, 19 May 1960, folder 2, box 135, PBJ Papers; *DN*, 26 Mar. 1960.

18. Minutes, State Sovereignty Commission, 19 May 1960, folder 2, box 135, PBJ Papers; *CL*, 18 June 1960; *DN*, 28 Dec. 1955.

19. Audit, State Sovereignty Commission, 97-1-0-7-1-1-1 to 7-1-1, p. 7-1-1; "December 1961 Payroll," 7-3-0-8-1-1-1, both in MSSC Records; *ST*, 2 July 1960; *CL*, 2 July 1960; *DN*, 4 Aug. 1947.

20. Audit, State Sovereignty Commission, 97-1-0-5-1-1-1 to 7-1-1, p. 7-1-1; H. A. Boren to State Sovereignty Commission, 30 Nov. [Dec.] 1961, 7-0-4-

148-1-1-1; Albert Jones to Public Employees' Retirement System of Mississippi, 25 Apr. 1962, 7-0-5-63-1-1-1, all in MSSC Records; *TP*, 17 June 1960; *CL*, 21 Dec. 1961.

21. "December 1961 Payroll," 7-3-0-8-1-1-1, MSSC Records; Neil R. McMillen, *The Citizens' Council: Organized Resistance to the Second Reconstruction, 1954–1964* (Urbana: University of Illinois Press, 1971), 326.

22. *JS*, 1960, regular sess., 73, 75; *JH*, 1960, regular sess., 92–93; *LSM*, 1960, regular sess., 870–71.

23. James W. Silver, *Mississippi: The Closed Society* (New York: Harcourt, Brace, and World, 1964), 44.

24. McMillen, *The Citizens' Council*, 27.

25. *SSN*, Aug. 1960.

26. Albert Jones to Paul B. Johnson Jr., 22 July 1960, folder 2, box 57; "Citizen[s'] Council Grant," folder 1, box 137, both in PBJ Papers; *TP*, 17 June 1960; *DN*, 30 Dec. 1960.

27. Hodding Carter, *The South Strikes Back* (Garden City, N.Y.: Doubleday, 1959), 188.

28. Statement, State Sovereignty Commission, 7-0-1-148-1-1-1 to 2-1-1, p. 2-1-1; Albert Jones to Paul Johnson, 7 July 1960, 7-0-1-148-1-1-1 to 2-1-1, p. 1-1-1, both in MSSC Records; *SSN*, Aug. 1960.

29. *ST*, 17 July 1960.

30. Mississippi Advisory Committee to the United States Commission on Civil Rights, *Report on Mississippi*, Jan. 1963, 4-0-1-82-1-1-1 to 36-1-1, p. 31-1-1, MSSC Records; *CL*, 10 July 1960.

31. Richard P. Ellerbrake to Albert Jones, 8 July 1960, 7-0-1-152-1-1-1, MSSC Records.

32. Albert Jones to Richard B. [*sic*] Ellerbrake, 11 July 1960, 7-0-1-153-1-1-1, MSSC Records.

33. Albert Jones to file, memo, 11 July 1960, 2-56-1-49-1-1-1, MSSC Records.

34. J. E. Stockstill to Richard Ellerbrake, 11 July 1960, 7-0-1-156-1-1-1 to 3-1-1, p. 1-1-1; Stockstill to Albert Jones, 13 July 1960, 7-0-1-161-1-1-1; Jones to Aubrey Bell, 14 July 1960, 7-0-1-162-1-1-1 to 2-1-1, p. 2-1-1, all in MSSC Records.

35. J. E. Stockstill to Albert Jones, 13 July 1960, 7-0-1-161-1-1-1; Jones to Stockstill, 14 July 1960, 7-0-1-162-1-1-1 to 2-1-1, p. 1-1-1, both in MSSC Records.

36. Earl Evans Jr. to Albert Jones, 15 July 1960, 2-56-1-55-1-1-1, MSSC Records.

37. Herman B. DeCell to Albert Jones, 15 July 1960, 2-56-1-56-1-1-1, MSSC Records.

38. Mississippi Advisory Committee, *Report on Mississippi*, 4-0-1-82-1-1-1 to 36-1-1, pp. 31-1-1, 36-1-1, MSSC Records.

39. *DN*, 14 Nov. 1959.

40. "Statement of William L. Higgs," folder 25, Schutt Papers; Complaint, *C. E.*

Shaffer, et al., v. Citizens' Council Forum, et al., Jackson Division, Southern District of Mississippi, U.S. District Court, 9-11-1-64-1-1-1 to 17-1-1, pp. 3-1-1, 9-1-1; A. L. Hopkins, investigative report, 16 May 1961, 2-55-2-48-1-1-1, both in MSSC Records; *Arkansas Gazette*, 8 Jan. 1961; *CL/DN*, 8 Jan. 1961; *DN*, 9 Jan. 1961.

41. *DDT*, 17 Jan. 1961; *DN*, 17 Jan. 1961.
42. *DN*, 23 Jan. 1961.
43. *DDT*, 31 Jan. 1961.
44. A. L. Hopkins, investigative report, 18 Feb. 1963, 1-76-0-54-1-1-1 to 4-1-1, MSSC Records; *DN*, 19 Oct. 1962; Silver, *Mississippi*, 96–98; Seth Cagin and Philip Dray, *We Are Not Afraid: The Story of Goodman, Schwerner, and Chaney and the Civil Rights Campaign for Mississippi* (New York: Macmillan, 1988), 252; John Dittmer, *Local People: The Struggle for Civil Rights in Mississippi* (Urbana: University of Illinois Press, 1994), 132, 150–51, 459; Charles M. Payne, *I've Got the Light of Freedom: The Organizing Tradition and the Mississippi Freedom Struggle* (Berkeley: University of California Press, 1995), 244–45.
45. *DN*, 25 Apr. 1961; *DDT*, 25 May 1961.
46. McMillen, *The Citizens' Council*, 339.
47. Erle Johnston Jr. to Albert Jones and members of the State Sovereignty Commission, proposal, n.d.; Johnston to Heber Ladner, 11 July 1960, both in vol. 542, subject files, Ladner Papers; Jones to Paul B. Johnson Jr., 7 June 1960, folder 2, box 135, PBJ Papers.
48. Erle Johnston Jr. to Albert Jones and members of the State Sovereignty Commission, proposal, n.d., vol. 542, subject files, Ladner Papers.
49. *JH*, 1960, regular sess., 51.
50. Johnston, oral history, vol. 276, pt. 2, transcript, 6, MOHP; *DN*, 24 Sept. 1960.
51. *A Report on the First Eighteen Months of the Public Relations Program*, 99-139-0-1-1-1-1 to 40-1-1, p. 2-1-1, MSSC Records.
52. Erle Johnston Jr. to Albert Jones and members of the State Sovereignty Commission, proposal, n.d., vol. 542, subject files, Ladner Papers.
53. "The Message from Mississippi: Talk Prepared for Speakers Bureau of Public Relations Department, Mississippi State Sovereignty Commission," *FF*, July 1961 to June 1962, roll no. 14, N14 3635–43. Besides this nine-page 1960 version of "The Message from Mississippi," there are at least two more versions with differences among them. These two other versions are: the thirteen-page "Message from Mississippi: Address Prepared for Volunteer Speakers of the Mississippi State Sovereignty Commission," which can be found in the vertical file "Sovereignty Commission, Mississippi State," Mississippiana Collection, and in the file "Mississippi Sovereignty Commission," administrative files, ASSC Records; and the eleven-page "Message from Mississippi: Address Prepared for Volunteer Speakers of the Mississippi State Sovereignty Commission,"

which is located in the appendices to Johnston, oral history, vol. 276, transcript, 110–20, MOHP.

54. "The Message from Mississippi: Talk Prepared for Speakers Bureau of Public Relations Department, Mississippi State Sovereignty Commission," *FF*, July 1961 to June 1962, roll no. 14, N14 3635–43.

55. *TP*, 22 July 1960; *DN*, 22 July 1960.

56. Erle Johnston Jr., *I Rolled with Ross: A Political Portrait* (Baton Rouge, La.: Moran, 1980), 47.

57. *A Report on the First Eighteen Months of the Public Relations Program*, 99-139-0-1-1-1-1 to 40-1-1, p. 2-1-1, MSSC Records.

58. *A Message from Mississippi: Are You Curious?*, 99-140-0-11-1-1-1 to 3-1-1, MSSC Records. The same pamphlet can also be found in the file, "Mississippi Sovereignty Commission," administrative files, ASSC Records; and in *FF*, July 1961 to June 1962, roll no. 14, N14 3586–88.

59. *A Report on the First Eighteen Months of the Public Relations Program*, 99-139-0-1-1-1-1 to 40-1-1, p. 2-1-1, MSSC Records.

60. Ibid., pp. 2-1-1 to 3-1-1; O. H. Barnett to Erle Johnston, 24 Aug. 1987, folder 5, box 9, Johnston Papers; *TP*, 10 Aug. 1960; *CL/DN*, 14 Aug. 1960.

61. William D. McCain to Erle Johnston, 27 Aug. 1987, folder 5, box 9, Johnston Papers; *DN*, 9 Sept. 1960.

62. *DN*, 29 Oct. 1960.

63. *ST*, 27 Jan. 1961.

64. *Birmingham (Ala.) News*, 9 Jan. 1961; *New York Herald Tribune*, 9 Jan. 1961; *CA*, 15 Jan. 1961.

65. J. W. Jones to State Sovereignty Commission, 3 Aug. 1960, 9-16-0-84-1-1-2; "Negro Offers to Be Speaker for Bureau," newspaper unknown, n.d., 9-16-0-93-1-1-1, both in MSSC Records.

66. J. W. Jones to Erle Johnston Jr., 12 Aug. 1960, 9-16-0-86-1-1-1 to 5-1-1, p. 1-1-1; "Why We Should Keep Mississippi Segregated," 9-16-0-86-1-1-1 to 5-1-1, pp. 2-1-1 to 5-1-1, both in MSSC Records.

67. *TP*, 19 Oct. 1961.

68. Albert Jones to John Bell Williams, 20 June 1961, 7-0-4-61-1-1-1, MSSC Records.

69. See the "Requisition on the Auditor of Public Accounts" forms in the following documents: 97-99-1-54-1-1-1 to 5-1-1; 97-99-1-37-1-1-1 to 2-1-1; 97-99-1-33-1-1-1 to 2-1-1; 97-98-2-264-1-1-1 to 7-1-1; 97-98-2-247-1-1-1 to 2-1-1; 97-98-2-182-1-1-1 to 2-1-1; 97-98-2-166-1-1-1 to 2-1-1; 97-98-2-121-1-1-1 to 3-1-1, all in MSSC Records.

70. *TP*, 19 Oct. 1961; *DN*, 19 Oct. 1961.

71. *NYT*, 19 Oct. 1961.

72. Erle Johnston Jr. to Aubrey Bell, 20 Oct. 1961, 7-0-4-132-1-1-1 to 2-1-1, p.

1-1-1, MSSC Records; Johnston, oral history, vol. 276, pt. 2, transcript, 20, MOHP; Johnston, letter to the author, 23 Dec. 1993.

73. Aubrey H. Bell to Albert Jones, 19 Oct. 1961, 7-0-4-130-1-1-1; Bell to Erle Johnston Jr., 21 Oct. 1961, 7-0-4-133-1-1-1 to 2-1-1, p. 1-1-1; Jones to Bell, 25 Oct. 1961, 7-0-4-135-1-1-1, all in MSSC Records.

74. Erle Johnston Jr. to Aubrey Bell, 20 Oct. 1961, 7-0-4-132-1-1-1 to 2-1-1, p. 1-1-1, MSSC Records.

75. Aubrey H. Bell to Albert Jones, 19 Oct. 1961, 7-0-4-130-1-1-1, MSSC Records.

76. Erle Johnston Jr. to Aubrey Bell, 20 Oct. 1961, 7-0-4-132-1-1-1 to 2-1-1, p. 1-1-1; Albert Jones to Wilburn Hooker, 24 Oct. 1961, 7-0-4-137-1-1-1, both in MSSC Records.

77. Wilburn Hooker to Albert Jones, 21 Oct. 1961, 7-0-4-134-1-1-1, MSSC Records.

78. Aubrey H. Bell to Erle Johnston Jr., 27 Oct. 1961, 7-0-4-138-1-1-1, MSSC Records.

79. Daniel Schechter to State Sovereignty Commission, 10 Jan. 1962, 3-38A-1-139-1-1-1; Albert Jones to Schechter, 22 Jan. 1962, 3-38A-1-140-1-1-1, both in MSSC Records.

80. Minutes, State Sovereignty Commission, 18 July 1963, 7-5-0-7-1-1-1 to 2-1-1, p. 1-1-1; "Agenda for Sovereignty Commission Meeting, July 18, 1963," 99-55-0-1-1-1-1 to 2-1-1, p. 1-1-1, both in MSSC Records. These documents can also be located in folder 4, box 135, PBJ Papers.

81. *A Report on the First Eighteen Months of the Public Relations Program*, 99-139-0-1-1-1-1 to 40-1-1, p. 2-1-1, MSSC Records.

82. "Questions Asked, and Answers Given, by Sovereignty Commission Volunteer Speakers," 99-139-0-7-1-1-1 to 5-1-1, MSSC Records. The same document can also be found in the vertical file "Sovereignty Commission, Mississippi State," Mississippiana Collection.

83. Johnston, oral history, vol. 276, pt. 2, transcript, 19, MOHP. As far as the Sovereignty Commission's official records attest, the speakers bureau did not utilize any women as its volunteer speakers.

84. *A Report on the First Eighteen Months of the Public Relations Program*, 99-139-0-1-1-1-1 to 40-1-1, p. 2-1-1, MSSC Records.

85. Erle Johnston Jr. to Paul B. Johnson Jr., memo, 12 Oct. 1964, folder 5, box 136, PBJ Papers.

86. Thomas P. Brady, oral history, interviewed by Orley B. Caudill, 4 Mar. 1972, vol. 2, pt. 1, transcript, 25, MOHP.

87. Johnston, oral history, vol. 276, transcript, 71, MOHP.

88. Ibid.; William J. Simmons, oral history, interviewed by Orley B. Caudill, 26 June 1979, vol. 372, transcript, 49–51, 56, 59, MOHP.

89. Albert Jones to Erle Johnston Jr., 24 Apr. 1962, 7-0-5-61-1-1-1; Johnston to Bill Simmons, 1 May 1962, 7-0-5-66-1-1-1, both in MSSC Records.

90. *A Report on the First Eighteen Months of the Public Relations Program*, 99-139-0-1-1-1-1 to 40-1-1, p. 23-1-1, MSSC Records.

91. Mike Martinson to Albert Jones, 19 July 1960, 7-0-2-107-1-1-1 to 2-1-1, MSSC Records; *DN*, 22 July 1960; *TP*, 22 July 1960.

92. Minutes, State Sovereignty Commission, 20 June 1956, 99-13-0-3-1-1-1 to 4-1-1, p. 4-1-1; minutes draft, State Sovereignty Commission, 20 June 1956, 99-13-0-4-1-1-1 to 4-1-1, p. 4-1-1, both in MSSC Records.

93. *DN*, 16 Dec. 1960.

94. Mike Martinson to Albert Jones, 19 July 1960, 7-0-2-107-1-1-1 to 2-1-1, MSSC Records; Erle Johnston Jr. to Albert Jones and members of the State Sovereignty Commission, proposal, n.d., vol. 542, subject files, Ladner Papers; *Memphis (Tenn.) Press-Scimitar*, 16 Dec. 1960.

95. "Report of Special Committee on Cost of Film, 'The Mississippi Story,'" 7-0-2-93-1-1-1 to 7-1-1, p. 6-1-1, MSSC Records.

96. *Charlotte (N.C.) Observer*, 13 Jan. 1961.

97. *The Message from Mississippi*, prod. Public Relations Department, Mississippi State Sovereignty Commission, Jackson, 1960, videocassette, in the author's possession.

98. Ibid.

99. Ibid.

100. Ross R. Barnett to Tom Watkins, 21 Dec. 1960, 7-0-2-102-1-1-1, MSSC Records; *Memphis (Tenn.) Press-Scimitar*, 16 Dec. 1960.

101. *A Report on the First Eighteen Months of the Public Relations Program*, 99-139-0-1-1-1-1 to 40-1-1, p. 23-1-1, MSSC Records; *Available to You without Cost!: "The Message from Mississippi," FF*, July 1961 to June 1962, roll no. 14, N14 3589–90.

102. *DN*, 13 Jan. 1961; *CA*, 15 Jan. 1961; *ST*, 5 Feb. 1961.

103. *A Report on the First Eighteen Months of the Public Relations Program*, 99-139-0-1-1-1-1 to 40-1-1, p. 23-1-1, MSSC Records.

104. Erle Johnston Jr. to Ross Barnett, 6 June 1962, 7-0-6-3-1-1-1 to 3-1-1, MSSC Records. The same document is located in folder 2, box 58, PBJ Papers.

105. Johnston, oral history, vol. 276, transcript, 75, MOHP.

106. Johnston, *Mississippi's Defiant Years*, 119.

107. James W. Silver, *Running Scared: Silver in Mississippi* (Jackson: University Press of Mississippi, 1984), 70.

108. Johnston, oral history, vol. 276, transcript, 75, MOHP.

109. See, for example, Virgil Downing, investigative report, 6 Feb. 1961, 2-46-0-19-1-1-1 to 2-1-1, MSSC Records.

110. Albert Jones to Ross Barnett, 23 Jan. 1962, 2-46-0-39-1-1-1; Barnett to Jones, 24 Jan. 1962, 2-46-0-40-1-1-1, both in MSSC Records.

111. John Barksdale to Albert Johes [*sic*], 19 Mar. 1962, 2-46-0-66-1-1-1; Albert Jones to Barksdale, 26 Mar. 1962, 2-46-0-67-1-1-1, both in MSSC Records.

112. *Citizens of Color in Meridian, Mississippi*, 9-30-0-1-1-1-1 to 27-1-1; John Barksdale to Albert Jones, 20 Aug. 1962, 7-0-6-10-2-1-1, both in MSSC Records.

113. John Barksdale to Albert Jones, 20 Aug. 1962, 7-0-6-10-2-1-1; Jones to Barksdale, 23 Aug. 1962, 7-0-6-11-1-1-1, both in MSSC Records.

114. R. Fairley to gentlemen, n.d., 7-0-2-6-1-1-1 to 2-1-1; Albert Jones to Ross R. Barnett, 30 Nov. 1960, 7-0-2-4-1-1-1; "Requisition on the Auditor of Public Accounts," 30 Nov. 1960, 97-99-2-150-1-1-1 to 2-1-1, all in MSSC Records.

115. Johnston, oral history, vol. 276, transcript, 81, MOHP.

116. Wayne A. Clark, *An Analysis of the Relationship between Anti-Communism and Segregationist Thought in the Deep South, 1948–1964* (Ann Arbor, Mich.: University Microfilms, 1976), 47–48, 58.

117. Numan V. Bartley, *The Rise of Massive Resistance: Race and Politics in the South during the 1950's* (Baton Rouge: Louisiana State University Press, 1969), 185.

118. Clark, *An Analysis of the Relationship between Anti-Communism and Segregationist Thought*, 66.

119. James O. Eastland, oral history, interviewed by Joe B. Frantz, 19 Feb. 1971, AC 76-9, transcript, 3–4, LBJ Library; Richard M. Fried, *Nightmare in Red: The McCarthy Era in Perspective* (New York: Oxford University Press, 1990), 176; *NYT*, 30 Jan. 1956. The James O. Eastland Collection housed in the Law School Archives at the University of Mississippi is probably one of the most important primary source materials to fully comprehend many intriguing aspects of Mississippi's and the South's anti-civil rights crusades. Unfortunately, however, the Eastland Collection has not yet been processed and open to the public as of early 2001. John Sobotka [assistant to the dean, University of Mississippi School of Law], "Eastland Papers," e-mail to the author, 28 Feb. 2001.

120. *DN*, 3 Mar. 1956.

121. "Segregation and the South" [documentary film script], 1957, 17, folder 4, box 112, FR Archives; *Segregation and the South*, prod. George M. Martin Jr., Newsfilm Project, Fund for the Republic, Los Angeles, 1957, videocassette, CSDI Collection. See also *SSN*, Dec. 1956.

122. Dittmer, *Local People*, 58.

123. *LSM*, 1958, regular sess., 780–81.

124. See, for example, Michael Smith, oral history, interviewed by Reid Derr, 16 June 1993, vol. 448, transcript, 11–12, MOHP.

125. Horace H. Harned Jr., oral history, interviewed by Yasuhiro Katagiri, 3 Nov. 1993, vol. 355, pt. 2, transcript, 14, MOHP. The transcript of the author's oral history interview with Harned can also be read on-line at <http://www.lib.usm.edu/~spcol/crda/oh/harnedtrans.htm> in *Oral Histories in the Civil Rights in Mississippi Digital Archives* series, William D. McCain Library and

Archives, University of Southern Mississippi, Hattiesburg, consulted 1 Dec. 2000 <http://www.lib.usm.edu/~spcol/crda/oh/index.html>.

126. "Statement of Governor Ross R. Barnett of Mississippi before U.S. Senate Commerce Committee, July 12, 1963," 99-69-0-12-1-1-1 to 9-1-1, pp. 2-1-1, 9-1-1, MSSC Records.

127. Edwin King, oral history, interviewed by Yasuhiro Katagiri, 17 Aug. 1993, incomplete transcript, in the author's possession. The audiocassettes of the interview have been deposited in the Mississippi Oral History Program at the Center for Oral History and Cultural Heritage of the University of Southern Mississippi.

128. Lewis M. Killian, *White Southerners* (New York: Random House, 1970), 6.

129. Erle Johnston Jr. to Paul B. Johnson Jr., memo, 12 Oct. 1964, folder 5, box 136, PBJ Papers.

130. Progress report, State Sovereignty Commission, Mar. 1961, 7-0-3-156-1-1-1 to 2-1-1, MSSC Records; *NYT*, 31 Mar. 1961.

131. *DN*, 19 May 1961; Silver, *Mississippi*, 8.

132. Press release, State Sovereignty Commission, 8 Jan. 1961, 7-0-2-68-1-1-1, MSSC Records.

133. Albert Jones to Horace H. Harned Jr., 3 Mar. 1961, 7-0-3-82-1-1-1 to 2-1-1, p. 1-1-1, MSSC Records.

134. Albert Jones to Walter Sillers, 12 Jan. 1961, 7-0-2-40-1-1-1, MSSC Records.

135. Minutes, Independent Women's Organization, 8 Dec. 1960, 7-0-3-2-1-1-1 to 3-1-1, p. 1-1-1, MSSC Records.

136. Minutes, Paul Revere Ladies, 14 Dec. 1960, 7-0-3-2-1-1-1 to 3-1-1, p. 2-1-1, MSSC Records.

137. Ibid., pp. 2-1-1 to 3-1-1.

138. *ST*, 27 Apr. 1961(?), 7-0-3-87-1-1-1, MSSC Records.

139. Press release, State Sovereignty Commission, 8 Jan. 1961, 7-0-2-68-1-1-1; Mrs. Harry Scrivner, "Report to Sovereignty Commission," 17 Jan. 1961, 7-0-2-82-1-1-1 to 2-1-1, p. 1-1-1, both in MSSC Records.

140. Press release, State Sovereignty Commission, 8 Jan. 1961, 7-0-2-69-1-1-1 to 2-1-1, p. 1-1-1; press release, State Sovereignty Commission, 11 Jan. 1961, 7-0-2-70-1-1-1, both in MSSC Records.

141. Press release, State Sovereignty Commission, 8 Jan. 1961, 7-0-2-69-1-1-1 to 2-1-1; Mrs. Harry Scrivner, "Report to Sovereignty Commission," 17 Jan. 1961, 7-0-2-82-1-1-1 to 2-1-1, both in MSSC Records.

142. Mrs. Harry Scrivner, "Report to Sovereignty Commission," 17 Jan. 1961, 7-0-2-82-1-1-1 to 2-1-1, p. 2-1-1, MSSC Records.

143. Ibid.

144. Albert Jones to file, memo, 19 Feb. 1961, 7-0-3-78-1-1-1 to 3-1-1, p. 1-1-1; press release, State Sovereignty Commission, 19 Feb. 1961, 7-0-3-78-1-1-1 to

3-1-1, p. 3-1-1; Virgil Downing, investigative report, 14 Mar. 1961, 7-0-3-79-1-1-1 to 2-1-1, all in MSSC Records.

145. Walter Sillers to Albert Jones, 9 Jan. 1961, 7-0-2-39-1-1-1; press release, State Sovereignty Commission, 19 Feb. 1961, 7-0-3-78-1-1-1 to 3-1-1, pp. 2-1-1 to 3-1-1, both in MSSC Records.

146. Walter Sillers to Albert Jones, 9 Jan. 1961, 7-0-2-39-1-1-1; press release, State Sovereignty Commission, 19 Feb. 1961, 7-0-3-78-1-1-1 to 3-1-1, pp. 2-1-1 to 3-1-1, both in MSSC Records.

147. Mrs. Harry Scrivner, undated report on speaking engagements of Myers Lowman, 7-0-3-80-1-1-1 to 5-1-1, pp. 2-1-1 to 3-1-1, MSSC Records.

148. Horace H. Harned Jr. to director, State Sovereignty Commission, 28 Feb. 1961, 7-0-3-81-1-1-1 to 2-1-1, MSSC Records.

149. Gordon H. Scherer to Albert Jones, telegram, 2 Mar. 1961, 7-0-3-84-1-1-1 to 2-1-1; Jones to Horace H. Harned Jr., 3 Mar. 1961, 7-0-3-82-1-1-1 to 2-1-1, both in MSSC Records.

150. "State Paying for Anti-Red Lectures," newspaper unknown, n.d., 7-0-3-135-1-1-1 to 3-1-1, p. 2-1-1; Albert Jones to Tom Lee Gibson, 20 Mar. 1961, 7-0-3-136-1-1-1, both in MSSC Records.

151. *TP*, 5 Mar. 1961.

152. *ST*, 27 Apr. 1961(?), 7-0-3-87-1-1-1, MSSC Records.

153. Press release, State Sovereignty Commission, n.d., 7-0-4-31-1-1-1, MSSC Records.

154. "To the Members of the State Sovereignty Commission, and to the Senate and House of Representatives of the State of Mississippi," 7-3-0-12-1-1-1 to 7-1-1, pp. 4-1-1, 6-1-1, MSSC Records; untitled expenditure list, State Sovereignty Commission, folder 10, box 135, PBJ Papers.

155. "Education and Information Program," 7-3-0-9-1-1-1 to 2-1-1, MSSC Records; *DN*, 19 May 1961.

156. Albert Jones to Washington Video Productions, Inc., 10 Mar. 1961, 7-0-3-98-1-1-1, MSSC Records; *DN*, 4 Mar. 1961.

157. "Education and Information Program," 7-3-0-9-1-1-1 to 2-1-1, MSSC Records; Corey T. Lesseig, "Roast Beef and Racial Integrity: Mississippi's 'Race and Reason Day,' October 26, 1961," *Journal of Mississippi History* 56 (Feb. 1994): 1–15.

158. "Education and Information Program," 7-3-0-9-1-1-1 to 2-1-1, p. 2-1-1, MSSC Records.

159. Erle Johnston Jr. to Tom Watkins, 12 Apr. 1963, 7-0-7-43-1-1-1; *Biennial Report of the Mississippi State Sovereignty Commission to the Legislature of Mississippi*, 7-3-0-13-1-1-1 to 9-1-1, p. 5-1-1, both in MSSC Records.

160. Mrs. Harry Scrivner, "Report to Sovereignty Commission," 17 Jan. 1961, 7-0-2-82-1-1-1 to 2-1-1, p. 2-1-1, MSSC Records.

161. *Montgomery (Ala.) Advertiser*, 26 Mar. 1961.

Chapter 4. The Greatest States' Rights State: Helping Ross Keep Mississippi Sovereign

1. *Boynton v. Virginia*, 364 U.S. 454 (1960); Alexander Bloom and Wini Breines, eds., *"Takin' It to the Streets": A Sixties Reader* (New York: Oxford University Press, 1995), 25.

2. "Ain't Scared of Your Jails, 1960–61," in *Eyes on the Prize: America's Civil Rights Years* series, Blackside, Boston, 1987, videocassette; Juan Williams, *Eyes on the Prize: America's Civil Rights Years, 1954–1965* (New York: Penguin, 1987), 159; Paul D. Escott and David R. Goldfield, eds., *Major Problems in the History of the American South*, vol. 2 (Lexington, Mass.: D. C. Heath, 1990), 544.

3. Bill Minor, "A Poignant Summer Reunion," *Reckon* 1 (Premiere 1995): 57.

4. Alan Greenblatt, "Crossing the Line in the Dust," *Congressional Quarterly*, 13 May 1995, 1295; John Dittmer, "The Mississippi Summer Project in Retrospect," paper presented at the sixtieth annual meeting of the Southern Historical Association, Louisville, Ky., 9 Nov. 1994, 4.

5. Arthur M. Schlesinger Jr., *Robert Kennedy and His Times* (Boston: Houghton Mifflin, 1978), 299.

6. Edwin O. Guthman and Jeffrey Shulman, eds., *Robert Kennedy in His Own Words: The Unpublished Recollections of the Kennedy Years* (New York: Bantam, 1988), 96–97.

7. Irving Bernstein, *Promises Kept: John F. Kennedy's New Frontier* (New York: Oxford University Press, 1991), 67.

8. "Ain't Scared of Your Jails, 1960–61."

9. *DN*, 23 June 1961.

10. *LSM*, 1962, regular sess., 1007–8, 1011–12, 1017–18.

11. Erle Johnston Jr., "The Practical Way to Maintain a Separate School System in Mississippi," 25 May 1962, 1, 5–6, 8–9, folder 2, box 58, PBJ Papers. This nine-page speech draft can also be located in the folder "Sovereignty Commission, 1960–1977," box 13, Minor Papers; and in *FF*, July 1961 to June 1962, roll no. 14, N14 3596–604.

12. *DDT*, 1 June 1962.

13. Albert Jones to Erle Johnston Jr., 24 Apr. 1962, 7-0-5-61-1-1-1; Johnston to Bill Simmons, 1 May 1962, 7-0-5-66-1-1-1, both in MSSC Records.

14. *Scott County (Miss.) Times*, 6 June 1962.

15. C. W. McGowen to State Sovereignty Commission, 4 June 1962, 7-0-5-99-1-1-1, MSSC Records.

16. V. E. Fewell to Albert Jones, 4 June 1962, 7-0-5-97-1-1-1, MSSC Records.

17. R. K. Daniel to Mississippi Sovereignty Commission, 8 June 1962, 7-0-5-101-1-1-1, MSSC Records.

18. *Memphis (Tenn.) Press-Scimitar*, 1 June 1962.

19. *Scott County (Miss.) Times*, 6 June 1962.

20. Erle Johnston Jr. to Ross Barnett, 6 June 1962, 7-0-6-3-1-1-1 to 3-1-1, MSSC Records. The same letter can be found in folder 2, box 58, PBJ Papers.
21. Erle Johnston Jr. to Paul B. Johnson Jr., 14 June 1962, folder 2, box 58, PBJ Papers.
22. *DDT*, 17 June 1962.
23. Robert B. Patterson to Thatcher Walt, 18 June 1962, folder 2, box 58, PBJ Papers.
24. Wilburn Hooker to Ross R. Barnett, telegram, 11 June 1962, 7-0-5-105-1-1-1, MSSC Records.
25. Wilburn Hooker to Albert Jones, 22 June 1962, 7-0-6-6-1-1-1 to 5-1-1, pp. 4-1-1 to 5-1-1, MSSC Records; Erle Johnston Jr., oral history, interviewed by Yasuhiro Katagiri, 13 Aug. 1993, vol. 276, pt. 2, transcript, 34, MOHP.
26. Wilburn Hooker to Ross R. Barnett, 22 June 1962, 7-0-6-6-1-1-1 to 5-1-1, pp. 2-1-1 to 3-1-1, MSSC Records.
27. Erle Johnston Jr. to Ross Barnett, 19 Oct. 1962, 8-17-0-28-1-1-1; Aubrey H. Bell to Johnston, 25 Oct. 1962, 7-0-6-25-1-1-1 to 3-1-1, p. 2-1-1, both in MSSC Records.
28. See, for instance, "Sovereignty Group Retains Johnston," *DN*, 20 July 1962; and "Johnston Kept in State Post: Segregation Unit Refuses to Fire Controversial Publicity Agent," *CA*, 20 July 1962.
29. Walter Sillers to Albert Jones, 19 July 1962, 7-0-5-122-1-1-1 to 2-1-1, p. 1-1-1; resolution, State Sovereignty Commission, n.d., 7-0-5-122-1-1-1 to 2-1-1, p. 2-1-1, both in MSSC Records.
30. Albert Jones to Ross R. Barnett, 20 July 1962, 7-0-5-131-1-1-1; Aubrey H. Bell to Jones, n.d., 7-0-5-140-1-1-1, both in MSSC Records.
31. *LSM*, 1962, regular sess., 61; *Memphis (Tenn.) Press-Scimitar*, 10 May 1962.
32. *DN*, 10 May 1962; *Memphis (Tenn.) Press-Scimitar*, 10 May 1962.
33. David G. Sansing, *Making Haste Slowly: The Troubled History of Higher Education in Mississippi* (Jackson: University Press of Mississippi, 1990), 162; Sansing, *The University of Mississippi: A Sesquicentennial History* (Jackson: University Press of Mississippi, 1999), 289.
34. Jack Bass, *Unlikely Heroes* (New York: Simon and Schuster, 1981), 178; "Fighting Back, 1957–62," in *Eyes on the Prize* series.
35. James H. Meredith, oral history, interviewed by Yasuhiro Katagiri, 11 Jan. 1994, B-M559mo, transcript, 4, MDAH.
36. *CR*, 83d Cong., 2d sess., 27 May 1954, 7256.
37. Guthman and Shulman, *Robert Kennedy in His Own Words*, 160.
38. Schlesinger, *Robert Kennedy and His Times*, 319.
39. Gerald S. Strober and Deborah H. Strober, *"Let Us Begin Anew": An Oral History of the Kennedy Presidency* (New York: Harper Collins, 1993), 302.
40. Meredith, oral history, B-M559mo, transcript, 10–11, MDAH.
41. Ross R. Barnett, "A Statewide Address on Television and Radio to the People

of Mississippi by Governor Ross R. Barnett, 7:30 P.M., September 13, 1962,"
12-37-0-3-1-1-1 to 7-1-1, pp. 1-1-1 to 2-1-1, 4-1-1, 6-1-1, MSSC Records.
The full text of the governor's address can also be found in the folder "Barnett,
Ross—Miscellaneous, 1962–1963," Godwin Collection; and in folder 50, box
2, Toler Papers.

42. *JH*, 1962, first extraordinary sess., 4; *LSM*, 1962, first extraordinary sess., 18.

43. *JS*, 1962, first extraordinary sess., 8; *JH*, 1962, first extraordinary sess., 5;
Joseph E. Wroten, oral history, interviewed by Yasuhiro Katagiri, 4 Nov. 1993,
vol. 476, transcript, 36, MOHP; Karl Wiesenburg, oral history, interviewed
by H. T. Holmes, 9 Aug. 1976, OH 77-04, transcript, 29, MDAH; Wiesenburg, *The Oxford Disaster: Price of Defiance* (Pascagoula, Miss.: Advertiser Printing, 1962), 2.

44. Wiesenburg, oral history, OH 77-04, transcript, 29, MDAH; Adam Nossiter,
Of Long Memory: Mississippi and the Murder of Medgar Evers (Reading, Mass.:
Addison-Wesley, 1994), 68.

45. Paul B. Johnson Jr., oral history, interviewed by T. H. Baker, 8 Sept. 1970,
AC 80-63, transcript, 13, LBJ Library.

46. Burke Marshall, oral history, interviewed by T. H. Baker, 28 Oct. 1968, AC
74-215, transcript, 22, LBJ Library; John R. Salter Jr., with Edwin King, oral
history, interviewed by John Jones, 6 Jan. 1981, OH 81-06, transcript, 103,
MDAH; untitled document, State Sovereignty Commission, 99-77-0-13-1-
1-1 to 2-1-1, p. 2-1-1, MSSC Records.

47. A. L. Hopkins, investigative report, 18 Aug. 1961, 1-76-0-23-1-1-1 to 3-1-1;
Virgil Downing, investigative report, 14 Feb. 1962, 1-67-1-2-1-1-1 to 3-1-1,
both in MSSC Records; Hopkins, investigative report, 11 July 1962; Downing,
investigative report, 12 July 1962, both in folder 8, box 5, Faulkner Collection.

48. *TP*, 2 Oct. 1972.

49. Untitled expenditure list, State Sovereignty Commission; "Outstanding Expenditures or Outstanding Projects of This Commission," both in folder 10, box
135, PBJ Papers.

50. Russell H. Barrett, *Integration at Ole Miss* (Chicago: Quadrangle, 1965), 107–8;
Erle Johnston Jr., *Mississippi's Defiant Years, 1953–1973: An Interpretive Documentary with Personal Experiences* (Forest, Miss.: Lake Harbor, 1990), 150; James
H. Meredith, *Three Years in Mississippi* (Bloomington: Indiana University Press,
1966), 188–89.

51. Item #4A1, dictabelt #4A, transcript; item #2, audiotape #27, audiocas-
sette, both in "Integration of the University of Mississippi," Presidential Recordings, President's Office File, John F. Kennedy Presidential Papers, John F.
Kennedy Presidential Library, Boston.

52. "Voting Rights and Jury Discrimination," in *The Civil Rights Movement and the
Law: A National Symposium* series, University of Mississippi, University, 1989,

videocassette; Horace H. Harned Jr., oral history, interviewed by Tom Healy, 3 Oct. 1978, vol. 355, transcript, 48, MOHP; Meredith, *Three Years in Mississippi*, 196.

53. "Fighting Back, 1957–62."

54. Burke Marshall to Robert F. Kennedy, memo, 27 Sept. 1962, folder "Telephone Transcripts, Sept. 27, 1962," box 20, Marshall Papers.

55. Ibid.

56. *CA*, 27 Sept. 1962.

57. Burke Marshall to Robert F. Kennedy, memo, 27 Sept. 1962, folder "Telephone Transcripts, Sept. 27, 1962," box 20, Marshall Papers.

58. *LSM*, 1962, first extraordinary sess., 29–30; *JS*, 1962, first extraordinary sess., 42, 44; *JH*, 1962, first extraordinary sess., 30.

59. "Agency Purchase Order," 31 Oct. 1962, 97-11-0-222-1-1-1, MSSC Records; "Outstanding Expenditures or Outstanding Projects of This Commission," folder 10, box 135, PBJ Papers; *Nashville Tennessean*, 2 Oct. 1962.

60. Virgil S. Downing, report, 2 Oct. 1962, 7-0-6-63-1-1-1, MSSC Records.

61. "Outstanding Expenditures or Outstanding Projects of This Commission," folder 10, box 135, PBJ Papers.

62. *Nashville Tennessean*, 2 Oct. 1962.

63. Sansing, *Making Haste Slowly*, 186.

64. Ibid., 186, 188.

65. "Fighting Back, 1957–62."

66. *CL/DN*, 30 Sept. 1962; *MOSR*, 1996–2000, 489–90.

67. Taylor Branch, *Parting the Waters: America in the King Years, 1954–63* (New York: Simon and Schuster, 1988), 659.

68. "Telephone Conversation between Attorney General and Governor Barnett, Governor Barnett Called Sunday, 12:45 P.M., September 30, 1962," folder "Telephone Transcripts, Sept. 28–Oct. 1, 1962," box 20, Marshall Papers.

69. "Additional Conversation with Governor on September 30, 1962," folder "Telephone Transcripts, Sept. 28–Oct. 1, 1962," box 20, Marshall Papers.

70. Ross R. Barnett, "Statement of Governor Ross R. Barnett," folder "Legal Briefs," box 170, PBJ Papers.

71. Ibid.

72. *Public Papers of the Presidents of the United States: John F. Kennedy, 1962* (Washington, D.C.: GPO, 1963), 726–28.

73. Ibid., 728.

74. Tom Scarbrough, investigative report, 9 Oct. 1962, 1-67-3-16-1-1-1 to 7-1-1, p. 6-1-1, MSSC Records.

75. Virgil S. Downing, report, 2 Oct. 1962, 7-0-6-63-1-1-1, MSSC Records.

76. Thomas P. Brady, oral history, interviewed by Orley B. Caudill, 17 May 1972, vol. 2, pt. 2, transcript, 22, MOHP.

77. Mississippi State General Legislative Investigating Committee, *A Report by the General Legislative Investigating Committee to the Mississippi State Legislature concerning the Occupation of the Campus of the University of Mississippi, September 30, 1962, by the Department of Justice of the United States*, 1963, 5, in the author's possession; Theodore C. Sorensen, *Kennedy* (New York: Harper and Row, 1965), 547. The legislative committee's report can be found in George M. Yarbrough, oral history, interviewed by Orley B. Caudill, 21 Feb. 1980, vol. 367, transcript, 59–85, MOHP.

78. Sorensen, *Kennedy*, 547.

79. Henry Hampton and Steve Fayer, *Voices of Freedom: An Oral History of the Civil Rights Movement from the 1950s through the 1980s* (New York: Bantam, 1990), 121.

80. "At Ole Miss: Echoes of a Civil War's Last Battle," *Time*, 4 Oct. 1982, 8, 11.

81. Hampton and Fayer, *Voices of Freedom*, 122.

82. Virgil S. Downing, report, 5 Oct. 1962, 7-0-6-64-1-1-1; Downing, report, 22 Oct. 1962, 7-0-6-65-1-1-1, both in MSSC Records.

83. Albert Jones to George Singleman [*sic*], 2 Oct. 1962, 7-0-6-19-1-1-1, MSSC Records; Neil R. McMillen, *The Citizens' Council: Organized Resistance to the Second Reconstruction, 1954–1964* (Urbana: University of Illinois Press, 1971), 230–31.

84. Erle Johnston Jr. to Ross Barnett, 19 Oct. 1962, 8-17-0-28-1-1-1, MSSC Records.

85. Ross R. Barnett to Erle Johnston, 12 Dec. 1962, 8-17-0-30-1-1-1, MSSC Records.

86. "The Message from Mississippi: Address Prepared for Volunteer Speakers of the Mississippi State Sovereignty Commission," 12, vertical file "Sovereignty Commission, Mississippi State," Mississippiana Collection. The entire text of this newer version of "The Message from Mississippi" can also be located in the file "Mississippi Sovereignty Commission," administrative files, ASSC Records.

87. *DDT*, 27 Mar. 1963.

88. "The Message from Mississippi," 5, 9.

89. Ibid., 9–10.

90. Michael L. Carr Jr., oral history, interviewed by Yasuhiro Katagiri, 28 Oct. 1993, vol. 469, transcript, 12–16, MOHP; Erle Johnston Jr. to Carr, 10 Nov. 1962, 7-0-6-36-1-1-1, MSSC Records; *Springfield (Mass.) Union*, 4 Dec. 1962; *CL*, 4 Dec. 1962. The transcript of the author's oral history interview with Carr can also be read on-line at <http://www.lib.usm.edu/~spcol/crda/oh/carrmtrans.htm> in *Oral Histories in the Civil Rights in Mississippi Digital Archives* series, William D. McCain Library and Archives, University of Southern Mississippi, Hattiesburg, consulted 1 Dec. 2000 <http://www.lib.usm.edu/~spcol/crda/oh/index.html>.

91. Untitled document, State Sovereignty Commission, 7-0-6-82-1-1-1, MSSC Records.

92. Erle Johnston Jr. to Ross Barnett, 21 Nov. 1962, 7-0-6-52-1-1-1, MSSC Records; *Greenwood (Miss.) Commonwealth*, 25 Jan. 1963.

93. Albert Jones to Vernon H. Broom, 1 Dec. 1961, 2-31-0-14-1-1-1; Erle Johnston Jr. to Bill Simmons, 1 May 1962, 7-0-5-66-1-1-1; "Voucher for Reimbursement of Expenses Incident to Official Travel," 97-98-1-101-1-1-1 to 5-1-1, pp. 2-1-1 to 3-1-1, all in MSSC Records.

94. *Free At Last: A History of the Civil Rights Movement and Those Who Died in the Struggle* (Montgomery, Ala.: Southern Poverty Law Center, 1989), 46–47.

95. "Questions Asked, and Answers Given, by Sovereignty Commission Volunteer Speakers," 99-139-0-7-1-1-1 to 5-1-1, p. 1-1-1, MSSC Records; James W. Silver, *Mississippi: The Closed Society* (New York: Harcourt, Brace, and World, 1964), 8; Howard Smead, *Blood Justice: The Lynching of Mack Charles Parker* (New York: Oxford University Press, 1986), 201.

96. Neil R. McMillen, *Dark Journey: Black Mississippians in the Age of Jim Crow* (Urbana: University of Illinois Press, 1989), 252.

97. "Requisition on the Auditor of Public Accounts," 17 May 1962, 97-98-1-101-1-1-1 to 5-1-1, p. 1-1-1; "Original Proposed Budget for Fiscal Year Beginning July 1, 1963," 7-3-0-14-1-1-1, both in MSSC Records.

98. *Greenwood (Miss.) Commonwealth*, 25 Jan. 1963.

99. Walter Sillers to Erle Johnston, 11 Aug. 1963, 7-0-7-168-1-1-1; "Original Proposed Budget for Fiscal Year Beginning July 1, 1963," 7-3-0-14-1-1-1; "Agenda for Sovereignty Commission Meeting, August 15, 1963," 99-56-0-2-1-1-1 to 2-1-1, p. 2-1-1; "Report to Sovereignty Commission Meeting of September 19, 1963," 99-65-0-1-1-1-1 to 3-1-1, p. 2-1-1, all in MSSC Records.

100. News release, Citizens' Councils of America, 24 Sept. 1963, 99-30-0-116-1-1-1 to 2-1-1, MSSC Records; *Birmingham (Ala.) News*, 1 Mar. 1963; *DN*, 8 Mar. 1963.

101. Albert Jones to all Commission members, memo, n.d., 8-12-0-5-1-1-1, MSSC Records; Erle Johnston Jr., oral history, interviewed by Orley B. Caudill, 16 July 1980 and 30 July 1980, vol. 276, transcript, 69, MOHP; *CL*, 22 Mar. 1963.

102. *CA*, 19 Mar. 1963.

103. Johnston, oral history, vol. 276, transcript, 69; Johnston, oral history, vol. 276, pt. 2, transcript, 9–10, both at MOHP; *Tupelo (Miss.) Daily Journal*, 22 Mar. 1963; *Greenwood (Miss.) Commonwealth*, 23 Mar. 1963.

104. *CL*, 22 Mar. 1963.

105. Erle Johnston Jr. to Ross R. Barnett, 22 Mar. 1963, 7-0-7-30-1-1-1, MSSC Records.

106. Herman B. DeCell to Erle Johnston Jr., 25 Mar. 1963, 7-0-7-8-1-1-1, MSSC Records.

107. Johnston, oral history, vol. 276, pt. 2, transcript, 10, MOHP; *DDT*, 27 Mar. 1963.

108. General Legislative Investigating Committee, *A Report by the General Legislative Investigating Committee*, in the author's possession; *DDT*, 8 May 1963; *CL*, 11 May 1963.

109. Johnston, *Mississippi's Defiant Years*, 166.

110. Erle Johnston Jr. to Russell Fox, 17 May 1963, 99-88-0-6-1-1-1; Fox to Ross R. Barnett, 12 Aug. 1963, 7-0-8-36-1-1-1, both in MSSC Records. See also minutes, State Sovereignty Commission, 18 July 1963, folder 4; "Agenda for Sovereignty Commission Meeting, August 15, 1963," folder 4; untitled expenditure list, State Sovereignty Commission, folder 10; "Outstanding Expenditures or Outstanding Projects of This Commission," folder 10, all in box 135, PBJ Papers.

111. Patrick M. Sims to State Sovereignty Commission, 10 Dec. 1962, 10-102-0-2-1-1-1 to 2-1-1, MSSC Records. The film, *Oxford, U.S.A.*, can be viewed in reel no. 53, *CCFF*.

112. Erle Johnston Jr. to Elizabeth Lippoth, 3 Mar. 1964, 99-115-0-154-1-1-1; Johnston, "Address by Erle Johnston Jr.," 13 May 1964, 6-36-0-26-1-1-1 to 13-1-1, p. 3-1-1, both in MSSC Records. Johnston's address can also be found in folder 17, box 3, CC/CR Collection.

113. "Expenditures as Compared to Proposed Budget through June 30, 1963," folder 4; untitled expenditure list, State Sovereignty Commission, folder 10; "Outstanding Expenditures or Outstanding Projects of This Commission," folder 10, all in box 135, PBJ Papers.

114. "Agenda for Sovereignty Commission Meeting, July 18, 1963," folder 4, box 135; Erle Johnston Jr. to Paul B. Johnson Jr. and all members of the Sovereignty Commission, memo, 1 Sept. 1964, folder 4, box 136, both in PBJ Papers. See also folder 99-115, MSSC Records.

115. "Expenditures as Compared to Proposed Budget through June 30, 1963"; "Expenditures as Compared to Proposed Budget through November 1963," both in folder 4, box 135, PBJ Papers.

116. Theodore C. Sorensen, *"Let the Word Go Forth": The Speeches, Statements, and Writings of John F. Kennedy, 1947 to 1963* (New York: Delacorte, 1988), 199, 201.

117. Erle Johnston Jr. to Ross R. Barnett and all members of the Sovereignty Commission, memo, 27 June 1963, folder 3, box 135, PBJ Papers; John C. Satterfield to Palmer Lipscomb, 28 June 1963, 99-51-0-34-1-1-1 to 3-1-1, MSSC Records.

118. Erle Johnston Jr. to John U. Barr Jr., 4 May 1964, 6-70-0-165-1-1-1 to 2-1-1, p. 1-1-1, MSSC Records.

119. Erle Johnston Jr. to Ross R. Barnett and all members of the Sovereignty Commission, memo, 27 June 1963, folder 3, box 135, PBJ Papers.
120. *DN*, 18 Nov. 1955.
121. Russell L. Fox to Ross R. Barnett, 12 Aug. 1963, 7-0-8-36-1-1-1, MSSC Records; *CL*, 13 Mar. 1963.
122. Coordinating Committee for Fundamental American Freedoms, "An Analysis of 'the Civil Rights Act of 1963,' " vertical file "Sovereignty Commission, Mississippi State," Mississippiana Collection.
123. Ibid.; "Collection of Material concerning Formation and Activities of the Coordinating Committee for Fundamental American Freedoms," folder 4, box 135, PBJ Papers; Erle Johnston Jr. to John U. Barr Jr., 4 May 1964, 6-70-0-165-1-1-1 to 2-1-1, p. 1-1-1, MSSC Records; *NYT*, 4 Nov. 1963.
124. Minutes, State Sovereignty Commission, 18 July 1963, 7-5-0-7-1-1-1 to 2-1-1, p. 2-1-1, MSSC Records. The same minutes can be found in folder 4, box 135, PBJ Papers.
125. *TP*, 9 Feb. 1964.
126. John C. Satterfield to Erle Johnston, 22 July 1963, 99-126-0-19-1-1-1; Johnston to Jim Eastland, 23 July 1963, 99-126-0-20-1-1-1 to 2-1-1, both in MSSC Records.
127. Untitled expenditure list, State Sovereignty Commission; "Outstanding Expenditures or Outstanding Projects of This Commission," both in folder 10, box 135, PBJ Papers.
128. "Agenda for Sovereignty Commission Meeting, August 15, 1963," folder 4, box 135, PBJ Papers.
129. Erle Johnston Jr. to Ross Barnett, memo, 18 Oct. 1963, 99-66-0-3-1-1-1, MSSC Records; Johnston to members, State Sovereignty Commission, memo, 10 Oct. 1963, folder 4, box 135, PBJ Papers; Johnston, *Mississippi's Defiant Years*, 242; *SSN*, Nov. 1963.
130. "Expenditures as Compared to Proposed Budget through November 1963," folder 4, box 135, PBJ Papers.
131. "Statement by James H. Meredith on the Death of Medgar Evers—June 12, 1963," 99-98-0-18-1-1-1, MSSC Records; Meredith, *Three Years in Mississippi*, 305.
132. J. D. Williams to the faculty, staff, and students of the University of Mississippi, 31 Jan. 1963, 99-98-0-2-1-1-1 to 8-1-1, p. 7-1-1, MSSC Records; *CA*, 10 July 1963.
133. Minutes, State Sovereignty Commission, 20 June 1963, folder 4, box 9, Johnston Papers; resolution, State Sovereignty Commission, 20 June 1963, 1-67-4-24-1-1-1 to 4-1-1, p. 4-1-1, MSSC Records.
134. Untitled document [press release(?)], State Sovereignty Commission, 1-67-4-25-1-1-1 to 2-1-1, p. 1-1-1, MSSC Records.
135. "Report to Sovereignty Commission on Action of Board of Trustees for Institu-

tions of Higher Learning in Response to Sovereignty Commission's Resolution Asking for an Investigation of Remarks Made by Student, James Meredith," 99-56-0-1-1-1-1 to 2-1-1, p. 1-1-1, MSSC Records; *DDT*, 19 Aug. 1963; Sansing, *Making Haste Slowly*, 207.

136. Erle Johnston Jr. to Ross R. Barnett, 15 July 1963, 99-98-0-12-1-1-1; E. R. Jobe to Johnston, 24 July 1963, 99-98-0-13-1-1-1, both in MSSC Records.

137. "Report to Sovereignty Commission on Action of Board of Trustees," 99-56-0-1-1-1-1 to 2-1-1, p. 1-1-1; untitled document [press release(?)], State Sovereignty Commission, 1-67-4-26-1-1-1 to 3-1-1, p. 1-1-1, both in MSSC Records.

138. University of Mississippi, "A Report Prepared for the Board of Trustees, Institutions of Higher Learning of the State of Mississippi," 14 Aug. 1963, 99-98-0-2-1-1-1 to 8-1-1, p. 5-1-1, MSSC Records.

139. "Report to Sovereignty Commission on Action of Board of Trustees," 99-56-0-1-1-1-1 to 2-1-1, MSSC Records; James P. Coleman and Verner S. Holmes, oral history, interviewed by David G. Sansing, 16 June 1979, transcript, 150, box 6, Holmes Collection; Barrett, *Integration at Ole Miss*, 221; Johnston, *Mississippi's Defiant Years*, 231.

140. Meredith, *Three Years in Mississippi*, 322; Sansing, *Making Haste Slowly*, 195.

141. Meredith, oral history, B-M559mo, transcript, 18, MDAH.

142. Allan K. Chalmers to dear friend, 3 Dec. 1962, folder 40, box 1, King Collection; Dittmer, *Local People: The Struggle for Civil Rights in Mississippi* (Urbana: University of Illinois Press, 1994), 82–83.

143. *Student Printz* [campus newspaper at the University of Southern Mississippi], 14 Oct. 1993.

144. Bradford Daniel and John Howard Griffin, "Why They Can't Wait: An Interview with a White Negro," *Progressive*, July 1964, 18–19.

145. Dittmer, *Local People*, 142.

146. "Members of the Faculty at the University of Mississippi, Who Offered a Resolution Protesting Attempts to Blame U.S. Marshals for Rioting on the Campus Sunday Night, September 30, 1962," 1-67-3-26-1-1-1 to 5-1-1, pp. 4-1-1 to 5-1-1, MSSC Records.

147. James W. Silver, "Mississippi: The Closed Society," *Journal of Southern History* 30 (Feb. 1964): 3–34.

148. *Memphis (Tenn.) Press-Scimitar*, 8 Nov. 1963.

149. Erle Johnston Jr. to Tom Tubb, 2 Dec. 1963, 99-137-0-8-1-1-1 to 2-1-1, MSSC Records. The same letter can also be found in folder 4, box 135, PBJ Papers.

150. Thomas J. Tubb to Erle Johnston Jr., 6 Dec. 1963, folder 4, box 119, PBJ Papers.

151. "Director's Report to Sovereignty Commission Members, December 1963," folder 4, box 135, PBJ Papers.

152. M. M. Roberts to Erle Johnston Jr., 4 Dec. 1963, 99-137-0-3-1-1-1; Johnston to file, memo, 9 Dec. 1963, 99-137-0-4-1-1-1, both in MSSC Records.

153. Sansing, *Making Haste Slowly*, 201; Sansing, *The University of Mississippi*, 312.

154. *CL*, 20 Mar. 1964.

155. James W. Silver to A. Eugene Cox, 14 June 1963, folder 4A, box 6, Cox Collection; Silver, "Mississippi Must Choose," *NYTM*, 19 July 1964, 8, 54–55.

156. Sansing, *Making Haste Slowly*, 202.

157. James W. Silver, *Running Scared: Silver in Mississippi* (Jackson: University Press of Mississippi, 1984), 103–4.

158. John D. Callaway to Erle Johnston Jr., 12 Mar. 1965, folder 3, box 137, PBJ Papers.

159. "On October 30, 1962, Professor Russell H. Barrett Made the Following Statements to the Students in One of His Classes," 3-9-1-69-1-1-1, MSSC Records; Erle Johnston Jr. to Paul B. Johnson Jr. and all members of the Sovereignty Commission, memo, 1 Sept. 1964, folder 4, box 136, PBJ Papers.

160. "Agency Purchase Order," 29 Oct. 1965(?), 97-12-0-252-1-1-1, MSSC Records.

161. A. L. Hopkins, investigative report, 7 Mar. 1962, 2-50-0-32-1-1-1 to 3-1-1; Hopkins, investigative report, 23 Mar. 1962, 2-50-0-42-1-1-1 to 2-1-1, both in MSSC Records.

162. Albert Jones to file, memo, n.d., 2-99-0-23-1-1-1; Billy Engram to Ross Barnett, 23 Feb. 1962, 2-101-0-20-1-1-1 to 3-1-1, pp. 1-1-1 to 2-1-1, both in MSSC Records.

163. Virgil S. Downing, investigative report, 16 May 1962, 2-101-0-26-1-1-1 to 3-1-1, MSSC Records.

164. A. L. Hopkins and Tom Scarbrough, investigative report, 19 July 1963, 2-34-0-23-1-1-1 to 3-1-1, p. 2-1-1, MSSC Records.

165. A. L. Hopkins, investigative report, 10 July 1963, 2-34-0-20-1-1-1 to 5-1-1, pp. 1-1-1 to 4-1-1, MSSC Records.

166. A. L. Hopkins and Tom Scarbrough, investigative report, 19 July 1963, 2-34-0-23-1-1-1 to 3-1-1, MSSC Records.

167. Erle Johnston Jr. to James O. Eastland, 12 July 1963, 2-34-0-22-1-1-1, MSSC Records.

168. *DN*, 18 May 1954.

169. Mr. and Mrs. Howard Johnson to Ross R. Barnett, 11 June 1962, 2-92-0-25-1-1-1; Tom Scarbrough, investigative report, 26 June 1962, 2-92-0-23-1-1-1 to 4-1-1, both in MSSC Records.

170. Albert Jones to file, memo, n.d., 3-81-0-4-1-1-1, MSSC Records.

171. A. L. Hopkins and Tom Scarbrough, investigative report, n.d., 3-81-0-5-1-1-1 to 4-1-1; "Duties of Investigators of the State Sovereignty Commission," 99-202-0-4-1-1-1 to 4-1-1, p. 3-1-1, both in MSSC Records.

172. John K. Bettersworth, "The Home Front, 1861–1865," in *A History of Missis-*

sippi, vol. 1, ed. Richard A. McLemore (Hattiesburg: University and College Press of Mississippi, 1973), 521–24; V. O. Key Jr., *Southern Politics in State and Nation* (New York: Knopf, 1949), 328.

173. Erle Johnston Jr. to Jack Tubb and F. Gordon Lewis, memo, 12 Dec. 1963, 99-68-0-2-1-1-1 to 9-1-1, pp. 1-1-1 to 2-1-1, 9-1-1, MSSC Records.

174. Ibid., pp. 2-1-1 to 5-1-1, 7-1-1; Tom Scarbrough and Virgil Downing, investigative report, 27 Nov. 1963, 3-81-0-7-1-1-1 to 4-1-1, p. 1-1-1, both in MSSC Records.

175. F. James Davis, *Who Is Black?: One Nation's Definition* (University Park: Pennsylvania State University Press, 1991), 9.

176. Erle Johnston Jr. to Jack Tubb and F. Gordon Lewis, memo, 12 Dec. 1963, 99-68-0-2-1-1-1 to 9-1-1, p. 1-1-1, MSSC Records.

177. "Report to Sovereignty Commission Meeting, November 21, 1963," 99-67-0-1-1-1-1 to 2-1-1, p. 1-1-1, MSSC Records.

178. Erle Johnston Jr. to file, memo, 26 Nov. 1963, 3-81-0-6-1-1-1, MSSC Records.

179. Tom Scarbrough and Virgil Downing, investigative report, 27 Nov. 1963, 3-81-0-7-1-1-1 to 4-1-1, p. 4-1-1, MSSC Records.

180. Erle Johnston Jr. to Jack Tubb and F. Gordon Lewis, memo, 12 Dec. 1963, 99-68-0-2-1-1-1 to 9-1-1, pp. 6-1-1 to 7-1-1, MSSC Records.

181. A. L. Hopkins and Erle Johnston Jr., investigative report, 19 Dec. 1963, 3-81-0-15-1-1-1 to 3-1-1, pp. 1-1-1 to 2-1-1, MSSC Records.

182. Erle Johnston Jr. to Jack Tubb and F. Gordon Lewis, memo, 12 Dec. 1963, 99-68-0-2-1-1-1 to 9-1-1, pp. 7-1-1 to 8-1-1, MSSC Records.

183. Erle Johnston Jr. to file, memo, 6 Jan. 1964, 3-81-0-17-1-1-1; "Report to Sovereignty Commission Members—Meeting, January 16, 1964," 99-69-0-1-1-1-1 to 2-1-1, p. 2-1-1, both in MSSC Records; "Director's Report to Sovereignty Commission Members, December 1963," folder 4, box 135, PBJ Papers.

184. Erle Johnston Jr. to all members of the Sovereignty Commission, memo, 24 Jan. 1964, 3-81-0-18-1-1-1 to 2-1-1; Johnston to file, memo, 3 Feb. 1964, 3-81-0-23-1-1-1, both in MSSC Records.

185. J. M. Tubb to Erle Johnston Jr., 4 Feb. 1964, 3-81-0-24-1-1-1, MSSC Records.

186. Erle Johnston Jr. to Paul B. Johnson and Carroll Gartin, memo, 14 Feb. 1964, 3-81-0-29-1-1-1 to 2-1-1, MSSC Records.

187. *JH*, 1964, regular sess., 21–22.

188. "Resolution of Commendation," 99-69-0-7-1-1-1; "Governor Barnett's Comment to Members of the Sovereignty Commission at His Last Meeting as Chairman," 99-69-0-6-1-1-1, both in MSSC Records.

Chapter 5. Feelings Run Deep and Blood Runs Hot: Submerging the State Sovereignty Commission

1. *CL*, 7 Sept. 1960, 22 Oct. 1963.
2. See, for example, the front-page editorial entitled "Let's Stand Tall with Paul" and written by James M. Ward in *DN*, 28 Aug. 1963.
3. Paul B. Johnson Jr., "Speech of Lieutenant Governor Paul B. Johnson to Jackson Citizens['] Council, May 17, 1963," 2–3, folder 8, box 91, PBJ Papers.
4. *MOSR*, 1964–1968, 424.
5. "The Dialogue," *Newsweek*, 14 Oct. 1963, 36.
6. Erle Johnston Jr., *Politics: Mississippi Style* (Forest, Miss.: Lake Harbor, 1993), 159.
7. Paul B. Johnson Jr., "Address of Lieutenant Governor Paul B. Johnson, Citizens' Councils of America Leadership Conference, Friday, October 25, 1963," 2, folder 10, box 91, PBJ Papers.
8. *MOSR*, 1964–1968, 440.
9. *NYT*, 22 Jan. 1964.
10. *JH*, 1964, regular sess., 43. The text of Governor Johnson's inaugural address can also be found in folder 17, box 91, PBJ Papers.
11. *NYT*, 22 Jan. 1964; "Words Make News in Mississippi," *Life*, 7 Feb. 1964, 4. See also "Mississippi: 'God Bless Everyone,' " *Time*, 31 Jan. 1964, 22.
12. Cecil L. Sumners, *The Governors of Mississippi* (Gretna, La.: Pelican, 1980), 117–20.
13. Theodore H. White, *The Making of the President 1964* (New York: New American Library, 1965), 218–19. See also Sumners, *The Governors of Mississippi*, 132–34.
14. Neil R. McMillen, *The Citizens' Council: Organized Resistance to the Second Reconstruction, 1954–1964* (Urbana: University of Illinois Press, 1971), 349.
15. Paul B. Johnson Jr., "Address of Governor Paul B. Johnson to Joint Session of the Mississippi Legislature, March 3, 1964," 9, folder 26, box 91, PBJ Papers.
16. McMillen, *The Citizens' Council*, 349; Reid S. Derr, *The Triumph of Progressivism: Governor Paul B. Johnson, Jr., and Mississippi in the 1960s* (Ann Arbor, Mich.: University Microfilms, 1994), 213. As an example of addresses made by Governor Johnson's administrative assistants for the Citizens' Council gatherings, see Frank D. Barber, "Remarks of Senator Frank D. Barber, Lexington Citizens['] Council, April 6, 1964," folder 14, box 101, PBJ Papers.
17. Erle Johnston Jr., oral history, interviewed by Orley B. Caudill, 16 July 1980 and 30 July 1980, vol. 276, transcript, 79, MOHP.
18. Erle Johnston Jr., oral history, interviewed by Yasuhiro Katagiri, 13 Aug. 1993, vol. 276, pt. 2, transcript, 12; Herman Glazier, oral history, interviewed by Reid Derr, 10 Sept. 1993, vol. 485, transcript, 31–32, both at MOHP; Derr, *The Triumph of Progressivism*, 438; *CL/DN*, 23 Jan. 1966.

19. Johnston, oral history, vol. 276, pt. 2, transcript, 12; Glazier, oral history, vol. 485, transcript, 10, both at MOHP.

20. Erle Johnston Jr. to Paul B. Johnson Jr. and all members of the Sovereignty Commission, memo, 1 Sept. 1964, folder 4, box 136, PBJ Papers.

21. *LSM*, 1964, regular sess., 136.

22. Horace H. Harned Jr., oral history, interviewed by Yasuhiro Katagiri, 3 Nov. 1993, vol. 355, pt. 2, transcript, 2, MOHP; Zack J. Van Landingham to Kenneth Williams, 27 Jan. 1959, 2-9-0-49-1-1-1, MSSC Records; *DN*, 29 Mar. 1965.

23. Paul B. Johnson Jr., "Press Release, Governor Paul B. Johnson, April 23, 1965," folder 1; Johnson, "Press Release, Governor Paul B. Johnson, May 7, 1965," folder 2, both in box 104, PBJ Papers; Semmes Luckett, oral history, interviewed by Thomas Healy, 14 Sept. 1977, vol. 370, transcript, 27, MOHP; *CL*, 9 Aug. 1966.

24. *CA*, 4 Jan. 1966; *Tupelo (Miss.) Daily Journal*, 27 July 1966; *DN*, 1 Aug. 1966; *CL*, 20 Dec. 1966; Paul B. Johnson Jr., press release, 17 Apr. 1967, vol. 1138, PBJ (MDAH) Papers.

25. Albert Jones to Kenneth Stewart, 27 Feb. 1964; Stewart to Jones, 12 Mar. 1964, both in folder 7, box 135, PBJ Papers; *CA*, 4 July 1965; Johnston, oral history, vol. 276, pt. 2, transcript, 13, MOHP.

26. "Salaries," 17 Mar. 1964, folder 7, box 135, PBJ Papers.

27. "Agenda for Sovereignty Commission Meeting, July 18, 1963," folder 4, box 135; minutes, State Sovereignty Commission, 18 July 1963, folder 4, box 135; Tom Scarbrough to members, State Sovereignty Commission, memo, 1 Aug. 1963, folder 4, box 135; Erle Johnston Jr. to Herman Glazier, memo, 29 Mar. 1965, folder 3, box 137; minutes, State Sovereignty Commission, 10 Nov. 1966, folder 6, box 139, all in PBJ Papers. See also Johnston, oral history, vol. 276, pt. 2, transcript, 24, MOHP.

28. Audit, State Sovereignty Commission, 97-1-0-11-1-1-1 to 7-1-1, p. 6-1-1, MSSC Records.

29. Ibid., 97-1-0-5-1-1-1 to 7-1-1, p. 5-1-1; "Report to Sovereignty Commission Meeting of September 19, 1963," 99-65-0-1-1-1-1 to 2-1-1, p. 1-1-1; "Report to Sovereignty Commission Members—Meeting, January 16, 1964," 99-69-0-1-1-1-1 to 2-1-1, p. 1-1-1; audit, State Sovereignty Commission, 97-1-0-10-1-1-1 to 8-1-1, p. 5-1-1, all in MSSC Records.

30. A. L. Hopkins to Erle Johnston Jr., memo, 1 May 1963, folder 10, box 2, Faulkner Collection.

31. James P. Walker Jr. to Erle Johnston, 8 June 1965, 2-82-0-60-1-1-1; Johnston to Walker, 14 June 1965, 2-82-0-61-1-1-1, both in MSSC Records.

32. A. L. Hopkins to Erle Johnston Jr., memo, 13 June 1966, 7-0-9-67-1-1-1, MSSC Records.

33. Erle Johnston Jr. to file, confidential memo, 26 May 1963, 7-0-7-79-1-1-1, MSSC Records.

34. Ralph D. Day to Albert Jones, 11 Jan. 1963, 7-0-6-62-1-1-1; untitled document, State Sovereignty Commission, 97-88-0-257-1-1-1 to 3-1-1, p. 2-1-1; Erle Johnston Jr. to Robert H. Pendleton, 8 Oct. 1964, 7-0-8-153-1-1-1; Louie Risk to State Sovereignty Commission, statement, 18 Mar. 1964, 99-99-0-103-1-1-1; Johnston to file, memo, 15 Aug. 1967, 7-0-10-78-1-1-1; Johnston to file, memo, 7 Aug. 1967, 9-31-7-15-1-1-1, all in MSSC Records; Johnston to Herman Glazier, memo, 23 Mar. 1965, folder 3, box 137; Johnston to John D. Sullivan, 9 Aug. 1966, folder 3, box 139, both in PBJ Papers. See also Erle Johnston Jr., television interview, interviewed by Marva York and Gwen Belton, *Saddler Report*, WJTV, Jackson, Miss., 23 Dec. 1990, videocassette, Special Collections, Coleman Library.

35. Erle Johnston Jr. to file, memo, 18 May 1964, 9-32-0-4-1-1-1, MSSC Records; Johnston to Herman Glazier, memo, 23 Mar. 1965, folder 3, box 137, PBJ Papers.

36. Erle Johnston Jr. to Herman Glazier, memo, 27 Apr. 1965, 9-35-0-1-1-1-1 to 2-1-1; "Informant Z," investigative report, 24 Apr. 1965, 9-35-0-2-1-1-1; "Informant Z," investigative report, 28 Apr. 1965, 9-35-0-3-1-1-1; "Special Report," 7 May 1965, 9-34-0-2-1-1-1, all in MSSC Records.

37. "Organization and Administration, State Sovereignty Commission," 7-0-5-21-1-1-1 to 3-1-1, p. 2-1-1, MSSC Records; minutes, State Sovereignty Commission, 19 May 1960, folder 2, box 135, PBJ Papers.

38. Johnston, oral history, vol. 276, pt. 2, transcript, 25, MOHP.

39. Erle Johnston Jr. to Herman Glazier, memo, 23 Mar. 1965, folder 3, box 137, PBJ Papers.

40. Theodore C. Sorensen, *"Let the Word Go Forth": The Speeches, Statements, and Writings of John F. Kennedy, 1947 to 1963* (New York: Delacorte, 1988), 195.

41. Hugh D. Graham, *Civil Rights and the Presidency: Race and Gender in American Politics, 1960–1972* (New York: Oxford University Press, 1992), 73–74.

42. Erle Johnston Jr., *Mississippi's Defiant Years, 1953–1973: An Interpretive Documentary with Personal Experiences* (Forest, Miss.: Lake Harbor, 1990), 243. A few days before President Johnson appeared before Congress and urged the "earliest possible passage of the civil rights bill," the new president invited Senator Richard B. Russell from Georgia, his old friend and political mentor, to the White House. Realizing that Russell would launch his vigorous opposition to the bill in the Senate, Johnson conveyed his determination to Russell that he intended to seek strong civil rights legislation despite their mutual friendship and respect. The president quietly told the senator: "Dick, you've got to get out of my way. I'm going to run over you. I don't intend to cavil or compromise. I don't want to hurt you. But don't stand in my way." Disheartened, Russell replied: "You may do that, but by God, it's going to cost you the South

and cost you the [1964 presidential] election." "If that's the price I've got to pay," said Johnson, "I'll pay it gladly." See *NYT*, 2 July 1989; Gilbert C. Fite, *Richard B. Russell, Jr., Senator from Georgia* (Chapel Hill: University of North Carolina Press, 1991), 408–15.

43. John C. Satterfield to Paul B. Johnson Jr., 25 Mar. 1964, folder 7, box 135, PBJ Papers; "Congress: Backdoor Battle," *Newsweek*, 30 Mar. 1964, 17.

44. *TP*, 9 Feb. 1964; *CL*, 10 Feb. 1964; *SSN*, Nov. 1963; *Wall Street Journal*, 11 June 1999; Barry Mehler and Keith Hurt, "Race Science and the Pioneer Fund," Institute for the Study of Academic Racism, Lansing, Mich., 1998, consulted 30 July 2000 <http://www.ferris.edu/isar/Institut/pioneer/search.htm>; "The Pioneer Fund, Inc.," Pioneer Fund, New York, consulted 3 Aug. 2000 <http://www.pioneerfund.org>.

45. *CL/DN*, 22 Mar. 1964.

46. John C. Satterfield to Paul B. Johnson Jr., 4 Mar. 1964, folder 7; Satterfield to Johnson, 1 Apr. 1964, folder 8, both in box 135, PBJ Papers.

47. Seven months after the Supreme Court's *Brown II* ruling, delegates from twelve southern states—the eleven former Confederate states and West Virginia—met in Memphis, Tennessee, in late December 1955 to form a regionwide group named the Federation for Constitutional Government, whose purpose was the "preservation of constitutional government." The federation elected John U. Barr of New Orleans—a prominent leader of the 1948 Dixiecrat movement in his native state—as chair of its executive committee. The executive committee was comprised of twelve members—one from each member state—and State Circuit Judge Tom Brady represented Mississippi on the committee. Included in the federation's one hundred–member advisory committee were: Senator James Eastland from Mississippi; Senator Strom Thurmond from South Carolina, a former governor who was the States' Rights Democratic Party's (the Dixiecrat Party's) presidential nominee in 1948; Governor Marvin Griffin of Georgia; six United States representatives from the South, including John Bell Williams from Mississippi; and nine former southern governors, including Fielding Wright, vice presidential nominee for the Dixiecrats. Speaking before the crowd gathered at the federation's organizational meeting as a keynote speaker and projecting the restoration of "Americanism" and local self-government as the fight for the preservation of the "culture and the institutions of the Anglo-Saxon race," Eastland brought white southerners' "racial fear" into play. "Generations of Southerners yet unborn will cherish our memory," Eastland roared, "because they will realize that the fight we now wage will have preserved for them their untainted racial heritage." In order to "institutionalize" the southern movement that Eastland had in mind, the federation envisaged "[c]oordinating efforts of the 'literally hundreds of patriotic organizations' across the nation, maintaining a lobby in Washington, [and] undertaking [a] large-scale public relations program." But inadequate finances hindered

much of the federation's ambitious activities, and it never "fulfilled the . . . role envisioned by Eastland and other promoters" of the group. After its ill-fated third party campaign in the 1956 presidential election, which was a much more scaled-down version of the 1948 Dixiecrat movement, the Federation for Constitutional Government faded from public view. See Numan V. Bartley, *The Rise of Massive Resistance: Race and Politics in the South during the 1950's* (Baton Rouge: Louisiana State University Press, 1969), 121–23, 130–31; Hodding Carter, *The South Strikes Back* (Garden City, N.Y.: Doubleday, 1959), 61–62; *NYT*, 30 Dec. 1955; "South Increases Propaganda," *New South* 14 (May 1959): 5; folder 21: "Federation for Constitutional Government," box 1, Cox Collection.

48. *NYT*, 4 Nov. 1963.

49. "Report to Sovereignty Commission Meeting, November 21, 1963," 99-67-0-1-1-1-1 to 2-1-1, p. 1-1-1, MSSC Records; *TP*, 31 July 1963; *Baton Rouge (La.) State Times*, 1 Aug. 1963; *Memphis (Tenn.) Press-Scimitar*, 25 Jan. 1964.

50. "Brief Summary of Activities of the Coordinating Committee for Fundamental American Freedoms," folder 8, box 135, PBJ Papers; *DN*, 25 Apr. 1964.

51. Erle Johnston Jr. to Paul B. Johnson Jr., memo, 27 Mar. 1964, folder 7, box 135, PBJ Papers.

52. Erle Johnston Jr. to Paul B. Johnson Jr., Carroll Gartin, and Elson K. Collins, memo, 10 Mar. 1964, folder 7, box 135, PBJ Papers.

53. Ibid.; David G. Sansing, *Making Haste Slowly: The Troubled History of Higher Education in Mississippi* (Jackson: University Press of Mississippi, 1990), 61; John Dittmer, *Local People: The Struggle for Civil Rights in Mississippi* (Urbana: University of Illinois Press, 1994), 2; *CL*, 27 Apr. 1964.

54. Dittmer, *Local People*, 234; Charles Marsh, *God's Long Summer: Stories of Faith and Civil Rights* (Princeton, N.J.: Princeton University Press, 1997), 116–51.

55. A. L. Hopkins, investigative report, 26 Nov. 1962, 2-55-10-23-1-1-1, MSSC Records.

56. Johnston, *Mississippi's Defiant Years*, 301; Reed Massengill, *Portrait of a Racist: The Man Who Killed Medgar Evers?* (New York: St. Martin's, 1994), 220.

57. Erle Johnston Jr. to Tom Watkins, 31 Jan. 1964, 3-74-1-53-1-1-1, MSSC Records.

58. Erle Johnston Jr. to file, memo, 3 Mar. 1964, 3-74-1-61-1-1-1, MSSC Records.

59. Erle Johnston Jr. to Paul B. Johnson Jr., Carroll Gartin, and Elson K. Collins, memo, 10 Mar. 1964, folder 7, box 135, PBJ Papers.

60. Ibid., 26 Mar. 1964, folder 7, box 135, PBJ Papers.

61. John D. Sullivan to Mississippi Sovereignty Commission, memo, 14 Mar. 1964; Erle Johnston Jr. to file, memo, 16 Mar. 1964, both in folder 11, box 2, Faulkner Collection; Johnston to Paul B. Johnson Jr. and all members of the Sovereignty Commission, memo, 1 Sept. 1964, folder 4, box 136, PBJ Papers.

62. Untitled informant's report, 24 Mar. 1964, 3-74-2-11-1-1-1, MSSC Records.
63. A. L. Hopkins, investigative report, 5 Apr. 1964, 3-74-2-10-1-1-1 to 2-1-1, MSSC Records.
64. Erle Johnston Jr. to file, memo, 17 Apr. 1964, 99-62-0-55-1-1-1; "Faculty Members of Tougaloo College," 3-74-1-59-1-1-1 to 5-1-1, p. 5-1-1, both in MSSC Records; Johnston to file, memo, 13 Apr. 1964, folder 8, box 135, PBJ Papers. The Sovereignty Commission's use of Tougaloo's faculty members as its informants was not new. For instance, in the late spring of 1962, the state agency began its dubious relations with a Cuban refugee, Jose R. Cid, who was an associate professor of chemistry at Tougaloo. Through an arrangement made by another Cuban refugee, Commission Director Jones and Investigator Hopkins met with Cid at the agency's office on May 9. The Sovereignty Commission's new acquaintance, who told Jones and Hopkins that sociology Professor Salter at Tougaloo was "a socialist and possibly a Communist," promised them that he "would make an effort to learn more about Salter" and "report his findings" to the state agency. However, Cid's contract with Tougaloo apparently expired at the end of May 1962, and their relationship was short-lived. See A. L. Hopkins and Albert Jones, investigative report, 11 May 1962, 1-73-0-18-1-1-1 to 3-1-1; untitled document, State Sovereignty Commission, 3-74A-0-5-1-1-1, both in MSSC Records.
65. Erle Johnston Jr. to Wesley A. Hotchkiss, memo, 17 Apr. 1964; Johnston to file, memo, 17 Apr. 1964; Johnston to Herman Glazier, memo, 28 Apr. 1964, all in folder 8, box 135, PBJ Papers.
66. Erle Johnston Jr. to file, memo, 24 Apr. 1964; Shelby R. Rogers, confidential report, n.d., both in folder 8, box 135, PBJ Papers.
67. Erle Johnston Jr. to Herman Glazier, memo, 28 Apr. 1964, folder 8; Johnston to Paul B. Johnson Jr. and Carroll Gartin, memo, 5 May 1964, folder 9, both in box 135, PBJ Papers; Johnston, oral history, vol. 276, transcript, 83, MOHP.
68. Erle Johnston Jr. to file, memo, 31 Dec. 1964, folder 7, box 136, PBJ Papers.
69. Dittmer, *Local People*, 235.
70. Erle Johnston Jr. to Wesley A. Hotchkiss, memo, 17 Apr. 1964, folder 8, box 135, PBJ Papers.
71. Minutes, executive session, Tougaloo College Board of Trustees, 16 Jan. 1964, Minutes of Tougaloo College Board of Trustees Meetings, Special Collections, Coleman Library.
72. Ibid., 24 Apr. 1964.
73. Clarice T. Campbell and Oscar A. Rogers Jr., *Mississippi: The View from Tougaloo* (Jackson: University Press of Mississippi, 1979), 217; *NYT*, 29 July 1968.
74. "Information about Dr. A. D. Beittel Requested by Senator Jim Eastland," 1 Mar. 1966, 1-84-0-20-1-1-1 to 2-1-1, p. 1-1-1, MSSC Records.
75. John Dittmer, "The Politics of the Mississippi Movement, 1954–1964," in *The*

Civil Rights Movement in America, ed. Charles W. Eagles (Jackson: University Press of Mississippi, 1986), 73–74.

76. Doug McAdam, *Freedom Summer* (New York: Oxford University Press, 1988), 4; Steven F. Lawson and Charles Payne, *Debating the Civil Rights Movement, 1945–1968* (Lanham, Md.: Rowman and Littlefield, 1998), 126–27.

77. "Report on Mississippi State Sovereignty Commission (1964–1967)," folder 1, box 141, PBJ Papers.

78. "List of State Laws, Mississippi State Sovereignty Commission to Mississippi Law Enforcement Officers," file "Mississippi Sovereignty Commission," administrative files, ASSC Records.

79. "List of State Laws, Mississippi State Sovereignty Commission to Mississippi Law Enforcement Officers," FF, July 1963 to June 1964, roll no. 12, N12 10247–48.

80. Erle Johnston Jr., "Talk Delivered at State-Wide Meeting Sponsored by Mississippi Economic Council, June 4, 1964, Arlington Room, Robert E. Lee Hotel, Jackson, Mississippi," 99-36-0-30-1-1-1 to 3-1-1, p. 2-1-1, MSSC Records; Johnston to Boyce G. Bratton, 30 Apr. 1964, folder 8, box 135, PBJ Papers; *Tylertown (Miss.) Times*, 28 May 1964.

81. Tom Scarbrough, investigative report, 5 May 1964, folder 9, box 135, PBJ Papers.

82. Informant's report, "Re: Student Non-Violent Co-Ordinating [*sic*] Committee," 10 Feb. 1964, folder 6, box 135, PBJ Papers; informant's report, "Re: Student Non-Violent Co-Ordinating [*sic*] Committee," 10 Feb. 1964 [on the same subject with the same date, but with slightly different contents from the above report], folder 10, box 5, Faulkner Collection.

83. Untitled informant's report, 15 Mar. 1964, folder 7, box 135, PBJ Papers.

84. Informant's report, "Re: Special Report," 23 Apr.–9 May 1964, folder 8, box 135, PBJ Papers; informant's report, "Re: Special Report," 13 May 1964, 9-32-0-2-1-1-1 to 2-1-1, MSSC Records.

85. Informant's report, "Re: Special Report," 13 May 1964, 9-32-0-2-1-1-1 to 2-1-1, MSSC Records. The same report can also be found in folder 9, box 135, PBJ Papers.

86. Informant's report, "Re: Jackson Case #J-64-5-2-U," 28 Aug. 1964, 9-32-0-25-1-1-1; Erle Johnston Jr. to Robert H. Pendleton, 8 Oct. 1964, 7-0-8-153-1-1-1, both in MSSC Records. The same informant's report can also be found in folder 2, box 136, PBJ Papers.

87. Erle Johnston Jr. to file, memo, 27 Mar. 1964, 99-36-0-58-1-1-1; Johnston to Ernest Cochrane, memo, 3 Sept. 1965, 99-86-0-9-1-1-1, both in MSSC Records; Johnston to Paul. B. Johnson Jr. and all members of the Sovereignty Commission, memo, 1 Sept. 1964, folder 4; Johnston to Johnson, memo, 12 Oct. 1964, folder 5, both in box 136, PBJ Papers.

88. Erle Johnston Jr. to file, memo, 27 Mar. 1964, 99-36-0-58-1-1-1, MSSC Records.

89. John S. Kochtitzky Jr. to *Communist Viewpoint*, 20 Aug. 1964, 99-86-0-7-1-1-1; Kochtitzky to editor, *Inter-Racial Review*, 6 Apr. 1964, 99-86-0-33-1-1-1; Kochtitzky to news editor, *Journal of Negro History*, 6 Apr. 1964, 99-86-0-34-1-1-1, all in MSSC Records.

90. Erle Johnston Jr. to Ernest Cochrane, memo, 3 Sept. 1965, 99-86-0-9-1-1-1, MSSC Records; Johnston to Paul B. Johnson Jr. and all members of the Sovereignty Commission, memo, 1 Sept. 1964, folder 4, box 136, PBJ Papers.

91. DISCARD to Thomas N. Burbridge, telegram, 14 Apr. 1964, 6-42-0-1-1-1-1; C. Fain Kyle to T. W. Rogers, 27 Apr. 1964, 6-42-0-3-1-1-1, both in MSSC Records.

92. Erle Johnston Jr. to C. Fain Kyle, 4 May 1964, 6-42-0-4-1-1-1, MSSC Records.

93. C. Fain Kyle to Erle Johnston Jr., 8 May 1964, 6-42-0-6-1-1-1 to 2-1-1, MSSC Records.

94. Ibid., 11 Nov. 1964, 6-42-0-10-1-1-1; Johnston to Kyle, 16 Nov. 1964, 6-42-0-11-1-1-1; Kyle to Johnston, 23 Nov. 1964, 6-42-0-15-1-1-1 to 2-1-1, all in MSSC Records.

95. Johnston, "Talk Delivered at State-Wide Meeting Sponsored by Mississippi Economic Council," 99-36-0-30-1-1-1 to 3-1-1, p. 2-1-1, MSSC Records.

96. James F. Findlay Jr., *Church People in the Struggle: The National Council of Churches and the Black Freedom Movement, 1950–1970* (New York: Oxford University Press, 1993), 85; Nicolaus Mills, *Like a Holy Crusade: Mississippi 1964—The Turning of the Civil Rights Movement in America* (Chicago: Ivan R. Dee, 1992), 86.

97. Johnston, oral history, vol. 276, transcript, 84, MOHP.

98. Paul B. Johnson Jr. oral history, interviewed by T. H. Baker, 8 Sept. 1970, AC 80-63, transcript, 27, LBJ Library.

99. Untitled informant's report, 26 June 1964, folder 10, box 135, PBJ Papers; "Breakdown on Expenses, June 1964," folder 11, box 5, Faulkner Collection.

100. *Meridian (Miss.) Star*, 12 July 1964.

101. Florence Mars, *Witness in Philadelphia* (Baton Rouge: Louisiana State University Press, 1977), 80.

102. Seth Cagin and Philip Dray, *We Are Not Afraid: The Story of Goodman, Schwerner, and Chaney and the Civil Rights Campaign for Mississippi* (New York: Macmillan, 1988), 1–46, 345–56; Len Holt, *The Summer That Didn't End: The Story of the Mississippi Civil Rights Project of 1964* (New York: William Morrow, 1965), 207.

103. A. L. Hopkins, investigative report, 23 June 1964, 2-112-1-38-1-1-1 to 3-1-1, p. 3-1-1, MSSC Records.

104. A. L. Hopkins, investigative report, 29 June 1964, folder 10, box 135, PBJ Papers.

105. Erle Johnston Jr. to Herman Glazier, memo, 3 July 1964, folder 1; A. L. Hopkins, investigative report, 6 Aug. 1964, folder 2, both in box 136, PBJ Papers.

106. FBI memo, "Subject: MIBURN, Re: KKK," 2 July 1964, folder 15, box 3, Johnston Papers; Mars, *Witness in Philadelphia*, 80, 82.

107. Erle Johnston Jr. to file, memo, 17 Mar. 1964, folder 11, box 2, Faulkner Collection; G. L. Butler to Andy Hopkins, supplementary offense report, 19 Mar. 1964, 2-46-0-79-1-1-1; Hopkins, investigative report, 23 Mar. 1964, 2-46-0-77-1-1-1 to 2-1-1; Johnston to Betty Jane Long, 24 Mar. 1964, 2-46-0-75-1-1-1; Hopkins, investigative report, 9 Apr. 1965, 2-46-0-90-1-1-1 to 2-1-1, p. 1-1-1, all in MSSC Records; Hopkins, investigative report, 9 July 1964, folder 1, box 136, PBJ Papers. Investigator Hopkins's report dated 23 March and Director Johnston's 24 March letter addressed to Representative Long can also be found in William A. Link and Marjorie S. Wheeler, eds., *The South in the History of the Nation: A Reader*, vol. 2 (Boston: Bedford/St. Martin's, 1999), 243–45.

108. "Convesation 3820 with Rep. John McCormack (D-MA), Speaker of the House, Date: 6/23/64, Time: 12:45 PM," <http://www.c-span.org/ram/lbj/lbj2306.ram>; "Conversation 4280 with Senator Russell Long (D-LA), Date: 7/20/64, Time: 5:32 PM," <http://www.c-span.org/ram/lbj/lbj2819.ram>, both in *LBJ White House Tapes* series, C-SPAN, Washington, D.C., consulted 28 Nov. 2000 <http://www.c-span.org/lbj> Real Audio. See also Michael R. Beschloss, ed., *Taking Charge: The Johnson White House Tapes, 1963–1964* (New York: Simon and Schuster, 1997), 426–27, 444, 458.

109. Burke Marshall, oral history, interviewed by T. H. Baker, 28 Oct. 1968, AC 74-215, transcript, 30, LBJ Library; Paul B. Johnson Jr., "Press Release, Governor Paul B. Johnson, June 23, 1964," folder 21, box 103, PBJ Papers; John Stennis to Johnson, 27 June 1964, folder 11, box 2, Faulkner Collection; "Conversation 3845 with Sen. James Eastland (D-MS), Date: 6/23/64, Time: 4:25 PM," <http://www.c-span.org/ram/lbj/lbj2319.ram>; "Conversation 3878 with Governor Paul Johnson (D-MS), Date: 6/23/64, Time: 8:21 PM," <http://www.c-span.org/ram/lbj/lbj2418.ram>; "Conversation 3891 with J. Edgar Hoover, FBI Director, and Sen. John Stennis (D-MS), Date: 6/24/64, Time: 5:30 PM," <http://www.c-span.org/ram/lbj/lbj2426.ram>; "Conversation 3893 with J. Edgar Hoover, FBI Director, Date: 6/24/64, Time: Unknown," <http://www.c-span.org/ram/lbj/lbj2427.ram>, all in *LBJ White House Tapes* series. See also Beschloss, *Taking Charge*, 440; *NYT*, 24 June 1964.

110. Erle Johnston Jr. to Paul B. Johnson Jr. and all members of the Sovereignty Commission, memo, 1 Sept. 1964, folder 4, box 136, PBJ Papers; "Conversation 3919 with Paul Johnson governor of Mississippi, and between Allen Dulles and Governor Johnson, Date: 6/26/64, Time: 1:05 PM," <http://www.c-span.org/ram/lbj/lbj2505.ram>; "Conversation 3921 with J. Edgar Hoover,

FBI Director, and between Mr. Hoover and Allen Dulles, Date: 6/26/64, Time: 1:17 PM," <http://www.c-span.org/ram/lbj/lbj2506.ram>, both in *LBJ White House Tapes* series.

111. Erle Johnston Jr. to Paul B. Johnson Jr. and all members of the Sovereignty Commission, memo, 1 Sept. 1964, folder 4, box 136; Johnson, "Press Release, Governor Paul B. Johnson, June 26, 1964, 2:30 P.M.," folder 21, box 103; Johnston to file, memo, 2 July 1964, folder 1, box 136, all in PBJ Papers.

112. Al Richburg to T. B. Birdsong, report, 26 June 1964, folder 11, box 2, Faulkner Collection.

113. "Conversation 4138 with J. Edgar Hoover, FBI Director, Date: 7/2/64, Time: 5:02 PM," <http://www.c-span.org/ram/lbj/lbj2708.ram>, *LBJ White House Tapes* series; Dittmer, *Local People*, 250. See also Beschloss, *Taking Charge*, 450.

114. Burke Marshall to Dan H. Shell, 15 July 1964, folder 12, box 2, Faulkner Collection; Johnson, oral history, AC 80-63, transcript, 30, LBJ Library; *NYT*, 6 Oct. 1964.

115. *CL*, 3 Aug. 1964.

116. "Conversation 3836 with Sen. James Eastland (D-MS), Date: 6/23/64, Time: 3:59 PM," <http://www.c-span.org/ram/lbj/lbj2314.ram>, *LBJ White House Tapes* series. See also Beschloss, *Taking Charge*, 432.

117. A. L. Hopkins, investigative report, 6 Aug. 1964, folder 2, box 136, PBJ Papers.

118. Ben Chaney, "Schwerner, Chaney, and Goodman: The Struggle for Justice," *Human Rights* 27 (spring 2000), American Bar Association, Chicago, consulted 1 Aug. 2000 <http://www.abanet.org/irr/hr/spring00humanrights/chaney.html>.

119. "Schwerner['s] Car on White Citizens['] Council List" [FBI investigative report(?)], folder 2, box 9, Faulkner Collection; Delmar D. Dennis, letter to the author, 4 May 1995. See also Delmar D. Dennis, *To Stand Alone: Inside the KKK for the FBI* (Sevierville, Tenn.: Covenant House, 1991); Don Whitehead, *Attack on Terror: The FBI against the Ku Klux Klan in Mississippi* (New York: Funk and Wagnalls, 1970), 186–91.

120. Graham, *Civil Rights and the Presidency*, 74; *CL*, 3 July 1964; *CL/DN*, 5 July 1964.

121. A. L. Hopkins, investigative report, 9 July 1964, folder 1, box 136, PBJ Papers; *CL/DN*, 1 July 1984; Shirley Tucker, *Mississippi from Within* (New York: Arco, 1965), 16–17; Johnston, *Mississippi's Defiant Years*, 246.

122. Charles Sallis and John Q. Adams, "Desegregation in Jackson, Mississippi," in *Southern Businessmen and Desegregation*, ed. Elizabeth Jacoway and David R. Colburn (Baton Rouge: Louisiana State University Press, 1982), 243.

123. Ibid., 243–44.

124. *DN*, 9 July 1964.

125. Robert A. Sedler, "Civil Rights Act of 1964," in *The Oxford Companion to the*

Supreme Court of the United States, ed. Kermit L. Hall (New York: Oxford University Press, 1992), 148.

126. DN, 7 July 1964; Carter, *The South Strikes Back*, 208–9.

127. *Meridian (Miss.) Star*, 26 Aug. 1964.

128. *NYT*, 6 Oct. 1964.

129. Press release, Jackson Citizens' Council, 12 Oct. 1964, 99-30-0-134-1-1-1, MSSC Records.

130. Frank R. Parker, *Black Votes Count: Political Empowerment in Mississippi after 1965* (Chapel Hill: University of North Carolina Press, 1990), 23.

131. Erle Johnston Jr. to file, memo, 9 Nov. 1965, 3-81-0-38-1-1-1 to 2-1-1, MSSC Records.

132. Erle Johnston Jr. to Herman Glazier, memo, 20 Sept. 1965, 3-81-0-37-1-1-1, MSSC Records.

133. *NYT*, 4 Sept. 1957.

134. Ibid., 20 Dec. 1964.

135. Paul B. Johnson Jr., "Statement of Governor Paul B. Johnson before the U.S. Commission on Civil Rights, Jackson, Mississippi, February 16, 1965," 1–2, folder 11, box 93, PBJ Papers. See also Paul B. Johnson Jr., "Statement of Governor Paul B. Johnson, February 9, 1965," vol. 1138, PBJ (MDAH) Papers.

136. Paul B. Johnson Jr., "Address by Governor Paul B. Johnson to Southern Association of Chamber of Commerce Executives Annual Conference, March 22, 1965," folder 21, box 93, PBJ Papers.

137. Erle Johnston Jr. to Herman Glazier, memo, 11 Feb. 1965, folder 2, box 137, PBJ Papers.

138. Jim Edmondson to Earl [*sic*] Johnston Jr., 1 Feb. 1965; Johnston to Herman Glazier, memo, 5 Feb. 1965; Johnston to Glazier, memo, 12 Feb. 1965; Johnston to Edmondson, 16 Feb. 1965, all in folder 2, box 137, PBJ Papers.

139. Erle Johnston Jr. to file, memo, 5 Mar. 1965, folder 3; "Report of Principal Activities and Policies from September 1, 1964, through May 31, 1965," folder 4, both in box 137, PBJ Papers.

140. Untitled public relations proposal, folder 5, box 137, PBJ Papers.

141. Erle Johnston Jr. to Herman Glazier, memo, 22 Apr. 1965, folder 4, box 137, PBJ Papers.

142. Ibid.; Johnston to C. W. Gusewelle, 23 Apr. 1965, 99-84-0-4-1-1-1, MSSC Records.

143. *CL*, 2 May 1965.

144. Johnston, oral history, vol. 276, pt. 2, transcript, 22, MOHP.

145. R. C. Cook to Erle Johnston, memo, 24 May 1965, 99-118-0-8-1-1-1 to 2-1-1; Johnston to Paul B. Johnson, memo, 25 May 1965, 99-34-0-14-1-1-1 to 2-1-1, both in MSSC Records; Johnston to Herman Glazier, memo, 28 May

1965, folder 5; untitled public relations proposal, folder 5; Johnston to file, memo, 7 June 1965, folder 6, all in box 137, PBJ Papers.

146. Johnston, oral history, vol. 276, pt. 2, transcript, 23, MOHP; *CL*, 2 May 1965.

147. Erle Johnston Jr. to Paul B. Johnson, memo, 25 May 1965, 99-34-0-14-1-1-1 to 2-1-1, p. 1-1-1, MSSC Records. The same memo can also be found in folder 5, box 137, PBJ Papers.

148. Erle Johnston Jr. to Herman Glazier, memo, 15 June 1965, folder 6, box 137, PBJ Papers.

149. Erle Johnston Jr. to Paul B. Johnson, members of the Mississippi State Sovereignty Commission, and members of the Mississippi legislature, 2 Dec.1965, 8-17-0-56-1-1-1, MSSC Records. The same document can also be found in folder 5, box 138, PBJ Papers.

150. Erle Johnston Jr. to Herman Glazier, memo, 30 Dec. 1965, folder 5, box 138, PBJ Papers.

Chapter 6. Officially but Discreetly: Dealing with Unreconstructed Forces

1. Erle Johnston Jr., "Address by Erle Johnston, Jr.," 6-36-0-26-1-1-1 to 13-1-1, pp. 2-1-1 to 3-1-1, 7-1-1, MSSC Records. See also "Report on Mississippi State Sovereignty Commission (1964–1967)," folder 1, box 141, PBJ Papers; *DDT*, 13 May 1964; *Madison County (Miss.) Herald*, 21 May 1964. Johnston's address can also be found in folder 17, box 3, CC/CR Collection.

2. *Tylertown (Miss.) Times*, 28 May 1964.

3. Erle Johnston Jr., "Talk Delivered at State-Wide Meeting Sponsored by Mississippi Economic Council, June 4, 1964, Arlington Room, Robert E. Lee Hotel, Jackson, Mississippi," 99-36-0-30-1-1-1 to 3-1-1, pp. 1-1-1, 3-1-1, MSSC Records. See also Erle Johnston Jr. to file, memo, 5 June 1964, 99-36-0-29-1-1-1, MSSC Records.

4. James W. Williams and Rowland N. Scott to Erle Johnston Jr., 20 June 1964, 6-36-0-10-1-1-1 to 2-1-1, MSSC Records. The same letter can also be found in folder 10, box 135, PBJ Papers.

5. Minutes, Americans for the Preservation of the White Race, 13 May 1963, 6-36-0-1-1-1-1 to 8-1-1, pp. 2-1-1 to 4-1-1, MSSC Records.

6. Charter of incorporation, Americans for the Preservation of the White Race, 25 June 1963, 6-36-0-1-1-1-1 to 8-1-1, pp. 1-1-1, 5-1-1 to 7-1-1, MSSC Records.

7. Reed Massengill, *Portrait of a Racist: The Man Who Killed Medgar Evers?* (New York: St. Martin's, 1994), 254.

8. *CL*, 19 July 1965.

9. Americans for the Preservation of the White Race, *White Patriot*, n.d., 16.

10. Americans for the Preservation of the White Race, "The Only Reason You Are

White Is Because Your Ancestors Believed In and Practiced Segregation," n.d., folder 5, box 141, PBJ Papers.

11. Erle Johnston Jr. to Paul B. Johnson Jr., special report, 1 May 1964, folder 9, box 135, PBJ Papers; Andy L. Hopkins, investigative report, 1 May 1964, 6-36-0-2-1-1-1 to 2-1-1, MSSC Records; Virgil Downing to Johnston, memo, 1 May 1964, folder 11, box 2, Faulkner Collection. Investigator Hopkins's report can also be found in folder 9, box 135, PBJ Papers.

12. Erle Johnston Jr. to file, memo, 2 July 1964, 6-36-0-15-1-1-1, MSSC Records. The same memo can also be found in folder 1, box 136, PBJ Papers.

13. James W. Williams and Rowland N. Scott to Erle Johnston Jr., 20 June 1964, 6-36-0-10-1-1-1 to 2-1-1, MSSC Records.

14. Erle Johnston Jr. to file, memo, 24 July 1964, folder 1, box 136, PBJ Papers.

15. Erle Johnston Jr. to Herman Glazier, memo, 23 July 1964; Johnston to Glazier, memo, 30 July 1964, both in folder 1, box 136, PBJ Papers.

16. "Observations and Recommendations Made by Director, Sovereignty Commission, to Business and Professional Leaders of Carthage, Mississippi," 6-36-0-26-1-1-1 to 13-1-1, pp. 1-1-1 to 5-1-1, MSSC Records. Johnston's "Observations and Recommendations" can also be found in folder 1, box 135, PBJ Papers.

17. Erle Johnston Jr. to file, memo, 3 Aug. 1964, folder 2, box 136, PBJ Papers.

18. Ibid., 17 Aug. 1964, folder 2, box 136, PBJ Papers.

19. Erle Johnston Jr. to file, memo, 24 Aug. 1964, 6-36-0-20-1-1-1, MSSC Records. The same memo can also be found in folder 2, box 136, PBJ Papers.

20. See folder 3 entitled "August 1964—Letters Requesting Dismissal of Erle Johnston, Prepared by the Americans for the Preservation of the White Race, Inc.," in box 136, PBJ Papers.

21. A total of sixty-four of these protest letters, whose senders were not confined to the residents of Carthage, can be found in folder 3, box 136, PBJ Papers, and folder 4 in the same box contains one letter.

22. Rowland N. Scott to Earle [*sic*] Johnston Jr., 2 Sept. 1964, 6-36-0-21-1-1-1; Johnston to Scott, 3 Sept. 1964, 6-36-0-22-1-1-1, both in MSSC Records.

23. Erle Johnston Jr. to file, memo, 14 Sept. 1964, 6-36-0-25-1-1-1 to 3-1-1, p. 2-1-1, MSSC Records.

24. Ibid., pp. 1-1-1, 3-1-1; Rowland N. Scott to Johnston, 21 Sept. 1964, 6-36-0-29-1-1-1; Johnston to Scott, 24 Sept. 1964, 6-36-0-30-1-1-1, all in MSSC Records.

25. Erle Johnston Jr. to Paul B. Johnson Jr., memo, 12 Oct. 1964, folder 5, box 136, PBJ Papers.

26. Erle Johnston Jr., untitled speech, 12 Dec. 1964, folder 5, box 142, PBJ Papers. See also *TP*, 13 Dec. 1964; *CA*, 13 Dec. 1964.

27. Erle Johnston Jr., untitled speech, 12 Dec. 1964, folder 5, box 142, PBJ Pa-

pers. See also Erle Johnston Jr. to Carter C. Parnell Jr., 12 July 1965; Parnell to Johnston, 13 July 1965, both in folder 7, box 137, PBJ Papers.

28. A. L. Hopkins, investigative report, 18 Dec. 1964, folder 12, box 5, Faulkner Collection.

29. Erle Johnston Jr. to file, memo, 17 Nov. 1964, folder 6, box 136, PBJ Papers.

30. Erle Johnston Jr. to file, memo, 17 Nov. 1964 [on the same subject with the same date, but with different contents from the above memo], folder 6, box 136, PBJ Papers.

31. *TP*, n.d., folder 10, box 104, PBJ Papers; *Memphis (Tenn.) Press-Scimitar*, 26 July 1965.

32. *Southern Review*, 27 Oct. 1964.

33. See, for instance, the article entitled "Americans for the Preservation of the White Race" in the January 1965 issue of the *Southern Review*.

34. *Southern Review*, Jan. 1965.

35. Ibid., 27 Oct. 1964.

36. Erle Johnston Jr. to file, memo, 5 Apr. 1965, 6-43-0-22-1-1-1 to 2-1-1, MSSC Records.

37. Sam Talbert to Erle Johnston Jr., 31 Mar. 1965, folder 4, box 137, PBJ Papers; Johnston, "Members of the Mississippi Scholastic Press Association, Teachers, Dr. Talbert, and Guests," 1 May 1965, 99-139-0-14-1-1-1 to 6-1-1, pp. 3-1-1 to 4-1-1, MSSC Records. Johnston's address can also be found in folder 4, box 137, PBJ Papers.

38. Johnston, "Members of the Mississippi Scholastic Press Association," 99-139-0-14-1-1-1 to 6-1-1, p. 6-1-1, MSSC Records.

39. Erle Johnston Jr. to Herman Glazier, memo, 22 Apr. 1965; Johnston to Glazier, memo, 27 Apr. 1965, both in folder 4, box 137, PBJ Papers.

40. *CL*, 4 May 1965.

41. Ibid.

42. Erle Johnston Jr., "Public Relations Association of Mississippi—Tuesday, August 24, 1965," 1, folder 1, box 138, PBJ Papers.

43. Erle Johnston Jr., "Remarks by Erle Johnston Jr., Director, Sovereignty Commission, before Belzoni Rotary Club, Noon, October 1, 1965," 99-139-0-17-1-1-1 to 6-1-1, MSSC Records; Johnston, "Speech, Exchange Club, Cleveland, Mississippi, December 2, 1965, Noon," folder 5, box 138, PBJ Papers.

44. Erle Johnston Jr. to Paul B. Johnson Jr., special report, 1 May 1964, folder 9, box 135, PBJ Papers.

45. In April 1961, for example, Representative William Johnson, a Commission member, and William Simmons of the Council appeared before the House Ways and Means Committee of the South Carolina state legislature by invitation, where a House bill "to establish a continuing committee on States['] Rights" was being discussed. The bill was calling for a $100,000 appropriation to establish the committee, which would be "charged with promoting an un-

derstanding of Southern attitudes on constitutional government, racial segregation and related issues." See *Charleston (S.C.) News and Courier*, 12 Apr. 1961.

46. "Citizen[s'] Council Grant," 99-30-0-46-1-1-1 to 2-1-1, MSSC Records. The
same document can also be found in folder 1, box 137, PBJ Papers.

47. Erle Johnston Jr. to Paul B. Johnson Jr., memo, 6 Feb. 1964, folder 6, box
135, PBJ Papers; Johnston, oral history, interviewed by Orley B. Caudill, 16
July 1980 and 30 July 1980, vol. 276, transcript, 79, MOHP.

48. Johnston, oral history, vol. 276, transcript, 108, MOHP; *LSM*, 1964, regular
sess., 136.

49. Erle Johnston Jr. to Paul B. Johnson Jr., memo, 12 Oct. 1964, folder 5, box
136, PBJ Papers.

50. Earl Evans Jr. to Erle Johnston Jr., 18 Jan. 1965, folder 1; Evans to Johnston,
19 Feb. 1965, folder 2, both in box 137, PBJ Papers.

51. Erle Johnston Jr. to William J. Simmons, 23 Feb. 1965, folder 2, box 137,
PBJ Papers.

52. William J. Simmons to Erle Johnston Jr., 15 Mar. 1965, folder 63-A, box 1,
Cox Collection.

53. Earl Evans Jr. to Erle Johnston Jr., 16 Mar. 1965, folder 63-A, box 1, Cox
Collection.

54. Erle Johnston Jr., oral history, interviewed by Yasuhiro Katagiri, 13 Aug.
1993, vol. 276, pt. 2, transcript, 13, MOHP. See also Erle Johnston Jr. to
Herman Glazier, memo, 18 Mar. 1965; Johnston to Joe T. Patterson, 23 Mar.
1965, both in folder 3, box 137, PBJ Papers.

55. *DN*, 29 Mar. 1965; *CA*, 29 Mar. 1965.

56. "Financial Statement, State Sovereignty Commission, July 1, 1964, through
January 31, 1965," folder 1, box 137, PBJ Papers; "Citizen[s'] Council Grant,"
99-30-0-46-1-1-1 to 2-1-1, MSSC Records.

57. William J. Simmons to Erle Johnston Jr., 18 Nov. 1987, folder 9, box 2,
Johnston Papers.

58. Roy K. Moore to Paul B. Johnson Jr., 23 Sept. 1965; Moore to Johnson, 31
Mar. 1966, both in folder 1, box 142, PBJ Papers.

59. B. M. Duncan, Mississippi Livestock Theft Bureau case report, 30 Oct. 1964,
folder 12, box 5; Mississippi Bureau of Identification case report, 12 July 1965,
folder 11, box 7, both in Faulkner Collection; Reid S. Derr, *The Triumph of
Progressivism: Governor Paul B. Johnson, Jr., and Mississippi in the 1960s* (Ann
Arbor, Mich.: University Microfilms, 1994), 424.

60. A. L. Hopkins, investigative report, 29 July 1965, 2-112-2-19-1-1-1 to
3-1-1, MSSC Records. See also A. L. Hopkins, investigative report, 26 Oct.
1965, folder 3, box 138, PBJ Papers.

61. A. L. Hopkins to Erle Johnston, memo, 12 Apr. 1965, folder 13, box 2, Faulkner Collection.

62. FBI memo, "Subject: MIBURN, Re: KKK," 2 July 1964; FBI memo, "Sub-

ject: Erle Johnston Jr.," 4 May 1967; FBI memo, "Subject: Earle [*sic*] Ennis Johnston," 31 Jan. 1968; FBI memo, "Subject: Erle Ennis Johnston," 5 Sept. 1968, all in folder 15, box 3, Johnston Papers. See also Kenneth O'Reilly, *"Racial Matters": The FBI's Secret File on Black America, 1960–1972* (New York: Free Press, 1989), 173. Though information is excised from the documents to protect personal privacy, the identity of confidential sources, and national security, the FBI's "MIBURN" files can be read at the bureau's "Freedom of Information Act Electronic Reading Room," <http://foia.fbi.gov/miburn.htm>.

63. *DN*, 1 Aug. 1966.

64. Erle Johnston Jr. to Herman Glazier, memo, 17 Apr. 1967, folder 3, box 140, PBJ Papers; Johnston to Glazier, memo, 4 May 1967, 7-0-10-47-1-1-1, MSSC Records.

65. Paul B. Johnson Jr., "Message to the Legislature, Governor Paul B. Johnson, January 5, 1966," 20, folder 1, box 96, PBJ Papers.

66. *NYT*, 9 Jan. 1966.

67. Paul B. Johnson Jr., "Press Release, Governor Paul B. Johnson, April 23, 1965," folder 1, box 104; Johnson to Edward J. Currie Sr., 23 Apr. 1965, folder 4, box 137; Currie to Johnson, 24 Apr. 1965, folder 2, box 80; Johnson, "Press Release, Governor Paul B. Johnson, May 7, 1965," folder 2, box 104, all in PBJ Papers.

68. *CA*, 1 July 1965.

69. Horace H. Harned Jr. to Paul B. Johnson Jr., 25 Jan. 1965; Johnson to Harned, 1 Feb. 1965, both in folder 2, box 137, PBJ Papers.

70. *CA*, 1 July 1965; *DDT*, 12 July 1965.

71. *CA*, 4 Jan. 1966.

72. *JH*, 1966, regular sess., 65; *MOSR*, 1964–1968, 87, 101; *CL*, 19 Jan. 1966; *CL/DN*, 23 Jan. 1966.

73. *JS*, 1966, regular sess., 67; Herman B. DeCell, oral history, interviewed by Orley B. Caudill, 9 June 1977, vol. 207, transcript, 37, MOHP; *DN*, 20 Jan. 1966; *CL*, 21 Jan. 1966; *TP*, 21 Jan. 1966.

74. *DN*, 20 Jan. 1966; *CL*, 21 Jan. 1966.

75. *CL/DN*, 23 Jan. 1966.

76. Untitled signed statement, 7-0-9-86-1-1-1, MSSC Records; *CA*, 22 Jan. 1966; *DN*, 22 Jan. 1966. The statement can also be found in folder 6, box 138, PBJ Papers.

77. "Mississippians for Mississippi" to the members of the Mississippi State Legislature, open letter, n.d., folder 5, box 142, PBJ Papers.

78. Ibid.

79. Erle Johnston Jr., letter to the author, 18 Oct. 1993; Johnston, oral history, vol. 276, pt. 2, transcript, 23, MOHP.

80. *JS*, 1966, regular sess., 313; Erle Johnston Jr. to file, memo, 1 Mar. 1966, folder 8, box 138, PBJ Papers; *CL*, 13 May 1966.

81. *LSM*, 1966, regular sess., 155–56; Erle Johnston Jr. to Paul B. Johnson Jr., memo, 12 July 1966, 7-3-0-24-1-1-1, MSSC Records.

82. *CL*, 26 May 1966.

83. *LSM*, 1966, regular sess., 155.

84. Johnston, oral history, vol. 276, pt. 2, transcript, 16, MOHP.

85. *DN*, 1 Aug. 1966.

86. *CL*, 9 Aug. 1966.

87. Minutes, State Sovereignty Commission, 8 Aug. 1966, folder 3, box 139, PBJ Papers.

88. Ibid.

89. Ibid.; *CA*, 9 Aug. 1966.

90. Walter Sillers to Erle Johnston Jr., 17 Aug. 1966; Sillers, "Proposed Policy Statement for Sovereignty Commission," both in folder 3, box 139, PBJ Papers.

91. Walter Sillers to Erle Johnston Jr., 17 Aug. 1966, folder 3, box 139, PBJ Papers.

92. Erle Johnston Jr. to Walter Sillers, 19 Aug. 1966, folder 3, box 139, PBJ Papers.

93. Erle Johnston Jr., "Address by Erle Johnston, Jr., Director, State Sovereignty Commission, before the Annual Convention of the Mississippi Association of Chamber of Commerce Executives at Biloxi, August 18, 1966," 99-122-0-7-1-1-1 to 8-1-1, pp. 4-1-1 to 5-1-1, MSSC Records. This address can also be found in folder 3, box 139, PBJ Papers.

94. *Southern Review*, 1 Oct. 1966.

95. "Petition for Impeachment of Paul B. Johnson, Governor of Mississippi, to the House of Representatives, State of Mississippi," 6-43-0-31-1-1-1 to 2-1-1, MSSC Records; Kenneth L. Dean to Erle Johnston Jr., 29 Feb. 1988, folder 3, box 3, Johnston Papers.

96. Erle Johnston Jr. to Paul B. Johnson Jr., memo, 23 Nov. 1966, 6-43-0-30-1-1-1; A. L. Hopkins, investigative report, 1 May 1964, 6-36-0-2-1-1-1 to 2-1-1, p. 1-1-1, both in MSSC Records; *CL*, 14 Feb. 1966.

97. Minutes, State Sovereignty Commission, 11 Oct. 1966, folder 5, box 139, PBJ Papers; Horace Harned Jr. to Semmes Luckett, 23 July 1965, 99-118-0-36-1-1-1 to 2-1-1, p. 2-1-1, MSSC Records.

98. Horace H. Harned Jr., oral history, interviewed by Yasuhiro Katagiri, 3 Nov. 1993, vol. 355, pt. 2, transcript, 17–18, MOHP.

99. Minutes, State Sovereignty Commission, 11 Oct. 1966, folder 5, box 139, PBJ Papers.

100. Ibid., 14 Feb. 1967, folder 1, box 140, PBJ Papers. See also Edward J. Currie to Erle Johnston Jr., 14 Jan. 1967; Johnston to Currie, 23 Jan. 1967; Johnston

to Paul B. Johnson Jr., memo, 30 Jan. 1967, all in folder 8, box 139, PBJ Papers; Johnston, letter to the author, 18 Oct. 1993.

101. Joe T. Patterson, memo, 17 Feb. 1967, folder 1, box 140, PBJ Papers.

102. John J. Nosser to Earl Johnson [*sic*], 3 May 1967, folder 4, box 140, PBJ Papers; Johnston, oral history, vol. 276, pt. 2, transcript, 34, MOHP.

103. Minutes, State Sovereignty Commission, 11 May 1967, folder 4, box 140, PBJ Papers.

104. Ibid., 13 June 1967, folder 5, box 140, PBJ Papers; Erle Johnston Jr. to investigative staff, memo, 14 June 1967, 7-0-10-55-1-1-1, MSSC Records.

105. Harned, oral history, vol. 355, pt. 2, transcript, 19, MOHP.

106. Erle Johnston Jr., *Mississippi's Defiant Years, 1953–1973: An Interpretive Documentary with Personal Experiences* (Forest, Miss.: Lake Harbor, 1990), 336.

107. Minutes, State Sovereignty Commission, 13 June 1967, folder 5; Erle Johnston Jr., "Address by Erle Johnston, Jr., Director, State Sovereignty Commission, before the Mississippi Methodist Student Movement State Conference at Jackson, Mississippi, March 4, 1967," folder 2; Johnston to Herman Glazier, memo, n.d., folder 2, all in box 140, PBJ Papers.

108. Johnston, oral history, vol. 276, pt. 2, transcript, 39, MOHP; Johnston to George M. Yarbrough, 5 July 1967, folder 6; Johnston to members, State Sovereignty Commission, memo, 28 July 1967, folder 6; Johnston to members, State Sovereignty Commission, memo, 1 Sept. 1967, folder 8, all in box 140, PBJ Papers.

109. See, for example, Paul B. Johnson Jr. to Kenneth O. Williams, 24 Oct. 1967, folder 1, box 141, PBJ Papers.

110. *CL/DN*, 14 May 1967.

111. "The Barnett Record," vol. 1, no. 2 (July–Aug. 1967), supplement to *CL/DN*, 30 July 1967.

112. Earl Black, *Southern Governors and Civil Rights: Racial Segregation as a Campaign Issue in the Second Reconstruction* (Cambridge: Harvard University Press, 1976), 182; *DN*, 7 Aug. 1967.

113. Black, *Southern Governors and Civil Rights*, 183; *DN*, 7 Aug. 1967; William F. Winter, oral history, interviewed by Orley B. Caudill, 9 Aug. 1978, vol. 417, transcript, 41, MOHP.

114. Black, *Southern Governors and Civil Rights*, 182; Erle Johnston Jr., *Politics: Mississippi Style* (Forest, Miss.: Lake Harbor, 1993), 218; *CL*, 30 July 1967.

115. *MOSR*, 1968–1972, 449.

116. Ibid., 458.

117. Black, *Southern Governors and Civil Rights*, 388; *MOSR*, 1968–1972, 460.

118. *CL*, 18 Sept. 1967.

119. Paul B. Johnson Jr. to Kenneth O. Williams, 24 Oct. 1967, folder 1, box 141, PBJ Papers.

120. Herman B. DeCell to Paul B. Johnson Jr., 27 Oct. 1967, folder 1, box 141, PBJ Papers.
121. Johnston, oral history, vol. 276, pt. 2, transcript, 30, MOHP.
122. *CL/DN*, 21 Feb. 1982.
123. Johnston, oral history, vol. 276, pt. 2, transcript, 1, 17–18, MOHP.
124. *TP*, 5 May 1968.
125. *NYT*, 6 July 1968.

Chapter 7. The Last Hurrah: Cracking Down on New Subversives

1. *JH*, 1968, regular sess., 42–43.
2. *LSM*, 1968, regular sess., 194–95.
3. *MOSR*, 1968–1972, 25.
4. John R. Junkin to W. Webb Burke, 9 Sept. 1968, 7-0-10-155-1-1-1; Junkin to Burke, 6 Feb. 1970, 7-0-11-190-1-1-1, both in MSSC Records; *MOSR*, 1968–1972, 100.
5. Horace H. Harned Jr., oral history, interviewed by Yasuhiro Katagiri, 3 Nov. 1993, vol. 355, pt. 2, transcript, 12, 24, MOHP.
6. Minutes, State Sovereignty Commission, 19 Mar. 1971, folder 3, box 10, Faulkner Collection.
7. *CA*, 14 Aug. 1968.
8. *DN*, 27 Aug. 1968; *CA*, 28 Aug. 1968; *Birmingham (Ala.) News*, 28 Aug. 1968.
9. W. Webb Burke to John Bell Williams, memo, 5 Feb. 1970, 7-0-11-189-1-1-1 to 4-1-1, p. 3-1-1; Burke, untitled document, 14 July 1972, 7-0-12-284-1-1-1; minutes, State Sovereignty Commission, 17 Nov. 1972, 99-216-0-16-1-1-1 to 6-1-1, p. 4-1-1; Burke to Francis Geoghegan, memo, 5 July 1973, 97-94-0-1-1-1-1 to 2-1-1, p. 1-1-1, all in MSSC Records.
10. Erle Johnston Jr. to file, memo, 4 Feb. 1964, 2-64-1-64-1-1-1; Louie Risk to State Sovereignty Commission, statement, 18 Mar. 1964, 99-99-0-103-1-1-1; Leland E. Cole Jr. to W. Webb Burke, 28 Jan. 1969, 99-44-0-8-1-1-1, all in MSSC Records; William F. Dukes, oral history, interviewed by Orley B. Caudill, 23 Jan. 1973, vol. 40, transcript, 35–36, MOHP.
11. "Application for Employment, State of Mississippi: Cole, Lee E. Jr., Investigator, Sovereignty Commission," 24 Aug. 1964, folder 2, box 80, PBJ Papers; "Answer to Garnishment," Jan. 1969, 99-44-0-5-1-1-1, MSSC Records. See also Erle Johnston Jr. to file, memo, 16 Sept. 1966, 99-44-0-28-1-1-1, MSSC Records.
12. W. Webb Burke to John Bell Williams, memo, 5 Jan. 1970, 99-208-0-8-1-1-1 to 2-1-1, p. 1-1-1; minutes, State Sovereignty Commission, 16 Apr. 1971, 99-102-0-14-1-1-1 to 8-1-1, p. 1-1-1; minutes, State Sovereignty Commis-

sion, 20 Aug. 1971, 99-130-0-16-1-1-1 to 6-1-1, p. 1-1-1, all in MSSC Records.

13. W. Webb Burke to John Bell Williams, memo, 5 Jan. 1970, 99-208-0-8-1-1-1 to 2-1-1, p. 1-1-1, MSSC Records.

14. Ibid., 5 Feb. 1970, 7-0-11-189-1-1-1 to 4-1-1, p. 4-1-1, MSSC Records.

15. *MOSR*, 1968–1972, 375.

16. Kenneth W. Fairly to Webb Burke, 16 Oct. 1968, 99-26-0-7-1-1-1 to 2-1-1; Fairly to Bill Rist, Burke, Rex P. Armistead, and M. D. Pierce, 28 May 1969, 1-95-0-37-1-1-1 to 2-1-1; Fairly to Armistead, Burke, and Julian Ervin, 11 June 1969, 2-158-4-20-1-1-1 to 8-1-1, all in MSSC Records.

17. Minutes, State Sovereignty Commission, 19 Nov. 1971, 99-130-0-6-1-1-1 to 10-1-1, p. 1-1-1, MSSC Records. See also Edgar C. Fortenberry, "Weekly Activity Report, 16–21 May 1971," 2-30-0-78-1-1-1 to 3-1-1, p. 3-1-1, MSSC Records.

18. W. Webb Burke, untitled document, 14 July 1972, 7-0-12-284-1-1-1, MSSC Records.

19. "Agency Purchase Order," 23 Apr. 1970, 97-13-0-15-1-1-1; 1 June 1970, 97-13-0-4-1-1-1; 13 Mar. 1970(?), 97-13-0-244-1-1-1; Security Consultants, Inc., investigative report, n.d., 99-135-0-5-1-1-1 to 15-1-1, all in MSSC Records.

20. Herman Glazier to Erle Johnston Jr., 2 June 1965, folder 6, box 137, PBJ Papers.

21. Erle Johnston Jr. to file, memo, 24 June 1965, 9-31-4-3-1-1-1, MSSC Records. The same memo can also be located in folder 6, box 137, PBJ Papers.

22. "Requisition for Issuance of Warrant," 4 Sept. 1968; Day Detectives, Inc., untitled document, 31 Aug. 1968; Ralph Day to Elizabeth Arnold, memo, n.d., all in 97-88-0-257-1-1-1 to 3-1-1, MSSC Records.

23. Untitled report, 15 May 1973, 9-31-10-124-1-1-1, MSSC Records; "Day Detective Reports to State Sovereignty Commission, 1970s," folder 1, box 3, Faulkner Collection. The Charles H. Griffin Collection at Mississippi State University contains three folders concerning the Sovereignty Commission, which include approximately sixty investigative reports prepared by the Commission's informants for the period between March 1968 and August 1968. See the folders entitled "Mississippi State Sovereignty Committee [*sic*]" in box 54.

24. Edgar C. Fortenberry to director, Sovereignty Commission, memo, 14 July 1969, 2-31-0-26-1-1-1 to 3-1-1, pp. 2-1-1 to 3-1-1; Fortenberry to director, memo, 11 Aug. 1969, 13-25-1-38-1-1-1 to 3-1-1, p. 2-1-1; Fortenberry, "Weekly Activity Report, 16–21 May 1971," 2-30-0-78-1-1-1 to 3-1-1, p. 2-1-1, all in MSSC Records; *MOSR*, 1968–1972, 372.

25. W. Webb Burke to J. W. Jones, 6 Nov. 1968, 9-16-0-118-1-1-1, MSSC Records.

26. J. W. Jones to Erle Johnston Jr., 4 Mar. 1965, 9-16-0-113-1-1-1, MSSC Records.

27. See, for example, W. Webb Burke to Luce Press Clippings, Inc., 15 Oct. 1968, 7-0-10-171-1-1-1, MSSC Records.

28. Audit, State Sovereignty Commission, 97-1-0-15-1-1-1 to 7-1-1, p. 6-1-1; 97-1-0-16-1-1-1 to 5-1-1, p. 5-1-1; 97-1-0-17-1-1-1 to 6-1-1, p. 5-1-1; 97-1-0-18-1-1-1 to 8-1-1, p. 6-1-1, all in MSSC Records.

29. Joanne Grant, ed., *Black Protest: History, Documents, and Analyses, 1619 to the Present*, 2d ed. (New York: Ballantine, 1974), 415–25; James M. Washington, ed., *A Testament of Hope: The Essential Writings and Speeches of Martin Luther King, Jr.* (New York: Harper Collins, 1986), 231–44.

30. Alexander Bloom and Wini Breines, ed., *"Takin' It to the Streets": A Sixties Reader* (New York: Oxford University Press, 1995), 342.

31. Erle Johnston Jr. to file, memo, 6 Mar. 1967, folder 2, box 140, PBJ Papers.

32. "Republic of New Africa (RNA)," 99-131-0-30-1-1-1 to 5-1-1, p. 1-1-1, MSSC Records.

33. Ibid.; "Republic of New Africa," 13-25-2-43-1-1-1, both in MSSC Records.

34. Peter B. Mastin to chief special investigator, memo, 9 July 1971, 13-25-2-50-1-1-1 to 18-1-1, pp. 1-1-1, 18-1-1; "Republic of New Africa (RNA)," 99-131-0-30-1-1-1 to 5-1-1, p. 3-1-1, both in MSSC Records.

35. Edgar C. Fortenberry to director, Sovereignty Commission, memo, 11 Aug. 1969, 13-25-1-38-1-1-1 to 3-1-1, p. 2-1-1; director to Herman Glazier, memo, 5 Aug. 1970, 13-25-2-3-1-1-1 to 4-1-1, p. 2-1-1; Peter B. Mastin to chief special investigator, memo, 9 July 1971, 13-25-2-50-1-1-1 to 18-1-1; "Republic of New Africa," 13-25-2-43-1-1-1, all in MSSC Records.

36. "Republic of New Africa (RNA)," 99-131-0-30-1-1-1 to 5-1-1, p. 5-1-1; "Civil Rights Disorders in Mississippi within the Past Decade," 3-17A-3-6-1-1-1 to 3-1-1, p. 3-1-1, both in MSSC Records.

37. *Gadfly*, 15 Jan. 1968, 99-48-0-221-1-1-1 to 2-1-1; Erle Johnston Jr. to file, memo, 9 Feb. 1968, 10-105-0-44-1-1-1; Johnston to file, memo, 12 Feb. 1968, 99-48-0-186-1-1-1, all in MSSC Records.

38. Terry H. Anderson, *The Movement and the Sixties* (New York: Oxford University Press, 1995), 349–51; James W. Loewen and Charles Sallis, eds., *Mississippi: Conflict and Change*, rev. ed. (New York: Pantheon, 1980), 319–20.

39. Garner J. Cline to Charles Griffin, staff memo, 3 Mar. 1969, 9-20-0-62-1-1-1; Griffin to John Bell Williams, 4 Mar. 1969, 9-20-0-61-1-1-1, both in MSSC Records.

40. W. Webb Burke to James O. Eastland, 28 Mar. 1969, 99-63-0-5-1-1-1; Burke to Betty Jane Long, 8 Apr. 1969, 7-0-11-78-1-1-1; Subcommittee on Immigration and Naturalization to Eastland, 14 Apr. 1969, 9-20-0-65-1-1-1, all in MSSC Records. See also James M. Mohead, "Weekly Report, May 19, 1969, to May 24, 1969," 1-109-0-14-1-1-1 to 4-1-1, pp. 1-1-1 to 3-1-1;

Mohead, "Weekly Report, June 9, 1969, to June 13, 1969," 2-38-2-14-1-1-1 to 5-1-1, p. 1-1-1, both in MSSC Records.

41. O. P. Lows to dear parents, 31 Jan. 1970, 9-20-0-75-1-1-1; "An Open Letter from Concerned Students at MVSC to President White," 9-20-0-74-1-1-1, both in MSSC Records.

42. Anonymous threatening letter to J. H. White, 9-20-0-80-1-1-1, MSSC Records; W. Webb Burke to file, memo, 13 Feb. 1970, folder 18, box 2, Faulkner Collection.

43. "History of Mississippi Valley State University," Mississippi Valley State University, Itta Bena, consulted 19 Dec. 1998 <http://www.mvsu.edu/history.html>.

44. *Reflector*, 6 Dec. 1968, 99-64-0-21-1-1-1, MSSC Records.

45. W. Webb Burke to file, memo, 12 Dec. 1968, 99-64-0-20-1-1-1 to 2-1-1, MSSC Records.

46. "Minutes of the First Interstate Sovereignty Commission Meeting," 99-83-0-3-1-1-1 to 3-1-1; untitled attendee list, 99-83-0-4-1-1-1 to 2-1-1; Erle Johnston Jr. to Eli Howell, 10 June 1968, 7-0-10-125-1-1-1; W. Webb Burke to Betty Jane Long, 7 Jan. 1969, 7-0-11-21-1-1-1, all in MSSC Records.

47. "Interstate Sovereignty Association," 99-83-0-2-1-1-1 to 3-1-1, MSSC Records.

48. W. Webb Burke to Betty Jane Long, 7 Jan. 1969, 7-0-11-21-1-1-1, MSSC Records.

49. "Interstate Sovereignty Group," 99-83-0-1-1-1-1; untitled minutes, 99-83-0-5-1-1-1 to 2-1-1, both in MSSC Records.

50. Untitled minutes, 99-83-0-5-1-1-1 to 2-1-1; untitled agenda proposal, 99-83-0-6-1-1-1 to 7-1-1; Eli H. Howell to Webb Burke, 27 Nov. 1968, 99-83-0-9-1-1-1 to 2-1-1; Howell to Burke, 9 Dec. 1968, 99-83-0-8-1-1-1 to 2-1-1, all in MSSC Records.

51. *Alexander v. Holmes County Board of Education*, 396 U.S. 19 (1969); Earl Black and Merle Black, *Politics and Society in the South* (Cambridge: Harvard University Press, 1987), 154.

52. *CA*, 4 Jan. 1970.

53. Charles C. Bolton, "The Last Stand of Massive Resistance: Mississippi Public School Integration, 1970," *Journal of Mississippi History* 61 (winter 1999): 329–50.

54. *LSM*, 1970, regular sess., 198–99; W. Webb Burke to John Bell Williams, memo, 5 Jan. 1970, 99-208-0-8-1-1-1 to 2-1-1, p. 2-1-1, MSSC Records.

55. *LSM*, 1971, regular sess., 47–48.

56. Minutes, State Sovereignty Commission, 16 July 1971, 99-130-0-15-1-1-1 to 8-1-1, pp. 2-1-1 to 3-1-1, MSSC Records; *CA*, 3 June 1971; *CL*, 4 June 1971; *Hattiesburg (Miss.) American*, 4 June 1971.

57. Edgar C. Fortenberry to W. Webb Burke, memo, 9 June 1971, 99-20-0-12-1-1-1, MSSC Records.

58. Rex Armistead to Giles Crisler and J. D. Gardner, memo, 4 June 1971, 99-20-0-14-1-1-1; Armistead to Crisler and Gardner, memo, 8 June 1971, 99-20-0-13-1-1-1 to 2-1-1; "Requisition for Issuance of Warrant," 28 Sept. 1971, 97-91-0-192-1-1-1 to 7-1-1, all in MSSC Records.

59. Marshall G. Bennett to W. Webb Burke, 12 July 1971, 6-77-0-56-1-1-1; minutes, State Sovereignty Commission, 16 July 1971, 99-130-0-15-1-1-1 to 8-1-1, pp. 5-1-1 to 6-1-1, both in MSSC Records.

60. See, for instance, W. Webb Burke to Betty Long, 11 Nov. 1971, 7-0-12-267-1-1-1, MSSC Records.

61. Minutes, State Sovereignty Commission, 19 Nov. 1971, 99-130-0-6-1-1-1 to 10-1-1, p. 1-1-1, MSSC Records.

62. *MOSR*, 1972–1976, 82, 448, 454–55.

63. Ibid., 449.

64. *DN*, 4 Aug. 1971.

65. *CL*, 26 Sept. 1971; *CA*, 18 Nov. 1971.

66. *DN*, 18 Jan. 1972.

67. *JH*, 1972, regular sess., 84.

68. *CL*, 24 Feb. 1993; Stephen D. Shaffer, "Party and Electoral Politics in Mississippi," in *Mississippi Government and Politics: Modernizers versus Traditionalists*, ed. Dale Krane and Stephen D. Shaffer (Lincoln: University of Nebraska Press, 1992), 84.

69. "State Sovereignty Commission," 97-53-0-1-1-1-1, MSSC Records; *LSM*, 1972, regular sess., 151–52; Jack Bass and Walter DeVries, *The Transformation of Southern Politics: Social Change and Political Consequence since 1945* (New York: Basic, 1976), 187; *DN*, 31 Aug. 1972.

70. *DN*, 31 Aug. 1972.

71. Minutes, State Sovereignty Commission, 17 Nov. 1972, 99-216-0-16-1-1-1 to 6-1-1, pp. 3-1-1 to 4-1-1, MSSC Records.

72. John R. Junkin to W. Webb Burke, 20 Oct. 1972, 99-216-0-17-1-1-1, MSSC Records.

73. W. Webb Burke to Perrin H. Purvis, 1 Nov. 1972, 7-0-12-287-1-1-1, MSSC Records.

74. William L. Waller to Heber Ladner, 22 Dec. 1972, 99-216-0-14-1-1-1, MSSC Records.

75. W. Webb Burke to Perrin H. Purvis, 1 Nov. 1972, 7-0-12-287-1-1-1; William F. Winter to Heber Ladner, 23 Jan. 1973, 99-216-0-12-1-1-1; Winter to Ladner, 9 Feb. 1973, 99-216-0-13-1-1-1, all in MSSC Records.

76. W. Webb Burke to William L. Waller, 1 Nov. 1972, 7-0-12-293-1-1-1; minutes, State Sovereignty Commission, 17 Nov. 1972, 99-216-0-16-1-1-1 to

6-1-1, p. 1-1-1; Burke to John R. Junkin, 1 Dec. 1972, 7-0-12-299-1-1-1, all in MSSC Records.

77. Minutes, State Sovereignty Commission, 17 Nov. 1972, 99-216-0-16-1-1-1 to 6-1-1; 11 Dec. 1972, 99-216-0-15-1-1-1 to 3-1-1; 28 Mar. 1973, 99-216-0-9-1-1-1 to 3-1-1; 27 Apr. 1973, 99-216-0-8-1-1-1 to 7-1-1; 17 May 1973, 99-216-0-7-1-1-1 to 3-1-1; 7 June 1973, 99-216-0-5-1-1-1 to 6-1-1; 22 June 1973, 99-216-0-4-1-1-1 to 3-1-1, all in MSSC Records. See also W. Webb Burke to William L. Waller, 16 Jan. 1973, 7-0-12-307-1-1-1; Burke to Waller, 14 Feb. 1973, 7-0-12-318-1-1-1, both in MSSC Records.

78. W. Webb Burke to William L. Waller, 1 Dec. 1972, 7-0-12-296-1-1-1, MSSC Records.

79. Minutes, State Sovereignty Commission, 11 Dec. 1972, 99-216-0-15-1-1-1 to 3-1-1, pp. 2-1-1 to 3-1-1, MSSC Records.

80. "State Sovereignty Commission," 97-53-0-1-1-1-1, MSSC Records; *JH*, 1973, regular sess., 11, 597; *MOSR*, 1972–1976, 75.

81. *JH*, 1973, regular sess., 635; *JS*, 1973, regular sess., 948.

82. *JH*, 1973, regular sess., 1278.

83. Minutes, State Sovereignty Commission, 7 June 1973, 99-216-0-5-1-1-1 to 6-1-1, pp. 1-1-1, 5-1-1, MSSC Records.

84. *DN*, 8 June 1973.

85. Minutes, State Sovereignty Commission, 17 Nov. 1972, 99-216-0-16-1-1-1 to 6-1-1, p. 3-1-1, MSSC Records; *CA*, 8 June 1973.

86. *CA*, 17 June 1973.

87. Minutes, State Sovereignty Commission, 22 June 1973, 99-216-0-4-1-1-1 to 3-1-1, MSSC Records.

88. *CA*, 23 June 1973.

89. *CL*, 28 July 1989.

Conclusion. To Grapple with the Past:
From "Mississippi Burning" to "Mississippi Learning"

1. *CL*, 17 Feb. 1977; *DDT*, 20 Feb. 1977.

2. *JH*, 1977, regular sess., 19, 158; *DN*, 28 Jan. 1977.

3. *MOSR*, 1976–1980, 58–59, 61; *DN*, 28 Jan. 1977; *CL*, 28 Jan. 1977.

4. *JH*, 1977, regular sess., 158.

5. *Lexington (Miss.) Advertiser*, 3 Feb. 1977.

6. *DN*, 17 Feb. 1977; *CL*, 17 Feb. 1977; *Tupelo (Miss.) Daily Journal*, 17 Feb. 1977.

7. *JS*, 1977, regular sess., 661–62; *JH*, 1977, regular sess., 627; *DDT*, 20 Feb. 1977; *CL*, 3 Mar. 1977; *DN*, 3 Mar. 1977.

8. *LSM*, 1977, regular sess., 447–48.

9. *DDT*, 20 Feb. 1977.

10. *JH*, 1978, regular sess., 138; Horace H. Harned Jr., oral history, interviewed by Tom Healy, 3 Oct. 1978, vol. 355, transcript, 55–56; Harned, oral history, interviewed by Yasuhiro Katagiri, 3 Nov. 1993, vol. 355, pt. 2, transcript, 25, both at MOHP.

11. Mississippi State Office of the American Civil Liberties Union, "ACLU/M Files Suit against State Spying," *ACLU/Memos* 3 (Mar./Apr. 1977): 1–2; Ken Lawrence, "The Mississippi Police State: A Report," both in folder "Sovereignty Commission, 1960–1977," box 13, Minor Papers; *CL*, 19 Feb. 1977.

12. Jack Bass, *Unlikely Heroes* (New York: Simon and Schuster, 1981), 166; *American Civil Liberties Union of Mississippi v. Cliff Finch*, 638 F2d 1336 (5th Cir. 1981). See also Calvin Trillin, "State Secrets," *New Yorker*, 29 May 1995, 58.

13. Untitled document, State Sovereignty Commission, 1-67-4-26-1-1-1 to 3-1-1, p. 3-1-1, MSSC Records; Adam Nossiter, *Of Long Memory: Mississippi and the Murder of Medgar Evers* (Reading, Mass: Addison-Wesley, 1994), 233.

14. *American Civil Liberties Union of Mississippi v. Kirk Fordice*, 969 F. Supp. 403 (S.D. Miss. 1994).

15. "Register of the John R. Salter, Jr., Papers, 1957–1982," John R. Salter Jr. Papers, Social Action Collection, Archives Division, State Historical Society of Wisconsin, Madison.

16. Peter J. Boyer, "The Yuppies of Mississippi: How They Took Over the Statehouse," *NYTM*, 28 Feb. 1988, 24; *The Neshoba County Fair*, prod. Tom Rieland and Marie Antoon, Communication and Resource Center, University of Mississippi, University, 1983, videocassette.

17. Erle Johnston Jr., *I Rolled with Ross: A Political Portrait* (Baton Rouge, La.: Moran, 1980), 131.

18. *CL/DN*, 26 Sept. 1982.

19. Boyer, "The Yuppies of Mississippi," 24.

20. *TP*, 22 June 1989; *CL*, 22 June 1989; Jesse Kornbluth, "The '64 Civil Rights Murders: The Struggle Continues," *NYTM*, 23 July 1989, 18, 54.

21. Dick Molpus, letter to the author, 9 May 1996.

22. Dick Molpus, "Remarks by Secretary of State Dick Molpus," 21 June 1989, 1–3, in the author's possession.

23. Ibid., 3.

24. *USA Today*, 22 June 1989.

25. *CL*, 24 Jan. 1994.

26. Gordon Lee Baum, letter to the author, 2 July 1990.

27. *American Civil Liberties Union of Mississippi v. Ray Mabus*, 719 F. Supp. 1345 (S.D. Miss. 1989).

28. Trillin, "State Secrets," 59.

29. Mississippi Religious Leadership Conference, untitled statement, in the author's possession.

30. Claude E. Fike to Paul B. Johnson Jr., 21 Jan. 1982; William D. McCain to

Fike, 31 Mar. 1982; Terry S. Latour to Michael C. Smith, memo, 5 May 1989; Latour to Aubrey K. Lucas, memo, 31 July 1989, all in Case File of the Paul B. Johnson Family Papers, McCain Library.

31. *Hattiesburg (Miss.) American*, 14 Oct. 1985.

32. Terry S. Latour to Michael C. Smith, memo, 15 Mar. 1989; Latour to Smith, memo, 11 Apr. 1989, both in Case File of the Paul B. Johnson Family Papers, McCain Library.

33. Leesha Cooper to the University of Southern Mississippi, 17 Apr. 1989; Aubrey K. Lucas to Mike Moore, 24 Apr. 1989, both in Case File of the Paul B. Johnson Family Papers, McCain Library.

34. Order, *Aubrey K. Lucas v. Arkansas Gazette Company*, Chancery Court, First Judicial District, Hinds County, Mississippi, civil action no. 138515 R-0, filed on 28 July 1989.

35. *American Civil Liberties Union of Mississippi v. State of Mississippi v. Edwin King and John Salter*, 911 F2d 1066 (5th Cir. 1990).

36. The author's memo taken at the court hearing.

37. *American Civil Liberties Union of Mississippi v. Kirk Fordice*.

38. Hank T. Holmes [director, Archives and Library Division, MDAH], letter to the author, 28 Feb. 1996.

39. *CL*, 11 Sept. 1994; *Cleveland (Tenn.) Daily Banner*, 18 Sept. 1994.

40. *NYT*, 28 Sept. 1995; *Biloxi (Miss.) Sun-Herald*, 29 Sept. 1995.

41. Erle Johnston Jr., unrecorded telephone interview by the author, 14 Aug. 1993, Forest, Mississippi (the author's memo).

42. Adib A. Shakir to Erle Johnston, 5 Dec. 1991; Johnston to Shakir, 15 Dec. 1991; Constance Slaughter-Harvey to Reuben Anderson, 14 Apr. 1992; Johnston to Slaughter-Harvey, n.d.; Slaughter-Harvey to Johnston, 12 Aug. 1992, all in folder 18, box 9, Johnston Papers.

43. Pamela Wilde, "A Team Again," folder 1; Erle Johnston Jr. to Lee Sampson, facsimile letter, n.d., folder 8; Johnston, untitled article, folder 8, all in box 1, Johnston Papers.

44. *DN*, 6 Dec. 1955.

45. Erle Johnston Jr., untitled article, folder 8, box 1, Johnston Papers; *DN*, 8 Dec. 1955.

46. "Welcome, COMPTON COLLEGE to the NEW Mississippi!" [banner design], folder 9, box 1, Johnston Papers.

47. *A Weekend in Mississippi: 40th Anniversary Reunion, 1955 Junior Rose Bowl Teams*, prod. Letter B Productions, Hattiesburg, Mississippi, Jones County Junior College, Ellisville, Mississippi, 1995, videocassette, folder 2, box 23, Johnston Papers.

48. *Biloxi (Miss.) Sun-Herald*, 22 Oct. 1995.

49. "Memorial Service for Erle Ennis Johnston, Jr., September 28, 1995"; Sid

Salter, "Eulogy for Erle Ennis Johnston, Jr., September 28, 1995," both in folder 3, box 10, Johnston Papers.

50. Order, *American Civil Liberties Union of Mississippi v. Edwin King v. Kirk Fordice*, U.S. Court of Appeals for the Fifth Circuit, New Orleans, no. 94-60425, filed on 11 June 1996; *Daily Corinthian (Miss.)*, 12 Mar. 1997. The *New York Times*, for example, ran the public notice by the Mississippi Department of Archives and History in its 20 January and 27 January 1997 issues.

51. Order, *American Civil Liberties Union of Mississippi v. Kirk Fordice*, Jackson Division, Southern District of Mississippi, U.S. District Court, civil action no. J77-0047(B), filed in Jan. 1998.

52. "Records of the Mississippi State Sovereignty Commission: Search and Access," MDAH; Sarah Rowe-Sims [special projects officer, MDAH], e-mail to the author, 8 Sept. 1999. Subsequently, some six thousand pages of additional documents were released by the state archives on 31 July 2000. This then was followed by the archives' release of some eighteen hundred pages which had remained sealed until January 18, 2001. As a result of these developments, practically all of the existing records of the Sovereignty Commission have become open to the public.

53. "Statement of Appropriated Funds and Unexpended Balances, May 1956–June 30, 1972," 97-58-0-22-1-1-1; "Financial Statement, July 1, 1972, through June 30, 1973," 97-58-0-2-1-1-1, both in MSSC Records.

54. Anne L. Webster, letter to the author, 14 Jan. 1998.

55. A. L. Hopkins, investigative report, 23 Mar. 1964, 2-46-0-77-1-1-1 to 2-1-1, MSSC Records; "Unsealing Mississippi's Past: The Sovereignty Commission, Racism, and State Terrorism," in *Building Bridges: Your Community and Labor Report* series, prod. Ken Nash and Mimi Rosenberg, Institute for Global Communications, San Francisco, consulted 1 Aug. 2000 <http://www.igc.org/wbai-labor/mississippi.html> Real Audio.

56. George B. Tindall, *The Ethnic Southerners* (Baton Rouge: Louisiana State University Press, 1976), 232; *CL*, 18 Apr. 2001.

57. *CL*, 8 Nov. 1999.

58. Molpus, "Remarks by Secretary of State," 3, in the author's possession.

BIBLIOGRAPHY

Archives

Alabama Department of Archives and History, Montgomery
    Alabama State Sovereignty Commission Records
John F. Kennedy Presidential Library, Boston
    Burke Marshall Papers
    John F. Kennedy Presidential Papers
Louisiana State Archives, Baton Rouge
    Louisiana State Joint Legislative Committee on Un-American Activities Records
Louisiana State University: Louisiana and Lower Mississippi Valley Collection, Hill Memorial Library, Baton Rouge
    Vertical Files
Mississippi Department of Archives and History: Archives and Library Division, Jackson
    Heber Ladner Papers
    James P. Coleman Papers
    Paul B. Johnson Jr. Papers
    Records of the Mississippi State Sovereignty Commission
    Subject Files
Mississippi State University: Special Collections, Mitchell Memorial Library, Mississippi State
    A. Eugene Cox Collection
    Charles H. Griffin Collection
    Citizens' Council Collection

Godwin Advertising Agency Collection

Kenneth Toler Papers

Vertical Files

Wilson F. "Bill" Minor Papers

Princeton University: Public Policy Papers, Department of Rare Books and Special Collections, Seeley G. Mudd Manuscript Library, Princeton, New Jersey

Fund for the Republic Archives

State Historical Society of Wisconsin: Social Action Collection, Archives Division, Madison

John R. Salter Jr. Papers

Tougaloo College: Special Collections, L. Zenobia Coleman Library, Tougaloo, Mississippi

Ed King Collection

Jane M. Schutt Papers

Minutes of Tougaloo College Board of Trustees Meetings

University of California at Santa Barbara: Department of Special Collections, Davidson Library, Santa Barbara

Center for the Study of Democratic Institutions Collection

University of Mississippi: Archives and Special Collections, John D. Williams Library, University

Verner S. Holmes Collection

University of Southern Mississippi: Archives and Manuscript Department, William D. McCain Library and Archives, Hattiesburg

Case File of the Paul B. Johnson Family Papers

Citizens' Council/Civil Rights Collection

Erle E. Johnston Jr. Papers

Leesha Faulkner Civil Rights Collection

Paul B. Johnson Family Papers

Vertical Files

Oral Histories

Except where noted, all interviews are from the Mississippi Oral History Program, Center for Oral History and Cultural Heritage, University of Southern Mississippi, Hattiesburg.

Barber, Mary Jane. "An Oral History with Mary Jane Barber." Recorded interview by Yasuhiro Katagiri, 30 Aug. 1998. Vol. 750, transcript.

Brady, Thomas P. "Interview with the Honorable Thomas P. Brady, Associate Justice, Mississippi Supreme Court." Recorded interview by Orley B. Caudill, 4 Mar. 1972. Vol. 2, pt. 1, transcript.

———. "Interview with the Honorable Thomas P. Brady, Associate Justice, Mississippi Supreme Court." Recorded interview by Orley B. Caudill, 17 May 1972. Vol. 2, pt. 2, transcript.

Carr, Michael L., Jr. "An Oral History with Mr. Michael L. Carr, Jr." Recorded interview by Yasuhiro Katagiri, 28 Oct. 1993. Vol. 469, transcript.

Cohen, James. "An Oral History with Mr. James Cohen." Recorded interview by Mike Garvey, 2 Feb. 1976. Vol. 705, transcript.

Coleman, James P. "An Oral History with the Honorable J. P. Coleman, Former Governor of Mississippi and Chief Judge (Ret.), the U.S. Court of Appeals for the Fifth Circuit." Recorded interview by Orley B. Caudill, 6 Feb. 1982. Vol. 203, pt. 2, transcript.

Coleman, James P., and Verner S. Holmes. Recorded interview by David G. Sansing, 16 June 1979. Transcript. Verner S. Holmes Collection, Archives and Special Collections, John D. Williams Library, University of Mississippi, University.

DeCell, Herman B. "An Oral History with the Honorable Herman B. DeCell." Recorded interview by Orley B. Caudill, 9 June 1977. Vol. 207, transcript.

Dukes, William F. "Interview with Mr. William F. Dukes, Native Mississippian, Lawyer and Former FBI Agent." Recorded interview by Orley B. Caudill, 23 Jan. 1973. Vol. 40, transcript.

Eastland, James O. Recorded interview by Joe B. Frantz, 19 Feb. 1971. AC 76-9, transcript. Lyndon B. Johnson Presidential Library, Austin, Texas.

Fairley, J. C., Mamie Phillips, and Charles Phillips. "An Oral History with J. C. Fairley, Mamie Phillips, and Charles Phillips." Recorded interview by Charles C. Bolton, 24 June 1998. Vol. 711, transcript.

Glazier, Herman. "An Oral History with Mr. Herman Glazier." Recorded interview by Reid Derr, 10 Sept. 1993. Vol. 485, transcript.

Harned, Horace H., Jr. "An Oral History with [the] Honorable Horace H. Harned, Jr." Recorded interview by Tom Healy, 3 Oct. 1978. Vol. 355, transcript.

————. "An Oral History with Mr. Horace H. Harned, Jr." Recorded interview by Yasuhiro Katagiri, 3 Nov. 1993. Vol. 355, pt. 2, transcript.

Johnson, Paul B., Jr. Recorded interview by T. H. Baker, 8 Sept. 1970. AC 80- 63, transcript. Lyndon B. Johnson Presidential Library, Austin, Texas.

Johnston, Erle, Jr. "Interview with Erle Johnston." Recorded interview by Betsy Nash, 26 Mar. 1991. Transcript. John C. Stennis Oral History Project, Mississippi State University, Mississippi State.

————. "An Oral History with Mr. Erle Johnston." Recorded interview by Orley B. Caudill, 16 July 1980 and 30 July 1980. Vol. 276, transcript.

————. "An Oral History with Mr. Erle Johnston." Recorded interview by Yasuhiro Katagiri, 13 Aug. 1993. Vol. 276, pt. 2, transcript.

King, Edwin. Recorded interview by Yasuhiro Katagiri, 17 Aug. 1993. Incomplete transcript.

Luckett, Semmes. Recorded interview by Thomas Healy, 14 Sept. 1977. Vol. 370, transcript.

Marshall, Burke. Recorded interview by T. H. Baker, 28 Oct. 1968. AC 74-215, transcript. Lyndon B. Johnson Presidential Library, Austin, Texas.

Meredith, James H. "An Oral History by James H. Meredith." Recorded interview by Yasuhiro Katagiri, 11 Jan. 1994. B-M559mo, transcript. Archives and Library Division, Mississippi Department of Archives and History, Jackson.

Salter, John R., Jr., with Edwin King. "An Interview with John R. Salter, Jr., with Rev. Edwin King." Recorded interview by John Jones, 6 Jan. 1981. OH 81-06, transcript. Archives and Library Division, Mississippi Department of Archives and History, Jackson.

Simmons, William J. "An Oral History with Mr. William J. Simmons." Recorded interview by Orley B. Caudill, 26 June 1979. Vol. 372, transcript.

Smith, Michael. "An Oral History Interview with Dr. Michael Smith." Recorded interview by Reid Derr, 16 June 1993. Vol. 448, transcript.

Wiesenburg, Karl. "An Interview with Karl Wiesenberg [*sic*]." Recorded interview by H. T. Holmes, 9 Aug. 1976. OH 77-04, transcript. Archives and Library Division, Mississippi Department of Archives and History, Jackson.

Winter, William F. "An Oral History with [the] Honorable William Winter." Recorded interview by Orley B. Caudill, 9 Aug. 1978. Vol. 417, transcript.

———. "An Oral History with [the] Honorable William Winter." Recorded interview by Yasuhiro Katagiri, 13 Aug. 1998. Vol. 417, pt. 2, transcript.

Wroten, Joseph E. "An Oral History with Mr. Joseph E. Wroten." Recorded interview by Yasuhiro Katagiri, 4 Nov. 1993. Vol. 476, transcript.

Yarbrough, George M. "An Oral History with [the] Honorable George M. Yarbrough." Recorded interview by Orley B. Caudill, 21 Feb. 1980. Vol. 367, transcript.

Audiovisual Materials

The American South Comes of Age. Produced by Alvin H. Goldstein. South Carolina Educational Television Network and Division of Continuing Education of the University of South Carolina, Columbia, 1985. 14 videocassettes.

The Civil Rights Movement and the Law: A National Symposium. University of Mississippi, University, 1989. 6 videocassettes.

Eyes on the Prize: America's Civil Rights Years. Blackside, Boston, 1986. 6 videocassettes.

"Integration of the University of Mississippi." Presidential Recordings, John F. Kennedy Presidential Library, Boston. 4 audiocassettes.

Johnston, Erle, Jr. Interview by Cal Adams. *Eyewitness News 16: Dateline.* WAPT, Jackson, Mississippi, n.d. Videocassette. Special Collections, L. Zenobia Coleman Library, Tougaloo College, Tougaloo, Mississippi.

———. Interview by Marva York and Gwen Belton. *Saddler Report.* WJTV, Jackson,

Mississippi, 23 Dec. 1990. Videocassette. Special Collections, L. Zenobia Coleman Library, Tougaloo College, Tougaloo, Mississippi.

The Message from Mississippi. Produced by Public Relations Department, Mississippi State Sovereignty Commission, Jackson, 1960. Videocassette. In the author's possession.

The Neshoba County Fair. Produced by Tom Rieland and Marie Antoon. Communication and Resource Center, University of Mississippi, University, 1983. Videocassette.

Oxford, U.S.A. Reel no. 53. Citizens' Council Forum Films, Audio-Visual Records, Mississippi Department of Archives and History, Jackson.

Segregation and the South. Produced by George M. Martin Jr. Newsfilm Project, Fund for the Republic, Los Angeles, 1957. Videocassette. Center for the Study of Democratic Institutions Collection, Department of Special Collections, Davidson Library, University of California at Santa Barbara, Santa Barbara.

Separate but Equal. Produced by Stan Margulies. Directed by George Stevens Jr. New Liberty Production, 1991. Videocassette.

A Weekend in Mississippi: 40th Anniversary Reunion, 1955 Junior Rose Bowl Teams. Produced by Letter B Productions, Hattiesburg, Mississippi. Jones County Junior College, Ellisville, Mississippi, 1995. Videocassette. Folder 2, Box 23, Erle E. Johnston Jr. Papers, Archives and Manuscript Department, William D. McCain Library and Archives, University of Southern Mississippi, Hattiesburg.

"Who Is Agent X?" *Dateline.* NBC, New York, 18 Jan. 1995. Videocassette. Folder 2, Box 24, Erle E. Johnston Jr. Papers, Archives and Manuscript Department, William D. McCain Library and Archives, University of Southern Mississippi, Hattiesburg.

Internet Sources

Chaney, Ben. "Schwerner, Chaney, and Goodman: The Struggle for Justice." *Human Rights* 27 (spring 2000). American Bar Association, Chicago. Consulted 1 Aug. 2000. <http://www.abanet.org/irr/hr/spring00humanrights/chaney.html>.

"Freedom Is a Constant Struggle." *Democracy NOW!* Pacifica Radio, Arlington, Virginia, 29 Feb. 2000. Consulted 2 Aug. 2000. <http://www.webactive. com/web active/pacifica/demnow/dn20000229.html> Real Audio.

"History of Mississippi Valley State University." Mississippi Valley State University, Itta Bena. Consulted 19 Dec. 1998. <http://www.mvsu.edu/history.html>.

LBJ White House Tapes. C-SPAN, Washington, D.C. Consulted 28 Nov. 2000. <http://www.c-span.org/lbj> Real Audio.

Mehler, Barry, and Keith Hurt. "Race Science and the Pioneer Fund." Institute for the Study of Academic Racism, Lansing, Michigan, 1998. Consulted 30 July 2000. <http://www.ferris.edu/isar/Institut/pioneer/search.htm>.

"MIBURN (Mississippi Burning)." *Freedom of Information Act Electronic Reading Room.*

Federal Bureau of Investigation, Washington, D.C. Consulted 3 Dec. 1999. <http://www.foia.fbi.gov/miburn.htm>.

Oral Histories in the Civil Rights in Mississippi Digital Archive. William D. McCain Library and Archives, University of Southern Mississippi, Hattiesburg. Consulted 1 Dec. 2000. <http://www.lib.usm.edu/~spcol/crda/oh/index.html>.

"The Pioneer Fund, Inc." Pioneer Fund, New York. Consulted 3 Aug. 2000. <http://www.pioneerfund.org>.

"Unsealing Mississippi's Past: The Sovereignty Commission, Racism, and State Terrorism." *Building Bridges: Your Community and Labor Report.* Produced by Ken Nash and Mimi Rosenberg. Institute for Global Communications, San Francisco. Consulted 1 Aug. 2000. <http://www.igc.org/wbai-labor/mississippi.html> Real Audio.

Books and Articles

Anderson, Terry H. *The Movement and the Sixties.* New York: Oxford University Press, 1995.

Ashmore, Harry S. *Hearts and Minds: A Personal Chronicle of Race in America.* Cabin John, Md.: Seven Locks, 1988.

"At Ole Miss: Echoes of a Civil War's Last Battle." *Time,* 4 Oct. 1982, 8, 11.

Barrett, Russell H. *Integration at Ole Miss.* Chicago: Quadrangle, 1965.

Bartley, Numan V. *The Rise of Massive Resistance: Race and Politics in the South during the 1950's.* Baton Rouge: Louisiana State University Press, 1969.

Bass, Jack. *Unlikely Heroes.* New York: Simon and Schuster, 1981.

Bass, Jack, and Walter DeVries. *The Transformation of Southern Politics: Social Change and Political Consequence since 1945.* New York: Basic, 1976.

Beschloss, Michael R., ed. *Taking Charge: The Johnson White House Tapes, 1963–1964.* New York: Simon and Schuster, 1997.

Black, Earl. *Southern Governors and Civil Rights: Racial Segregation as a Campaign Issue in the Second Reconstruction.* Cambridge: Harvard University Press, 1976.

Black, Earl, and Merle Black. *Politics and Society in the South.* Cambridge: Harvard University Press, 1987.

Bloom, Alexander, and Wini Breines, eds. *"Takin' It to the Streets": A Sixties Reader.* New York: Oxford University Press, 1995.

Bolton, Charles C. "The Last Stand of Massive Resistance: Mississippi Public School Integration, 1970." *Journal of Mississippi History* 61 (winter 1999): 329–50.

———. "Mississippi's School Equalization Program, 1945–1954: 'A Last Gasp to Try to Maintain a Segregated Educational System.' " *Journal of Southern History* 66 (Nov. 2000): 781–814.

Boyer, Peter J. "The Yuppies of Mississippi: How They Took Over the Statehouse." *New York Times Magazine,* 28 Feb. 1988, 24–27, 40, 43, 76.

Brady, Tom P. *Black Monday.* Brookhaven, Miss.: n.p., 1954.

Branch, Taylor. *Parting the Waters: America in the King Years, 1954–63.* New York: Simon and Schuster, 1988.

Cagin, Seth, and Philip Dray. *We Are Not Afraid: The Story of Goodman, Schwerner, and Chaney and the Civil Rights Campaign for Mississippi.* New York: Macmillan, 1988.

Campbell, Clarice T., and Oscar A. Rogers, Jr. *Mississippi: The View from Tougaloo.* Jackson: University Press of Mississippi, 1979.

Capers, Charlotte, ed. "Mississippi Bicentennial Celebration: The Address of Judge James Plemon Coleman." *Journal of Mississippi History* 39 (Feb. 1977): 51–61.

Carter, Hodding. "Citadel of the Citizens['] Council." *New York Times Magazine,* 12 Nov. 1961, 23, 125–27.

———. *The South Strikes Back.* Garden City, N.Y.: Doubleday, 1959.

Cash, W. J. *The Mind of the South.* New York: Knopf, 1941. Reprint, New York: Vintage, 1991.

Clark, Wayne A. *An Analysis of the Relationship between Anti-Communism and Segregationist Thought in the Deep South, 1948–1964.* Ann Arbor, Mich.: University Microfilms, 1976.

Cobb, James C. *The Most Southern Place on Earth: The Mississippi Delta and the Roots of Regional Identity.* New York: Oxford University Press, 1992.

Cohodas, Nadine. *Strom Thurmond and the Politics of Southern Change.* New York: Simon and Schuster, 1993.

"Congress: Backdoor Battle." *Newsweek,* 30 Mar. 1964, 17.

The Constitution of the State of Mississippi. Jackson: Mississippi Secretary of State's Office, 1992.

Cunnigen, Donald. *Men and Women of Goodwill: Mississippi's White Liberals.* Ann Arbor, Mich.: University Microfilms, 1988.

Daniel, Bradford, and John Howard Griffin. "Why They Can't Wait: An Interview with a White Negro." *Progressive,* July 1964, 15–19.

Daniel, Pete. *Standing at the Crossroads: Southern Life in the Twentieth Century.* Baltimore: Johns Hopkins University Press, 1996.

Davis, F. James. *Who Is Black?: One Nation's Definition.* University Park: Pennsylvania State University Press, 1991.

DeLaughter, Bobby. *Never Too Late: A Prosecutor's Story of Justice in the Medgar Evers Case.* New York: Scribner, 2001.

Dennis, Delmar D. *To Stand Alone: Inside the KKK for the FBI.* Sevierville, Tenn.: Covenant House, 1991.

Derr, Reid S. *The Triumph of Progressivism: Governor Paul B. Johnson, Jr., and Mississippi in the 1960s.* Ann Arbor, Mich.: University Microfilms, 1994.

"The Dialogue." *Newsweek,* 14 Oct. 1963, 36.

Dittmer, John. *Local People: The Struggle for Civil Rights in Mississippi.* Urbana: University of Illinois Press, 1994.

———. "The Mississippi Summer Project in Retrospect." Paper presented at the sixtieth annual meeting of the Southern Historical Association, Louisville, Ky., 9 Nov. 1994.

Eagles, Charles W. "Toward New Histories of the Civil Rights Era." *Journal of Southern History* 66 (Nov. 2000): 815–48.

———, ed. *The Civil Rights Movement in America*. Jackson: University Press of Mississippi, 1986.

Erenrich, Susie, ed. *Freedom Is a Constant Struggle: An Anthology of the Mississippi Civil Rights Movement*. Montgomery, Ala.: Black Belt, 1999.

Escott, Paul D., and David R. Goldfield, eds. *Major Problems in the History of the American South*. Vol. 2. Lexington, Mass.: D. C. Heath, 1990.

Findlay, James F., Jr. *Church People in the Struggle: The National Council of Churches and the Black Freedom Movement, 1950–1970*. New York: Oxford University Press, 1993.

Fite, Gilbert C. *Richard B. Russell, Jr., Senator from Georgia*. Chapel Hill: University of North Carolina Press, 1991.

Franklin, John Hope, and Alfred A. Moss Jr. *From Slavery to Freedom: A History of African Americans*. 7th ed. New York: McGraw-Hill, 1994.

Free At Last: A History of the Civil Rights Movement and Those Who Died in the Struggle. Montgomery, Ala.: Southern Poverty Law Center, 1989.

Fried, Richard M. *Nightmare in Red: The McCarthy Ear in Perspective*. New York: Oxford University Press, 1990.

Goldinger, Carolyn, ed. *Presidential Elections since 1789*. 5th ed. Washington, D.C.: Congressional Quarterly, 1991.

Graham, Hugh D. *Civil Rights and the Presidency: Race and Gender in American Politics, 1960–1972*. New York: Oxford University Press, 1992.

Grant, Joanne, ed. *Black Protest: History, Documents, and Analyses, 1619 to the Present*. 2d ed. New York: Ballantine, 1974.

Greenblatt, Alan. "Crossing the Line in the Dust." *Congressional Quarterly*, 13 May 1995, 1295–97.

Guthman, Edwin O., and Jeffrey Shulman, eds. *Robert Kennedy in His Own Words: The Unpublished Recollections of the Kennedy Years*. New York: Bantam, 1988.

Hall, Kermit L., ed. *The Oxford Companion to the Supreme Court of the United States*. New York: Oxford University Press, 1992.

Hampton, Henry, and Steve Fayer. *Voices of Freedom: An Oral History of the Civil Rights Movement from the 1950s through the 1980s*. New York: Bantam, 1990.

Hollander, Ronald A. "One Mississippi Negro Who Didn't Go to College." *Reporter*, 8 Nov. 1962, 30–34.

Holt, Len. *The Summer That Didn't End: The Story of the Mississippi Civil Rights Project of 1964*. New York: William Morrow, 1965.

Huey, Gary. *Rebel with a Cause: P. D. East, Southern Liberalism, and the Civil Rights Movement, 1953–1971*. Wilmington, Del.: Scholarly Resources, 1985.

Jacoway, Elizabeth, and David R. Colburn, eds. *Southern Businessmen and Desegregation*. Baton Rouge: Louisiana State University Press, 1982.

Johnson, Donald B., comp. *National Party Platforms*. Vol. 1. Rev. ed. Urbana: University of Illinois Press, 1978.

Johnston, Erle, Jr. *I Rolled with Ross: A Political Portrait*. Baton Rouge, La.: Moran, 1980.

————. *Mississippi's Defiant Years, 1953–1973: An Interpretive Documentary with Personal Experiences*. Forest, Miss.: Lake Harbor, 1990.

————. *Politics: Mississippi Style*. Forest, Miss.: Lake Harbor, 1993.

Kelly, Alfred H., and Winfred A. Harbison. *The American Constitution: Its Origins and Development*. 5th ed. New York: Norton, 1976.

Key, V. O., Jr. *Southern Politics in State and Nation*. New York: Knopf, 1949.

Killian, Lewis M. *White Southerners*. New York: Random House, 1970.

Kluger, Richard. *Simple Justice: The History of* Brown v. Board of Education *and Black America's Struggle for Equality*. New York: Knopf, 1976.

Kornbluth, Jesse. "The '64 Civil Rights Murders: The Struggle Continues." *New York Times Magazine*, 23 July 1989, 16–18, 46, 48, 54, 60, 62–63.

Krane, Dale, and Stephen D. Shaffer, eds. *Mississippi Government and Politics: Modernizers versus Traditionalists*. Lincoln: University of Nebraska Press, 1992.

Lawson, Steven F., and Charles Payne. *Debating the Civil Rights Movement, 1945–1968*. Lanham, Md.: Rowman and Littlefield, 1998.

Lesseig, Corey T. "Roast Beef and Racial Integrity: Mississippi's 'Race and Reason Day,' October 26, 1961." *Journal of Mississippi History* 56 (Feb. 1994): 1–15.

Link, William A., and Marjorie S. Wheeler, eds. *The South in the History of the Nation: A Reader*. Vol. 2. Boston: Bedford/St. Martin's, 1999.

Loewen, James W., and Charles Sallis, eds. *Mississippi: Conflict and Change*. Rev. ed. New York: Pantheon, 1980.

Lord, Walter. *The Past That Would Not Die*. New York: Harper and Row, 1965.

Lovejoy, Gordon W. "In Brotherhood Week: A Look at the South." *New York Times Magazine*, 17 Feb. 1957, 13, 50, 52, 54, 56.

Lowery, Charles D., and John F. Marszalek, eds. *Encyclopedia of African-American Civil Rights: From Emancipation to the Present*. New York: Greenwood, 1992.

Maass, Peter. "The Secrets of Mississippi." *New Republic*, 21 Dec. 1998, 21–25.

Mars, Florence. *Witness in Philadelphia*. Baton Rouge: Louisiana State University Press, 1977.

Marsh, Charles. *God's Long Summer: Stories of Faith and Civil Rights*. Princeton, N.J.: Princeton University Press, 1997.

Massengill, Reed. *Portrait of a Racist: The Man Who Killed Medgar Evers?* New York: St. Martin's, 1994.

McAdam, Doug. *Freedom Summer*. New York: Oxford University Press, 1988.

McClenaghan, William A., rev. *Magruder's American Government*. 55th ed. Boston: Allyn and Bacon, 1972.

McDonald, Forrest. *States' Rights and the Union: Imperium in Imperio, 1776–1876*. Lawrence: University Press of Kansas, 2000.

McGuiness, Colleen, ed. *National Party Conventions, 1831–1988*. Washington, D.C.: Congressional Quarterly, 1991.

McLemore, Richard A., ed. *A History of Mississippi*. 2 vols. Jackson: University and College Press of Mississippi, 1973.

McMillen, Neil R. *The Citizens' Council: Organized Resistance to the Second Reconstruction, 1954–1964*. Urbana: University of Illinois Press, 1971.

———. *Dark Journey: Black Mississippians in the Age of Jim Crow*. Urbana: University of Illinois Press, 1989.

———, ed. *Remaking Dixie: The Impact of World War II on the American South*. Jackson: University Press of Mississippi, 1997.

Meredith, James H. *Three Years in Mississippi*. Bloomington: Indiana University Press, 1966.

Mills, Nicolaus. *Like a Holy Crusade: Mississippi 1964—The Turning of the Civil Rights Movement in America*. Chicago: Ivan R. Dee, 1992.

Minor, Bill. "A Poignant Summer Reunion." *Reckon* 1 (Premiere 1995): 57.

"Mississippi: 'God Bless Everyone.' " *Time*, 31 Jan. 1964, 22.

Nossiter, Adam. *Of Long Memory: Mississippi and the Murder of Medgar Evers*. Reading, Mass.: Addison-Wesley, 1994.

"On the Spot." *Time*, 22 Oct. 1956, 54.

O'Reilly, Kenneth. *"Racial Matters": The FBI's Secret File on Black America, 1960–1972*. New York: Free Press, 1989.

Oshinsky, David, and Richard Rubin. "Should the Mississippi Files Have Been Reopened?" *New York Times Magazine*, 30 Aug. 1998, 30–37.

Parker, Frank R. *Black Votes Count: Political Empowerment in Mississippi after 1965*. Chapel Hill: University of North Carolina Press, 1990.

Payne, Charles M. *I've Got the Light of Freedom: The Organizing Tradition and the Mississippi Freedom Struggle*. Berkeley: University of California Press, 1995.

Piliawsky, Monte. *Exit 13: Oppression and Racism in Academia*. Boston: South End, 1982.

President's Committee on Civil Rights. *To Secure These Rights: The Report of the President's Committee on Civil Rights*. Washington, D.C.: GPO, 1947.

Public Papers of the Presidents of the United States: John F. Kennedy, 1962. Washington, D.C.: GPO, 1963.

Roche, Jeff. *Restructured Resistance: The Sibley Commission and the Politics of Desegregation in Georgia*. Athens: University of Georgia Press, 1998.

Rotch, William. "Cotton, Cordiality and Conflict [part 1]." *New South* 12 (Feb. 1957): 9–11.

———. "Cotton, Cordiality and Conflict [part 2]." *New South* 12 (Mar. 1957): 6–9.

Rowe-Sims, Sarah. "The Mississippi State Sovereignty Commission: An Agency History." *Journal of Mississippi History* 61 (spring 1999): 29–58.

Sansing, David G. *Making Haste Slowly: The Troubled History of Higher Education in Mississippi*. Jackson: University Press of Mississippi, 1990.

———. *The University of Mississippi: A Sesquicentennial History*. Jackson: University Press of Mississippi, 1999.

Schlesinger, Arthur M., Jr. *Robert Kennedy and His Times*. Boston: Houghton Mifflin, 1978.

Silver, James W. "Mississippi: The Closed Society." *Journal of Southern History* 30 (Feb. 1964): 3–34.

———. *Mississippi: The Closed Society*. New York: Harcourt, Brace, and World, 1964.

———. "Mississippi Must Choose." *New York Times Magazine*, 19 July 1964, 8, 54–55.

———. *Running Scared: Silver in Mississippi*. Jackson: University Press of Mississippi, 1984.

Skates, John R. *Mississippi: A Bicentennial History*. New York: Norton, 1979.

Smead, Howard. *Blood Justice: The Lynching of Mack Charles Parker*. New York: Oxford University Press, 1986.

Smith, Frank E. *Congressman from Mississippi*. New York: Pantheon, 1964.

Sorensen, Theodore C. *Kennedy*. New York: Harper and Row, 1965.

———. *"Let the Word Go Forth": The Speeches, Statements, and Writings of John F. Kennedy, 1947 to 1963*. New York: Delacorte, 1988.

"South Increases Propaganda." *New South* 14 (May 1959): 5.

Strober, Gerald S., and Deborah H. Strober. *"Let Us Begin Anew": An Oral History of the Kennedy Presidency*. New York: Harper Collins, 1993.

Sumners, Cecil L. *The Governors of Mississippi*. Gretna, La.: Pelican, 1980.

Thompson, Julius E. *The Black Press in Mississippi, 1865–1985*. Gainesville: University Press of Florida, 1993.

———. *Percy Greene and the* Jackson Advocate*: The Life and Times of a Radical Conservative Black Newspaperman, 1897–1977*. Jefferson, N.C.: McFarland, 1994.

Tindall, George B. *The Ethnic Southerners*. Baton Rouge: Louisiana State University Press, 1976.

"To All on Equal Terms." *Time*, 24 May 1954, 9.

Trillin, Calvin. "State Secrets." *New Yorker*, 29 May 1995, 54–64.

Tucker, Shirley. *Mississippi from Within*. New York: Arco, 1965.

Washington, James M. *A Testament of Hope: The Essential Writings and Speeches of Martin Luther King, Jr*. New York: Harper Collins, 1986.

White, Theodore H. *The Making of the President 1964*. New York: New American Library, 1965.

Whitehead, Don. *Attack on Terror: The FBI against the Ku Klux Klan in Mississippi*. New York: Funk and Wagnalls, 1970.

Whitfield, Stephen J. *A Death in the Delta: The Story of Emmett Till*. New York: Free Press, 1988.

Wiesenburg, Karl. *The Oxford Disaster: Price of Defiance*. Pascagoula, Miss.: Advertiser Printing, 1962.

Williams, Juan. *Eyes on the Prize: America's Civil Rights Years, 1954–1965*. New York: Penguin, 1987.

Williams, Kenneth H. *Mississippi and Civil Rights, 1945–1954*. Ann Arbor, Mich.: University Microfilms, 1985.

Wilson, Paul E. *A Time to Lose: Representing Kansas in* Brown v. Board of Education. Lawrence: University Press of Kansas, 1995.

Woodward, C. Vann. *The Burden of Southern History*. Rev. ed. Baton Rouge: Louisiana State University Press, 1968.

———. "Teaching American History." *American Scholar* 67 (winter 1998): 105–6.

"Words Make News in Mississippi." *Life*, 7 Feb. 1964, 4.

INDEX

Johnson, Lyndon B., 150, 151, 165, 166, 212

Johnson, Paul B., Jr., 145, 146, 192, 196–98, 200–02; and aftermath of Neshoba County murders, 165; APWR criticism of, 184, 205; background, 143–44; and Carthage school desegregation, 180–82; and Citizens' Council, 141, 142, 145; Civil Rights Act, reaction to, 168, 171; on Commission and white extremist groups, 191; Commission funding to Citizens' Council continued by, 188; Commission, praise of, 205; on Commission's inactivity, 193; and Commission's new direction, 198–99; and Commission's use of detective agencies, 210; and Coordinating Committee for Fundamental American Freedoms, 151; DeCell, defended by, 194; and DISCARD, 162; donation of family papers of, 234–35; elected, 142; and Freedom Summer Project, 162; gubernatorial candidacy, 140, 141–42; impeachment, call for, 199–200; inaugural address, 142–43; Johnston, defended by, 184; Johnston, support for, 119; and Johnston's calls for moderation, 186; and Johnston's conflicts with APWR, 182; law-and-order policies, 144, 171, 192; lieutenant governor, candidacy for (1967), 205; Klan members, list provided to FBI by, 166; and Lowman's speaking tours, 90; and Meredith crisis, 109, 111, 141; in *Oxford, U.S.A.*, 120; political setbacks, 170; school desegregation enforced by, 199; segregation, attitudes toward, 144; *Southern Review* on, 185, 199; and white extremist groups, investiga-

tion of, 190. *See also* Johnson Family Papers

Johnson, Paul B., Sr., 143

Johnson, William H., Jr.: appointment to Commission, 9, 67; Johnston, support for, 119; monthly meetings, support for, 34; and speakers bureau, 77; and VA hospital controversy, 25

Johnston, Bubby, 239

Johnston, Erle E., Jr.: appointed director, 119, 120, 198, 237; appointed public relations director, 67–68; APWR, conflict with, 177–78, 180–81, 182–83, 184, 187, 195; background, 68, 82; and Baez concert investigation, 154; and Beittel case, 155–57; and BIG program, 173–74; and Carthage school desegregation, 180–81; on challenge to Gore's directorship, 11; Citizens' Councils, feud with, 98–99, 101–02, 187–88; civil rights legislation, opposition to, 122, 150; civil rights movement, affects on white people, 237–38; and COFO investigation, 162, 176; on Commission, 206, 207–08; Commission funding for Citizens' Council, attempts to stop, 187–90; Commission's image, attempts to change, 173–74; and Commission's new direction, 197–99; and Committee on the Preservation of Civil Rights Papers, 238; and Compton Community College–Jones County College reunion game, 238–39; and Coordinating Committee for Fundamental American Freedoms, 124; and CORE investigation, 163, 164; criticism of, 174–75, 195, 200–01; death, 237, 239; and detective agencies used by Commission, 148–49; and DISCARD, 162; Dulles, meeting with,